TOLKIEN ON FILM

D1104351

TOLKIEN ON FILM: ESSAYS ON PETER JACKSON'S THE LORD OF THE RINGS

EDITED BY
JANET BRENNAN CROFT

THE MYTHOPOEIC PRESS
ALTADENA, CALIFORNIA

THE MYTHOPOEIC PRESS is an imprint of: The Mythopoeic Society, P.O. Box 6707, Altadena CA 91003 (www.mythsoc.org). Orders and inquiries may be directed to: The Mythopoeic Press, 920 N. Atlantic Blvd. #E, Alhambra CA 91801.

Printed in the United States of America.
First Printing   2004.
Second Printing   2010.

LIBRARY OF CONGRESS CATALOGING-IN-PUBLICATION DATA

Tolkien on film : essays on Peter Jackson's The lord of the rings / edited by Janet Brennan Croft.
       p. cm.
 Includes bibliographical references and index.
 ISBN-13: 978-1-887726-09-2
 ISBN-10: 1-887726-09-8 (alk. paper)
 1. Lord of the Rings films--History and criticism. 2. Jackson, Peter, 1961- I. Croft, Janet Brennan.
 PN1995.9.L58T66 2004
 791.43'75--dc22

                         2004022039

Cover illustration by Patrick Wynne. Cover design by Eleanor M. Farrell. Set in Palatino Linotype and Copperplate Gothic.

"The Lord of the Rings: A Source-Critical Analysis" by Mark Shea is reprinted with permission from CRISIS Magazine, where it appeared in January 2004.

TABLE OF CONTENTS

INTRODUCTION

Peter Jackson's three blockbuster films based on J.R.R. Tolkien's classic *The Lord of the Rings* inspired a wide range of reactions from general viewers and readers and from scholars of Tolkien and film. At one extreme are people who love the movies as much as (or more than) the books, and are delighted at their commercial success and the vast number of film industry awards they garnered. On the other hand are those who find them profoundly antithetical, or even sacrilegious, to Tolkien's text and themes and almost too painful to watch. Very few readers of Tolkien are entirely neutral about Jackson's epic undertaking and its effect on public perceptions of Tolkien's work. For this book, the first collection of critical essays on the Peter Jackson *Lord of the Rings* films, we tried to solicit strong and convincingly argued opinions on all sides; we hope we have not served you any weak tea, though we expect that not all the views represented here will be to every reader's taste.

We start with an overview examining the place of Jackson's trilogy in the history of film, and specifically in the genre of "Imperial Cinema." J.E. Smyth shows how *The Lord of the Rings* is thematically related to two of the greatest films in this genre, the Korda brothers' *The Four Feathers* and David Lean's *Lawrence of Arabia,* but also can be read as an updated political response to the question of imperialism in an age of terrorism, and are particularly interesting as a product of the filmmaking industry of the former British imperial colonies of New Zealand and the United States.

After this we look at problems of adaptation and revision: how a film evolves from book to script, and what is lost or gained in the process. David Bratman applies convincing and logical arguments to a refutation of defenders of the films who see them as ideal adaptations of Tolkien's works, along the way looking at issues of directorial vision, media colonization, and methods of judging art. In my own essay, I look more specifically at two ways in which Jackson's films are less satisfying than the book: Jackson's inclination to decrease surprise and tension by anticipating later events and revealing them earlier in the script than Tolkien did in the book, and his propensity for flattening out Tolkien's characters and dialogue. Diana Paxson counters with a working author's understanding of the process of revision, and how Jackson's films can be seen as an extension of Tolkien's own tendency to constantly revise his creation even after publication. Her conclusion is that a great story has the resilience to withstand even the sort of changes Jackson made, and that new versions can add richness to an established work.

Paxson's essay concludes with an examination of Jackson's treatment of Aragorn, which leads naturally into the next group of three essays on heroism and leadership as depicted in the books and on film. One criticism of the films is that they have made Aragorn more conflicted and Frodo less mature than in the book, creating what are in effect entirely different characters from those Tolkien so carefully crafted. Kayla McKinney Wiggins looks at heroism in general, its place in fantasy, and how Jackson's modernized heroes, meant to be more relevant to today's movie audience, may strike us as oddly distant and not a convincing fulfillment of our human need for classic heroism. Daniel Timmons explores Jackson's depiction of Frodo and how it in some ways fails to convince us that Frodo is the best and only choice for the Ringbearer, as Tolkien's text so abundantly does. Judith Kollmann concludes this section by examining the concept of counsel, the part it plays in collaborative decision-making and consultative leadership in Tolkien's world, and what Jackson's re-stagings of Tolkien's scenes of council and counsel imply.

One of the most obvious changes made in the films was the expansion of Arwen's role, and Jackson also made a point of including parts of Éowyn's and Galadriel's roles which were often cut from previous adaptations. Jackson's increased emphasis on female characters is a thought-provoking rereading of Tolkien. Jane Chance leads off this section with an explication of how Jackson changed the focus of the story from Frodo's journey and the theme of "the ennoblement of the humble" to Aragorn and Arwen's love story, and how this decision may or may not be supported by evidence from the legendarium and Tolkien's letters. Cathy Akers-Jordan and Victoria Gaydosik both look at the implications of Arwen's greatly changed character; Akers-Jordan gives us a detailed reading of Jackson's portrayal and its roots in Arwen's ancestry, and Gaydosik examines what she terms the "new Psyche" paradigm in films and television and how these recent depictions of powerful women (and the lack of models for interactions between them) may have influenced Jackson's decisions. And Maureen Thum shows us that Jackson's interpretation of Galadriel, Arwen, and Éowyn is not really that much of a departure from the heroic and stereotype-breaking women Tolkien depicted in the whole corpus of his work, and especially in the *Silmarillion*.

And what of the fans? Tolkien has always had a vocal and active fan base, and fan fiction has been a part of Tolkienian "fanac" since the beginning. Susan Booker takes us on a guided tour of the fan fiction universe, introducing us to the varieties and vocabulary of fanfic and providing some eye-opening statistics about the amount of material available on the World Wide Web. Amy Sturgis takes a more focused look at the effect of the movies on fan fiction, particularly how it has divided fanfic into "bookverse" and "movieverse," and how writers deal with the two overlapping and sometimes contradictory canons.

Finally, for the "lucky number," we have a short and amusing but thought-provoking hobbit of a piece by Mark Shea, postulating a future where Tolkien and Jackson are just two among many sources making up the "Matter of Middle-earth." Is this just a dystopian vision, or is it a foretaste of the natural evolution of what has become a mythology for our time?

These are movies about which it is hard to hold no opinion, and these essays are surely but the first of many. The films provide a rich mine for future academic work enriching our understanding of both Tolkien and how the changes in our culture in the fifty years since he wrote *The Lord of the Rings* have influenced depictions of his work on screen.

References to the book *The Lord of the Rings* are to page numbers in the one-volume 1994 edition (with introduction and note on the text by Douglas A. Anderson). Book and chapter numbers are provided for those consulting other editions. References to the movies are to scene numbers in the extended edition DVDs for *The Fellowship of the Ring* and *The Two Towers*, and the theatrical release DVD for *The Return of the King*, with scene titles included for readers who might be referring to other versions.

I'd like to thank the editorial board at The Mythopoeic Press for proposing this fascinating project, and my contributors for putting up with the foibles of a first-time editor. Joe Christopher and Joan Marie Verba were wonderfully sharp-eyed proofreaders. Beth Russell in particular made outstanding editorial suggestions, and I thank her, both as the editor of this volume and as a contributor, for her assistance in making all these essays, including mine, the best they could be.

Janet Brennan Croft
August 2004

A NOTE ON THE SECOND PRINTING

We are delighted to be faced with the pleasant task of ordering a second printing of *Tolkien on Film*. This collection remains, we feel, the most important gathering of criticism on the film from a literary studies perspective, as opposed to a film studies perspective. Film studies has different aims and concerns, a different vocabulary, and different theoretical underpinnings from those the reader will encounter in this book. Readers interested in film studies might want to look at *The Lord of the Rings: Popular Culture in Global Context* and *From Hobbits to Hollywood: Essays on Peter Jackson's Lord of the Rings*, both edited by Ernest Mathijs, *Peter Jackson in Perspective* by Greg Wright, or *The Frodo Franchise* by Kristin Thompson. While we feel that anyone can appreciate our more book-based approach to criticism of the films, it is perhaps more appropriate for use in literature classes than film classes. We are pleased with its continuing success, and hope the forthcoming *Hobbit* films will generate more critical interest in Jackson's *The Lord of the Rings* as an adaptation of Tolkien's classic.

Janet Brennan Croft
April 2010

PART I:

FILM
HISTORY

THE THREE AGES OF IMPERIAL CINEMA
FROM THE DEATH OF GORDON TO
THE RETURN OF THE KING

J.E. SMYTH

The Great War may have been the beginning of the end of the British Empire, but it formed the creative impetus for the regeneration of the British film industry and the dominance of imperial cinema from the early sound era to the present day. From 1914 to 1918, three brothers lived through the desolation of the Austro-Hungarian Empire; two suffered in the trenches, while the elder, unfit for military service, struggled to maintain Hungary's "national" film industry in the face of debilitating military defeats. A shy Oxford archaeologist, seconded to British military intelligence in Cairo, helped to lead an Arab revolt against the Turkish Empire, and became a popular hero in an age and a war which threatened to obliterate any concept of traditional heroism. Another Oxford student-turned-soldier fought in the Battle of the Somme, lost some of his closest friends in the course of the war, and began to construct his fantastic history of the fall of the Elvish and Númenórean Empires, *The Silmarillion* (Carpenter 98-100; White 62-70).

The careers and cinematic legacies of the Korda brothers, T.E. Lawrence, and J.R.R. Tolkien were all deeply marked by their war experience and the subsequent collapse of the British Empire. Their ensuing impact on Western film culture has determined much of the structure of twentieth-century cinema's imperial imagination. Reconfronting the historical and imperial discourses of *The Four Feathers* (1939), *Lawrence of Arabia* (1962), and *The Lord of the Rings* (2001-2003) reveals some significant problems in traditional formulations of "classical" imperial cinema and the global Hollywood phenomenon. At the height of the so-called "classical" era in filmmaking, the Kordas' popular and critically successful production of *The Four Feathers* questioned the discourse of imperialism. In the wake of the twin collapse of the Hollywood studio system and the British Empire, David Lean would deconstruct the concept of the imperial hero, T.E. Lawrence. Many films would attempt to mimic *Lawrence of Arabia*'s ambivalent attitude toward imperial history and heroes, and with lasting consequences. For most recently, imperial cinema has abandoned the pretense of representing traditional history in favor of legitimizing imperial fantasy. The year 2001 marked the beginning of the Third Age of Imperial Cinema, to borrow a phrase from its unconscious architect, J.R.R. Tolkien; and in a time of renewed Eastern terror and conflict, imperialism has been reborn.

THE FIRST AGE: ZOLTAN KORDA, A.E.W. MASON, AND EARLY IMPERIAL DOUBT

It is one of the great ironies of film history that one of Britain's most powerful producers, the man responsible for revitalizing the British historical film and internationalizing the industry in the early sound era, was a left-wing Hungarian director. Alexander Korda directed his first films during the war, and in 1918 the post-war interim government appointed him commissioner of film production. When the conservative Horthy government came to power in 1920, he was forced to leave Hungary. After filmmaking stints in Vienna, Hollywood, and Paris, Korda eventually settled in the heart of the British Empire. In 1932, he formed London Film Productions and chose the tolling Big Ben as the company's logo. Although nominally an independent producer, Korda, like other British studio executives, was dependent on Hollywood distribution. The British film industry's attempt to restrict Hollywood's colonization of British theatres in the early sound era with quota acts did little to improve the caliber of British filmmaking. Alone among his peers, Korda courted Hollywood in order to secure international markets for his new British productions. Of all the major production and distribution companies, United Artists had the most to gain from the energetic Korda; the major partners, silent stars Mary Pickford, Douglas Fairbanks, D.W. Griffith, and Charles Chaplin, produced too infrequently for the company's solvency. Through his successful approach to UA, Korda captured an international status and independence unknown to other British producers (Low). Several months after the agreement, Korda's first release, *The Private Life of Henry VIII* (1933), jolted Britain out of its provincial cinema status. *The Observer*'s C.A. Lejeune predicted that *The Private Life of Henry VIII* was "more likely to bring prestige to the British Film Industry, both at home and abroad, than anything we have done in the whole history of filmmaking" (Lejeune). United Artists' investment paid off; the historical

4

spectacle was a huge critical and popular success in America and was the first "foreign" film to win a major American Academy Award.

The film provided the momentum for London Films' subsequent lavish historical productions. Korda, together with his two younger brothers Zoltan and Vincent, competed with Hollywood's successful genre of historical "prestige" pictures during the 1930s, and *The Private Life of Catherine the Great* (1934) and *The Private Life of Don Juan* (1934) were successful alternatives to Twentieth Century-Fox's *The House of Rothschild* (1934) and *Cardinal Richelieu* (1935). But the Kordas would achieve their greatest success when London Films turned to the territories of the empire. The British press, headlining "He Hopes to Win Empire for British Talkies," cast Korda in the role of a twentieth-century imperial hero, artfully turning Britain's burgeoning international film prestige into a new imperial success ("He Hopes"). Even as the worldwide economic depression and growth of the Indian nationalist movement hastened the decay of the British Empire, the film industry's representations of the territories of the empire and events in British imperial history became a major independent national genre. During the 1930s, American studios struggled to mimic the lavish biopics and British imperial epics of Korda and Michael Balcon (*Rhodes of Africa*, 1936; *King Solomon's Mines*, 1936), but they seemed more like overseas Westerns. These American efforts like *Lives of a Bengal Lancer* (1936) and *Gunga Din* (1939) not only marginalized or ignored the engagement with historical contexts that often characterized the work of Korda and Balcon, but also unequivocally reinforced the most repressive racial discourses of imperialism.

Yet late twentieth-century film criticism has persisted in viewing British and American imperial films as one category, a bastion of popular imperialism and propaganda (Richards, "Imperial"; Slotkin). The Korda brothers' British Empire features have been generally dismissed as "expressions of official rhetoric," promoters of consensus, and manifestations of juvenile fiction's militarist and racial stereotypes (Armes; MacKenzie, *Propaganda*; Richards, "Boys Own" and *Films*). British imperial films of this era have suffered from three scholarly prejudices within Film and Cultural Studies: they are often historical films, they are empire films, and they fall within the "classical Hollywood" film era and style. All three categories are considered to replicate a mythic view of the national past that reconciles cultural contradiction and dissent in order to reinforce the dominant ideology (Ray; Bordwell). Additionally, the narrative structures of "classical Hollywood" cinema, classified as genres constructed of almost immutable formulas, depend on a process of symbolization which drains its mythic subject of historical reality. Within this scholarly vacuum, any reading of a classical empire film that would suggest its possession of an independent and critical historical argument would not only be spurious but impossible. It is time to revise this classical scholarship, which, in its rigidity and reductive theoretical justifications, deserves the "classical" epithet far more than the designated cinema. Even within the context of the pre-war studio era, within the gates of the most empire-driven film mogul, there was a deliberate sense of imperial ambiguity and doubt.

Although Alexander Korda publicly admired Britain and its empire, his memories of the post-war collapse of the Austro-Hungarian Empire and the rapid growth of right-wing governments framed his attitude. For Korda, a strong British Empire in the post-war era served as the only bulwark against the rise of European fascism (Tabori 157-8). Zoltan Korda, however, had many doubts, misgivings, and criticisms of Britain's imperial past and present, attitudes he would express throughout his directorial career in *The Four Feathers* and later in his production of Alan Paton's *Cry, the Beloved Country* (1951). In the late 1930s, the writings of A.E.W. Mason reconciled the Korda brothers' diverging responses to empire and served as the basis for London Films' most successful imperial epics, beginning with *Fire over England* (1937), a denunciation of the oppressive sixteenth-century Spanish Empire; *The Drum* (1938), a story of contemporary India; and culminating in *The Four Feathers* (1939).

Mason was a popular and prolific historical novelist, and over the years his work has provided an astounding resource for American and British film companies.[1] However, he is best remembered for *The Four Feathers* (1902) and *The Broken Road* (1907), two acutely critical representations of British imperialism in Africa and India (Lancelyn Green 107-8). *The Four Feathers* was his first major critical success. It is the story of Harry Feversham, a career army officer who resigns his commission on the eve of General Kitchener's plan to retake the Sudan in 1898. The young man is repulsed by imperial ambition and jingoism, but his peers attribute his decision to pure cowardice and send him white feathers. In order to avenge his personal honor, Harry travels to the Sudan, disguises himself as a Sengali native, and eventually saves the lives of his former friends in Omdurman's prison, the House of Stones.

Mason's novel was based on events surrounding the murder and avenging of one of Britain's most famous military figures, General Charles

---

[1] *The Four Feathers* has been remade seven times (1915, 1921, 1929, 1939, 1955, 1979, 2002), and *Clementina, At the Villa Rose, House of the Arrow, Miranda, The Truants,* and *The Broken Road* were also filmed several times as silent pictures in Britain and America.

Gordon. In 1884, Prime Minister William Gladstone sent Gordon to relieve Khartoum, long threatened by a powerful native religious uprising led by the Mahdi. Gordon remained through early 1885, determined to hold the city. The Mahdi's forces overran Khartoum in January, and Gordon was slain. Gordon remains a haunting figure in British imperial history, a professional soldier but an avowed anti-imperialist, a deeply religious man whose hatred of slavery and attempts to end the slave trade in North Africa earned the Mahdi's wrath and indirectly cost Gordon his life. His murder and the fall of Khartoum were devastating blows to imperial prestige. Then in 1898, the government finally sent General Kitchener to retake the Sudan and avenge Gordon's death. Kitchener reclaimed the area, and soon it was safe for British travelers. Mason was among the first civilians to visit the city in 1900. Within a few weeks, he began constructing *The Four Feathers* from stories he heard about Kitchener's campaign (Lancelyn Green 87). Mason, like many of his countrymen, was fascinated with Gordon, and one of his two protagonists, the solitary, desert-loving Jack Durrance, bears a close resemblance to the popular heroic conception of Gordon. Indeed, Gordon's solitary heroism and courageous death are a likely inspiration for Durrance's quiet courage and unaffected endurance. While in the desert, Durrance contemplates "the history of that honest, great, impracticable soldier, who, despised by officials and thwarted by intrigues, a man of few ties and much loneliness, had gone unflaggingly about his work, knowing the while that the moment his back was turned the work was in an instant all undone" (Mason 79).

Yet in his novel, Mason also expressed deep ambivalence toward the empire and military establishment. Young Harry Feversham shrinks from his pugilistic father, and Mason links the boy's sensitivity to the character of his deceased mother. But rather than forcing a pro-imperial, male-female, empire builder-empire outsider dichotomy, Mason attacked the patriarchal, imperial war ethic and its strong continuities with national identity. Early in the narrative, Harry walks through his family picture gallery, the military portraits functioning as emblems of national continuity and imperial glory. Yet it is a continuity and glory that Mason rejects.

> Father and son, the Fevershams had been soldiers from the very birth of the family . . . in lace collars and bucket boots, in Ramillies wigs and steel breastplates . . . they looked down, summoning him to the like service. They were men of one stamp . . . without the subtleties, or

> nerves, or that burdensome gift of imagination; sturdy
> men, a little wanting in delicacy, hardly conspicuous for
> intellect . . . (Mason 12-13)

Even Durrance, the model soldier and Harry's best friend, serves as a foil for Mason's critique of imperialism. Durrance is blinded during his campaign in Africa, and his handicap functions as an analogy for British imperial and military blindness. Although now considered one of the "classics" of imperial literature (Richards, "Visions" 23), Mason's novel is neither a justification for empire nor a heroic study of two men's separate adventures in the British dominions. In Mason's view, Britain's imperial blindness and political intrigue killed General Gordon, made an intelligent boy more afraid of fear than death, and crippled a dedicated soldier.

Alexander Korda purchased the rights to *The Four Feathers* in 1937; his production, scripted and shot in 1938 and released in 1939, would be the fourth version of the film.[2] American documentary-prone filmmaker, Merian C. Cooper, had released the last remake of Mason's book in 1929. Cooper made a full-blown action feature out of Mason's novel, obliterating Mason's original critique of imperialism and militarism with a surfeit of battle sequences and shots of murderous hippopotamuses. The Kordas were more interested in projecting Britain's turn-of-the-century imperial history as accurately as possible. Alexander Korda allowed Zoltan to film *The Four Feathers* in the Sudan, and with the permission of the Governor General, crews shot around Omdurman and Khartoum (Waugh 898). Zoltan, weary of his brother's meddlesome patriotism, was determined to preserve Mason's original critique of the empire. He had just finished directing *The Drum*, a contemporary tale of British India that Mason had written to Alex Korda's specifications in 1937-8. Hampered by location shooting in Wales and his brother's zealous project to fight fascism with stories of imperial strength, Zoltan Korda had little freedom to express his own view of the raj.

Zoltan's last two films set in the territories of the empire, *Sanders of the River* (1935) and *The Drum*, while possessing sympathetic African (Paul Robeson) and Indian (Sabu Dastigir) leads, were hardly critiques of imperialism. However, Zoltan did manage to convey some of his and Mason's repressed sympathy for the Indian population. Sabu's Prince Azim exerts the primary narrative agency in the film's tale of rebellion (Street 43-6). While British soldiers are powerless to fight the rebels in a hostile mountainous terrain, it is Prince Azim who puts down his

---

[2] Previous productions released in 1915, 1921, 1929.

8

usurping uncle's insurrection. Though acting in British interests, he is also acting in his own, effectively guaranteeing his succession to his father's kingdom. There is no significant critique of the empire (beyond the device of revolt) in either *Sanders* or *The Drum*, but these films were contemporary narratives. Any cinematic attack on current imperial governance would have awakened the British censors (Pronay). *The Four Feathers* gave Zoltan Korda both physical and historical distance from potential contemporary constraints on imperial critique.

Within that first "classical" era of imperial filmmaking, *The Four Feathers* stands out as both the epitome of the genre and the harbinger of the anti-imperialist epics of the post-Suez era. It is neither the contemporary adventure of *Sanders of the River, The Drum*, and *King Solomon's Mines*, nor the exotic child's fantasy of *Elephant Boy* (1937) and *The Thief of Bagdad* (1940), nor the historical eulogy of Balcon's *Rhodes of Africa*, nor the American imperial panegyric, *Lives of a Bengal Lancer*. *The Four Feathers'* stunning location shooting, color technology, and epic battle sequences may link it to the most prestigious imperial-historical filmmaking of the era, but the film also represents a hitherto unacknowledged apex of the empire genre in its engagement with history, national myth, contemporary imperial decay, and international popularity. The apex of classical British imperial cinema ironically constituted the genre's most thorough critique of imperial history. Part of the credit must go to Korda's screenwriter, R.C. Sherriff, author of the anti-war play and film *Journey's End* (1931). Together they followed A.E.W. Mason's original intent, questioning the discourse of imperialism through the narrative's tortured outsider and anti-hero, Harry Faversham.[3] Twenty years later, David Lean would similarly designate T.E. Lawrence as the emblem of his imperial critique.

When Mason published *The Four Feathers* in 1902, the novel was a contemporary account and critique of the British Empire. By 1938, the Battle of Omdurman was part of the text of imperial history. Consequently, R.C. Sherriff and Zoltan Korda constructed *The Four Feathers* as a historical film rather than a timeless adventure. Following the practice of prestigious classical Hollywood historical films of the 1930s, Korda began *The Four Feathers* with a foreword and historical prologue set in 1885 Khartoum.[4] While previous scholarship has dismissed Sherriff and

---

[3] Sherriff changed the spelling of Feversham's last name for the movie.

[4] Cutting continuity (April 1939), British Film Institute; in the final shooting script (14 July 1938), the prologue was much longer, involving a House of Commons' debate and a lengthier death for General Gordon (1-4). These and other scenes were later cut after the preview in the

Korda's device as "setting the imperial context," the use of an opening text "foreword" when sound technology had rendered projected text obsolete in 1927-8, not only proclaimed the film's historical nature and textual accuracy, but also self-consciously allied the narrative with the more traditional and respected form of written history. Mason's novel, while indirectly mentioning General Gordon and Khartoum, did not include any historical prologue. Instead, Sherriff and Korda reinforced the film's historical status and engagement with the structural devices associated with prestigious historical filmmaking. The foreword introduces the infamous events of 1885: the rise of the Mahdi, the return of the slave trade, the British abandonment of Khartoum, and Gordon's lonely death. The textual foreword then dissolves to a silent montage of Gordon's assassination on the steps of the palace. He holds a Bible rather than a gun, and a native spears him through the heart. Although no evidence exists determining how Gordon died, Korda's portrayal of Gordon as a Christian martyr to the empire cinematically reinforced the view popularized by G.W. Joy's 1894 painting, *The Death of Gordon*, and justified the "avenging" of Khartoum by Kitchener in 1898 (Johnson; Joy). Yet Gordon's status as a successful professional soldier conflicted with both his pre-Khartoum reputation as an anti-imperialist, anti-slave trade crusader and his popular deification as a passive victim of native aggression.

The instability of Gordon's imperial image was not only part of *The Four Feathers'* historical legacy, but also influenced the characterization of the film's fictional critic of empire, Harry Faversham. Early in the film, after hearing of the news of Gordon's death, the militant General Faversham considers what was wrong with Gordon is also wrong with his son Harry: "He wasn't hard enough." The brand of heroism shared by Gordon and Harry was not the conventional type. But unlike Gordon, Harry expresses his contempt for the empire and the military directly: he resigns his commission in 1898. The basis of Mason's novel and Harry's adventure in the Sudan is his direct questioning of the value of the British Empire. Korda and Sherriff embellished these criticisms. They are not implied or unconscious ambiguities but direct statements. Harry Faversham (John Clements) speaks for the filmmakers when he tells his fiancée why he resigned his commission and refused to participate in Kitchener's reconquest of the Sudan. He remained in England, he says, because he felt he owed it more love and loyalty than a country and

---

interest of length, and the Kordas implemented the impressive text foreword and historical montage.

people he had never seen. He stays to save his family's decaying estate and "to save all those people who've been neglected by my family because they preferred glory in India, glory in China, glory in Africa" (Sherriff, *Feathers* shooting script 26). In this sequence, Sherriff enhanced Mason's conflict between military stupidity and personal courage. Harry's speech is not merely an excuse for cowardice. Although initially fearful, he eventually travels alone to the Sudan in search of Kitchener's army. He has no dramatic patriotic epiphany. His remarkable deeds in Africa are not for the Crown, but for personal reasons, for revenge upon his three former friends and his fiancée who sent him white feathers of cowardice when he resigned his commission.

Although *The Four Feathers* articulates a resistant anti-imperial argument, the film's imperial ambivalence emerges from within the ranks of the establishment. In spite of the impressive shots of the Khalifa's army, Korda did not present the Sudanese populations with their own subjective perspective. However, Harry Faversham learns what it is like to be a native under both the Khalifa and the British flag. Having abandoned his British uniform, Harry disguises himself as a Sengali incapable of speech and travels with the Khalifa's army in search of Kitchener. This performing of native identity is not simply an exhibition of the Orientalist discourse that enables the Western hero to experience the exotic and unlimited potentialities of the East. Considered slave labor by both the Sudanese and the British, Harry experiences little of the so-called liberating and seductive freedom Westerners experienced in performing native identity (Said 159). In one panoramic shot of the borders of the Nile, Harry is hardly noticeable among the Sudanese laborers forced to haul the British army's barges up the river. Africans repeatedly whip the writhing but mute Harry. Eventually, his own former commanding officer will also abuse him, mistaking him for a Sengali thief. Still Harry cannot speak in the face of this cross-cultural abuse, and his unique identity displacement draws attention to the absent, mute perspective of the Sudanese in 1898 under both the British and Islamic "empires." Even in Britain, Harry's position is likened to that of a slave. While Ethne understands his contempt for the empire, she reminds him that unlike other men and women, those belonging to military families are "not born free . . . We were born into a tradition, a code which we must obey even if we do not believe" (Sheriff, *Feathers* shooting script 32). The military classes, the so-called guardians of empire, are actually the British Empire's slaves. Ethne's desperate justification has no effect on Harry beyond confirming his belief in the "emptiness" and "futility" of imperial and military tradition.

Though he succeeds in rescuing his friends and regaining his fiancée's favor, Harry does not abandon his original attitudes toward the empire and the military. Neither does the film's romantic restoration "correct" Harry's ideological deviation. In the film's final sequence, Harry destroys the most cherished war myth of his future father-in-law, General Burroughs. On two separate occasions in the narrative, the old Crimean campaigner tells the amusing, vainglorious tale of his key role in winning a major action and illustrates the event at the dinner table with fruit and nuts. Harry interrupts his third attempt, corrects him, and tells a more accurate, though less heroic story. Burroughs's great order to charge the Russians was actually his horse's idea, after an exploding shell sent the terrified animal headlong into the enemy's front line. Harry, still the critic of heroism and the British Empire, finds imperfections in the dominant discourse, and in the final shots, Zoltan Korda and R.C. Sherriff added a comical corrective to the heroic discourse and events of imperial history.

THE SECOND AGE: LEAN'S LAWRENCE AND THE FATE OF THE IMPERIAL HERO

The Kordas' next project was to have been another empire film, the first film treatment of T.E. Lawrence, who had died tragically in 1935. They selected John Clements, who played the anti-imperialist Harry Faversham, to star as Lawrence. In fact, Clements learned of their decision while he was in the Sudan shooting *The Four Feathers* (Tabori 202-03). Mason and Korda's anti-imperialist hero and T.E. Lawrence had a great deal in common. Like Harry, Lawrence was an outsider, a man who refused a commission, who hated the establishment and doubted the intentions of the imperial elite. The project was shelved, and Korda was left to reach audiences with more contemporary tales of national and international displacement, like *Perfect Strangers* (1945) and *The Third Man* (1949).

Why did Alexander Korda abandon the project? Now that Lawrence was dead, he had permission to make the film. The heart of the answer lies in Lawrence himself. He was an unconventional imperial hero, to say the least. During the Arabian campaign and even after the war, when he shunned all interviews and the press, Lawrence loved to pose for the camera and for the painters, perhaps amused by the discrepancy between his rather unheroic photographic appearance and the romantic imaginings of painters like Augustus John and Eric Kennington. Although a public figure, he was an intensely private man, and after he wrote *The Seven*

12

Pillars of Wisdom in the early 1920s, he refrained from writing about himself. Although Lawrence was the subject of massive press attention, there was a corresponding mystery about his precise role in the Arab revolt and his relationship with the British government. As Jeremy Wilson has pointed out in a more recent biography, the official documents and correspondence about Lawrence and the Arab Revolt were not available until the late 1960s (Wilson 1). This ambiguity undoubtedly fueled the Lawrence of Arabia myth in the post-war era, a myth largely created by American reporter Lowell Thomas, who first constructed Lawrence's heroic public image in motion picture lectures (Thomas, *With Lawrence* and *A Boy's Life*). The myth was created as an antidote to the horror of the trenches in Europe, to the unprecedented conditions that threatened to destroy the concepts of traditional heroism and history.

At the same time, the American Expeditionary Force was struggling to find the public an American war hero who would last the course of the war. When the *Saturday Evening Post* reported the remarkable story of Sergeant Alvin York, who had captured 132 Germans in a raid in the Argonne forest, General Pershing and many other high-ranking soldiers were reputedly annoyed. York was not a professional soldier, and had even fought his draft as a conscientious objector before patriotism got the better of him. His heroism and the speedy conclusion of the war transformed him into one of the nation's most famous war heroes. His autobiography and biographies articulated a simple patriotic creed and faith in national history and pioneer ancestors. In 1941, Warner Brothers' screenwriters easily circumvented York's religious pacifism by making him read another book, *The History of the United States*. York (Gary Cooper), with a Bible in one hand and *U.S. History* in the other, became "the last of the long hunters," the modern descendant of Daniel Boone and Abraham Lincoln.

Britain had more difficulty manipulating the elusive Lawrence, the academic, the archaeologist, the border-crosser. He wouldn't be forced into the mold of the everyman-hero like Alvin York. Lawrence's war memoir was not a guileless, patriotic story of faith and courage, but a complex and strikingly impersonal history of the Arab Revolt. As friend and biographer Robert Graves wrote in 1927,

> People like Lawrence are in fact an obvious menace
> to civilization; they are too strong and important to
> be dismissed as nothing at all, too capricious to be
> burdened with a position of responsibility, too sure

> of themselves to be browbeaten, but then too
> disdainful of themselves to be made heroes of.
> (Graves 54-55)

Korda, although unafraid of producing a challenging imperial film like *The Four Feathers*, was forced to abandon his biography of Lawrence in 1939. Although the reasons are unknown, it is very likely that wartime censorship would prohibit a film with such overt anti-imperial possibilities.

It would take another twenty years for Lawrence's life to reach the screen and one of Korda's protégés, David Lean, to accomplish it. After working in Britain for years, Lean obtained the financial support of Columbia Pictures in the late 1950s. In many ways, Lean seemed to have inherited Korda's mantle as Britain's imperial filmmaker. With Columbia's money behind him and the era of widescreen epics well underway, Lean possessed the publicity machinery and international distribution networks that Korda had always dreamed of. But times had changed for British filmmaking. Korda lost control of his studio in the late 1930s even as he gained an imperial foothold in financing American movies (Low 226-7). While David Lean may have operated his small production company like a small empire, he lacked the independence Korda had once guarded at his studio. Lean and his films lived under the imperial dominion of Hollywood, but even the studio system was in decline. Rising costs, the closing of most overseas markets during the Second World War, and growing post-war international competition impinged upon Hollywood's former monopoly, but the *Paramount* decree dealt the harshest blow of all. In 1948, the Supreme Court ordered the studios to divest themselves of their theater holdings. Seeking some means of combating this territorial loss and the repressive domestic tax laws, in the 1950s and 1960s, many studios turned to overseas filmmaking.

The British Empire and the imperial hero suffered an even harder fate after the Second World War. Curiously, T.E. Lawrence's own heroic triumphs and disillusionment provided some of the impetus for post-war imperial decay. Winning the Great War may have left Britain territorially richer, but its imperial grip was weakened as Indian and Pan-Arab nationalist movements grew. The loss of India in 1947 and the ignominious result of the Suez Crisis prepared the way for David Lean's harsher look at imperial history. In the midst of the Suez Crisis in 1955, Zoltan Korda remade *The Four Feathers*, but retitled the film with grim irony, *Storm on the Nile*. As Harry once again questioned the need for empire in 1898, film audiences in 1955 reaped the harvest of imperial doubt. As Suez fell, even the reputation of Britain's most legendary imperial hero was in jeopardy. Although the press and biographers had exhausted themselves investigating the enigma of Lawrence of Arabia, most agreed he was a magnificent enigma. Lawrence was rather unpopular in the political and military establishment, and there had been a great deal of hearsay and gossip about the man who "went native," who crossed too many borders and never went first class. For years, this antagonism remained out of print, but in 1955, Richard Aldington's biography released a torrent of revisionist invective, claiming Lawrence was both a pathological liar and megalomaniac (Aldington; Caton 110). Aldington reputedly hated Lawrence with such passion that he chose tendentious sources with often unsubstantiated claims (Wilson 8; 980-81). The book's shock-value served Aldington well. His biography would be screenwriters Michael Wilson and Robert Bolt's major source for *Lawrence of Arabia* (Caton 110).

Terrence Rattigan's play *Ross* was equally powerful in its attack on the heroic Lawrence. Alec Guinness's performance, one of the earliest public reinventions of Lawrence's life, stunned audiences. A headliner in the Haymarket's 1960 season, Rattigan and Guinness explored Lawrence's heroic ambiguity and homosexuality. Guinness, small, spare, and with a well-known penchant for disappearing from private view and averting his personality, was actually a lot like the real Lawrence. A protégé of David Lean, Guinness became an international star playing the obsessive military dictator Colonel Nicholson in *Bridge on the River Kwai* (1957). He was the obvious choice to play Lawrence on the screen. Yet by 1960, Lean's regard may have cooled, due partially to Guinness's overwhelming international popularity. Lean prevented Guinness from playing Lawrence in his upcoming production, and instead cast the more impish, but far less-known Peter O'Toole. Although the youthful casting certainly emphasized a dichotomy between the aged, corrupt imperial bureaucracy (Claude Rains's Dryden and Jack Hawkins's Allenby) and its betrayal of one of the young "Lost Generation," Alec Guinness's more accurate physical resemblance and elusive shyness would have made a more nuanced and sympathetic protagonist. Instead, Lean picked an actor who was nearly a foot taller than the real T.E. Lawrence, dyed O'Toole's dark hair Prussian blond, and had him act out and perform the multiple roles of the British outsider, the imp, the hero, and the jaded butcher.

T.E. Lawrence has been called Britain's "last imperial hero," but in a recent study of *Lawrence of Arabia*, cultural anthropologist Steven C. Caton has questioned whether David Lean and screenwriters Michael Wilson and Robert Bolt believed that Lawrence was a hero. While acknowledging the film's post-war widescreen epic antecedents and Hollywood financing,

Caton has disputed the tendency within film scholarship to dismiss *Lawrence of Arabia* as a traditional imperial epic supporting both the hegemonic ideologies of Hollywood cinema and British imperialism. Calling for a more dialectical reading, Caton proposed that the film generates multiple perspectives critical of imperial heroism and the Hollywood epic, and that Lean and his screenwriters deliberately created an Orientalist but deeply anti-imperialist film focusing on a sado-masochistic, fascist anti-hero (Caton 102; 134). Caton has also offered an astute critique of Ella Shohat's work, later reproduced in the much-praised *Unthinking Eurocentrism*, charging her for a reductive reading of Anglo-American imperial films (Shohat 145-46). In their project to "unthink" Eurocentrism, Shohat and Robert Stam were guilty of a reductive, even tendentious approach that damned all Anglo-American films as bulwarks of the dominant discourses of imperialism and Orientalism. Although tending to reinforce an exceptional reading of *Lawrence of Arabia* that ignores the question of classical films' potential for critical imperialism, Caton's work suggests that a British imperial film is capable of critical agency and deliberate historiographic voice.

But the cost to the historical empire feature may have been too high. In the twenty years since Harry Faversham's painful rejection of imperial and military glory, Lean's Lawrence had plumbed the depths of imperial anti-heroism and decay. With Aldington's biography, long-term imperial "appeasement," the Suez Crisis, and other evidence of imperial collapse serving as their sources, Lean, Wilson, and Bolt transformed Lawrence into a conflicted imperial megalomaniac. Caton has brilliantly located a significant part of the film's critique of heroism within Lawrence's moments of performed megalomania; namely, his participation in Jackson Bentley's (Lowell Thomas) construction of his public image (Caton 128; 138). By 1962, Lawrence could be portrayed and criticized; yet one might argue that Lean's complex but flawed and fascist protagonist served the agenda of the very establishment that preferred to obliterate his popular legend. Like Korda, Lean still depended on British imperial history to frame his critical narrative, but his subject and his hero were so fraught with ambivalence, lies, war myths, and countermyths, that any search for the real Lawrence, any attempt to use cinema as a vehicle for historical truth, was futile. Lean alludes to this ambiguity repeatedly with the multiplicity of Lawrence's masks, his staged funeral service, his many portrait sittings, and most poignantly, the moment when he emerges from the Sinai Desert. A patrolling soldier sees Lawrence from across the Nile and shouts, "Who are you?" Lawrence stares mute and immobile, his face marbleized by desert sand and despair. A bitter visual allusion to the tradition of heroic public sculpture, it was Lean's "monumental" view of the imperial hero. If Lawrence is a conflicted and shadowy legend, the empire he serves and thwarts is far worse. Treacherous, decayed, effete, Dryden and Allenby are the old men with old ideas sending young men off to their deaths. They are killing the empire even as they serve their country. In 1962, as the British Empire disintegrated, *Lawrence of Arabia* articulated the disillusionment and decay of the Second Age of Imperial Cinema.

Imperial films continued to appear, and just as in the First Age, British filmmakers were often backed with Hollywood money. Cy Endfield's *Zulu* (1964) and Basil Dearden's *Khartoum* (1966) built upon Lawrence's legacy in more ways than one, returning to the ambivalent imperial hero, Charles Gordon, who fought alone against powerful and often triumphant native nationalist movements. To give Shohat and Stam their due, it is true that these films do not depict the Zulu or Sudanese perspective except for a few abbreviated longshots of burning military compounds. The narratives always focus on an empire, however decayed and disillusioned, under siege. Sometimes the filmmakers diverted attention from their imperial narratives by focusing on the tensions between working class Welsh soldiers and English officers, as in *Zulu*, or revealing the government's betrayal of a decent man and anti-imperialist like Charles Gordon, as in *Khartoum* (Richards, "Imperial" 138-40). Decayed outposts on the brink of isolated destruction: these were the imperial tales of Isandlwana and Khartoum. By the 1970s, imperialism seemed as dead in the theaters as it was around the globe. The rebirth of British cinema in 1981 either sublimated the empire as in *Chariots of Fire* (1981) or demonized it as in *Gandhi* (1982), *A Passage to India* (1984) and *Howard's End* (1993). The historical imperial epic seemed to be doomed. Even an attempted American remake of *The Four Feathers* collapsed at the box office in 2002.

The Third Age: The Return of "the Kings of Old"

Recently though, the old-fashioned imperial film has returned. The great irony is that a former colony of Great Britain has made it, and in an age of multiple national cinemas, the film has dominated every film market in the world. The film is *The Lord of the Rings*, produced and directed by New Zealand's Peter Jackson. But the real creator is of course J.R.R. Tolkien.

Tolkien was at Oxford only a few years after Lawrence. Like Lawrence, he fought in the Great War, and afterwards returned to the isolated world of Oxbridge to teach. His war experience would also have as great an effect on the shaping of imperial cinema. Like the Kordas and Lawrence, Tolkien witnessed the fall of empires, the horrors of the trenches and massive European kin killing, the wreck of great cities, and the ensuing economic and political decline of his own nation. He transformed Britain's years of imperial decay into the saga of Middle-earth. Abandoning the constraints of traditional historiography, he created his own fantastic history of a legendary race of Elves and Men (Númenóreans), once possessors of an enormous empire approximating the size of Europe and Russia. Yet old grudges and fears set off a wave of kin killing, Men betrayed the Elves, the Elves died or fled, and the forces of evil in the East grew, pillaging westward and attacking the territories of the empire.

As with much criticism of imperial cinema, there has been a tendency to marginalize Tolkien's work as nothing but a captivating epic fantasy in the tradition of *The Iliad* and *The Odyssey*, *The Elder Edda*, and Wagner's *Ring of the Nibelungs* (Carter). Paul Fussell's classic study of the Great War's influence on postwar literature, *The Great War and Modern Memory*, ignores Tolkien entirely (Fussell). Tolkien often denied that *The Lord of the Rings* was an allegory. Doubtless he was greatly irritated by the attempts to see the Ring as a symbol of nuclear power and Mordor as Russia, since these readings tended to ignore his text's linguistic genius and historical invention. As he put it, "I much prefer history, true or feigned, with its varied applications to the thought and experience of readers" (xvii; Foreword to second edition). Tolkien began the story of "The Fall of Gondolin," the stronghold of the Elves, shortly after recuperating from action in the Battle of the Somme (Carpenter 100). The Great War's destabilization of traditional views of the past, empire, and heroism is crucial in understanding Tolkien's acknowledged recreation of history and *The Lord of the Rings'* current popular impact on imperial cinema. C.S. Lewis, Tolkien's close friend and colleague, recognized the connection between Tolkien's war experience and his writings. In his review of *The Two Towers* for *Time and Tide*, he mused,

> This war has the very quality of the war my generation knew. It is all here: the endless, unintelligible movement, the sinister quiet of the front when "everything is now ready," the flying civilians, the lively, vivid friendships, the background of something like despair and the merry foreground, and such heaven-sent windfalls as a *cache* of

> choice tobacco "salvaged" from a ruin. The author has told
> us elsewhere that his taste for fairy-tale was wakened into
> maturity by active service; that, no doubt, is why we can
> say of his war scenes (quoting Gimli the Dwarf), "There is
> good rock here. The country has tough bones." (Lewis 1373-
> 4)

While Lewis agreed that some of the proposed allegories of the trilogy
were absurd, he acknowledged the universal quality of Sauron, and the
constant necessity of having to defeat him again and again. "Every time
we win we shall know that our victory is impermanent," he wrote, but
that has always been the "unchanging predicament by which heroic ages
have lived." Curiously, Lewis titled his review "The Dethronement of
Power," and the leading article and editorial in that issue of *Time and Tide*,
titled "Storm in the Desert," responded to Britain's own ignominious
dethronement in Egypt. But rather than likening the empire to Mordor, the
editor angrily denounced appeasement in Egypt, predicting, "We must
face the fact that soon there will develop in the Middle East a threat to the
security of us all" ("Storm"). Tolkien's tales of the decline of the Elvish and
Númenórean Empires, and their eventual Pyrrhic victory with the
coronation of Aragorn in *The Return of the King*, were born out of one
British imperial catastrophe and published in the middle of yet another
crisis between empire and appeasement. Lewis noticed how "real events
began, horribly, to conform to the pattern he had freely invented." His
words would resonate again a few short weeks before America's New
Line Cinema released Peter Jackson's *Fellowship of the Ring* (2001). The late
twentieth-century West's Eastern threat materialized on September 11
with the terrorist destruction of the Twin Towers.

Jackson's film, though glorying in the special computer-generated
effects and exotic prosthetics needed to create Hobbits, Elves, Dwarves,
and Ringwraiths, follows many of the structural characteristics of the
classic imperial film. There is an omniscient historical prologue narrated
by one of the oldest and wisest Elves, Lady Galadriel of Lothlórien, a
melancholy account of Middle-earth's loss of history. There is an epic
battle between Good and Evil, an unresolved balance of power, a sense of
decline and despair, when "History became legend, legend became myth
. . . " Such was the narrative of British imperial cinema from the days of
Korda to the days of Lean and the decline of the imperial film. But the
greatest continuity lies in *The Lord of the Rings'* Númenórean heir and hero.
Those familiar with the old, conflicted imperial hero from Charles Gordon
to Harry Faversham to T.E. Lawrence will recognize Aragorn. An outsider
and a scion of the kings of old, he is forced from his isolated, anonymous

life to fight the Eastern evil of Mordor and reclaim the empire of his forefathers. In *The Fellowship of the Ring*, Jackson often frames him with the ruins of his ancestors' empire. There are frequent shots of former imperial outposts, leveled watchtowers, and marble kings guarding gates that now any evil can penetrate. Boromir and Aragorn, sporting the beards and shoulder-length hair of Norman crusaders, make despairing references to the impending doom of the "white" imperial city of Gondor and take a grim pride in seeing the vestiges of the old empire. The petrified ruins of the "immortal" Elvish Empire serve as a constant reminder to Aragorn. Elrond and Galadriel live in a fading world of autumnal decay and twilight and remind him that one day he may also "fall into darkness, with all that is left of [his] kin."

Why did it take cinema nearly fifty years to transform narratives that seem ideal for the classical cinematic epic? Can imperialism only remain viable on screen by retreating into fantasy, far from the sneers of New Labor and the sublime contempt of the American Left? Or has it returned as an unsettling historical analogy, as new Eastern terrors arise and old empires of men dissolve? Whatever the reason, this retreat from history to fantasy, this reformulation of the imperial, this valorizing of the old empires, the old values of the Elves, the old wisdom of the wizard Gandalf, so key to imperial discourse, if not always to classical imperial cinema, is too obvious to ignore. Jackson and his team at Wingnut Films have remade memories of Western imperialism as the only honorable alternative to an evil Eastern Empire, something which both Zoltan Korda and David Lean conspicuously avoided. The second installment of the film, *The Two Towers* (2002), reedited after September 11, makes the allusions to terrorism and genocide, to veiled aggressors from the East, even more explicit. Those men who fight for Sauron, swarthy, draped in black, turbaned, and veiled, could be Middle-earth's equivalent of Saracens or Bedouin. The narrative focuses almost exclusively on the pale-haired Rohan people's last stand at Helm's Deep, an event that merits only a chapter in Tolkien's *Two Towers*. Saruman's (Christopher Lee's) battle speech to his new army of dark orc and goblin invaders projects a panoramic and spectacular menace reminiscent of Leni Riefenstahl's view of the Nuremberg rallies, but also resonates with the more contemporary and insidious racial terrors of dark, aberrant, but invisible enemies.

In 1915, as Tolkien lost faith in history, he imagined a great age of imperialism, glorious fallen empires, and rising imperial threats. British imperial cinema, increasingly preoccupied with imperial critiques from *The Four Feathers* to Lean's last feature, *A Passage to India*, still anchored its narratives within a recognizable British past. It was the remembrance and portrayal of the British Empire that gave British cinema some measure of independence from Hollywood. Imperialism's new lease on film-life, following the collapse of the studio system and wrought from the apparent abandonment of British history, still records many of the concerns of the previous two eras of imperial filmmaking. The writing and recording of history matters; in fact, Jackson concluded *The Return of the King* with shots of Bilbo and Frodo's historical accounts, *There and Back Again* and *The Lord of the Rings*. However, *The Lord of the Rings* looks upon imperial decay with nostalgia and regret. In *The Fellowship of the Ring*, Lord Elrond questioned the world of men, "Who will you look to when we've gone?" (*Fellowship*, scene 24: "The Fate of the Ring"). Tolkien and Jackson's solution was *The Return of the King* and the coronation of Aragorn in the white imperial city of Gondor. Imperial cinema may have lost its historians, classical critics, bitter skeptics, Zoltan Korda, A.E.W. Mason, and David Lean—it may even have ceded its British imperial identity to Hollywood and New Zealand—but Jackson's *The Lord of the Rings* may owe as much to Alexander Korda as to J.R.R. Tolkien. In the late 1930s, Korda believed that imperialism was the only reliable bulwark against fascism. In the Third Age of Imperial Cinema, is it the only certain defense against Eastern terrorism? In the world of corporate filmmaking, this at least is certain: imperial cinema will never disappear while it earns a multibillion-dollar worldwide gross.

WORKS CITED

Aldington, Richard. *Lawrence of Arabia: A Biographical Enquiry.* Chicago: Henry Regnery, 1955.

Armes, Roy. *A Critical History of the British Cinema.* New York: Oxford University Press, 1978.

Bordwell, David, et al. *The Classical Hollywood Cinema: Film Style and Mode of Production to 1960.* London: Routledge, 1985.

Carpenter, Humphrey. *Tolkien: A Biography.* Boston: Houghton Mifflin, 1977.

Carter, Lin. *Tolkien: A Look Behind the Lord of the Rings.* New York: Ballantine Books, 1969.

Caton, Steven C. *Lawrence of Arabia: A Film's Anthropology.* Berkeley: University of California Press, 1999.

Davis, Natalie Zemon. *Slaves on Screen.* Cambridge: Harvard University Press, 2001.

Drazin, Charles. *Korda: Britain's Only Movie Mogul.* London: Sidgwick & Jackson, 2002.

Fussell, Paul. *The Great War and Modern Memory.* New York: Oxford University Press, 1975.

Graves, Robert. *Lawrence and the Arabs.* London: Jonathan Cape, 1927..

"He Hopes to Win Empire for British Talkies." Korda microfiche, British Film Institute National Library. 28 January 1955.

Johnson, D.H. "The Death of Gordon: A Victorian Myth." *Journal of Imperial and Commonwealth History* X (May 1982): 285-310

Joy, G.W. *The Work of G.W. Joy, with an Autobiographical Sketch.* London: Cassell & Co., Ltd, 1904.

Judd, Denis. *Empire.* Basic Books, 1996.

Kanya-Forstner, A.S. "The War, Imperialism, and Decolonialism." *The Great War and the Twentieth Century.* Eds. Jay Winter, Geoffrey Parker, and Mary R. Habeck. New Haven: Yale University Press, 2000. 231-262.

Lancelyn Green, Roger. *A.E.W. Mason: The Adventure of a Story-Teller.* London: Max Parrish, 1952.

Lejeune, C.A. n.t. *The Observer* 29 October 1933 (from British Film Institute National Library clipping file, no page available).

Lewis, C.S. "The Dethronement of Power." *Time and Tide* 22 October 1955: 1373-4. Rpt. in *On Stories and Other Essays on Literature.* C.S. Lewis. San Diego: Harcourt, 1982.

The Lord of the Rings: The Fellowship of the Ring. Special Extended DVD Edition. Screenplay by Peter Jackson, Fran Walsh, and Philippa Boyens. New Line Home Entertainment, 2002.

Low, Rachel. *Film-Making in 1930s Britain.* London: George Allen & Unwin, 1985.

Mackenzie, John, ed. *Imperialism and Popular Culture.* Manchester University Press, 1986.

—. *Propaganda and Empire: The Manipulation of British Public Opinion, 1880-1960.* Manchester UP, 1984.

Mason, A.E.W. *The Four Feathers.* London: Smith, Elder, 1902.

Pronay, Nicholas. "The Political Censorship of Films in Britain Between the Wars." *Propaganda, Politics, and Film, 1918-1945.* Eds. Nicholas Pronay and D.W. Spring. London: Macmillan Press, Ltd., 1982. 98-125.

Ray, Robert. *A Certain Tendency of the Hollywood Cinema.* Princeton University Press., 1985.

Richards, Jeffrey. "Boys Own Empire: Feature Films and Imperialism in the 1930s," *Imperialism and Popular Culture.* Ed. John Mackenzie. Manchester University Press, 1986. 140-164.

—. *Films and British National Identity.* Manchester University Press, 1997.

—. "Imperial Heroes for a Post-Imperial Age: Films and the End of Empire." *British Culture and the End of Empire.* Ed. Stuart Ward. Manchester University Press, 2001. 128-44.

—. *Visions of Yesterday.* London: Routledge & Kegan Paul, 1973.

Rosenstone, Robert A. *Visions of the Past: The Challenge of Film to Our Idea of History.* Cambridge: Harvard University Press, 1995.

Said, Edward. *Culture and Imperialism.* New York: Knopf, 1993.

Sherriff, R.C. *The Four Feathers,* final shooting script. 14 July 1938. British Film Institute National Library.

—. *The Four Feathers,* cutting continuity. April 1939. British Film Institute National Library.

Shohat, Ella and Robert Stam. *Unthinking Eurocentrism: Multiculturalism and the Media.* London: Routledge, 1994.

Skeyhill, Tom. *Sergeant York: His Own Life Story and War Diary,* Garden City, NY: Doubleday, Doran, and Company, 1928.

—. *Sergeant York: Last of the Long Hunters,* Philadelphia: John C. Winston Company, 1930.

Slotkin, Richard. *Gunfighter Nation: The Myth of the Frontier in Twentieth Century America.* Norman: University of Oklahoma Press, 1992.

Street, Sarah. *British National Cinema,* London: Routledge, 1997.

—. "Stepping Westward: the Distribution of British Feature Films in America, and the Case of *The Private Life of Henry VIII.*" *British Cinema, Past and Present.* Eds. Justine Ashby and Andrew Higson. London: Routledge, 2000. 51-79.

"Storm in the Desert." *Time and Tide* 36:43 (22 October 1955): 1355-56

Tabori, Paul. *Korda.* New York: Living Books, 1966.

Thomas, Lowell. *A Boy's Life of Lawrence.* New York: The Century Co, 1927.

—. *With Lawrence in Arabia.* New York: The Century Co, 1925.

Tolkien, J.R.R. *The Lord of the Rings.* 2nd ed. With Note on the Text by Douglas A. Anderson. Boston: Houghton Mifflin, 1994.

Waugh, Alex. "Filming *The Four Feathers.*" *The Listener* 27 April 1939: 898-900.

White, Michael. *Tolkien: A Biography.* New York: Little, Brown & Co., 2001.

Wilson, Jeremy. *Lawrence of Arabia: The Authorized Biography of T.E. Lawrence,* London: Heineman, 1989.

PART II:

ADAPTATION
AND
REVISION

SUMMA JACKSONICA: A REPLY TO DEFENSES OF PETER JACKSON'S *THE LORD OF THE RINGS* FILMS, AFTER ST. THOMAS AQUINAS

DAVID BRATMAN

Never judge a book by its movie — Attrib. to J.W. Eagan

I begin to feel that I am shut up in a madhouse — J.R.R. Tolkien (Letters 363)

Scholars of J.R.R. Tolkien's work have noted, particularly in the cosmological sections of *The Silmarillion*, the influence of the theology of the great 13th century Catholic scholastic philosopher St. Thomas Aquinas. So it is perhaps appropriate to pursue a philosophical dispute involving Tolkien by using the *quaestio* format best known from Aquinas's masterwork, the *Summa Theologica*. In this format, we begin by posing the question at hand and laying out the objections to the position we will defend. Then we quote from Scripture or an authoritative master to show the contrary, expand on this in our own detailed response, and finally reply to the specific objections posed at the beginning.

Our topic in this paper is the *Lord of the Rings* films directed by Peter Jackson and their relationship to a book of the same title. Under this heading there are two points of inquiry:

(1) What are these films — a worthy rendition of J.R.R. Tolkien's novel into a different medium, or a travesty divorced from their claimed source?

(2) If they are a travesty, was this necessary for the purposes of film?

We proceed thus to the First Article:

WHETHER THE FILMS BE A TRAVESTY?

Objection 1: It would seem that the films are not a travesty, because the film-makers worked so hard and were so dedicated to their project and to Tolkien's spirit.

Objection 2: Further, that the films are Jackson's vision, not Tolkien's. A film is not a book.

Objection 3: Further, that the popularity of Jackson's films has brought new readers to the novel.

Objection 4: Further, that Jackson made accessible a boring old book that nobody liked anyway.

Objection 5: Further, that the films are a curate's egg. The story goes that a humble curate, visiting his bishop, was inadvertently given a stale egg to eat. Asked how he liked it, he meekly replied, "Parts of it are excellent."

Objection 6: That Tolkien did not object to films being made of his story. He sold the rights, and he wrote: "Can a tale not conceived dramatically but (for lack of a more precise term) epically, be dramatized—unless the dramatizer is given or takes liberties, as an independent person?" (*Letters* 255). And he also wrote, "I would draw some of the great tales in fullness, and leave many only placed in the scheme, and sketched. The cycles should be linked to a majestic whole, and yet leave scope for other minds and hands, wielding paint and music and drama" (*Letters* 145).

On the contrary, J.R.R. Tolkien also wrote,

> The failure of poor films is often precisely in exaggeration, and in the intrusion of unwarranted material owing to not perceiving where the core of the original lies. . . . One of [the writer's] chief faults is his tendency to anticipate scenes or devices used later, thereby flattening the tale out. . . . He has cut the parts of the story upon which its characteristic and peculiar tone principally depends, showing a preference for fights. (*Letters* 270-71)

I answer that, How close Peter Jackson came to making a great adaptation! How badly he muffed it!

The heartbreak of these films has been how easily Jackson could have created something to make Tolkien readers proud. His excision of Tolkien's moral fiber and nobility was so unnecessary: only small changes—or, more accurately, lack of changes—would have made all the difference. These films could have been the perfect treatment of Tolkien's epic story, without losing one touch of the thrilling adventure they so brilliantly are, without losing any of their popular appeal. What a shame, what a tragedy, what a lost opportunity!

Each year as I sat in the theatre, I felt as if I were seeing two films at once: one in the visuals which was faithful and true to Tolkien and another in the script and the general tone and style, which was so unfaithful as to be a travesty.

Much of the set design is absolutely beautiful. Not all—Lórien is dark and drab and not at all in Tolkien's image—but much is. But the tone and style bear almost no relationship to the book I have read and loved. The films are about war tactics: the novel is about moral issues that transcend the details of the war. The films dwell intensely on images of evil: the novel focuses lovingly on the Elves and Hobbits, giving attention to the beautiful things, and the homely pleasures, that will be lost should the Ring be taken. Everything about the beauty and wonder of the Elven lands has been cut down beyond any demands of plot or atmosphere.

They're good films. They just aren't *The Lord of the Rings*, and that's true *far* beyond the extent to which no film is the book from which it's made. Jackson could even have made better films *as film* if he'd been truer to Tolkien in many places and aspects where he wasn't. I grade Jackson an A on visuals and props, a B on the films as independent pieces of work divorced from the book, a C on faithfulness to Tolkien's story and detail, and a D (but only because I won't give an F when the student has shown evidence of trying) on faithfulness to Tolkien's spirit and tone.

Did Tolkien have a preternatural vision of Jackson's films in the above quote? No, but he might as well have had. What he's eviscerating here is a film scenario by Morton Grady Zimmerman sent him in 1958. Many of its flaws are deftly avoided in the Jackson films, but these particular comments are uncannily appropriate to Jackson. In *The Fellowship of the Ring* alone, think of the violent attacks by the Ringwraiths *in the Shire*, instead of their being left a vague menace, and the onscreen appearance of their attack in Bree, which flatten out their later real attack on Weathertop. Think of the discovery that the dwarves are dead at the *entrance* to Moria, flattening out the arrival at Balin's tomb. And most of all, think of that completely and utterly superfluous and time-wasting falling bridge immediately before the Bridge of Khazad-dûm. What was Jackson thinking? This even fails on the level of film-as-film, as well as on the level of film-as-adaptation of Tolkien. This scene is barely recognizable as an utter distortion and exaggeration of a reference to the company jumping over a seven-foot gap earlier in Moria (303; II:4). As for fights, the films' battle scenes go on and on, while the stays in Rivendell and Lórien are scanted: the novel depicts the battles briefly and in a detached style (as described by Matthew T. Dickerson in the first chapter of his book

Following Gandalf), leaving whole chapters for the beauties of the Elven lands, which despite their lack of "action" are many readers' favorites.

The book is more than its plot, and far more than its action scenes. As Elizabeth R. Milner wrote, "The crux of the matter to me is that *The Lord of the Rings* is an action adventure in the same way that the Bible is a book about sex." Jackson doesn't agree with this. The actual monster scenes in the book are few and far between, especially in the first volume. Even in them, Tolkien never puts the emphasis on fleeing. Jackson's focus on the fights distorts the whole. Hatchet journalists know this very well: you can write a profile of any person that will make them look like a fool, while containing no lies, regardless of what the person's really like. If a film has time for only, say, 10% of a book, Jackson chose his 10% almost entirely from a 20% selection of the original, ignoring everything that was in the other 80%.

None of this makes it bad as film. Compared with most recent blockbusters, Jackson's work is quite enjoyable. I'm a film-goer who was bored silly by the classic *Raiders of the Lost Ark*, and felt like crawling the walls during *The Phantom Menace*, but I was rarely bored by Jackson. But this is a series of pseudo-historical medieval war films, like *Braveheart*, also an enjoyable film that ludicrously trashed its sources. The book smells of elves; the movies reek of orcs.

Reply to Objection 1: An A for effort is not a final grade. An intent of capturing Tolkien's spirit does not equal an accomplishment of this. It certainly must be difficult to capture Tolkien's spirit, as Jackson, for all his efforts, failed to do so.

Jackson's film trilogy is a remarkable work: a remarkable work of the type of adventure fantasy known as "sword-and-sorcery." But Tolkien did not write a sword-and-sorcery novel. Except for the broadest of plot motives and themes, and the simplest of adventure, the films are totally unlike the book. Some will say otherwise. I'm sorry to insult such people, but they can't know the book very well. Within the realm of script and tone, it was the superficial and least important points which were most faithfully adhered to, and the deeper meanings, and those matters which set Tolkien apart from run-of-the-mill fantasists, that were most altered or dropped. Tolkien's moral sense has been nearly completely lost, and the story reduced to a series of battles which are carefully avoided or distanced in Tolkien's narration, when they're in the book at all. All that's left that's any good is the exciting adventure story, and some part of the riot of invention. That's not enough to separate Tolkien from the average cracking adventure fantasist, and he's much more than that.

The film-makers say they are devotees of the book. I believe they mean this, though I am astonished to hear it. To my mind, the claim proves merely that they do not understand the work they are adapting. And the more they claim they're keeping true to it, the more it proves they don't understand it. For an example on the most superficial level, apparently Jackson depicted Sauron as a giant protoplasmic eye on top of Barad-dûr because he genuinely failed to recognize Tolkien's phrase "The Eye of Sauron" as a synecdoche like *all hands on deck* (see Ansen and Giles 64). (Gollum refers to Sauron as the Black Hand twice [624, 627; IV:3]; one could just as well use that to justify depicting Sauron as Thing from the Addams Family movies.) Tolkien has often been criticized for leaving Sauron offstage, but he knew that in a book of this kind to bring his chief villain onstage in any form would only trivialize him. (Read Tolkien's early *Book of Lost Tales* to see how trivialized villains can be.) He showed restraint and wisdom.

There is no vitriol being spilled at Jackson just for daring to think he could succeed at translating the book to the screen. If vitriol is being spewed, it is for his failure to achieve this, and his belief that he succeeded. Nor is there refusal to enjoy an entertainment just for being an entertainment. Many critics did not find the films entertaining on any level. They can hardly be accused of sneering at "pure entertainment" if they weren't entertained. The humorist Dave Barry, for instance, called *The Two Towers*—to my taste the most exciting and fast-moving of the three—"*Lord of the Rings II: A* Lot *More Stuff Happens.* . . . Yes, this is a classic movie, the kind that makes you laugh, makes you cry, makes you wonder, over and over, if this would be a good time to go to the bathroom." Others, including myself, were entertained and have repeatedly said so. Our criticism is of their claim to have anything seriously to do with Tolkien.

I really wonder what spirit or "themes" *The Lord of the Rings* has that they think the movies preserve. They preserve a summary of the plot; they convey a big, complex world; they show danger and heroism (in the broadest sense); parts look like Tolkien. That's about it.

The author Michael Swanwick has written of his experience reading *The Lord of the Rings* aloud to his nine-year-old son. He became aware that the story the boy was hearing was not the same as the one he was reading. To the boy, it was just an exciting adventure story, but to the man it was ever so much more (35-36).

Peter Jackson has a nine-year-old's understanding of Tolkien. I expect more than that.

Reply to Objection 2: It isn't Tolkien's vision? You can say that again.

Artistic vision is personal interpretation. Either Jackson and his crew were devotees of the original text and setting, and did their best to keep true to the text and spirit of Tolkien, or they were determined to put their interpretation on the text, to make the movies uniquely theirs. You can't have it both ways.

There's plenty of room for creative imagination and originality in adapting Tolkien to film, especially in what it will look like, and visual design—the aspect in which Tolkien left the most room for a director to express himself—is what Jackson did best. I'm very happy with about 80-90% of what these films look like, including the actors, and the rest I'm willing to accept, chalking it up to differences in taste, or minor lapses that are forgivable within the whole. That's not the case with the script, which is 90% travesty from start to finish.

To defend Jackson by saying his films aren't Tolkien's *The Lord of the Rings* is not an answer to criticism, but a throwing up of the argument in mute agreement. It defies the clear statements in each film's credits, "Based on the book by J.R.R. Tolkien." And to say that it's Jackson's *The Lord of the Rings* is tautological. The question is, what *is* Jackson's *Lord of the Rings*? As his defenders say, any director will necessarily pursue his own vision. So what *is* his own vision? The answer turned out to be something incompatible with Tolkien's vision, and the solution would have been a director whose own vision was more compatible with Tolkien's.

Compatibility doesn't mean faithful reverence. It does not imply mechanically reproducing the book's plot, but conveying its spirit. If you can't do that, choose another book. A director who approaches his film with a spirit only of reverence, and not of creativity and imagination, will make a dead work no matter what the source. That's what happened to the first two *Harry Potter* films: a bad director tied rigidly to the text made dull movies out of sparkling books. But part of that is because the bright, witty spirit of Rowling's *Harry Potter* was edited out of those scripts as ruthlessly as the noble spirit of Tolkien was edited out of Jackson's. They just kept more of the plot in.

Faithfulness to the spirit is not at all the same as strict adherence to the letter. A book on *Jane Austen in Hollywood* contains many essays showing the films of her novels wildly deviating from their spirit while remaining relatively close to their letter. Austen scholars Carol M. Dole, Suzanne Ferriss, and Nora Nachumi all spontaneously agree that the true spirit and temperament of Austen are more to be found in the film

Clueless, a thoroughly whimsical modern updating of *Emma* set in a tony high school (Troost and Greenfield 72; 123; 136). While it is doubtful that a modern fable applying Tolkien's morality to, say, the atomic bomb could have carried his spirit, the real point is not to confuse adherence to the letter with faithfulness to the spirit.

There are subjectivities here, and none of it would matter so much if there were other movies being made of Tolkien on a regular basis. (Though that would be a shudder-inducing reality for other reasons.) Or if, having been made, they were seen and then dropped off the cultural radar. The frequent productions of Shakespeare's plays show that some directors have individual visions compatible with Shakespeare's and some don't. Playgoers learn from experience to avoid the latter; if you make a mistake and go to a bad one, you shrug and say "Better luck next time." But a giant blockbuster film trilogy doesn't have the ephemeral quality of a stage production. These are the officially authorized, one-and-only (at least for this generation), massively publicized film series. You can't ignore a 500-pound gorilla.

I'm not particularly bothered by bad Tolkien artwork, for instance, because I can glance at it and throw it away, and there's plenty more Tolkien artwork that may be more to my taste. None of that is true of a film, and no other form of art grabs so many senses—the eyes, the ears, the aesthetic senses of spectacle and drama and music, and the implanted sense of repetition of all these things as you re-watch it—as a film does. Film is a powerful tool, and, as Tolkien tells us, power must be used only with great caution.

Jackson's saga was marketed from the beginning as an authentic, true-to-the-book story, a fan's version, a prestige project and not just another Hollywood blockbuster. There would always have remained some disagreements among fans, of course. But given the effort involved, it would have been no harder to have made films that would have been true to Tolkien's spirit, that pleased us to some degree. The films' attractive qualities are quite different from Tolkien's, so a person who might like Tolkien could easily be repelled by the films and never realize that he or she might like the books. That would certainly be the case with several people I know, particularly women, who are attracted to the book for its beauty and wonder, and by its remarkable lack (for a war story) of long gruesome depictions of battles. Here the films are very different.

Jackson is aware of the necessity for fidelity. He has said, "We experimented with the idea of trying to make Sauron more of a physical presence but we found whenever we went too far away from what Tolkien wrote, it just didn't feel right" (Jackson and Boyens).

Indeed. It sure enough didn't.

Reply to Objection 3: It's pleasing that sales of the book have increased, and that (one hopes) more people are reading it. But it's not as if, as some film-boosters have been heard to say, the films have been moving sales of a book product that was not selling all that well: as if Jackson were somehow doing Tolkien a favor; as if *The Lord of the Rings* were some obsolete old thing that nobody read any more, half-forgotten, needing to be rescued from near-oblivion by the kindly hand of Peter Jackson. This is utter rot, but it keeps appearing. *The Lord of the Rings* has been a staple of book-of-the-century lists since before the films showed up (Shippey, *J.R.R.* xxi), and is perhaps the best-selling work of fiction of its time. That's a wide enough audience that a film isn't needed to keep it wide. And the number of people who will read Tolkien because of Jackson is surely smaller than the number who will see Jackson and think, wrongly, that they therefore know Tolkien's work.

It would be possible to make this argument differently: one might say something like, "There's one ironic silver lining to all this: sales of the book are up. Maybe that'll help wash the taste of the films out of people's minds." But nobody who's made the point has written anything at all like that. They all put it in the context of praising the movies. They may not realize that a better film would have attracted even more readers.

New readers have come to Tolkien from worse imitations than Peter Jackson, and yes, that's good fortune from dross. But this no more makes those sources admirable than Gollum's role in destroying the Ring makes him admirable. Bad does not become good because its existence leads to a good result. Destruction of the Ring was not Gollum's intent; nor was increased sales of the book Peter Jackson's intent. The only difference is that presumably Jackson isn't unhappy about it. It's not as if the book has been lacking readers. True, it's been read by fewer people than will have seen the films, but that's because films are measured on a different scale. If Jackson's changes were necessary to popularize the story, then it follows that the book would also have been more popular if Tolkien had had the sense to write a story that followed the spirit and letter of Jackson's script.

But this would be nonsense. Dozens of lesser heroic fantasies that are written like Jackson's films have been forgotten. The survival of *The Lord of the Rings* is due to its being different. People were reading it long before Jackson's time, and I hope they will still be reading it when his films look like cheesy dated spectacles, as I'm convinced they will. One review of Jackson's *Return of the King* says it makes *Star Wars* "look like stick figures in a bad, Japanese-made Saturday-morning cartoon" (Edelstein). Remember what an awesome thing *Star Wars* was in its day? Jackson's CGI Gollum, so dazzling to its first viewers, will look equally moth-eaten in twenty-five years. As George Lucas is now, Peter Jackson one day will be, and they're both susceptible to this because they're both ultimately derivative. Tolkien is an original, and has lasted.

The harm wreaked by Jackson's films appears tragically in Tom Shippey's essay "Another Road to Middle-earth," in which he turns his mighty brain to the task of justifying Jackson's changes—and comes a cropper, because even the mightiest brain can't do it. Language like "Arwen's defiance [while] rhetorically cheaper than Frodo's . . . perhaps offers a moment for female viewers to place themselves in the story" (237), and excuses for "sequences designed for the teenage market" (237) because they "pass quickly" and do not affect the "core of the original" (238)—a doubtful proposition at best—reek of Sarumanian accomodationism. When the dean of Tolkien scholars uses such language, something is wrong. The premises are false, anyway. The book's supposed lack of "moment[s] for female viewers to place themselves in the story" have not prevented millions of women of all ages from loving it, and the book so strongly appeals to "the teenage market" that some of Tolkien's hostile critics have accused it of not appealing to anything else. Saying that films have to appeal to more people than books begs the question of whether a film actually resembling Tolkien's book would so appeal—all the evidence leans towards the conclusion that it would. Even Shippey concludes, desperately, with the hope that the film's viewers will turn to the book.

I just hope that readers who come to the book through the films will be able to appreciate it. My own experience as a 12-year-old trying Charles Dickens in a rush of enthusiasm from the film *Oliver!* was a case of mental whiplash so severe that I've never gotten over it. Word so far is that readers coming to Tolkien from Jackson have generally not been repelled, and I am glad to hear it, though the early chapters of hobbitry and Tom Bombadil have always put some readers off.

They may be outnumbered by those who just want to use the book—and the films—as a basis for daydreams. This is not the first occasion on which people have been enchanted by Tolkien in a way that others thought misapplied. Tolkien had a few choice words for the more dubious appropriations made by his early fans. He was embarrassed by their over-praise and deeply repelled by much of the form that appreciation took—I suspect, but do not know, that it showed him they didn't really appreciate it at all. C.S. Lewis had some good, and not entirely critical, comments on those who would rather pine for sexy characters than appreciate the story: see chapter 6 on fantasizing in his *An Experiment in Criticism*. Folks who want to swoon over actor Orlando Bloom are welcome to do so, but they should not delude themselves into thinking they are thereby appreciating *The Lord of the Rings* (even the films, let alone the book). If it leads them to learn to appreciate the book, so much the better—stranger things have happened—but first it has to lead them there.

Reply to Objection 4: Yes, Jackson has actually been praised by demeaning Tolkien. After extolling their own faithfulness to the novel in the commentary tracks on the DVD of *The Fellowship of the Ring*, and being rightly excoriated for it, Jackson's crew changed their tune with the DVD of *The Two Towers* and started boasting of how much better-written their script was than the book.

And they've not lacked for fellow-travelers in print. Those who have noticed how high *The Lord of the Rings* ranks in literary polls of public opinion may find it hard to believe that the spirits of early obtuse critics like Philip Toynbee and Edmund Wilson (Shippey, *J.R.R.* 306-07) still walk the land, but they do:

> ∞ Peter Jackson has taken a gnarly, blustering and at times haughtily didactic doorstopper chock full of stilted dialogue and winding diversion and brought it to vibrant, thrilling life. —Nina Rehfeld

> ∞ Tolkien's book moves at a deliberate pace and features a hero (Frodo Baggins) who eventually loses the sympathy of most readers. —Eli Lehrer

Other critics don't hate the book, they just don't think it measures up:

> ∞ Tolkien was a very fine artist, as the enduring popularity of his books testifies. But he was not as fine an artist as Peter Jackson is. The films are mightier by far than the books; indeed they stand as the greatest achievement in the history of cinema. —Kevin Myers

> ∞ Jackson's picture is an improvement on its source material, if only because Jackson's film language is subtler, more sophisticated and certainly more contemporary than the stilted, deliberate archaisms of J.R.R. Tolkien's descriptive prose and, even more problematically, of his

dialogue. (I am a big fan of the book version of *The Lord of the Rings*, but nobody ever read Tolkien for the writing.)
—Salman Rushdie

To these two gentlemen, I can only say: Let's meet again in another twenty-five years and see which achievement stands up better then. I know which one I'm betting on. *Nobody* ever read Tolkien for the writing? Speak for yourself, Mr. Rushdie. How much greater Sméagol's agony is in the book, how much more moving and better-written than the films, how much more sense it makes when his two personalities simply reflect that he's in two minds about his role and aren't trying to send each other physically into exile. "Leave now and never come back . . . leave now and never come back . . . leave now and never come back," says Film-Sméagol, yes, three times (*Towers*, scene 29: "Gollum and Sméagol"). What subtle, sophisticated dialogue, eh, Mr. Rushdie? What a mighty achievement in cinematic art, eh, Mr. Myers?

What's striking about Lehrer and Rushdie is, as Tom Shippey has noted of their predecessors, "that they should insist so perversely in making statements not about literary merit, where their opinions could rest undisprovable, but about popular appeal, where they can be shown up beyond all possibility of doubt" (*Road* 1-2).

Reply to Objection 5: Unlike the curate's stale egg, parts of these films *are* excellent. What's heart-breaking is how good the excellent parts are. After the rushed, battle-filled *Fellowship of the Ring*, I was delighted with the perfectly paced, beautifully modulated *Two Towers*, a work of cinematic craft its director can be proud of. And the epilogue of *The Return of the King* gives full weight to Tolkien's long, elegiac coda. After seeing what Jackson has done with "The Grey Havens," the book's final chapter, I'm almost ready to forgive him for anything. It was maudlin, but in context it worked well. It might have been changed, here and there, or made closer to the book—if it were set at dusk, for instance, or if Sam's final line had been given context by showing him earlier telling Rosie he wouldn't be gone long—but it could not have been made better. It took its time, but not too much time. This was from some other *Lord of the Rings* film, the one I'd been hoping Jackson would make. Why didn't he show such sensitivity to the rest of the book?

But this is all mixed up inextricably with egregious horrors: the interminable battle scenes, the scanting of Elven wonder, the uncanonical failures of nerve, the relentless trivialization of the story, the superficial appreciation of the book thinly veiling a profound lack of comprehension. While my filmgoing self was cheering, my Tolkien reader was wincing—

simultaneously, a most peculiar sensation. You can't eat just the good parts of this egg: Jackson isn't serving it that way.

Another way of putting the "curate's egg" defense is to say, "We got half a loaf. Let's not criticize the half a loaf we didn't get." But we didn't get half a loaf. A half loaf is still a loaf, it's just smaller than a regulation loaf, and just as edible. With these films, we didn't get a smaller amount of good, we got bad mixed inextricably up with good. It's more like a poisoned glass of milk: all the vitamins and calcium are still there, but it's not nutritious.

Reply to Objection 6: Before deducing what Tolkien would have thought of these films, let's make a clear distinction amongst what one considers legally permissible, morally admirable, and aesthetically desirable. Nobody is disputing Jackson's legal right to make these films. But it in no sense follows that the result must therefore be morally admirable or aesthetically desirable. Junk e-mail may be legal (for now), but only junk e-mailers mistake this for an argument that it's admirable.

By contrast, one is free to admire the aesthetic quality of, say, some rip-off piece of fan fiction that's openly in violation of copyright law; and on occasion a wholly illegal act may be morally entirely admirable: for an example in *The Lord of the Rings*, consider Beregond's bloody rescue of Faramir (833-4; V:7) and the judgment passed upon him (947; VI:5).

There's no question: Tolkien disapproved of the notion of a film being made ("I think the book quite unsuitable for 'dramatization'" [*Letters* 228]) and accepted the idea only insofar as he wanted the money and was able to shrug off the desecration. He never thought a film would actually be made:

> Brass bands playing, big drums thumping, the publicity circus for the mythology-movie *Lord of the Rings* draws near; but all I can hear is the chuckle of John Ronald Reuel Tolkien, 30 years ago, telling me that he had consented to a film rights deal with one of the big studios. 'Not that there's any chance of a film being made,' he said. But the deal meant, at least, that film company lawyers would save him from the distraction of guarding his copyrights from people making Hobbit T-shirts or plastic Gandalf toys, and let him get on with his work. (Cater)

Tolkien is asking the question, not giving an answer, when he writes of "the dramatizer [who] is given or takes liberties, as an independent person" (*Letters* 255). As advice to a dramatizer (of the 1956 BBC radio version), it is very minimal and grudgingly given. Tolkien did not wish to take responsibility for an adaptation he elsewhere describes as "not well done" (*Letters* 229) and "sillification" (*Letters* 257), when writing in frankness to friends instead of in politeness to the show's producer.

Describing what he would "leave scope for other minds and hands" to do, he is recalling what "once upon a time . . . [he] had a mind" to do, adding "my crest has long since fallen" (144). And his final word on this original intent to beget a shared mythology? "Absurd" (145). It is interesting that Tolkien had no objection to music inspired by his work, even if he didn't happen to like the music (*Letters* 350), but then music was not his art. Visual art and narrative story were his arts, and those kinds of retellings he expected to show faithfulness to his spirit. About illustrations he could be very grumpy (*Letters* 362-63), but he could also be very pleased: he was utterly delighted with Pauline Baynes's work for *Farmer Giles of Ham*, for instance (*Letters* 133).

In the second chapter of *The Lord of the Rings*, Frodo wishes that the Ring had never been found (58; I:2). Similarly, it would have been better had a film never been made. But as the Ring has been found, the question becomes what to do with it. And though it lies not within our power to cast these films into a fiery pit, we can wish for ones that are true to Tolkien's spirit.

We proceed thus to the Second Article:

WHETHER THE TRAVESTY WAS NECESSARY
FOR THE PURPOSES OF FILM?

Objection 1: It would seem that a travesty was necessary, for films aren't books, and must bow to the financial, commercial, and story-telling conventions of Hollywood.

Objection 2: Further, it could have been worse. It's a miracle that Jackson did as well as he did.

Objection 3: Further, a perfect film would have been 70 hours long.

Objection 4: Further, it doesn't matter because the book is still there to read. There's an anecdote about an author—in some tellings it's James M. Cain, in some it's somebody else—who was asked how he felt about Hollywood film versions having "ruined his books," and Cain replied, "My books aren't ruined. They're right there, sitting on the shelf."

Objection 5: Further, that Jackson's critics are just annoyed because Tom Bombadil was cut.

On the contrary, J.R.R. Tolkien wrote, "The canons of narrative art in any medium cannot be wholly different" (*Letters* 270). And "I think the book quite unsuitable for 'dramatization'" (*Letters* 228). And of Kenneth Grahame's sense of tone in *The Wind in the Willows*, he wrote,

> It is all the more remarkable that A.A. Milne, so great an admirer of this excellent book, should have prefaced to his dramatised version a 'whimsical' opening in which a child is seen telephoning with a daffodil. Or perhaps it is not very remarkable, for a perceptive admirer (as distinct from a great admirer) of the book would never have attempted to dramatise it. Naturally only the simpler ingredients, the pantomime, and the satiric beast-fable elements, are capable of presentation in this form. The play is, on the lower level of drama, tolerably good fun, especially for those who have not read the book; but some children that I took to see 'Toad of Toad Hall' [the Milne play] brought away as their chief memory nausea at the opening. For the rest they preferred their recollections of the book. (*Tree* 66-67)

And Ursula K. Le Guin, the greatest of post-Tolkienian fantasists, wrote,

> In art, the best is the standard. When you hear a new violinist, you do not compare him to the kid next door; you compare him to Stern and Heifetz. If he falls short, you will not blame him for it, but you will know what he falls short of. And if he is a real violinist, he knows it too. In art, 'good enough' is not good enough. (83-84)

I answer that, Why does it matter if the travesty was necessary? Why can't Tolkien go his way and let Jackson go his?

Because of media colonization. The book is being drowned out and substituted for by the films in any number of ways. It will eventually take over from Tolkien's book as the predominant public image of Middle-earth. This may seem unlikely, but it is already happening.

On a panel on Tolkien's books at the 2002 World Science Fiction Convention, one panelist, a community college English professor, had taught *The Hobbit* in class but admitted never having finished reading *The Lord of the Rings*. Yet she was ready to denounce *The Lord of the Rings* vehemently for plot problems she noticed in the first film, the only one then released—each of which was not a problem in the book for one reason or another, but despite the protests of the rest of the panel, this panelist would not stop. Clearly she didn't know enough not to judge a book by its movie, as the proverb has it. At least one of her criticisms—an incredulity that Aragorn would go on a quest leaving his beloved Arwen behind—is addressed not only by the book, in which Arwen is not an Action Figure, but (differently) by Jackson's second film, if only our professor had had the patience to wait for it.

Many new writings about Tolkien mix the book and films indiscriminately. Most prominent so far is *The Rough Guide to The Lord of the Rings*. This volume frankly covers both works, yet makes no effort to keep them separate, using stills and even production photos (67) to illustrate its discussion of the book. Its summary of the book is clearly of the book, not of the films, yet it describes Merry and Pippin as "exuberant" (88), says that Gandalf "throws [Wormtongue] out" (94), and claims that "Tolkien's imagination was fired by monsters" (105), all statements true of the films but highly dubious about Tolkien or his book. Indeed, one of the sharpest moral distinctions between book and film comes when the film's Wormtongue is literally thrown out of Edoras, where in the book even he is offered a chance to redeem himself in war (508; III:6). Tolkien used monsters in his story, but he did not focus on them. Jackson loves them for themselves.

The most blatant case I've yet seen of quoting from the films and attributing it to the book comes in a magazine article about Tolkien's understanding of environment and landscape. This begins:

> "Build me an army worthy of Mordor," commands Sauron in *The Fellowship of the Ring*. With a maniacal greed for power, the easily corrupted Saruman turns his cavernous lair beneath Isengard into a frenzied factory of orcs and armor, fueled by burning the region's trees, which he clear-cuts with reckless abandon. When an orc reports to Saruman, "The trees are strong, my lord; their roots grow deep," Saruman barks, "Take them all down," and down they come.
>
> Thus J.R.R. Tolkien draws the lines of evil in his wondrous tale, *The Lord of the Rings*. (Amodeo 36)

No, thus Peter Jackson draws them. His Saruman actually says "Rip them all down," not "Take." But aside from that minor point, this dialogue is exactly copied from Jackson's film (*Fellowship*, scene 18: "The Spoiling of Isengard"). Nothing like it occurs in the book. Tolkien's Saruman is known to cut down trees and raise orcish armies, but that's no excuse for the appalling sloppiness of quoting from Jackson and attributing it to Tolkien.

This might not be carelessness alone. Already, in almost every conversation I'm having about *The Lord of the Rings*, I have to say "the films do this but the book does that," because if I don't, people who know the films better than the book will think I'm misremembering the films. This is one reason why, as a Tolkien critic, I had to see the films even if I didn't want to: simply to avoid endless confusion in discussing the book. But the better I know the films, the more vigilance I must apply to myself. Marketers have been selling "Hadhafang™: The Sword of Arwen." In discussing the unloveliness of this name, I found myself trying to remember whether the sword had a name in the book. It took me a moment to remember that in the book Arwen had no sword whatever. Oops.

Films have colonized books before. The general public has no idea that the monster in Mary Shelley's *Frankenstein* is nothing like the one in the 1931 Universal film. Almost anyone reading Shelley's novel for the first time is in for a big surprise. The film has become that iconic. The better and more lasting Jackson's films are, the more Tolkien will be headed for a similar fate. I don't believe anyone who says that they can cast the films totally out of mind in these circumstances.

The Wonderful Wizard of Oz by L. Frank Baum is often cited as a book which has survived a film very different from it. But though the book is there to be read, it's been buried by the film. "I am sure I am not alone," says one Oz scholar, "when I say that it was the 1939 MGM motion picture that defined Oz for me" (Swartz ix). It should disturb Baum's faithful readers that most people—following the film—think Oz is a dream-world. Baum's biographer observes that making Oz a dream reduces "Dorothy's journey into . . . a mere projection of her wishes and fears." This is the "ultimate falsification . . . [of] Baum's view that the world of imagination has its own validity. Baum's Oz . . . should not be dismissed as a dream" (Rogers 253-54).

We were warned that this utter change in our view of Tolkien's book was coming. Cartoonist Scott Kurtz warned us: in an episode of his comic strip *PvP* published before Jackson's first installment was released, the middle-aged Cole urges the young Francis—who has never read the book—"You must read [*The Lord of the Rings*] now, *before* the movie. . . . Don't let the movie create the first images of these characters for you." But now, in the Age of Jackson, Francis would no longer have that choice. Tolkien scholar Douglas A. Anderson warned us: it is in practice no longer possible for a new reader to come to Tolkien uninfluenced by Peter Jackson, any more than a new reader can come to Baum's Dorothy Gale uninfluenced by Judy Garland (150). Since the films are so different from the book, and since the imagery of *any* film would be limiting to the imagination, this is a serious loss. "I am sure I am not alone," future scholars will write, "when I say that it was Peter Jackson's motion pictures that defined Middle-earth for me." We should pause and think about what this means.

Reply to Objection 1: A studio devoted to the financial bottom line wouldn't have allowed, let alone encouraged, Peter Jackson to make three films instead of one, let alone filming all three before getting any box-office feedback on the first one. That decision saved them lots of production money in the long run, but it also took an enormous risk of a kind and scale unprecedented in film history.

A director tied to Hollywood convention, focused on making the most cinematic film appealing to the widest possible audience wouldn't have put that twenty-minute epilogue on the end of *The Return of the King*. Nothing in the entire film saga was more true to the spirit of Tolkien's book, yet nothing was less cinematic, and nothing was pilloried more by critics who otherwise liked the films. Whenever I've complained about Jackson's trivialization of Tolkien, his apologists have said that I don't understand: movies have to appeal to a broader audience, there are certain conventions of movie storytelling that you just can't break if you want to sell the film, and so on. But the most basic convention of ending an action adventure film is this: one quick celebration scene and then wrap it up. The epilogue of *The Return of the King* is proof that, *when he wants to*, Jackson has the courage to defy not only cinematic convention, but also the critics who enforce it. Here he carries the Tolkien fans with him, and that's actually enough: the better a reviewer knows the book, the more that reviewer liked *The Return of the King*. Patrick Diehl showed keen perception when he wondered "how far the success of these scenes, for me, was due to the reflected glow of the same scenes in Tolkien's book, rather than their own virtues. The response from those who have not read the book seems to be quite different, and much less favorable, than mine."

A screenwriter named Linda Seger applied the conventional view of cinematic storytelling to the epilogue, demonstrating that she'd entirely missed Jackson's and Tolkien's point—in one of the few places where the author and director are in full agreement. "Here is where the structure breaks down," she wrote. "If *The Return of the King* had concluded [with Aragorn's coronation], the resolution would have been five minutes long, and would have told us everything we needed to know." Seger has forgotten that this is a story about Hobbits. "Everything we needed to know" excludes not only Sam's marriage, but Frodo's restlessness and departure oversea. And isn't this a rather small-minded comment? Isn't there more to a story, in film or in print, than a need-to-know basis? A twenty-minute epilogue is not unreasonable for a nine-to-eleven-hour saga. If your goal is to learn the plot facts you need to know, read the Cliffs Notes. To experience a film, or a book, is to immerse yourself in its atmosphere and style. This isn't a cram session for a test. If Jackson is to be criticized on this ground—one thing in plotting that he did right—he should be criticized for making three great, sprawling movies in the first place. A "what you need to know" version of the story could easily have been packed into a single 2½ hour film mainly about Frodo, discarding most of the parallel plots.

For once, Jackson knew better than that. He wanted, and got, a full-scale epic. Nor did he tear apart the entire storyline to stuff it into the mindless three-act structure which so many bad screenwriters insist is essential for cinematic success, but which too often merely produces bad, predictable films.

So let's not be too dogmatic about the story-telling and audience-appealing needs of cinema. When Jackson *does* change the story, don't blame what's dramatically or cinematically or structurally "necessary." He does it because he wants to. He didn't have to: there's general critical agreement that the extended edition of *The Fellowship of the Ring* is *both* truer to Tolkien *and* a better film than the original theatrical release, so it *is* possible to work towards both those goals at once. But Jackson didn't always want to do that.

There is insufficient rigor in film criticism in distinguishing between changes that actually are necessary because of the differences in the media, changes that are not necessary but are made to fit the director's or screenwriter's preferences (usually dignified as "expressing a vision"), and changes that are made purely out of guesswork or superstition about what will sell to movie audiences. The screenwriter William Goldman's first Law of Filmmaking is *"Nobody knows anything"* (39). Nobody knows what will be popular; nobody knows what will succeed or fail, or why it succeeded or failed; nobody knows whether something that worked in one film last year will replicate its popularity if repeated in some other film this year; nobody knows if your idea of what is dramatically necessary really is. Nobody knows whether *The Lord of the Rings* films could have been successful, or as successful, if they had stayed closer to the spirit of the book. I just would have liked to have seen them try: for there are two things we do know. One is that a dramatization truer to Tolkien's spirit is possible. It was done in the 1981 BBC radio adaptation by Brian Sibley and Michael Bakewell, which faced nearly all of Jackson's condensation problems (it's 13 hours long), plus the additional hurdles of being restricted to hour-long episodes and to the medium of sound alone. Yet it completely avoids the kind of storytelling horrors that most disfigure Jackson's films. Fidelity to Tolkien was also achieved by Orson Scott Card, whose readers' theatre adaptation takes only six hours to perform. It comes across as a chamber version, but respects both the spirit and letter of Tolkien while being dramatically interesting.

The other thing we know is that the book is successful the way Tolkien wrote it. No matter how many people out there found *The Lord of the Rings* difficult—and there's no novel ever written that appeals to everybody—it has overall been the most popular and lasting of its century. This suggests that whatever its literary merits—and critics like Harold Bloom most eager to deny its merits probably wouldn't care for the movies either—Tolkien did know something about story-telling and popular appeal. His story is constructed with tight, interwoven detail and a fine eye for both repetition and contrast. Thus any changes to his story made by film-makers, unless their literary artistry is greater than his, are liable to be for the worse.

If there is any truth to Goldman's Law, anybody who claims that Tolkien's story had to be altered this way or that to make it more "cinematic" or "dramatic" is talking through their hat. It's a cover for a personal preference for doing it that way, or an inability to write a better screenplay, or, worst of all, for a total lack of comprehension of what Tolkien was trying to do. We can see this in the screenwriters' defenses of their worst blunders. Co-author Philippa Boyens explains:

> The reason Frodo turns Sam away is what would happen to that story if he didn't do something? You would have a very long climb up the stairs and then you would have Sam getting lost in the tunnel, which happens in the book, which is not dramatic. (Jackson and Boyens)

It takes a strongly individual sense of the dramatic, to say the least, to mischaracterize the climactic chapters of Book 4 as "not dramatic," and then to spice them up with a scene which had critics sneering and audiences dropping their jaws in disbelief. Dramatic moments have to make sense. This one doesn't. One parodist nicely paraphrases the scene:

> GOLLUM. Fat hobbit wants Ring; yes, Master.
> SAM. I do not!
> FRODO. I think maybe you do. Gollum wouldn't lie to
>   me, after all.
> SAM. He's trying to kill us! We're walking straight
>   into a trap. I'm not going one step further.
> FRODO. Leave, then. I'm sick of your paranoid
>   delusions anyhow.

SAM. But I . . .

FRODO. Go on—get out of here. Good riddance.

SAM. But you . . .

FRODO. Have a nice death.

FRODO stomps off. Sam stays behind, weeping
piteously.

PEOPLE WHO HAVE READ THE BOOK. . . . the
f**k?? (Winter)

And in defense of the Faramir who behaved so far out of character in Jackson's *Two Towers* as to strike some viewers as an imposter, even as the Denethor of *The Return of the King* must have been the imposter's equally phony father, Jackson explains:

> At one point, [Tolkien's] Faramir says, 'Look, I wouldn't even *touch* the ring if I saw it lying on the side of the road.' For us, as filmmakers, that sort of thing creates a bit of a problem because we've spent a lot of time in the last film and in this one to establish this ring as incredibly powerful. Then to suddenly come to a character that says, 'Oh, I'm not interested in that', to suddenly go against everything that we've established ourselves is sort of going against our own rules. (qtd. in Rehfeld)

This is the most truly dismaying statement Jackson has made, because it demonstrates a complete lack of understanding of the moral imperatives of Tolkien's work. Jackson cannot comprehend that anyone would shun a powerful weapon for reasons of either morality or prudence: the same lesson that Boromir fails to learn. Tolkien's Faramir offers his own explanation: "I am wise enough to know that there are some perils from which a man must flee" (666; IV:5).

Some have said that these changes make Faramir more believable, more of a "real character." But all they make him is more modern, and shallower, with no more perception or depth than the evil characters. Tolkien's characters are not cardboard, and do not lack reality, if you read them with the proper understanding. Paul Kocher's chapter on Aragorn in *Master of Middle-earth* and Verlyn Flieger's essay on "Tolkien's Wild Men" demonstrate Tolkien's ability to mediate medieval ethics and personalities in a timeless modern prose. Most of Tolkien's readers understand this. His characters' steadfast morality, refreshingly different from drab contemporary situational ethics, explains a large part of Tolkien's popularity.

I don't believe Jackson made these changes from a desire to take the safe road to commercial success or from a general theory as to what is cinematic. I believe he did it because he wanted to tell the story that way. There's a bit of a chicken-and-egg problem here, for Jackson is a film director and consequently thinks like one. But many of his structural narrative choices do such violence to Tolkien's themes, without condensing the plot or changing the outcome, that adherence to cinematic narrative conventions can't explain it. They were unnecessary for that purpose.

Critics grasp that film is a different medium: their desire is for changes that are sensible, sensitive, and necessary. The filmmakers still need to show respect for the book, and the lack of respect is even more dismaying when it comes from filmmakers who had previously been boasting of their respect for the book. It is disturbing how little exaggeration there is in Scott Ott's caustic satire:

> "We wanted to bring Tolkien's incredibly intricate, poetic prose to the screen in a way that would be accessible to modern American moviegoers," said Mr. Jackson, a native New Zealander. "One of our scriptwriters suggested that the final epic battle between good and evil might best be portrayed by having the Dark Lord Sauron pursue Frodo and Sam (the ring-bearing Hobbits) in a spectacular car chase through Middle Earth. It really breathes new life into the literary fantasy-action-adventure genre."
>
> Asked how he's dealing with the withering criticism from Tolkien fans, Mr. Jackson bristled: "I can't live my life trying to satisfy the purists. What do these people want? We spent months shooting that car chase, and I used classic cars to make it authentic. I think it's true to the spirit of Tolkien."

Reply to Objection 2: Of course it could have been worse. It *was* worse. Ralph Bakshi's 1978 half-finished (in more than one respect) film of *The Lord of the Rings* was a poorer film in most ways, especially its visuals. But to be better than Bakshi is no great achievement. Jackson's miracle of achievement is merely a miracle against the odds of Hollywood. It doesn't require very much quality to be better than that.

But there is one all-important area where Jackson did not improve on Bakshi: the script. "Gems scattered amidst dross, set inappropriately, scarred and miscut. . . . The grotesque, the homely, and the comic are in easy reach of [the director's] grasp, but he fails utterly even to approach the noble. . . . This constant intrusion of technique draws the attention away from what is being presented to how it is being presented" (Ziegler

37). This could be an observant critic on Jackson. But it's actually about Bakshi.

Art is not graded on a curve. Lucius Shepard asks in his review of Jackson's *Return of the King*: does being "the finest high fantasy movie ever made . . . make it a great film or merely the winner of a beauty contest for goats?"

I don't rank a mere replication of the core story particularly high on the faithfulness meter. We were warned from the beginning that Jackson had the *legal* right to throw out the entire book and make something totally different under the title—this has actually happened in some of the James Bond films—but nobody really expected him to do that. Few film adaptations of books couldn't be described with some justice as replicating the core story. Bakshi well surpassed that level. Even Rankin-Bass's television *Hobbit* and *Return of the King* surpassed that level. But neither reached faithfulness to any degree that I would find it meaningful to use the word.

Jackson's apparent attempt to keep some of Tolkien's spirit can be more false to Tolkien than if he hadn't even tried. He has taken Tolkien's profoundest themes, and most moving sentiments, and recast and rephrased them into meaningless mush. This is a constant problem in his script, and there are many, many offending moments. On the page his dialogue, even when the sentiment is Tolkienian, is just one modernized, mushy banality after another:

> GALADRIEL. Even the smallest person can change the course of the future.
> (*Fellowship*, scene 39: "The Mirror of Galadriel")

> GIMLI. The Fellowship has failed.
> ARAGORN. Not if we hold true to each other.
> (*Fellowship*, scene 46: "The Road Goes Ever On . . . ")

> SAM. There's some good in this world, Mr. Frodo, and it's worth fighting for.
> (*Two Towers*, scene 60: "The Tales That Really Mattered . . . ")

Only the skill of the actors, and other production qualities of the films, make trite lines like these work at all. A good actor reading Tolkien's own words could be, and in talking books and other readings often has been, far more moving. Contrast Galadriel's film platitude above with its source, Elrond's stern and noble statement in the book:

> This quest may be attempted by the weak with as much
> hope as the strong. Yet such is oft the course of deeds that
> move the wheels of the world: small hands do them because
> they must, while the eyes of the great are elsewhere. (262;
> II:2)

These exact words need not have been put on film. But banality
should not have replaced them. The difference is important because
language was everything to Tolkien. "Fake feeling, fake grammar," as
Ursula K. Le Guin has put it (85). Or, as Tolkien himself wrote, defending
his not-really-very-archaic dialogue,

> People who think like [Théoden] just do not talk a modern
> idiom. . . . There would be an insincerity of thought, a
> disunion of word and meaning. For a King who spoke in a
> modern style would not really think in such terms at all. . . .
> Such 'heroic' scenes do not occur in a modern setting to
> which a modern idiom belongs. Why deliberately ignore,
> refuse to use the wealth of English which leaves us a choice
> of styles—without any possibility of unintelligibility.
> (*Letters* 226)

Philippa Boyens, who conceived Merry and Pippin's antics at
Bilbo's Farewell Party in *Fellowship* (scene 5: "A Long-expected Party"),
says in the extended edition DVD commentary that it's the sort of thing
these boys might have done at that time. That's a reasonable supposition.
The problem is that the scene is conceived, and written, in the form and
style of amateur fan fiction. This is true of most of the invented scenes.
Boromir telling Faramir over a cup of ale, "Remember today, little brother.
Today, life is good" (*Towers*, scene 41: "Sons of the Steward"), has a potent
lack of sincerity that could have come directly from a beer commercial. It's
not unreasonable to hypothesize an escapade of Merry and Pippin as
young scamps, or to imagine a scene showing the brotherly love of
Boromir and Faramir. It's just that the scenes we have are really badly
written. As amateur stories on a fanfiction web site, they would amuse
inoffensively, and be forgotten. But they're not on a fanfiction web site, are
they?

Jackson takes minor characteristics and vastly over-emphasizes
them. In the book, Treebeard begins his first conversation with the
Hobbits by apologizing for having momentarily mistaken them for orcs
(453; III:4). In the movies, he spends nearly the whole length of *The Two
Towers* suspecting them of being orcs. And Jackson has really run away
with minor evidences of Sam's crabbiness. Movie Sam is so unpleasant I

wouldn't want to take an afternoon hike with him, let alone a six-month trip to Mordor.

Jackson has a peculiar tendency to make characters false to themselves, losing their nerve before recovering it, in additions to the plot that make no difference to the outcome. This is particularly notable in *The Two Towers*. Legolas can't speak to the spirit of hope against odds without falling into despair first. (I thought he was having a nervous breakdown.) Théoden, immediately after grasping a sword, can't prepare for battle (as he does in the book): instead he decides to run away, then mysteriously recovers his nerve before having exactly the same battle as in the book. The Ents don't declare for war, they declare for peace, and have to be *tricked* into fighting the same battle they fight in the book. Frodo needlessly lies to Faramir about Gollum, Faramir himself prepares to send Frodo to Gondor (appropriating Denethor's foolish words about Boromir bringing him "a mighty gift"!—doesn't Jackson recall Gandalf's reply to that? [795; V:4]), and Aragorn (we learn) broke up with Arwen before leaving Rivendell. Only Wormtongue, who *should* lose his nerve, really acts in character. These people are all Wormtongues: this script has no faith in its source. This is probably what the screenwriters consider making the characters more modern, easier to identify with, giving them "human weaknesses," and so on. They've turned them into Wormtongues, and turned the story into routine sword-and-sorcery. This attitude, this result, is exactly what Tolkien considered the malaise of the 20th century, and it's exactly what he wrote *The Lord of the Rings* to counteract.

Jackson's Gandalf socks Denethor in the teeth. Had Tolkien's Gandalf done this, he would have fallen, and not succeeded at his larger task. For such arrogant bullying is a step along the road to becoming Saruman—whose response to Gandalf's arguments had been to imprison him. Frodo had shown a character flaw of this kind when, early on, he expresses a wish that Gollum had been killed, but that flaw is corrected when he sees Gollum and pities him. Tolkien's Gandalf pities Denethor; Jackson's does not. Instead, he follows up the sock by having Shadowfax push Denethor into his pyre. Jackson's Gandalf has learned nothing. Such scenes as this, and the Rohirrim literally throwing Wormtongue down the steps of Edoras, are from a world in which Boromir would have been right to seize the Ring. This is what shows that Jackson completely lacks any comprehension of Tolkien's morality. For Tolkien good was *different* from evil. This is not any old story of good vs. evil. What makes Tolkien's story stand out is what good is fighting for, and the way they're fighting.

Reply to Objection 3: The objective isn't to create a perfect replica of the book on screen, at 70 hours or any other length. That would be silly, and boring. The objective is to keep faith with the spirit and character of the story, to capture Tolkien's spirit in the medium of film. Style matches content.

Jackson could so easily have made something virtually indistinguishable from my ideal, without losing anything of the excitement and adventure (all admirable qualities) that he supposedly made his changes to enhance. The completely accurate, complete transcription, 70-hour (or whatever) movie, that satisfied everybody perfectly, could never have been made at any time by anybody. The film that would have satisfied me *could* have been made by Peter Jackson, and every once in a while, in glimpses, I can see him making it. The satisfactory film is not as much of an airy abstraction as the ideal Platonic film. Its absence is more regrettable because it was more possible. Even the absolute triumph of Jackson's version—the Oscars, the critical and popular acclaim—does not make it any less desirable to wish for a better film, or change what a better film would be like.

Succeeding at capturing Tolkien in a medium other than prose not only can be done, it's *been* done—and frequently. There's plenty of great Tolkien art out there—much of it by John Howe and Alan Lee, Jackson's conceptual artists, and their concepts and set design are the best thing about Jackson's films. There are some superb musical settings of his poetry that stick in my mind when re-reading even more than the films' images do. There's also bad and mediocre work in both fields, but the amount of excellent work is gratifyingly high. Even in dramatization of *The Lord of the Rings*, there's been fine work in the Orson Scott Card and BBC 1981 audio versions. If three or four film directors have not succeeded at capturing Tolkien, I'm inclined to think it's more the individuals than the medium.

The film-makers have argued that a film can't take a novel's leisurely pace at setting tone, and must get into the action quickly. I would have thought this would be the other way around, and indeed, some novelists will tell tyros that you must grab the reader with the first sentence and never let go. Proportionate to total length, a film doesn't need to grab attention quite as vividly, because the audience is already there. It's easy to put a book down; it's a lot harder to get up and walk out of the theatre; and if the film pays off in the end, word of mouth will still be good. In any case, the average film won't detain you for more than three hours, whereas only the shortest novel can be read that quickly. Actually, in *overall* structure, only the omission of the Bombadil episode makes Jackson's *Fellowship* much faster-paced than the book. In the theatrical cut, the Hobbits reach Bree, where the adventure really gets under way, at 49 minutes into a film of 2 hours 50 minutes (excluding closing credits): 29% of the way through. In the book, they get there on page 146 of the 382 pages that make up the text of *Fellowship*: 38%, but if you exclude the three Bombadil chapters (I:6-8, 39 pages), it's only 31%. Yet the film seems frenetic where the book lets you feel the world is explored. Why? Because of pacing and style. Both Orson Scott Card and the 1981 BBC radio version also eliminate Bombadil. Card even cuts the Birthday Party too, and gets Frodo to Bree on page 14 of his script, only 20% of the way through his version of volume 1. But neither adaptation feels hurried. Pacing and style make the difference.

A little relaxation in time can improve even an action film, making it go places instead of spinning its wheels impotently. It sets the atmosphere and contributes to the feeling that you're visiting a world, not just following a story. This is something Jackson conveys well in *The Two Towers* (where he had the space to do it), and even better in the epilogue to *The Return of the King* (where he *made* the space), but fails to convey in *The Fellowship of the Ring*. It's not just a matter of screen time. For instance, Jackson's Gandalf on entering Moria says, "It's a four day journey to the other side" (*Fellowship*, scene 34: "A Journey in the Dark"). But despite this statement, and the fact that over seven minutes—a long time in screen terms—pass before the orc attack, it doesn't feel like four days. I wonder if that's because of the absence of a little piece of cinematic vocabulary that brilliantly conveys the passage of time: the fade. It's been a long time since I've seen a fade in a new film. Perhaps it works too well at slowing down the pace, in a day when big-budget films must feel rushed-rushed-rushed. But just a quiet fade-out as the Fellowship set off through Moria, followed by a beat of silence, then a fade-in to the next scene somewhere in the mines, would have done wonders for conveying that they'd been there a while, at no cost in screen time. It would have contributed spaciousness, but not drag.

On a broader scale, a mere fifteen minutes added to *Fellowship* could have adequately conveyed Tolkien's sense of spaciousness. The material added to the extended edition of this film is not perfect in this regard, but it goes very much in the right direction. And lest it make the film longer than Jackson wanted the audience to sit in the theatre, the fifteen minutes could easily have been reclaimed from superfluous scenes of violence: the orc-spawning scenes, which anticipate and thus diminish the horror when the orcs actually appear in battle later, and flatten Saruman into a simple bad guy from Tolkien's complex wise man gone wrong; the "wizard-fu" battle scenes between Saruman and Gandalf, an absurd extrapolation from Gandalf's simple statement in the book, "They took me and they set me alone on the pinnacle of Orthanc" (254; II:2); the Watcher in the Water, not content to attack Frodo but compelled, like some creature from the nightmares of H.P. Lovecraft, to wave him around in the air a while; the superfluous extra bridge scene; and, above all, the battle with the cave-troll: not only overlong but tedious. These scenes prove, if proof were needed, that Jackson has no true love for Tolkien, but only for cheap horror.

A close examination of some of Jackson's choices of time allocation in this film reveals how prodigiously he spends time on monsters and running away from monsters. It's 48 seconds from the moment the Watcher attacks Frodo until his rescue, and a total of 72 seconds from the attack until the Watcher slams the door. It's 3 minutes 20 seconds from the moment the cave-troll enters the Chamber of Mazarbul until it finally keels over: an eternity in film terms. You could read the entire scene from the book *aloud* in that time. When Pippin, instead of merely dropping a rock in the well as in the book, manages to knock in a whole suit of armor, it takes an aching 34 seconds for the sound to stop echoing; but it's only 16 seconds after that (a whole ten pages in the book) that the first "Doom" sounds come rumbling.

It isn't picayune to measure time down to the second. Screen time is precious, and film editing must allocate it with a fine discernment. Above all, we have been told again and again that so much had to be cut and condensed. To lose so much of Tolkien as to eviscerate his spirit, and then to spend time prodigiously on this, reveals an unnecessarily distorted sense of priorities.

John Kovalic put it well in his comic strip *Dork Tower*:

> KAYLEIGH. You know, *The Lord of the Rings* is a good movie, but why does it have to be so *long*?
> MATT. Well, it has a lot of material to fit in. Think of it from the director's perspective. He had to have twenty minutes for the Shire, twenty minutes for Rivendell . . . an hour for Boromir's death scene . . .

Reply to Objection 4: The way I've heard the story, what James M. Cain said was "My books aren't ruined. They're right there, sitting on the shelf. *That's what I have to keep telling myself.*" In this version, Cain knows that his reply isn't a satisfactory answer to the complaint; it's merely a snappy comeback to keep his self-respect: "a modicum of solace," as Douglas A. Anderson puts it (149).

And indeed that's all it is. Cain knew perfectly well that his questioner wasn't under some delusion that Hollywood had snuck into his house and stolen his copies of the books. In some cases it's actually happened: though Hollywood can't steal the copies you already have, on occasion publishers have been known to remove the novel from print and replace it with *a novelization of the movie*. Conscientious bookstores place warning labels on their shelves in this situation: "This is not the original novel!"

Thanks to the vigilance of the Tolkien Estate, that won't happen to *The Lord of the Rings*. The book is on the shelf all right: with a film tie-in photo cover on it, ensuring to the best of the publishers' ability that you can't buy and read a new copy of the book without thinking of the films every time you look at the cover. These editions aren't entirely unavoidable, but they're as close to it as the publishers can make them. I do not consider it salutary to argue over exactly how unavoidable that is. Does this make any difference to the reading experience? Hollywood must think so, or they wouldn't have supplied the photos.

But even film tie-in covers are relatively rare, and like Burger King trinkets they too will pass, while the films, works of lasting artistic merit in their own right, will live on, burying the book by media colonization. "Devotees of Oz can be glad that the film *Wizard* popularized Baum's imaginative world, but they do not want to see the film supplant the greater work," says Baum's biographer, and devotees of Tolkien don't want it either (Rogers 254).

Readers talking about a book being ruined rarely phrase it in absolute terms as the patsy in the Cain anecdote does. They usually say, "The book was ruined *for me*," and as a purely personal reaction this cannot be gainsaid. It's as valid as any other viewer's response of enrichment, or of not being affected at all. This ruination can happen very easily. Many authors and critics have observed that writing is not just the words the author puts on paper. A novel is a dead thing so long as it sits on a shelf unread. It only comes alive as an active collaboration between writer and reader, to which readers bring their own mental experiences: a novel is what happens in the reader's head when he or she reads the book. If the reader is Michael Swanwick's nine-year-old son, it will be a different book than it is to the boy's father. And if the reader's head is filled with images and voices from a film, that collaboration is changed. Something *has* been done to the book, and if the reader doesn't like it, *ruined* is not too strong a word. If the physical book hasn't been ruined, the reader's experience of it has been, and the reader's experience is what counts.

At this point it is necessary to reply to those who claim that films don't affect them, and that anybody except the weak-minded, the weird, or the juvenile can simply will themselves not to think of the film version while reading the book from which it was made. An epic, detailed, captivating film dramatization of a book somehow has no effect whatever on the mental state or image of the reader. Anybody for whom that is true must be one of those rare people who can win at the game whose object is *not* to think of a purple elephant. Such iron-mindedness is simply not the experience of the common run of humanity. As evidence I offer:

⅋ Angelika Kirchschlager, an opera singer who prepared for the title role in Nicholas Maw's opera based on William Styron's novel *Sophie's Choice* by avoiding the famous movie based on the same novel. "I got the video and I started, but then gave up after 20 minutes because I realized Meryl Streep was so strong in that role I'd never get rid of the impression of how she did it" (qtd. in White 23). I like that word "never"—probably a rhetorical exaggeration; still, she said it.

⅋ The travel writer Bill Bryson, whose book *Bill Bryson's African Diary* begins with his account of how he didn't realize, until planning a trip to Africa, how much his image of that continent had been permanently shaped by watching Jungle Jim movies on television forty years earlier. He knew perfectly well they were completely fake, but they formed a lasting image anyway.

⅋ Children's book reviewer Polly Shulman, who found J.K. Rowling's *Harry Potter* stories ruined by the Chris Columbus films of the first two books. "The problem, in part, lies with the movies. Do you agree? For me, it's hard to read the books now without hearing those awful child actors flub the lines. And even though the films were full of actors I love . . . I resent having their faces superimposed on the characters I'd imagined. Even Rowling's witty touches—the talking portraits, the touchy ghosts, the Floo transportation system, the Every Flavor Beans—seem almost stale now, as if her sensibility has entered the mass mind and started to fade into cliché" (Edelstein and Shulman).

⅋ Film critic David Edelstein, who agreed with her. "Like you, I had a hard time getting the actors and the sets out of my head. . . . It's much more fun to visualize your own *Potter* universe than to have it all pinned down for you by the faces and the voices of actors—or, more damagingly, by director Chris Columbus and FX giant Industrial Light & Magic" (Edelstein and Shulman).

ᔆ Fantasy critic Alexei Kondratiev, who wrote, "It is entirely possible that readers who come to the book after the movie will be unable to imagine those characters as looking like anything other than those actors, and that this will eventually become a convention—a built-in tradition in Tolkien illustration, perhaps. The movie will definitely have restricted the potential scope of a reader's spontaneous imaginative response to Tolkien's words." Here, and in Shulman's "mass mind," we see films affecting the imaginations even of those who have not seen them.

ᔆ The legion of jokes in which youngsters claim that Jackson's film saga—or Tolkien's novel—is only a rip-off of earlier fantasy films: *Willow* or *Star Wars*.

Even Tolkien was not so secure in his mental image of his own work that nothing could disturb him. He winced with agony at almost every use of his mythology by someone else, even C.S. Lewis's intended homage of borrowing the name "Númenor" in *That Hideous Strength*, which he called "plagiarism" even though he knew that was an unfair charge (*Letters* 224).

So let's hear no more about the book being on the shelf. It doesn't matter where the book is, if the film is in the head.

Reply to Objection 5: I like Bombadil, and I miss him, but if any thread of the story could be removed without unraveling the whole tapestry, that was it. His removal was a wise condensation, since condensation was necessary.

Departures from the text are not what I'm worried about. I don't care what color someone's hair is, or where Merry got his sword. It didn't even bother me that much that Jackson turned the Hobbits into Irish peasants, though it would have infuriated Tolkien (see Ezard). It's departures from the spirit that I'm worried about.

Reviewer Andrew O'Hehir wrote: "The handful of Tolkien purists likely to pillory Jackson for his various departures from the sacred text are missing the point on a world-historical scale. . . . It's an interpretation that seeks to capture Tolkien's magic in a new vessel" (O'Hehir 2). Seeking is fine, but you haven't captured the magic if you drop the vessel. The richness and delight of Tolkien's world is a fragile, elven one: like fairy gold, it turns to dust when it is stolen away, as any number of Tolkien-imitation novelists have proven. Good intentions are not enough. Fragility of spirit is often characteristic of the greatest literature. The popular image of Genesis is still mostly formed by the interpretation given it by John

Milton in the 17th century, even though few today have read his *Paradise Lost*.

This isn't a matter of profaning a "sacred text." That's not it at all: that resembles the real point the way a Jackson plot resembles Tolkien's. The point is that he's taken out just about everything that makes *The Lord of the Rings* a strikingly unique work, one which we love, and reduced it to a generic sword-and-sorcery adventure story. If the book were written that way, I'd have read it, enjoyed it, and forgotten it. The films are so far from being in the same class as the novel that there's no comparison. They're the aesthetic equivalent of a Tolclone novel. Condensation is not the issue: the evisceration of Tolkien's spirit is the issue. This is not a matter of personal taste or point of view; it's as simple a fact as an aesthetic statement can be. It is the determination to express this as fact, not personal taste, that some may take as a form of religious devotion.

Peter Jackson, when asked about the faithfulness of the films, said, "Certain scenes are totally different. Certain lines are totally different." (*Certain* ones? It's the line that actually comes from the book that's the standout rarity in these films.) "It's all to do with how obsessive you are" (qtd. in Brooks). No, it's all to do with what you're obsessive about.

Jackson could have done with a bit more obsession with Tolkien's unique spirit and artistic vision. Instead, he relentlessly trivializes them. This is seen most clearly in his treatment of characters and their behavior. Consider his Aragorn. He never seemed very energetic to me, or much of anything else besides tough and sinewy. I kept waiting for the Ranger to turn into the King, but except for washing his hair before the coronation, he never did. The Aragorn who "seemed to have grown in stature while Éomer had shrunk; and in his living face [Gimli and Legolas] caught a brief vision of the power and majesty of the kings of stone" (423; III:2) is the aptly-named Sir Not Appearing In These Films. Jackson's Aragorn wants to distract the giant eyeball's attention so that it literally won't notice that Frodo and Sam are crawling across Mordor. In the book, that isn't the problem, and in fact the hobbits are caught again (a scene omitted from the film), but no-one says, "Aha, so there are the spies with the Ring." Tolkien's Aragorn, by contrast, wants to fool Sauron into thinking that *he* has the Ring, and is just not feeling ready to use it yet; and thus (for a longer period than depicted by Jackson) cause it not even to occur to Sauron that the West might be doing something totally different with the Ring.

Same facts on the ground, but a completely different meaning, a completely different feel.

There are matters of personal taste on which I don't care if Jackson's differs from mine. I do not insist that the films express my vision, and I don't care what Peter Jackson's vision is, so long as it's also Tolkien's vision. This is less paradoxical than it sounds. After Tolkien's Arda, I revere no fantasy creation more than Mervyn Peake's Gormenghast. The set design of the BBC television adaptation was not my vision. But within the freedom of artistic creativity it was unquestionably true to Peake's vision, and I was not merely content, but delighted. Where Jackson was true to Tolkien's vision I likewise was content, and sometimes delighted when I could set aside from my mind the wounds inflicted elsewhere.

Some matters I thought Jackson handled well. *The Fellowship of the Ring* clearly conveys the complexity of Boromir: not a villain, but a flawed hero. *The Two Towers* does well with the relationship between Wormtongue and Éowyn. That he is not above taking a crude sexual interest in her *is* textual (I think it's the only such reference in the entire book). Thankfully, Jackson does not overplay it, and the actor playing Wormtongue does not ham it up. Nor does Jackson overplay Sam's reunion with Frodo in the Tower of Cirith Ungol in *The Return of the King*. How much more tasteful this Ring scene is than Frodo's with Bilbo in Rivendell. Even a few of Jackson's additions made sense: in *Fellowship*, adding allusions to Rosie and Sam's romance, which in the book Sam does not mention until he's in Mordor; in *The Two Towers*, the added emphasis on the grief at the death of Théodred, which goes almost unnoticed in the book. I'd call both of these minor flaws on Tolkien's part.

Best of all are those few moments which come straight from the book, with some of Tolkien's original dialogue. In *Fellowship*, Frodo and Gandalf discussing the moral question of Gollum (even though placed in Moria instead of Bag End). In *The Two Towers*, Éowyn's defiant speech on fearing being locked up in a cage. In *The Return of the King*, Frodo's final scenes with Sam in Bag End and with Bilbo on the road. These are scenes from a different movie, the one I wish Jackson had made, the film that could have stood in a place of honor with Sibley and Bakewell's BBC version and Orson Scott Card's reader's theatre adaptation, the film that would have satisfied me. That's really all I wanted from a *Lord of the Rings* film.

See? I'm really not very picky at all. These scenes satisfied me. The scandal is that 99% of the time, Jackson couldn't even manage that much. Better luck with *King Kong*.

NOTE

Thanks to the members of the MythSoc e-mail list, especially the incisive Liz Milner, the magisterial Alexei Kondratiev, the inquisitive Susan Palwick, the steadfast Carl Hostetter, the persistent Janet Croft, and the indefatigable Mary Stolzenbach, for references and insights.

WORKS CONSULTED AND CITED

Amodeo, John. "Hobbit Sense." *Landscape Architecture* May 2003: 36-42. 23 April 2004 <http://www.asla.org/lamag/lam03/may/ecology.html>

Anderson, Douglas A. "Tolkien After All These Years." *Meditations on Middle-earth.* Ed. Karen Haber. New York: St. Martin's, 2001. 129-51.

Ansen, David, and Jeff Giles. "The New Visionaries." *Newsweek* 9 Feb. 2004: 58-68. 23 April 2004 <http://www.msnbc.msn.com/id/4120864/>

Aquinas, Thomas. *The Summa Theologica.* 1st complete American ed. Trans. Fathers of the English Dominican Province. 3 vols. New York: Benziger, 1947-48. 13 Aug. 2004 <http://www.ccel.org/a/aquinas/summa/home.html>

Barry, Dave. "The Long (and Short) of New 'Ring'." *San Jose Mercury News* 26 Jan. 2003: 14E.

Brooks, Xan. "The Ring Cycle." *Guardian Unlimited* 7 Dec. 2001. 23 April 2004. <http://film.guardian.co.uk/lordoftherings/storynav/0,11016,614629,00. html>

Bryson, Bill. *Bill Bryson's African Diary.* New York: Broadway, 2002.

Card, Orson Scott, adapter. *Lord of the Rings by J.R.R. Tolkien.* Adapted for readers' theatre. Unpublished playscript. Perf. Mythopoeic Conference 28. Pepperdine Univ., Malibu, Calif., Aug. 9, 1997.

Cater, Bill. "We Talked of Love, Death and Fairy Tales." *Daily Telegraph* [London] 4 Dec. 2001. 23 April 2004 <http://www.telegraph.co.uk/arts/main.jhtml? xml=%2Farts%2F2001%2F12%2F04%2Fbatolk04.xml>

Dickerson, Matthew T. *Following Gandalf: Epic Battles and Moral Victory in The Lord of the Rings.* Grand Rapids: Brazos, 2003.

Diehl, Patrick. "*The Lord of the Rings* and the Trials of Adaptation." *West by Northwest.org Online Magazine* 9 Jan. 2004. 23 April 2004 <http://westbynorthwest.org/artman/publish/article_677.shtml>

Edelstein, David. "To Mordor and Back." Rev. of *The Return of the King*, dir. Peter Jackson. *MSN Slate Magazine* 16 Dec. 2003. 23 April 2004 <http://slate.msn.com/id/2092700/>

Edelstein, David, and Polly Shulman. Review of *Harry Potter and the Order of the Phoenix* by J.K. Rowling. *MSN Slate Magazine* 23 June 2003. 23 April 2004 <http://slate.msn.com/id/2084660/entry/2084710/>

Ezard, John. "So, Would Tolkien Have Liked the Film?" *Guardian Unlimited* 14 Dec. 2001. 23 April 2004 <http://film.guardian.co.uk/lordoftherings/news/0,11016,618449,00.html>

Flieger, Verlyn. "Tolkien's Wild Men: From Medieval to Modern." *Tolkien the Medievalist*. Ed. Jane Chance. London: Routledge, 2003. 95-105.

Goldman, William. *Adventures in the Screen Trade: A Personal View of Hollywood and Screenwriting*. New York: Warner, 1983.

Jackson, Peter, and Philippa Boyens. Interview with Michael Bodey. *Daily Telegraph* [Sydney] 1 Jan. 2004. 3 Jan. 2004 <http://dailytelegraph.news.com.au/story.jsp?sectionid=1267&storyid=703823>

Kocher, Paul H. *Master of Middle-earth: The Fiction of J.R.R. Tolkien*. Boston: Houghton, 1972.

Kondratiev, Alexei. "Re: Public Response." Online posting. 1 Jan. 2003. MythSoc. 23 April 2004 <http://groups.yahoo.com/group/mythsoc/message/7292>

Kovalic, John. "Dork Tower." Comic strip. *Dork Tower Archive* 22 Feb. 2002. 23 April 2004 <http://archive.gamespy.com/comics/dorktower/archive.asp?nextform=viewcomic&id=538>

Kurtz, Scott. "PvP." Comic strip. *PvPonline.com* 21 March 2001. 23 April 2004 <http://www.pvponline.com/archive.php3?archive=20010321> Reprinted in *Beyond Bree* Aug. 2001: 1.

Le Guin, Ursula K. "From Elfland to Poughkeepsie." *The Language of the Night: Essays on Fantasy and Science Fiction*. Ursula K. Le Guin. Rev. ed. New York: Harper, 1989. 78-92.

Lehrer, Eli. "Tolkien at the Two Towers of Academia." *FrontPage Magazine.com* 10 Jan. 2003. 23 April 2004 <http://frontpagemag.com/Articles/Printable.asp?ID=5461>

Lewis, C.S. *An Experiment in Criticism*. Cambridge: Cambridge UP, 1961.

The Lord of the Rings. Screenplay by Peter S. Beagle and Chris Conkling. Dir. Ralph Bakshi. Fantasy Films, 1978.

The Lord of the Rings: The Fellowship of the Ring. Special Extended DVD Edition. Screenplay by Peter Jackson, Fran Walsh, and Philippa Boyens. Perf. Elijah Wood et al. Dir. Peter Jackson. United States: New Line Home Entertainment, 2002.

The Lord of the Rings: The Return of the King. Theatrical Release DVD. Screenplay by Peter Jackson, Fran Walsh, and Philippa Boyens. Perf. Elijah Wood et al. Dir. Peter Jackson. United States, New Line Home Entertainment, 2004.

The Lord of the Rings: The Two Towers. Special Extended DVD Edition. Screenplay by Peter Jackson, Fran Walsh, and Philippa Boyens. Perf. Elijah Wood et al. Dir. Peter Jackson. United States: New Line Home Entertainment, 2003.

Milner, Elizabeth R. "Re: Spotty Review." Online posting. 17 Jan. 2004. MythSoc. 23 April 2004 <http://groups.yahoo.com/group/mythsoc/message/11272>

Myers, Kevin. "No Oscars for the Actors of Our Greatest Drama." *Sunday Telegraph* [London] 1 Feb. 2004. 23 April 2004 <http://www.telegraph. co.uk/opinion/main.jhtml?xml=%2Fopinion%2F2004%2F02%2F01%2Fdo0 106.xml>

O'Hehir, Andrew. "The Fellowship of the Ravenous Movie Press." *Salon.com* 6 Dec. 2001. 23 April 2004 <http://www.salon.com/ent/movies/ feature/2001/12/06/lotr_junket/index.html>

Ott, Scott. "'Rings' Fans Awed by Sequel's Car Chase Scene." *ScrappleFace* 16 Dec. 2003. 23 April 2004 <http://www.scrappleface.com/MT/ archives/001422.html>

Rehfeld, Nina. "The Next Reel: Peter Jackson and Philippa Boyens." *Green Cine* 18 Dec. 2002. 23 April 2004 <http://www.greencine.com/article? action=view&articleID=62&>

Rogers, Katharine M. *L. Frank Baum: Creator of Oz.* New York: St. Martin's, 2002.

The Rough Guide to The Lord of the Rings. London: Rough Guides, 2003.

Rushdie, Salman. "Getting into Gang War." *Washington Post* 25 Dec. 2002: A29. 23 April 2004 <http://www.washingtonpost.com/wp-dyn/articles/A35424- 2002Dec24.html>

Seger, Linda. "*The Return of the King*: How Story and Structure Won 11 Oscars." *Creative Screenwriting* 16 Mar 2004. 23 April 2004 <http://www.creativescreenwriting.com/csdaily/craft/03_16_04.html>

Shepard, Lucius. "King Me." Review of *The Lord of the Rings: The Return of the King*, dir. Peter Jackson. *Electricstory.com* 6 Jan. 2004. 23 April 2004 <http://www.electricstory.com/reviews/rotk.asp>

Shippey, Tom. "Another Road to Middle-earth: Jackson's Movie Trilogy." *Understanding The Lord of the Rings: The Best of Tolkien Criticism.* Ed. Rose A. Zimbardo and Neil D. Isaacs. Boston: Houghton Mifflin, 2004. 233-254.

—. *J.R.R. Tolkien: Author of the Century.* London: Harper, 2000.

—. *The Road to Middle-earth.* Rev. and expanded ed. Boston: Houghton, 2003.

Sibley, Brian, and Michael Bakewell, adapters. *The Lord of the Rings.* By J.R.R. Tolkien. Prepared for BBC Radio. Dir. Jane Morgan and Penny Leicester. Rec. 1981. Audiocassette. BBC Audio, 1987.

Swanwick, Michael. "A Changeling Returns." *Meditations on Middle-earth.* Ed. Karen Haber. New York: St. Martin's, 2001. 33-46.

Swartz, Mark Evan. *Oz Before the Rainbow.* Baltimore: Johns Hopkins UP, 2000.

Tolkien, J.R.R. *The Letters of J.R.R. Tolkien.* Boston: Houghton Mifflin, 1981.

—. *The Lord of the Rings.* 2nd ed. With Note on the Text by Douglas A. Anderson. Boston: Houghton Mifflin, 1994.

—. *Tree and Leaf.* London: Unwin, 1964.

Troost, Linda, and Sayre Greenfield, ed. *Jane Austen in Hollywood*. 2nd ed. Lexington: UP of Kentucky, 2001.

White, Michael. "Choosing Sophie." *BBC Music Magazine* Jan. 2003: 23-26.

Winter, Molly. *"Return of the King*, Condensed Parody Version." Online posting. 18 Dec. 2003. Mollyringwraith LiveJournal. 23 April 2004 <http://www.livejournal.com/users/mollyringwraith/5635.html>

Ziegler, Dale. "Ring-Wrath: or Therein Bakshi Again." *Mythlore* 6.1 (whole no. 19, Winter 1979): 37-38.

MITHRIL COATS AND TIN EARS: "ANTICIPATION" AND "FLATTENING" IN PETER JACKSON'S *THE LORD OF THE RINGS* TRILOGY

JANET BRENNAN CROFT

BOOK TO SCRIPT: *"THE LORD OF THE RINGS* CANNOT BE GARBLED LIKE THAT"

Although J.R.R. Tolkien sold the film rights to *The Lord of the Rings* in 1969, he considered it "very unsuitable for dramatic . . . representation" (*Letters* 255). He did not approve a 1957 proposal for an animated version by Morton Grady Zimmerman, Forrest J. Ackerman, and Al Brodax (Carpenter 226), and aside from the 1978 Ralph Bakshi and 1980 Rankin and Bass animated films, no other effort to commit Tolkien's masterpiece to celluloid came to fruition until director Peter Jackson began working on a script for a live-action film in 1997 with his partner, Fran Walsh.

Jackson got his start making low-budget horror movies in his native New Zealand in the late 1980s. In an interview with *Creative Screenwriting*, he said he had read *The Lord of the Rings* once at the age of 18, and never looked at it again until "the whole idea of doing the film came up seventeen years later" (Bauer 6). His ambition was to make a fantasy film, not necessarily *The Lord of the Rings*, and he wanted to move away from horror and take advantage of modern computer special effects (Bauer 8; Thompson 46). He considered the monsters in *The Lord of the Rings* one of his "real motivations" for making the films (Thompson 49). Co-writer Philippa Boyens was more immersed in the story, having had "a childhood obsession" with *The Lord of the Rings* (Smith 4) and being an annual re-reader (*Fellowship*, appendix: "From Book to Script"), but had never worked on a screenplay before being asked by Jackson and Walsh to collaborate with them.

The publicity build-up for the first film was incredible, and it opened to (mostly) rave reviews on December 19, 2001. However, not everyone praised Jackson's vision, and viewer opinion is remarkably polarized about these films. Many long-time readers of Tolkien were deeply disappointed, after the wonders promised, to see how far Jackson deviated from Tolkien's creation, and even more so after the second and third films were released. Earlier attempts to film Tolkien's works also evoked the same response.

Why were these fans so upset? As one reviewer, writing about the Bakshi film, suggested, "the point is that we have been there; we can say 'Yes, that's just how it was,' or 'No, no, no, that's all wrong'" (Ziegler 37). A reviewer of the Rankin and Bass *Hobbit* (1978) said, "The original as it has become familiar to its audience stands in judgment of the imitation" (Hardy 137). What they see, to quote a critique of the Bakshi film, is "gems scattered amidst dross, set inappropriately, scarred and miscut" (Ziegler 37). A reviewer writes of the Jackson trilogy that it is "a substitute, one far inferior to the original vision. Our precious has been taken from us, and we hates it, yes, we hates it. . . . The subtleties, delights, and marvels of the book have been replaced with the predictable dimensions of a video game" (Jacobs). These readers feel that, while there may be scenes close to perfection in the Jackson films, they are unfortunately outweighed by moments where those familiar with the books, even when making an honest effort to look at Tolkien's works with a film-maker's eye, can see no compelling cinematic reason for Jackson's changes to the original text. Tolkien readers are not unique in this reaction to film adaptations; fans of Jane Austen, for example, may find that "the simplest visual choices for a film can easily remold the values of the novels" and "the social commentary loses subtlety and balance; the passions in the stories . . . suffer coarsening in their compression" (Troost and Greenfield 7).

Noted Tolkien scholar Wayne G. Hammond has this to say:

> In the moments in which the films succeed, they do so by staying close to what Tolkien so carefully wrote; where they fail, it tends to be where they diverge from him. . . . [T]he filmmakers sacrifice the richness of Tolkien's story and characters, not to mention common sense, for violence, cheap humor, and cheaper thrills. (qtd. in Kirst 2)

Jane Chance comments on the "infantilization" of several key characters (Chance 81); as Hammond has pointed out, "Most of the characters in the films are mere shadows of those in the books, weak and diminished (notably Frodo) or insulting caricatures (Pippin, Merry, and Gimli)" (qtd. in Kirst 2). Carl Hostetter notes the "systematic removal of all traces of nobility and faith from the most noble and faithful characters, and the concomitant angstifying [of Aragorn] and wimpifying [of Frodo]" (Hostetter).

A number of film critics and fans feel that Jackson has accurately represented Tolkien's broadest themes, and this should invalidate any criticism of other aspects of the adaptation. However, in Tolkien's writing both the broadest and most subtle themes are inextricably bound to the characters that represent them and the specific actions they take. In fact, Tolkien makes clear in his analysis of the Zimmerman script that the "perversion of the characters" was even worse than the "spoiling of the plot and scenery" (*Letters* 275). Aragorn, for example, personifies the theme of reclaimed and rightful hereditary kingship; in the book, his entire will is unwaveringly bent on the goal of regaining the throne of Gondor from the day he learns of his heritage, and he pursues it with sure and steady confidence. Denethor, Steward of Gondor, physically represents a cautionary lesson about nobility and greatness overcome by the sins of pride and despair. Frodo embodies courage and self-sacrifice, and shows that the meekest of exteriors may conceal great reserves of bravery and endurance, both physical and moral.

Tampering with the characters muddies these themes. In the Jackson movie, Aragorn's self-doubt and angst over his fitness to rule may suit our republican reservations about kings and divine right, but they are out of place in the world Tolkien created; and in any case, in the text Tolkien deliberately balanced Aragorn's steadfastness with Boromir's hubris on one hand and Faramir's humility on the other. Jackson eliminates this contrast by making the three characters too similar to each other, not only "angstifying" Aragorn, but at the same time placing an increased emphasis on Boromir's nobility and making Faramir as vulnerable to temptation as his brother.

Denethor exhibits little of his initial honorable and stern dignity in the movie, seeming from the start an emotional and self-indulgent petty tyrant, unshaven and twitchy, bowed and weeping over Boromir's horn and not caring overmuch for his city in his personal grief, instead of the book's "proud and subtle" ruler of ancient and noble blood (737; V:1), "kingly, beautiful, and powerful" (740; V:1), who slept fully armored in mail lest he weaken with age (800; V:4). Jackson eliminates the *palantír* which Denethor thought in his pride he could control, and which tempted him to despair. His character arc begins with his decline instead of before it, and his spiritual fall is from a far lesser height; Jackson replaces it with an exaggerated physical fall instead.

In Frodo's case, the uplifting message that one may find hidden reserves of strength, will, and leadership ability inside oneself, just waiting for the right moment, is undermined by Frodo's weakness, youth (which not everyone finds acceptable, Philippa Boyens's assertion to the contrary

[*Towers*, app.: "From Book to Script"]), and passivity in the movie. It may be more cinematically compelling to focus on his anguished fear and physical suffering, but the audience identifying with the hobbit is denied the chance to think that they themselves might have the ability to be strong in a crisis, or handle pain with grace.

PROBLEMS OF ADAPTATION: "NO EVIDENT SIGNS OF ANY APPRECIATION OF WHAT IT IS ALL ABOUT"

In the commentary on the extended edition DVD, Peter Jackson defends his changes to the film, saying "What does Old Man Willow contribute to the story of Frodo carrying the Ring? What does Tom Bombadil ultimately really have to do with the Ring?" (*Fellowship*, app.: "From Book to Script"). Many readers of Tolkien could answer these questions without a moment's hesitation: besides their obvious contributions to the mechanics of the plot (the acquisition of the enchanted swords two characters need to use later, Frodo's vision of the curtain of glass rolling back to reveal a far green country) and to our understanding of the Ring (why Bombadil is not affected by it, and what this means), the Bombadil chapters build relationships and develop characters, most especially in Frodo's confrontation with the Barrow-wight. The tapestry of Tolkien's Middle-earth is so closely woven that to carelessly pull out one string leads to holes in the picture elsewhere, weakening the whole fabric, unless the scriptwriter understands and compensates fully for the effects of each dropped scene.

Tolkien's extensive commentary on the 1957 Zimmerman script is especially interesting now that we have seen all three of Jackson's films. Tolkien's introductory comments ask the screenwriters to:

> make an effort of imagination sufficient to understand the irritation (and on occasion the resentment) of an author, who finds, increasingly as he proceeds, his work treated as it would seem carelessly in general, in places recklessly, and with no evident signs of any appreciation of what it is all about. (*Letters* 270)

Jackson and his co-authors may not have added a "fairy castle" to Lórien, or had characters traveling everywhere on giant Eagles (as Zimmerman did), but they did fall prey to the temptation to add "incantations, blue lights, and some irrelevant magic" (*Letters* 271). They are certainly guilty, in many places, of altering the original's "characteristic and peculiar tone" and "showing a preference for fights" (*Letters* 271).

As Tom Shippey has pointed out, in reference to the Zimmerman script, "What ruined everything for [Tolkien] was an endemic carelessness over detail, coupled with a probably unconscious urge to standardize everything in Middle-earth toward suburban norms" ("Temptations" 16). Jackson is guilty of something very similar, in his case standardizing the characters and action scenes to Hollywood fantasy norms. Hollywood currently demands that heroes must agonize over their power, and women must emulate the fighting ability of an Amazon princess, so Jackson delivered a conflicted Aragorn and a sword-wielding Arwen. Quiet, character-building moments, and the completion of character arcs for many secondary characters, were gutted or sacrificed because Hollywood requires ever more spectacular battle scenes; *The Return of the King* had to compete with the equally epic *Master and Commander* and *The Last Samurai* at the box office in December 2003.

Two concepts Tolkien mentions in his criticism of the 1957 script are "anticipation" and "flattening." Tolkien said that Zimmerman had a "tendency to anticipate scenes or devices used later, thereby flattening the tale out" (*Letters* 271). For example, Zimmerman has Eagles landing in the Shire before the hobbits' journey begins, thus reducing the surprise factor of the Eagle rescuing Gandalf from Orthanc and the pinnacle of Celebdil, as well as ruining the folkloric "third time pays for all" aspect of the climactic rescue of Sam and Frodo. Overusing this device throughout the script makes it stale and predictable. "Flattening" can also describe what happens to a character arc when a writer anticipates later character traits in earlier scenes, as when Denethor is presented from the start as not fully in control of himself. In addition, dialogue can be flattened; the scriptwriter may be tempted to reduce the many distinctive voices of Tolkien's characters to the colloquial mean of the younger Hobbits, in a (rather condescending) effort to make their speech intelligible to a wider audience. As an example, in the final film Aragorn is particularly ill-served by an uninspiring and incoherent "St. Crispin's Day" oration at the Gates of Mordor, and a banal coronation speech in Minas Tirith (*Return*, scene 48: "The Land of Shadow," and scene 57: "The Return of the King"), neither in the original. Tolkien is hardly the first author to whom this has happened; Charles Dickens was furious about a pirated retelling of *A Christmas Carol* which similarly changed his words and rendered them "weakened, degraded . . . tame, vile, ignorant, and mawkish" (Dickens and Hearn 24).

Consider the hobbits' first encounter with the Black Rider in the woods near Hobbiton. In the book, Frodo's only conscious desire is to make himself disappear, primarily out of annoyance at being followed, and his hand barely touches the chain from which the Ring hangs before the Rider turns away (74; I:3). In the Jackson movie, however, Frodo is seized by an uncontrollable urge to put on the Ring; his eyes roll back in his head and he appears nauseated, and Sam reaches out to stop his hand just before Merry throws the bag of mushrooms to distract the Rider (*Fellowship*, scene 13: "A Short Cut to Mushrooms"). In the book, Tolkien subtly and slowly strengthens Frodo's compulsion to put on the Ring. It has a cumulative effect; as Frodo gets closer to Mordor and grows weaker, the temptation builds. Sam does not have to help him physically resist it until they are on the slopes of Mount Doom itself (921; VI:3). By anticipating the Ring's later effect on Frodo, Jackson has left himself no room to build up to this pivotal scene, and in fact he drops it entirely.

Also, consider the hobbits' first glimpses of Bree and The Prancing Pony. In the book, it is a clear, starry night. Unsophisticated Sam is nervous about the height of the buildings, but Frodo reassures him that the inn comes highly recommended. From the outside, the inn "looked a pleasant house," and there are lights shining through the windows (149; I:9). They can hear singing inside, and they get a friendly welcome from the innkeeper. The first hint of anything sinister is Frodo's glimpse of Aragorn smoking quietly in a corner with his hood concealing his face (153; I:9). Aragorn's revelations and the later attack by the Black Riders are all the more frightening for happening in such a seemingly safe and comfortable place. This contrast is important to Frodo's decision to accept Aragorn's guidance. It reinforces Frodo's feeling that he is personally attracting danger to every safe refuge, and must leave to protect his friends and the Shire.

In Jackson's movie, however, Bree is threatening from the start. It is pouring rain when the travelers reach town; tall Men jostle them in the streets and a cart nearly runs them down. There is harsh laughter in the bar. The customers are unpleasantly dirty, and sloppy drinkers as well. It seems to anticipate the Shire under Sharkey (which Jackson also dropped), rather than being the pleasant multi-cultural town readers expected to see. And when the Ring slips onto Frodo's finger, we get the "Ring effect" of blue light and rushing wind, along with Sauron's searching Eye (*Fellowship*, scene 15: "At the Sign of the Prancing Pony"). In the book the Ring has absolutely no effect in this scene but to make Frodo disappear from sight (157; I:9). Again, this anticipates Frodo's experience of the Ring's effects on Weathertop and his vision of Sauron's Eye in Galadriel's mirror, making their later use stale and repetitive rather than startling and new.

One of the most blatant examples of anticipation in the Jackson films is the immediate revelation (*Return*, scene 26: "The Muster of Rohan") that Éowyn has ridden with the Rohirrim to Minas Tirith against King Théoden's orders. In the book, her disguise as the soldier Dernhelm fools even Merry, who shares a horse with her for several days, and she is revealed as Éowyn only when she confronts the Lord of the Nazgûl, in fulfillment of the ancient prophecy that no living man can harm him. In the movie, as soon as she scoops Merry up on to her horse, he recognizes her and calls her "my lady." And even earlier, Aragorn notices the sword she has hidden under her saddlebags. There is no mystery about this young soldier with "the face of one without hope who goes in search of death" (785; V:3), and the surprise exposure of her identity is ruined.

There is one place in *The Return of the King* where Jackson does the opposite of "anticipation" by hiding something which happens in plain sight in the book. In the film, Sam is not shown taking the Ring from Frodo's supposedly dead body after the attack by Shelob. In one way this increases the tension of the following scenes by making the audience fear, along with Frodo, that the orcs have found the Ring. But this is an assumption Frodo would not have made if he hadn't been so disoriented, because there would have been no reason for the orcs to have kept him alive in this case; in fact, the Ring would long since have been on Sauron's hand again if the orcs had found it.

However, in the book, we as readers know that Sam has saved the Ring. What we feel, on reading about Frodo's fear, is the far more subtle sense of "pity and terror" evoked by Greek drama. The worst effect of Jackson's decision is to deprive us of the scenes of Sam's terrible choice between going on with the quest, hunting down Gollum, or staying by his master's body, and his later temptation by the Ring on the edge of Mordor. It could be said that, purely in terms of plot, Tolkien has anticipated himself by showing Sam taking the Ring. But what the author gained by doing so has great importance in terms of theme and characterization. In the scenes where Jackson anticipates, there does not seem to be a similar artistic goal.

In some places, Zimmerman and Jackson treat the same incident in similar ways, "anticipating" and "flattening" the same events. The Weathertop scene is a major example. There is no grand battle on the hilltop in the original; the only blows struck are Frodo's at the hem of the Witch-king's robe, and his in return at Frodo's shoulder. Aragorn drives them back with fire alone. At this point Aragorn should not even have a sword, as Tolkien points out. But both Zimmerman and Jackson create an extended swordfight scene out of the encounter (*Fellowship*, scene 19: "A Knife in the Dark"). Tolkien felt that presenting it the way it was written "would seem to me far more impressive than yet one more scene of screams and rather meaningless slashings" (*Letters* 273). And indeed, that would have made the primarily non-physical nature of the menace of the Ringwraiths more obvious; at this point in the story, as Tolkien points out, their tactic is to inspire "unreasoning *fear*" (*Letters* 272, original italics).

Another change both Zimmerman and Jackson made was to intercut the two parallel stories in *The Two Towers* and *The Return of the King*. Intercutting may indeed seem appropriate, even inevitable, at first glance. Philippa Boyens called it "an easy decision" (*Towers*, app.: "From Book to Script"), and the Zimmerman, John Boorman, and Chris Conkling/Peter Beagle scripts in the collection at Marquette University all intercut these two books. In an interview, scriptwriter Fran Walsh said:

> I often wondered . . . what kind of movie it'd be if you played out one story, and then the other. But it's a narrative structure that lends itself to literature much more than film. When Tolkien was writing this book, intercutting wasn't something that was so prevalent in literature—though it is starting to be now, and partly I think because of the influence of film. (qtd. in Verini 37).

Tolkien's opinion was strongly worded on this point: "*It is essential that these two branches should each be treated in coherent sequence.* Both to render them intelligible as a story, and because they are totally different in tone and scenery. Jumbling them together entirely destroys these things" (*Letters* 275, original italics). There is also the fact that intercutting the two books flattens a nicely executed dramatic irony. The characters we follow in Book III—Aragorn, Legolas, Gimli, Gandalf, Merry, and Pippin—all build suspense by voicing their concerns about Frodo and Sam. The reader is repeatedly reminded that their fate after leaving the Company is unknown. Then in Book IV, the reader experiences the dramatic irony of knowing what happened to the rest of the Company every time Frodo and Sam worry about them. This subtle contrast is lost when the stories are intercut.

Intercutting may have been the easiest path to take, given the kind of mass-market movie Jackson was trying to make. But Tolkien's parallel story structure is not unknown in the movies; Quentin Tarantino, for example, proves that it can be done successfully and even brilliantly. His *Pulp Fiction* and *Kill Bill* challenge the viewer by telling overlapping stories in differing styles and out of chronological order, without losing momentum or overly confusing the audience, and provide a model for how Tolkien's two story lines could have been handled. By intercutting the two parts of both *The Two Towers* and *Return of the King* and adhering strictly to internal chronology, Jackson was forced to move the encounter with Shelob to the middle of the third movie instead of the end of the second, creating a rushed feeling in the second half of *The Return of the King*. The worst effect of Jackson's decision to intercut may be seen more in the pacing of the story than in the jumbling of tone and scenery; these might not have been as confusing to a modern movie audience as Tolkien thought they might be, but telling separate and overlapping stories might not have been as confusing as Jackson thought it would be either.

It is somewhat surprising to see an exact duplication of some of what Tolkien considered Zimmerman's scriptwriting mistakes in the Jackson films. I myself saw co-screenwriter Philippa Boyens look up a quotation in Tolkien's *Letters* at a conference I attended; she was familiar enough with them to page very quickly to the one she wanted (for another account, see Kelley 6), so she must have been familiar with Tolkien's criticisms of the Zimmerman script. But if several scriptwriters adapt the same scenes the same way, does that mean Tolkien was wrong, or just that most scriptwriters tend to think the same way about what will work on screen? It can be argued that a primarily narrative author like Tolkien, who was unacquainted with the specialized techniques of writing for film, would not have understood the best way to adapt his own work for the medium. Tolkien only published one dramatic work, "The Homecoming of Beorhtnoth Beorhthelm's Son," a quite competent short verse play which has been produced several times in England (and at least once in America, at an early Mythopoeic Society conference). He readily admitted his ignorance of filmmaking and scriptwriting, but had some ideas of his own about translating text into dramatic form. As Tolkien observed:

> The canons of narrative art in any medium cannot be wholly different; and the failure of poor films is often precisely in exaggeration, and in the intrusion of unwarranted matter owing to not perceiving where the core of the original lies. (*Letters* 270)

For many viewers, Jackson's adaptation fails in precisely this way: his focus on battles, spectacle, and his own interpolated material, is at the expense of the core matters of characterization and theme and their careful construction through the tone, language, and pacing of bridging scenes.

THE MINES OF MORIA: "[HE] MAY THINK HE KNOWS MORE ABOUT BALROGS THAN I DO, BUT HE CANNOT EXPECT ME TO AGREE WITH HIM"

A close study of the Mines of Moria sequence illustrates the above problems further, and shows how Jackson's preference for horror and fight scenes actually reduces tension and suspense. Tolkien's two chapters set in Moria, "A Journey in the Dark" and "The Bridge of Khazad-dûm," are brilliantly written. Tom Shippey comments on the "increasing tension" and "relative understatement" of this section of *The Fellowship of the Ring*:

> Unlike many of his imitators, Tolkien had realized that tension was dissipated by constant thrill-creation. Accordingly the dangers of Moria build up slowly: from the first reluctance of Aragorn, 'the memory is very evil' (never enlarged on), to the ominous knocking from the deep that answers Pippin's stone (was it a hammer, as Gimli says?—we never learn), to Gandalf's mention of Durin's Bane. The Balrog is also hinted at several times before it appears: the orcs hang back as if they are afraid of something on their own side, Gandalf contests with it and concedes 'I have met my match' before it is ever seen, and again the orcs and trolls fall back as it comes up to cross the bridge of Khazad-dûm. Even when it does come into focus, the focus is blurred. . . . What Tolkien does in such passages is to satisfy the urge to know more . . . while retaining and even intensifying the counterbalancing pleasure of seeming always on the edge of further discovery, looking into a world that seems far fuller than the little at present known. (Shippey, *Century* 86-7)

One of the most incomprehensible changes Jackson makes is immediately revealing the fate of Balin and his companions, thus eliminating one major aspect of the tension of the journey through Moria. Moria is no longer the haunted and disquieting scene of a dwarf-colony's mysterious disappearance; in Jackson's film, it is just a rather prosaically bloodstained killing ground. Echoes and cobwebs would have been far more intriguing and suspenseful than scattered bits of armor and bone (*Fellowship,* scene 33: "Moria," and app.: "Moria" on disc 3).

The flattening of dialogue is also troublesome in this sequence. As one reviewer points out, "Tolkien's dialogue was always very carefully crafted—he had a delicate ear for nuance—hitting the tone just right with impressive consistency. The screenwriters are clumsy by comparison. . . . I don't think Jackson has much faith in words" (Russell 2). For example,

Gimli's invented speeches about dwarf hospitality sound rather painfully forced: "Soon, Master Elf, you will enjoy the fabled hospitality of the Dwarves—roaring fires, malt beer, red meat off the bone" (*Fellowship*, scene 33: "Moria"). This dialog is inappropriately jolly and Disney-like for Tolkien's "tough, thrawn [and] secretive" race of Dwarves (1106; App. F:I), a race definitely not known for their hospitality to outsiders. Gandalf's original lines at the point the Company is lost are precise and in character: "I do not like the smell of the left-hand way; there is foul air down there, or I am no guide" (306; II:4). It is grating to hear this reduced to Jackson's colloquial "When in doubt, always follow your nose" (*Fellowship*, scene 34: "A Journey in the Dark"). It makes Gandalf sound like Toucan Sam™ chasing after Froot Loops™.

It is only when the screenwriters use Tolkien's own words, even shifted many chapters away from their origin or given to different characters (as described in *Towers*, appendix: "From Book to Script"), that the script comes close to soaring. Gandalf and Frodo's conversation about pity and mercy, the fate of Gollum, and how Bilbo was meant to find the Ring (*Fellowship*, scene 34: "A Journey in the Dark"), though displaced far from its source in the early chapter "The Shadow of the Past" and much rearranged, is more effective and moving than anything else Jackson has added to this scene. (This technique does not always work; having Sam paraphrase Frodo's lines about the improbability of any return journey from Mordor [610; IV:4] in the third movie [*Return*, scene 47: "The Land of Shadow"] is inappropriate to Sam's character, because he never entirely gives up hope that they will somehow survive and return.)

The battle in the Chamber of Mazarbul is another sequence Jackson rewrote drastically in order to add superfluous elements of horror and comedy (and possibly, as more than one viewer has pointed out, to provide fodder for the videogames associated with the movie franchise [Thompson 49]). As one reviewer put it, "[T]he Fellowship's fight with the Orcs and the cave Troll is a flurry of cuts and laboured humour" (Fuller 19). Instead of Pippin dropping a pebble in a well two days earlier, so that the Company forgets the drumming and tapping noises until it is too late, Pippin's pebble is changed into a farcical full skeleton in armor, and the drumming and attack are an immediate response to it. There is not actually a cave-troll in the battle in the book—it is simply an early speculation as to why the orcs are hanging back, and it turns out to be the Balrog that is frightening them. Aragorn's grim "We shall make them fear the Chamber of Mazarbul" (316; II:5) is transformed to Gimli's over-the-top "Let them come! There is one Dwarf left in Moria who still draws breath!" (*Fellowship*, scene 35: "Balin's Tomb"). In the book, Frodo does not hang back behind the other hobbits or hide behind a pillar; in fact, he stabs at the foot of the first orc who tries to force the doors. Likewise, Sam isn't a comic figure wielding a skillet; instead, he fells an orc with "a sturdy thrust with his Barrow-blade" (317; II:5). Jackson takes time to linger lovingly on Frodo's agony after the spear-thrust from the cave-troll for nearly fifteen seconds all told; in the book, Frodo says "I am bruised and in pain, but it is not too bad" (319; II:5). Jackson's rewrite needlessly expands what was a brief interlude in the book, and distracts from the far more important battle on the Bridge of Khazad-dûm. (Similarly, Jackson's focus on Legolas's invented fight with the mûmak [*Return*, scene 42: "Victory at Minas Tirith"] distracts the audience's attention from Éowyn's much more significant battle with the Witch-king.)

Another problem, which Jackson shares with Bakshi, is a predilection for over-using new and unproven special effects. Commenting on Bakshi's rotoscoping, one reviewer said, "[T]his constant intrusion of technique draws the attention away from what is being presented to how it is being presented" (Ziegler 37). The battle with the cave-troll is supposed to be a wonder of computer-generated imagery, but it frequently looks ridiculous, and the "forced perspective" technique used to make the Hobbits and Dwarves appear shorter is not always seamless. It is especially intrusive in the stiffly posed "group portrait" at the end of the Council of Elrond (*Fellowship*, scene 27), the crowd bowing to the hobbits at Aragorn's coronation, and during the farewell scene at The Grey Havens. When technique becomes obvious, the audience's willing suspension of disbelief fails and is difficult to recover.

Jackson's interpretation of the Moria sequence is also heavily influenced by his sense of humor. Tolkien's books are not without their humorous moments, but the kind of crude comedy Jackson adds works against the tension of highly serious scenes. Ursula K. Le Guin's influential essay on the language of fantasy, "From Elfland to Poughkeepsie," included this observation: "humor in fantasy is both a lure and a pitfall to imitators" (Le Guin 81). It is fatal to introduce contemporary humor, like Jackson's dwarf-tossing joke (*Fellowship*, scene 36: "The Bridge of Khazad-dûm"), to high fantasy. There is a type of comic fantasy, of which Terry Pratchett is the master, which can shade into high fantasy; but pure high fantasy takes itself seriously and cannot shade back into the comic without serious damage to its themes. Le Guin's words about another writer apply as well to Tolkien: "He never lets his creation down in order to make a joke, and he never shows a tin ear for tone" (Le Guin 82). Jackson unfortunately does show a tin ear for tone, particularly in Moria but also at other key moments. When Jackson adds a comic sequence not in the original, like Merry and Pippin's "Dumb and Dumber" misadventure with Gandalf's firecrackers (*Fellowship*, scene 5: "A Long-expected Party"), the viewer is "jerked back and forth between Elfland and Poughkeepsie" (Le Guin 81) and may find himself asking "We gave up Tom Bombadil, the gifts from Galadriel, and the Houses of Healing for *this*?" (Last).

The dwarf-tossing joke (repeated in the second movie but thankfully not in the theatrical release of the third), is especially egregious. Tom Shippey calls it an "error of tone. . . . One sees the joke, and the . . . audience laughed, but it is an anachronism beyond anything Tolkien allowed" ("Temptations" 16). As another reviewer observed, "Gimli was, in the books, somewhat comical, but never the parody he has become in the films" (Russell 2). Jackson was known for "corny in-joke[s]" (Davis 120) and a "taste for schlock horror" (Fuller 19) in his earlier movies, but they are out of place in high fantasy. Jackson said in one interview, "I have a sort of inherent dislike of things that take themselves too seriously and I just think there's a sort of pompousness that I'm always trying to avoid" (Bauer 10). Jackson admitted elsewhere that he used Gimli "as my kind of foil to get a bit of irreverent humour out there" (Bodey), and that he wanted "to have some fun" with the Balrog sequence (qtd. in Thompson 49). Humor was the inspiration for the "World Wizard Wrestling" scene in the first movie as well (*Fellowship* scene 12: "Saruman the White"), where the dignified Saruman and Gandalf have a knockdown physical fight: "I thought it would be funny, and more interesting, to see two old guys just beating the crap out of each other" (quoted in Thompson 51).

That is not a crime when the clear intent is satire; the *Harvard Lampoon's* hilarious but dated 1969 spoof *Bored of the Rings*, the dwarf cave sequence in Terry Pratchett's *Witches Abroad* (42-52), and innumerable fan fiction parodies are cases in point. However, Jackson said repeatedly that he was making a film as true to Tolkien as possible (for example, *Fellowship*, app.: "From Book to Script"), and to do this properly he should have maintained Tolkien's tone of high seriousness. As one reviewer pointed out,

> There is a simple truth that film-makers miss: fantasy works best when it's played straight. It was one of Tolkien's great contributions to the genre: he applied the methods of realism to a novel of the fantastic. Film-makers don't seem to be able to do it without feeling they must make it comic, or mock the genre. (Russell 1)

There are other errors in emotional tone in the Moria sequence as well. Gandalf's harsh treatment of Pippin is disturbing; in the book,

Gandalf calls Pippin "Fool of a Took!" quite frequently, but all his rebukes have a kindly, almost avuncular feel to them, and Pippin is "undaunted by the wizard's bristling brows," even when Gandalf threatens to use his head to open the doors of Moria (299; II:4). In the movie, after Pippin knocks the skeleton into the well, Gandalf cruelly sneers, "Throw yourself in next time and rid us of your stupidity," snatching his hat and staff back from the obviously ashamed young hobbit (*Fellowship*, scene 35: "Balin's Tomb"). The original "Throw yourself in next time, and then you will be no further nuisance" (305; II:4) is somewhat less harsh and not as personally insulting, particularly as it is preceded by a slightly humorous line and followed shortly after by kind words and Gandalf admitting he was not his usual self. Gandalf continues to be somewhat rougher with Pippin in *The Return of the King* than he is in the book.

The portrayal of Gimli throughout the movie is terribly off the mark (one reviewer calls him a "belching knucklehead from Edinburgh" [Kelly]), but this sequence especially is difficult to take. The grim, serious dwarf is made to talk gloatingly of the hospitality they will soon receive in Moria, in the sort of hubristic speech that invariably presages disaster in the movies, and then cries out in anguish when Gandalf's light reveals the dead bodies in the caves. This "anticipates" and "flattens" his later reaction at the tomb of Balin, where he drops to his knees in a paroxysm of grief, sobbing loudly (*Fellowship*, scene 35: "Balin's Tomb"). Surely, seeing all the dead dwarves lying about, he ought to have concluded that Balin was dead as well, and not been so shocked to see his tomb. In the book, his reaction is movingly stoic; he pulls up his hood to hide his face (312; II:4), and when they flee the chamber, Legolas must drag him away from the sarcophagus (317; II:5). Gimli is not only made into the butt of cheap humor, but must play the emotion-ruled sidekick as well, and in the third movie even dishonorably suggests that Aragorn not release the army of the Dead when their oath is fulfilled (*Return*, scene 44: "Oaths Fulfilled").

Jackson has been justifiably praised for allowing his male characters to show the same emotion and unselfconscious physical affection for each other that they demonstrate in the books, and Elijah Wood and Sean Astin do a particularly good job portraying this aspect of Frodo and Sam's friendship. But Jackson does at times go overboard, dwelling on a character's pain too long and disrupting the rhythm of a scene. For example, after Gandalf's fall in Moria, Frodo screams in slow-motion and is carried away by Boromir like a child having a tantrum (*Fellowship*, scene 36: "The Bridge of Khazad-dûm"). Dwelling on Frodo's beautiful but anguished face for just a beat too long makes all the difference to the pacing of this scene, just as dwelling on his injuries and subsequent agonies did at Weathertop and during the flight to Rivendell, in the cave-troll scene, and after he is stung by Shelob.

A director better known for suspense, rather than horror, might have handled the Moria sequence of the film differently. Imagine Alfred Hitchcock directing this section, perhaps even in black-and-white. He would have made the most of the spooky emptiness of the vast corridors and stairs, the slow building of tension, the half-seen shadows out of the corner of the eye, and the ominous sounds in the dark. The silent forcing of the door to the Chamber of Mazarbul, the frightening, bewildering battle in the dim dusty light, and the headlong race to the gates would have been well-suited to Hitchcock's style, and the Balrog would most likely have remained a menacing unfocused shadow in his hands, rather than a CGI monster with a well-defined shape. Directed like this, it could have been much truer to Tolkien's original vision.

CONCLUSION: "SIGHING FOR SOMETHING QUITE DIFFERENT — A MOON NO DOUBT"

In one of the notes to his well-known essay "On Fairy-stories," Tolkien recalls taking a group of children to see A.A. Milne's stage adaptation of Kenneth Grahame's *The Wind in the Willows*. As David Bratman has pointed out, his comments are oddly appropriate to the Jackson films:

> [A] perceptive admirer (as distinct from a great admirer) of the book would never have attempted to dramatize it. . . . The play is, on the lower level of drama, tolerably good fun, especially for those who have not read the book, but some children . . . brought away as their chief memory nausea . . . [T]hey preferred their recollection of the book. ("On Fairy-stories" 76)

What many readers worry about is that "mass exploitation . . . is likely to have a detrimental effect on Tolkien's literary status, shaky enough by dint of his ever-expanding popularity" (Fuller 20). Hammond says, "I wouldn't give [the movie] much thought except that so many of its reviewers have praised it as faithful to the book, or even superior to it, all of which adds insult to injury and is demonstrably wrong" (qtd. in Kirst 2).

An early reviewer of the Bakshi movie stated, "The mind of the initiate to Middle-earth is likely to fix on Bakshi's relatively limited images before his imagination has a chance to move through Tolkien's depth and complexity. . . . Bakshi's movie may leave future readers free to see only what Bakshi saw" (Walker 36). Shippey likewise says of the Jackson film, "It imposes alien visuals on the mind. . . . Jackson will replace Tolkien, even erase him; this is the fear of some of Tolkien's defenders" ("Temptations" 16). Fortunately, few people seem to carry the Bakshi images in their heads any longer. Perhaps Jackson's mistakes will fade from their memories as well, leaving only memories of the images and scenes that were miraculously right. The current permeation of the market with Jackson's images makes one pessimistic about this possibility, though. Margaret Mackey asks similar questions in her investigation into market representations of Peter Rabbit:

> [T]o what extent do the many spin-offs actually affect or possibly even damage responses to the original text? Does market saturation have esthetic consequences? For everybody? Just for some? How much does it matter? Do the copyright holders have any kind of duty to the public beyond a perceived requirement to maximize profit? (Mackey 119-20)

It is unlikely, but not impossible, that there will be another attempt to film *The Lord of the Rings* in our lifetimes. Viewers who were disappointed by Jackson's efforts can only hope that next director who tackles Tolkien will take note of the critics of the various film scripts, and create an adaptation truer to the spirit of the book and less attuned to the tastes of Hollywood's hypothetical mass audience. But as Tolkien commented after reading the 1956 B.B.C. radio script, we may be ineffectually "sighing for something quite different—a moon no doubt" (*Letters* 255).

NOTE

Versions of this paper were presented at the Southwest/Texas Popular Culture Association Annual Conference and at the Mythopoeic Society Annual Conference in 2003.

Works Cited

Bauer, Erik. "'It's Just a Movie': Erik Bauer Speaks with Peter Jackson." Rev. of *The Fellowship of the Ring*, dir. Peter Jackson. *Creative Screenwriting* 9.1 (2002): 6-12.

Bodey, Michael. "Riddles of the Rings Resolved." Rev. of *The Return of the King*, dir. Peter Jackson. *Daily Telegraph* 1 January 2004.

Bratman, David. *Tolkien on Dramatizations*. 2003. Mythsoc discussion group. 6 Jan. 2003 <http://groups.yahoo.com/group/mythsoc/message/7449>

Carpenter, Humphrey. *Tolkien : A Biography*. Boston: Houghton Mifflin, 1977.

Chance, Jane. "Is There a Text in This Hobbit? Peter Jackson's *Fellowship of the Ring*." Rev. of *The Fellowship of the Ring*, dir. Peter Jackson. *Literature/Film Quarterly* 30.2 (2002): 79-85.

Davis, Erik. "*The Fellowship of the Ring*." *Wired* (2001): 120-32.

Dickens, Charles, and Michael Patrick Hearn. *The Annotated Christmas Carol*. New York: Avenel Books, 1976.

Fuller, Graham. "Trimming Tolkien." Rev. of *The Fellowship of the Ring*, dir. Peter Jackson. *Sight and Sound* 12.2 (2002): 18-20, 49-52.

Hardy, Gene. "More Than a Magic Ring." Rev. of *The Hobbit*, dir. Arthur Rankin Jr. and Jules Bass. *Children's Novels and the Movies*. Ed. Douglas Street. New York: Ungar, 1983. 131-40.

Hostetter, Carl F. *Digest Number 1086*. 2003. Mythsoc discussion group. 6 Jan. 2003 <http://groups.yahoo.com/group/mythsoc/message/7188>

Jacobs, Deborah P. "They Took Our Precious." Rev. of *The Return of the King*, dir. Peter Jackson. *Boston Globe* 2 January 2004.

Kelley, Thomas. *Mythcon 32 and Meeting Philippa Boyens*. 2001. TheOneRing.Net. 13 Jan. 2003 <http://greenbooks.theonering.net/guest/files/110101.html>

Kelly, Martin. "One Triumph to Rule Them All." Rev. of *The Return of the King*, dir. Peter Jackson. *Washington Dispatch* 30 December 2003.

Kirst, Sean. "Tolkien Scholar Stings "Rings" Films." Rev. of *The Fellowship of the Ring* and *The Two Towers*, dir. Peter Jackson. *The Post-Standard* 4 February 2003.

Last, Jonathan V. "The End of the Ring." Rev. of *The Return of the King*, dir. Peter Jackson. *Weekly Standard* 22 December 2003.

Le Guin, Ursula K. "From Elfland to Poughkeepsie." *The Language of the Night*. 1973. Ed. Susan Wood. New York: Berkley, 1979. 73-86.

The Lord of the Rings: The Fellowship of the Ring. Special Extended DVD Edition. Screenplay by Peter Jackson, Fran Walsh, and Philippa Boyens. Perf. Elijah Wood et al. Dir. Peter Jackson. United States: New Line Home Entertainment, 2002.

The Lord of the Rings: The Return of the King. Theatrical Release DVD. Screenplay by Peter Jackson, Fran Walsh, and Philippa Boyens. Perf. Elijah Wood et al. Dir. Peter Jackson. United States, New Line Home Entertainment, 2004.

The Lord of the Rings: The Two Towers. Special Extended DVD Edition. Screenplay by Peter Jackson, Fran Walsh, and Philippa Boyens. Perf. Elijah Wood et al. Dir. Peter Jackson. United States: New Line Home Entertainment, 2003.

Mackey, Margaret. *The Case of Peter Rabbit: Changing Conditions of Literature for Children.* New York: Garland, 1998.

Pratchett, Terry. *Witches Abroad.* New York: Penguin, 1991.

Russell, Sean. *The Lord of the Rings: The Two Towers.* 2003. SF Site. 8 Jan. 2003 <http://www.sfsite.com/01a/2t143.htm>

Shippey, Thomas A. *J.R.R. Tolkien: Author of the Century.* Boston: Houghton Mifflin, 2001.

—. "Temptations for All Time." Rev. of *The Fellowship of the Ring,* dir. Peter Jackson. *Times Literary Supplement* 21 December 2001: 16-17.

Smith, Patricia Burkhart. "Ring Bearer: Patricia Burkhart Smith Talks with Philippa Boyens." *Creative Screenwriting* 8.2 (2001): 4, 6, 8.

Thompson, Kristin. "Fantasy, Franchises, and Frodo Baggins: *The Lord of the Rings* and Modern Hollywood." *The Velvet Light Trap.*52 (2003): 45-63.

Tolkien, J. R. R. *The Lord of the Rings.* 2nd ed. With Note on the Text by Douglas A. Anderson. Boston: Houghton Mifflin, 1994.

—. *The Letters of J.R.R. Tolkien: A Selection.* Ed. Christopher Tolkien. 1st Houghton Mifflin pbk. ed. Boston: Houghton Mifflin, 2000.

—. "On Fairy-Stories." *The Tolkien Reader.* New York: Ballantine, 1966. 3-84.

Troost, Linda, and Sayre Greenfield. "Introduction: Watching Ourselves Watching." *Jane Austen in Hollywood.* Eds. Linda Troost and Sayre Greenfield. Lexington: U. Press Kentucky, 1998. 1-12.

Verini, Bob. "Hobbit-Forming: Adapting *The Lord of the Rings.*" Scr(i)pt (2001): 34-37, 62-63.

Walker, Steven C. "Tolkien According to Bakshi." Rev. of *The Lord of the Rings,* dir. Ralph Bakshi. *Mythlore* 6.1 (1979): 36.

Ziegler, Dale. "Ring-Wrath: Or Therein Bakshi Again." Rev. of *The Lord of the Rings,* dir. Ralph Bakshi. *Mythlore* 6.1 (1979): 37-38.

RE-VISION: *THE LORD OF THE RINGS* IN PRINT AND ON SCREEN

DIANA PAXSON

Watching the films of *The Lord of the Rings* has been a fascinating, if sometimes mixed, experience. As a lover of the book, it is exhilarating to see with my eyes what I have so often tried to imagine, and frustrating when the vision falters. As a writer, I am delighted by the opportunity to compare the several versions of both book and film.

We are accustomed to receive a book or a film as holy writ, direct from the mind of the maker, but it takes time for a work's creator to see it thus. As Tolkien says in a letter to his son Christopher, "I knew I had written a story of worth in 'The Hobbit' when reading it (after it was old enough to be detached from me) I had suddenly in a fairly strong measure the 'eucatastrophic' emotion at Bilbo's exclamation: 'The Eagles! The Eagles are coming!'" (*Letters* 101). It is also apparently true for the creators of films. Producer Barrie Osborne comments: "When you see it now, you think, 'How could we ever have contemplated anything different?' But that is the process of movie making" (*Towers*, app.: "From Book to Script").

The notes and drafts of *The Lord of the Rings* published in *The History of Middle-earth* reveal Tolkien's successive "visions" of the story. The release of both the theatrical and the extended versions of the movies offer us alternate visions of the film. The filmmakers' commentaries give us insight into the cinematic creative process, just as Tolkien's notes and letters show how his concept of the work evolved. Thus, rather than simply comparing the book and the film, we may consider a multiplicity of visions.

The creative process is one of constant adjustment. The more recent the book, the easier it is to remember at which points the plot could have gone another way, all the times one had to cut and backtrack, and the places where, for good or for ill, changes were forced by editorial fiat. Until the galleys are turned in, a novel is mutable, and sometimes, if there are multiple editions, even after.

Each art form imposes its own constraints on focus and content. To cover every aspect of Tolkien's and Jackson's revisions would require a book. In this paper, therefore, I will confine myself to some of the major variations in Tolkien's and Jackson's visions of the work in general, and in particular, to the development of Aragorn.

CONSTRAINTS AND CONTENT

One of the most crucial constraints on the form and content of a tale is the number of words or minutes available to tell the story. Marketing constraints can determine the length of a book or a film. The shortage of paper during and after World War II had publishers enraging Tolkien by threatening to cut *The Lord of the Rings*; however, by the time the book was actually finished, the situation had eased, and Unwin was willing to adjust the publishing format to the manuscript instead of vice versa. This is fortunate, since given Tolkien's creative process, it took some time for the structure of the final product, which in turn determined its length, to emerge. In a letter written in October, 1948, he says, "I think there is a chance of it being published though it will be a massive book far too large to make any money for the publisher (let alone the author): it must run to 1200 pages. However length is no obstacle to those who like that kind of thing" (*Letters* 131), thus proving himself at once both a poor prophet and a good one.

Having seen the completed manuscript at last, Sir Stanley Unwin asked rather plaintively "whether there is any possibility of breaking the million words into, say, three or four to some extent self-contained volumes?" (*Letters* 139). As we know, this is in fact what happened, with the addition of the Appendices to fill out the third volume.

For the producers of the film, length was a major constraint as well. Even at the beginning, Jackson knew the story could not be told in a single film. His initial proposal was to do it in two. This was the form in which he presented it to New Line. At the end of the presentation, co-chairman Robert Shay turned to him and asked, "Aren't there three books? You should make three" (*Return*, app.: "A Filmmaker's Journey").

Retaining a three-part structure allowed the filmmakers to keep the focus of each story-line more or less the same as it was in the novel's three volumes — as it was described in one of the trailers, "A Journey Begins, A Fellowship is Broken, A King Returns." The length of a film destined for wide distribution in theaters is determined by the number of showings that can be fitted into a day. The usual upper limit for a single film is about two and a half hours, although the success of *The Fellowship of the Ring* allowed Jackson to extend that to three. Fortunately the extended versions integrate rather than simply add cut scenes, and provide a much more satisfying version of each film.

The length of time available for creation also has an impact on a work. Tolkien, resistant to the pleas of friends and publisher alike, continued to revise and polish *The Lord of the Rings* until he felt it was done. By the time he let it go, inconsistencies had been corrected, loose ends tied off, and the prose was well-nigh perfect. Although creating the films took eight years, Peter Jackson had only one year to complete the final version of each movie. In addition to the constant revisions during shooting, actors were brought back during post-production for "pick-up" shots which allowed the director to refine. Unfortunately, even with pick-ups, there was not always time to give the films the polish they needed. Some of the problems are addressed in the extended versions, but there are still points where the dialogue is clumsy or the plot logic falters (usually in places where the film departs from the original story line).

The impact of length on a film can be seen by comparing the running times of the theatrical and extended versions of the first and second films. For *Fellowship,* with the shortest theatrical time, thirty minutes of additional footage were added in the extended version. The popularity of this first extension encouraged Jackson to include an additional forty-three minutes of material in the extended version of *The Two Towers.* Although in each case the story line is unchanged, the addition of so much material affects the focus and flavor of the films. The theatrical version of *Fellowship,* for instance, is intentionally "Frodo-centric." In creating it, scenes which did not focus on Frodo were excised. In the extended version, the inclusion of those scenes allows the film to develop other characters in more detail. The film thus becomes the story of the Fellowship as a group rather than of Frodo alone.

VERSIONS AND REVISIONS

The Fellowship of the Ring. The first task of anyone seeking to translate a book to the screen is to identify the essential story line. The action of *The Lord of the Rings* consists of a quest and a war. The incidents which survive are those which significantly affect the ability of the hero or heroes to reach their goal.

The notes edited by Christopher Tolkien in *The Return of the Shadow* show that it took Tolkien some time to figure out whose story he was telling. After the surprising success of *The Hobbit,* both Tolkien and his publishers were eager for a sequel. In November of 1937 he discussed a number of possibilities at one of those literary lunches from which one returns trying to remember just what one has committed to, and whether, once the glow has worn off, it can in fact be done. The general conclusion was that he should tackle a direct sequel to *The Hobbit* rather than launching into the earlier mythology. By the beginning of 1938, he had written "A Long Expected Party." In a letter to Stanley Unwin dated February 17th of that year, Tolkien observes that:

> They say it is the first step that costs the effort. I do not find it so. I am sure I could write unlimited "first chapters." I have indeed written many. The Hobbit sequel is still where it was, and I have only the vaguest notions of how to proceed. Not ever intending any sequel, I fear I squandered all my favourite "motifs" and characters on the original "Hobbit." (*Letters* 29)

Between 1937 and 1939 the story underwent numerous false starts and revisions. Even at this point Tolkien was considering whether to make Bilbo or the character who eventually is named Frodo (we must all be eternally thankful that his original name of "Bingo" was rejected) the hero. The Ranger who protects him is a hobbit called Trotter (of whom more will be said later). Although Tolkien's notes indicate that he was still considering a wealth of alternatives for the early part of the story, the basic elements of future action were finally beginning to emerge.

Throughout 1940 the story continued to develop, following the characters through Moria and Lothlórien to the breaking of the fellowship at the falls of Rauros. Here, Tolkien's original plan was to have Frodo flee, followed by Sam, after being attacked by Boromir. Afterward, Aragorn and Boromir intend to head towards Gondor while Legolas and Gimli return north toward their homes. Merry and Pippin get lost and end up with Treebeard, who will take them to Minas Tirith. The important point here is that from now on, the story line must diverge into several strands.

The narrator of "A Filmmaker's Journey" (*Return,* app.) comments, "Tolkien himself might have deeply identified with the ongoing struggle to get each script right. Like the original novel, it was a process of constant revision." In any translation of narrative to drama, the adapter must focus on the *essence* of the story. Every episode has to do several jobs. In the commentary we learn that the early drafts of the *Rings* script fared even farther from the original story than the final form. As the producer, Barrie Osborne, observes,

> Sometimes they thought of going in a different direction from the book, and every time they tried to do that, gradually they would find that actually Tolkien knew what he was doing with the story and they would go back to where he had started. (*Fellowship*, app.: "From Book to Script")

From the directors' commentary on the extended *Fellowship* DVD, we learn that there was considerable debate regarding how and where to begin. When I first encountered the book in the sixties, Tolkien's choice to open with the Hobbits, whose culture is so closely modeled on that of traditional English country folk, seemed a brilliant way to ease the reader into Middle-earth. The Hobbits, like most readers, are essentially "muggles," and protagonists and readers together move from the "mundane" world of the Shire into realms of mystery and magic.

Ironically, by the time the film was made, the traditional English countryside, already disappearing when Tolkien wrote the book, had for most people receded into a mythic past. In the meantime, the success of *The Lord of the Rings* had introduced an entire generation to elves and dwarves, wizards and orcs and dragons. Through games like *Dungeons and Dragons* even those who had never read the books had become more familiar with settings like Moria or Lothlórien than they were with the Shire. Thus, although an extended sequence in the Shire was filmed which covers the same material as Tolkien's own prologue, the eventual decision was to begin with a different prologue which would provide much of the back-story which in the book is revealed gradually. Only after we have been introduced to Middle-earth does the film focus in on the Shire.

But even here we have two visions. In the theatrical release, we move directly from the history of the Ring to the moment when Frodo welcomes Gandalf to the Shire. From the point of view of the action, this is the true beginning—the last moment of equilibrium before the situation begins to fall apart. It establishes the "Frodo-centric" focus of the first film. However, in the extended version the Shire sequence begins with Bilbo, and it is Hobbits in general rather than Frodo who engage our interest.

Once the story begins, the viewer who knows the books well is gratified to note that a surprising number (by comparison with other film adaptations) of lines from the original dialogue have been retained, although they do not always appear in their original locations. Interestingly enough, in transporting dialogue, Walsh and Boyens were following Tolkien's example. As Christopher Tolkien observes,

> As often in the history of *The Lord of the Rings* much of the
> earliest writing remained, for example in the detail of
> conversation, and yet such conversation appears later
> shifted into new contexts, given to different speakers, and
> acquiring new resonance as the 'world' and its history grew
> and expanded. (*Return of the Shadow* 431)

In scripting *The Fellowship of the Ring,* Fran Walsh and Philippa
Boyens were required to refine the action even further, cutting any
episode that did not directly contribute to the main story line, thus, the
much-bewailed disappearance of the hobbits' adventures in the valley of
the Withywindle and on the Barrow-downs and their rescues by Tom
Bombadil. Having been forced to cut some of my own most exciting
passages because they did not in fact advance the story line, I can mourn
the loss, but I understand why they were excised.

The Two Towers. In the beginning, of course, Tolkien had no idea
that he was writing a trilogy. Thus he was to some extent spared the strain
of finding material to fill the gap between the beginning and the end. By
the winter of 1941 he had reached the point at which the final text of *The
Two Towers* begins. As he came to points in the story which had been
outlined earlier, many of them were changing. In early versions, after
meeting with Gandalf, Trotter and the other companions go to Minas
Tirith. What follows is summarized as, "Rest of war in which Gandalf and
/ on his eagle in white leads assault must be told later — partly a dream of
Frodo, partly seen by him (and Sam), and partly heard from orcs" (*The
Treason of Isengard* 389).

At this point, although Tolkien had long known that Gandalf
would reappear, he was unsure about his opponent on the Bridge of
Khazad-dûm, and for a time considered assigning the role to Saruman.
Christopher Tolkien describes his father's process at this point as ". . .
passages of very rough and piecemeal drafting being built into a
completed manuscript that was in turn heavily overhauled, the whole
complex advancing and changing at the same time —" (*The War of the Ring*
3). This made it difficult to keep track of the chronology, a problem that
was also to be faced by the makers of the film. Nonetheless, by the end of
1942 he had completed the destruction of Saruman and was moving the
characters toward Gondor. But at this point, inspiration failed, and it was
not until the spring of 1944 that he turned back to Frodo and Sam and got
the story going again.

In scripting and shooting *The Two Towers,* Jackson and his crew faced the same difficulties as Tolkien in filling in the gap between *Fellowship,* described by Jackson as "by comparison . . . a very linear straightforward 'road' movie," *(Return,* app.) and the resolution provided by *The Return of the King.* The middle part of a trilogy is always the hardest to create, and in the commentary on the extended DVD, both director and editors remark that *The Two Towers* was by far the most difficult of the three films to do.

In the book, Tolkien moves back and forth between the stories of Aragorn, Legolas, and Gimli, and of Merry and Pippin among the orcs and ents in Book IV, but puts the adventures of Frodo and Sam in Book V with no interruptions. Jackson felt that to maintain viewer interest he needed to intercut all three story lines. However this made it obvious that the chronology of the two books in Volume II is not in fact the same. The confrontation with Shelob actually takes place at the same time as Gandalf's arrival at Minas Tirith. Furthermore, Frodo's battle with Shelob and capture by the orcs is an emotional climax. If those scenes were intercut with the battle at Helm's Deep, Philippa Boyens believed that the two would cancel each other out.

One of the major changes made to the plot in the movie is in the character of Faramir. Since the film makers had been at pains to emphasize the corrupting effects of the Ring in *Fellowship,* they felt that to have Faramir resist its lure so easily would deny its power. In the book, it must be admitted that Faramir's character remains consistently (and perhaps not completely credibly) noble from beginning to end. The inclusion of the scene showing the relationship between Boromir, Faramir, and their father is one of the points in which the extended version of the film solves a problem created by the ruthless cutting of the theatrical version. Although there are still places where the logic falters, I must admit that this version adds more suspense, and the scene in which Frodo faces the Nazgûl is a memorable addition to the story.

Another important difference between the two film versions is the inclusion of additional footage of Treebeard, Merry and Pippin. For the most part this is extremely welcome, as in the theatrical version that part of the story seems rather thin. Here we have another example of transposition of text, in which Old Man Willow is magically transported to Fangorn Forest and some of Tom Bombadil's lines are spoken by Treebeard, a development which seems somewhat less shocking when one notes that Treebeard's characterization evolved drastically throughout the writing—in one early draft, *he* was the one who captured Gandalf and kept him from returning to the Shire.

By deleting the episode with Shelob, altering the characterization of Faramir, and developing the relationship between Aragorn and Arwen through flashbacks, the film makers created a story line that diverges in major ways from the book. To create a satisfying conclusion they needed an emotional climax. As Jackson points out, not having anyone die at the end was a disadvantage. His solution was to finish with the victory at Helm's Deep and the drowning of Isengard (which was also his reason for moving the "Flotsam and Jetsam" scene to the beginning of the third film).

The Return of the King. The capture of Frodo at the end of Volume Two of the novel not only stops Sam, it apparently stopped its author, for he accomplished almost nothing on the book between 1944 and 1946. In a letter to Christopher Tolkien dated 29 November, 1944, he states,

> Here is a small consignment of 'The Ring': the last two chapters that have been written, and the end of the Fourth Book of that great Romance, in which you will see that, as is all too easy, I have got the hero into such a fix that not even an author will be able to extricate him without labour and difficulty. . . .

Tolkien summarizes the story's events in much the same order as they eventually appeared, going on to say:

> With the destruction of the Ring, the exact manner of which is not certain—all these last bits were written ages ago, but no longer fit in detail, nor in elevation (for the whole thing has become much larger and loftier) . . . the clearing up of all loose threads, down even to Bill Ferny's pony, must take place. A lot of this work will be done in a final chapter where Sam is found reading out of an enormous book to his children . . . but the final scene will be the passage of Bilbo and Elrond and Galadriel through the woods of the Shire on their way to the Grey Havens. Frodo will join them and pass over the Sea . . . It will probably work out very differently from this plan when it really gets written, as the thing seems to write itself once I get going, as if the truth comes out then, only imperfectly glimpsed in the preliminary sketch . . . (*Letters* 103)

Clearly, Tolkien knew *what* was going to happen, but as many an author before and since has discovered, the problem was to figure out *how* it would occur. It is clear also that in the years since he first imagined the destruction of the Ring, the *why* had evolved as well. The changes between early and later drafts are therefore not so much in content as in presentation, as he discovered that scenes he thought might be summarized had to be shown, point of view characters shifted, and the exact order of and motivation for events in the story worked out.

By the end of 1946 he had completed Book V, and felt that he was now "'on the last chapters'; and greatly underestimating (as he had so often done before) how much needed to be told before he reached the end, he thought that he could finish it within the month" (*Sauron Defeated* 13). Book VI was not, in fact written until 1948. When Tolkien had described the feast at the Field of Cormallen, he sketched out the remaining events, which include the coronation and wedding of King Elessar, and (for the first time) the union of Faramir and Éowyn. On their way home, the hobbits meet and pardon Saruman, arrive in the Shire and eject the Sackville-Bagginses from Bag End. Frodo and Sam go to the Grey Havens, where Frodo and Bilbo sail away with the elves.

Here, we have the final major "re-visioning" in Tolkien's text. The suspicion that Lotho (here still called Cosimo) has been up to no good in the Shire mutates into its full-scale corruption, and the author discovers that the ruffian Sharkey is in fact Saruman. In the first version of this episode, it is Frodo who leads the fighting. Only later did Tolkien realize the extent to which "the Shire has been saved, but not for me" (1006; VI:9). The planned chapter in which Sam ties up loose ends by talking to his children was in fact written, but later deleted to preserve the impact of that final, "Well, I'm back" (1008; VI:9), and most of the information it contained included in the Appendices. As Tolkien observed in a letter written in 1954, "One must stop somewhere" (*Letters* 179).

With the film of *The Return of the King,* we are once more seeing a story which is (relatively) familiar to those who know the books. At this point, Tolkien himself was concerned with clarifying the chronological relationship between the various story lines. As Sam seeks to rescue Frodo from the Tower of Cirith Ungol he wonders what is happening to the others, and the author inserts a bit of omniscient narrative, "Out westward in the world it was drawing to noon upon the fourteenth day of March in the Shire-reckoning, and even now Aragorn was leading the black fleet from Pelargir, and Merry was riding with the Rohirrim down the Stonewain Valley, while in Minas Tirith flames were rising and Pippin watched the madness growing in the eyes of Denethor" (877; VI:1). Jackson's solution was to intercut the action of all three story lines.

Since the third volume of the novel actually has fewer chapters than the others, adding episodes from Volume Two to the third film made sense. Most of its scenes are based on material from the book. One addition is Arwen's decision to return to Rivendell instead of going to the

Grey Havens, inspired by a vision of the child the Appendix has told us she is destined to bear, leading to the reforging (finally!) of Narsil. Another (in my opinion less successful) change is the quarrel between Frodo and Sam on the stairs of Cirith Ungol.

The major alteration, however, is the deletion of the Scouring of the Shire. To leave it out loses some of Tolkien's most profound insights, but from a dramatic and structural point of view it works. In reading the books to my grandchildren, I find that the end of chapter 5 of Book VI ("The Field of Cormallen") is a natural stopping place. The story arc ends there. The explanations of what happened to everyone thereafter provide a natural epilogue. However, one hopes that other missing pieces, such as the disposition of Saruman, the relationship between Éowyn and Faramir, and additional dialogue in a great many of the existing scenes, will reappear in the extended version of the film.

Until the release of the extended version we will not have access to the director's and writers' commentaries; however, the Special Features included with the theatrical release provide some insight into their intentions. In "A Filmmaker's Journey," Peter Jackson says, "The journeys these characters have been going on, what they care about, what they have been fighting for, what some of their friends have died for, are all leading to the events that are taking place in this film" (*Return*, app.).

To maintain interest in a story which now has a cast of thousands, the focus must remain on the human drama within the spectacle. In the theatrical release version, the emphasis is on testing. For all the main characters, everything that has gone before can be considered as a preparation for the final test, in which, as Elijah Wood comments, "It's a massive pay-off, because these characters you've watched have to go to the ends of their abilities" (*Return*, app.).

THE EVOLUTION OF ARAGORN

The evolution of the character of Aragorn offers a particularly good opportunity to examine the process of revision in book and film. Not only do he and his role develop through the successive drafts of the book, the films' increased emphasis on his actions and motivation provide one of their most significant changes in vision.

The twelve volumes of *The History of Middle-earth* offer a unique window into a great writer's creative process, and make clear the fact that Tolkien continued to tinker with his mythos until the end. As David Bratman pointed out in his article "Top Ten Rejected Plot Twists from *The*

Lord of the Rings," for most of the changes made during its composition we must be profoundly grateful. In particular, the transformation of Trotter, the adventuring hobbit with the tortured feet and wooden shoes, into Aragorn son of Arathorn, heir to the throne of Gondor, transformed the story. The Ranger's evolution was to continue practically to the moment of publication

For the hobbits, the inn at Bree is the gateway to a wider world. They arrive at the Prancing Pony expecting to put themselves under the protection of Gandalf. Instead, in all versions of the story, they encounter an enigmatic Ranger. As Tolkien wrote in a letter to W.H. Auden,

> I met a lot of things on the way that astonished me. Tom Bombadil I knew already; but I had never been to Bree. Strider sitting in the corner at the inn was a shock, and I had no more idea who he was than had Frodo. (*Return of the Shadow* frontispiece; also *Letters* 216-7)

Some of the dialogue in the chapter "At the Sign of the Prancing Pony" survived from the first version written in the late 1930's to the final form of the book, and made it into the film as well. However, in the first version, the Ranger in question is a hobbit!

> Suddenly Bingo noticed that a queer-looking, brown-faced hobbit, sitting in the shadows behind the others, was also listening intently. He had an enormous mug (more like a jug) in front of him, and was smoking a broken-stemmed pipe right under his rather long nose. He was dressed in dark rough brown cloth, and had a hood on, in spite of the warmth — and, very remarkably, he had wooden shoes! (*Return of the Shadow* 137)

as compared to —

> Suddenly Frodo noticed that a strange-looking weather-beaten man, sitting in the shadows near the wall, was also listening intently to the hobbit-talk. He had a tall tankard in front of him, and was smoking a long-stemmed pipe curiously carved. His legs were stretched out before him, showing high boots of supple leather that fitted him well, but had seen much wear and were now caked with mud. A travel-stained cloak of heavy dark-green cloth was drawn close about him, and in spite of the heat of the room he wore a hood that overshadowed his face; but the gleam of his eyes could be seen as he watched the hobbits. (153; I:9)

At the end of 1939, Tolkien could still ask, "Who is Trotter?" and briefly consider making him a disguised elf, but a note on a scrap of paper from this period tells us, "Trotter's true name—as a Man: *Aragorn*. Trotter is a man of Elrond's race descendant of [*struck out at once* Túrin] the ancient men of the North, and one of Elrond's household. He was a hunter and wanderer. He became a friend of Bilbo. He knew Gandalf. He was intrigued by Bilbo's story, and found Gollum" (*The Treason of Isengard* 6-7). Shortly thereafter, Tolkien decided that he was a "real ranger" and a descendent of Elendil.

In the scene at Bree as it appears in the Fourth Phase of the story there is no mention of the broken sword, which does not appear until a revision made in 1940, when it is displayed at Bree. In fact, August of 1940 seems to have been the point at which Tolkien's vision of Aragorn's identity had solidified (*Treason* 161).

It is in Rivendell that the Sword is reforged, in a development which is paralleled but overshadowed by the scene that immediately follows in which Bilbo gives Frodo the sword Sting. In this first version, the new sword is given the name Branding, which is linguistically consistent with the alternate name then being used by Aragorn, "Ingold," since at that time Tolkien felt that all terms relating to Aragorn should come from human languages. The name of the sword was not changed to Andúril until the first typescript of the completed manuscript was made (*Treason* 294). When the Fellowship leaves Lothlórien, Galadriel's gift to Aragorn is a sheath to fit the sword (we are not told how he has been carrying it since they left Rivendell). The first mention of the sword's ancient name, Narsil, occurs when Aragorn lands with the Black Ships at Harlond.

It took some time for Aragorn's name(s) to be established. In *The Treason of Isengard,* pp. 277-78, Christopher Tolkien analyzes the tortuous progression of nomenclature through *"Aragorn (or Trotter)> Elfstone> Ingold> Elfstone> (Trotter)> Aragorn."* It is only when Tolkien had realized the significance of the "elfstone" that the reason for the name became clear. In 1942, his Elven name was given as Eldamir, corrected by Tolkien to Elessar later still.

By the time Tolkien began the chapters that became part of *The Two Towers,* he knew that Aragorn was the royal heir. A version written in 1941 has him telling Éomer, "And I am Aragorn Elfstone son of Arathorn Tarkil, the heir of Isildur Elendil's son of Ondor" (*The Treason of Isengard* 393). From this point on, Tolkien refers to him as "Aragorn." He continued to fiddle with the names of his characters until the very end, and "Trotter" was not replaced by "Strider" as Aragorn's nickname until the revision of the final chapters of the book, which themselves were not written until 1946-48.

Christopher Tolkien points out:

> It would obviously not be true to say merely that there was a role to be played in the story, and that at first this role was played by a Hobbit but afterwards by a Man. . . . I would be inclined to think that the original figure (the mysterious person who encounters the hobbits in the inn at Bree) was capable of development in different directions without losing important elements of his 'identity' as a recognisable character—even though the choice of one direction or another would lead to quite different historical and racial 'identities' in Middle-earth . . . [H]e had been potentially Aragorn for a long time; and when my father decided that Trotter *was* Aragorn and *was not* Peregrin Boffin his stature and his history were totally changed, but a great deal of the 'indivisible' Trotter remained in Aragorn and determined his nature. (*The Return of the Shadow* 431)

As Aragorn's true identity became more apparent, Tolkien began to realize that a royal heir would need a royal bride. In the earliest version of Aragorn's arrival at Meduseld, he is attracted to Éowyn and she to him. In a list of "matters to be explained before the end," we find "Aragorn weds Éowyn sister of Éomer (who becomes Lord of Rohan) and becomes King of Gondor." But this is soon followed by another note: "? Cut out the love-story of Aragorn and Éowyn. Aragorn is too old and lordly and grim. Make Éowyn the twin-sister of Éomund, a stern amazon woman . . . Probably Éowyn should die to avenge or save Théoden." Christopher Tolkien adds, "But my father added in a hasty scribble the possibility that Aragorn did indeed love Éowyn and never wedded after her death" (*The Treason of Isengard* 448).

But as Aragorn's elvish connections developed, an elven princess was needed to fill this role. Throughout much of the writing the daughter of Elrond was named Finduilas. In the 1946 revisions, this was changed to Arwen. Aside from a brief reference in an early version of the Lothlórien sequence, her first mention is as maker of the banner brought by her brothers to Aragorn along with Elrond's advice to take the Paths of the Dead. Her appearance in Rivendell was inserted later, and her back-story in the Appendices, later still. In the book, we do no more than glimpse the two of them together until the action is wrapped up at the very end.

Tolkien's handling of the relationship between Beren and Lúthien in *The Silmarillion* demonstrates his ability to develop and portray a great love story. That he did not do so in *The Lord of the Rings* is certainly in part because the scope and focus of the story in his final version leave no room for it. The emotional relationships in *The Lord of the Rings* are between the members of the fellowship in general and Frodo and Sam in particular. However, when one considers how long it took for Aragorn's full role in the book to develop, so important a connection may not have been addressed because it was added so late in the book's development. Although there is no evidence that Tolkien would have given more time to the Aragorn/Arwen relationship if he had put the book through yet another set of revisions, such a development is not inconsistent with his patterns of rewriting.

However, I am grateful to Beth Russell for bringing to my attention two quotations from the *Letters* that suggest that at least at the time of publication, Tolkien would not have considered doing so. In a letter written in early 1956 he says, ". . . I regard the tale of Arwen and Aragorn as the most important part of the Appendices; it is part of the essential story, and is only placed so, because it could not be worked into the main narrative without destroying its structure: which is planned to be 'hobbito-centric," that is, primarily a study of the ennoblement (or sanctification) of the humble" (*Letters* 237). And later the same year he restates the same thought: "This story is placed in an appendix, because I have told the whole tale more or less through 'hobbits' . . . " (*Letters* 246).

In the film of *The Fellowship of the Ring*, our first sight of Strider smoking in the corner, eyes gleaming in the glow from his pipe, is straight out of the book. In the scenes that follow he offers the hobbits the same information as he has done since his first incarnation as Trotter the hobbit long ago, and is treated with the same suspicion.

From here on, however, things begin to change. In the film, his sword is not broken, which is both more practical and avoids the unintended humor of Strider's presentation of Narsil's shards in the book. An awkward image that may be ignored in print is only too obvious on screen. The question of where and how Strider is carrying the shards of Narsil is a problem which the film solves quite appropriately by placing them in the shrine at Rivendell. This in turn introduces a new, and equally successful, shift in emphasis. Whereas in the book the broken sword suggested the broken line of the kings, in the film it becomes a symbol of Aragorn's own ambivalence about power, efficiently bearing much of the weight carried by other symbols (such as the *palantír*) in the book, and tightening the focus thereby.

In the book, Aragorn's character has been developed by many years of warfare and wandering. Only gradually do we, like the hobbits, realize that his rough exterior hides a kingly spirit.

> Frodo turned and saw Strider, and yet not Strider; for the weatherworn Ranger was no longer there. In the stern sat Aragorn son of Arathorn, proud and erect, guiding the boat with skilful strokes; his hood was cast back, and his dark hair was blowing in the wind, a light was in his eyes: a king returning from exile to his own land. (384; II:9)

This preference for disguise continues well into *The Return of the King*, when Aragorn furls his banner after the battle of the Pelennor Fields and enters Minas Tirith incognito. From the semi-comic Trotter he has become the king who gives his name to the third volume of the novel.

In the novel, Aragorn's noble essence is gradually *revealed*, but it does not *change*. The film's vision of Aragorn shows us the man behind the mask. Like Frodo, he has a "journey," in which he not only returns, but *becomes* the king. Several scenes in the film of *The Fellowship of the Ring* establish Aragorn's fear of royal power. In the theatrical release, Elrond comments that Aragorn turned aside from the path to kingship long ago. In the extended version, we learn more when Elrond comes upon Aragorn tending his mother's grave.

> ELROND. You cannot escape your fate. The skill of elves can reforge the Sword of Kings, but only you have the power to wield it.
> ARAGORN. I do not want that power. I have never wanted it.
> ELROND. You are the last of that bloodline. There is no other.
> (*Fellowship*, scene 28: "Gilraen's Memorial")

At the departure from Lothlórien, Galadriel tells him, "You have your own choice to make, Aragorn: to rise above the height of all your fathers since the days of Elendil, or to fall into darkness with all that is left of your kin . . . " (*Fellowship*, scene 41: "Farewell to Lórien").

It is because he *is* the heir of Elendil, and of Isildur, who fell to the lure of the Ring, that Aragorn doubts his own fitness to rule. When Boromir lies dying in despair, Aragorn takes the first step toward acceptance. "I do not know what strength is in my blood, but I swear to you I will not let the White City fall, nor our people fail" (*Fellowship*, scene 44: "The Breaking of the Fellowship").

In the film of *The Two Towers,* that commitment is tested. A flashback to Aragorn's days with Arwen in Rivendell reminds us of his uncertainty and her faith in him. One of the more successful changes made in the film was to make the information given about Arwen in the Appendix part of the action and develop the resulting dramatic tension. The film makers were faced with the problem of portraying a romance between two characters who spend most of the film apart. The idea of a psychic connection between Aragorn and Arwen didn't "sell" to the studio, so they not only wrote but filmed scenes in which Arwen comes to Helm's Deep with the elves and fights at Aragorn's side. However, the mere rumor of this development created so much furor among fans that Walsh and Boyens went back to the book, in this case to the Appendices, in search of an alternative.

In doing so, they realized that the love story did not have to follow a conventional pattern: ". . . you could tell the story as written [in the Appendix], with these two main characters apart from each other, because they were always [psychically] together." This psychic connection is in fact implied in "The Tale of Aragorn and Arwen," where we are told that "Arwen remained in Rivendell, and when Aragorn was abroad, *from afar she watched over him in thought* . . . " (1036; app. A.I.v, italics added).

Jackson compensated by "devising a way in which we could present flashbacks instead of forcing them together in the progression of the *Two Towers* story line" (*Towers,* appendix: "From Book to Script"). This connection creates problems as well as solving them. To Aragorn's ambivalence about his role as heir of Isildur is added the guilt of causing Arwen to lose her kindred and her immortality. The implications of "the choice of Lúthien" are presented early enough to give their decisions meaning.

The Return of the King completes his development. In "A Filmmaker's Journey" Jackson comments,

> Aragorn has been on a journey through these first two movies towards his taking of the throne of Gondor. It is not an easy journey for Aragorn, because he essentially doesn't have faith that he is doing the right thing by becoming the king. (*Return,* app.)

The message of the beacons (a truly wonderful scene developed from a mere hint in the book) signals that the time to go to Gondor has arrived, but will he do so as a Ranger, or a King?

In the book, the reforging of the sword, which marks an important milestone in Aragorn's life, takes place off-stage. In the film we see the elven smiths working on the blade. Elrond's journey to Dunharrow takes the place of the arrival of the Dúnedain as a call to action, and instead of a banner, he brings the Sword. To provide some extra motivation, he informs Aragorn that if Sauron is not defeated, Arwen will die. Furthermore, the only way to defeat the corsairs who are sailing toward Minas Tirith is to recruit the Dead. Elrond exhorts him to "Put aside the Ranger. Become who you were born to be. Take the Dimholt road!" Aragorn agrees, but he replies, "I give hope to men. I keep none for myself" (*Return*, scene 22: "Andúril – Flame of the West"). And indeed, when Éowyn tries to persuade him to stay, he tells her that, "It is but a shadow and a doubt that you love" (*Return*, scene 23: "Aragorn Takes the Paths of the Dead").

For Aragorn to accept the Sword of Kings is to accept his destiny. Structurally, his decision to take it parallels his decision to master the *palantír* in the book. The sword proves his right to command the ghosts on the Paths of the Dead, and when he confronts them, for the first time he claims his identity as Isildur's heir and Gondor's rightful king.

However, he still has no hope. He leads the army of the West to the Black Gate without expecting to survive the battle. In words which recall the old Germanic literature with which Tolkien was so familiar, he rallies his men:

> A day may come when the courage of men fails; when we forsake our friends and betray all bonds of fellowship, but it is not this day; an hour of wolves and shattered shields, when the Age of Men comes crashing down, but it is not this day. This day we fight. By all you hold dear on this good earth, I bid you stand, Men of the West!
> (*Return*, scene 48: "The Black Gate Opens")

As in the book, cleaned up he is a revelation to those who knew him only as a Ranger, but even in the coronation scene, Aragorn accepts the crown almost as one condemned to it. All good fairy-tales end with a wedding, but in the novel there would have been little point in showing his reunion with Arwen on stage, since we had seen her only from a distance and had no insight into their relationship. In the film, her appearance enables him, for the first time, to face the future with joy.

CONCLUSION

In bringing their own vision of *The Lord of the Rings* to the screen, have Peter Jackson, Fran Walsh and Philippa Boyens, along with the hundreds of other people who contributed images and ideas to the production, created a triumph or a travesty? Perhaps a better question is whether the filmed *Lord of the Rings* will bring more readers to the book from which it came. In my family it has certainly done so. Not only have the images in the film refreshed my own re-reading of the books, but my grandchildren clamored for the story. My oldest grandson asked me to read him the *Silmarillion*, and his brother wants to learn Elvish.

For me, the two visions are complementary. The film shows in rich detail things which were all too briefly described in the books, whereas the books provide all the additional dialogue and explanation that the films skip over. But is it valid to have more than one version, or vision, of a tale? I would say yes — if the most important thing about the book is in fact not the style, but the story. In "A Filmmaker's Journey," Tolkien expert Brian Sibley says,

> I see Peter Jackson as part of the process which was begun
> by Tolkien when he wrote the first line of the book. This is
> the story living in a different medium. What I hope is that
> people will see the film and see that what Peter Jackson has
> captured, what his actors have personified, is really the
> spirit and the heart of the book. (*Return*, app.)

Whether or not what Jackson has presented is *the* heart and spirit of *The Lord of the Rings*, the fact that his version appeals to so many people is in an odd way proof of Tolkien's success as a story-teller. Many an exquisitely crafted work of literature withers in libraries unread. The really great tales are those to which each new version adds richness. A story that can survive being retold transcends mere literature, and becomes legend.

WORKS CITED

Bratman, David. "Top Ten Rejected Plot Twists from *The Lord of the Rings:* A Textual Excursion into the 'History of *The Lord of the Rings*'." *Mythlore* 22:4 (2000): 13-37.

The Lord of the Rings: The Fellowship of the Ring. Special Extended DVD Edition. Screenplay by Peter Jackson, Fran Walsh, and Philippa Boyens. Perf. Elijah Wood et al. Dir. Peter Jackson. United States: New Line Home Entertainment, 2002.

The Lord of the Rings: The Return of the King. Theatrical Release DVD. Screenplay by Peter Jackson, Fran Walsh, and Philippa Boyens. Perf. Elijah Wood et al. Dir. Peter Jackson. United States, New Line Home Entertainment, 2004.

The Lord of the Rings: The Two Towers. Special Extended DVD Edition. Screenplay by Peter Jackson, Fran Walsh, and Philippa Boyens. Perf. Elijah Wood et al. Dir. Peter Jackson. United States: New Line Home Entertainment, 2003.

Tolkien, J. R. R. *The Lord of the Rings*. 2nd ed. With Note on the Text by Douglas A. Anderson. Boston: Houghton Mifflin, 1994.

—. *The Return of the Shadow*. Ed. Christopher Tolkien. Boston: Houghton-Mifflin Co., 1988.

—. *Sauron Defeated*. Ed. Christopher Tolkien. Boston: Houghton-Mifflin Co., 1992.

—. *The Treason of Isengard*. Ed. Christopher Tolkien. Boston: Houghton-Mifflin Co., 1989

—. *The War of the Ring*. Ed. Christopher Tolkien. Boston: Houghton-Mifflin Co., 1990

PART III:

HEROES AND LEADERS

THE ART OF THE STORY-TELLER AND THE PERSON OF THE HERO

KAYLA MCKINNEY WIGGINS

For each of us, there are transitional moments in our societal and personal history that we remember vividly. For fans and students of folklore and/or fantasy literature, one of those moments is their first introduction to the works of J.R.R. Tolkien. I was seventeen years old when I first discovered *The Hobbit*. I will admit that it took me a while to get into the book, a few pages, a chapter or two. At first I found myself wondering just what this could be about—small creatures with furry feet who lived in holes in the ground? But then the book took me to itself. I entered, heart and mind, into the world of the Shire and Middle-earth. I went on, of course, to read *The Lord of the Rings* and found myself absorbed on an even more fundamental level and in an even deeper way. I became compelled by characters living in a time and place I had never known that was yet somehow familiar, somehow timeless. Here was a depth and complexity of invention beyond anything I had ever imagined, a cast of characters that were as familiar as childhood friends and as lofty as gods. I found myself wondering in awe how anyone could ever have invented all this. And then of course I realized that Tolkien hadn't invented it, though he had definitely put his own stamp on the material available to him. When I learned that Tolkien's source material came from myth, I went on my own quest that took me through Greek and Roman lore and eventually to the myth, legend, and folklore of Britain and Northern Europe. For thirty years, I have been a student of folklore, and a loyal fan of Tolkien. I re-read all four books every year for a decade, and would read them every year for the rest of my life if time permitted. Like the folk literature at the heart of his writing, Tolkien's work resonates because it remains true to the human condition, because it provides touchstones, both human and artistic, that help us to understand our world and our place in it a little better. At the center of *The Lord of the Rings* is storytelling, and at the center of any good story is character. In contrast, at the center of any film

103

endeavor, by virtue of the medium, is the visual impulse. Despite its grandeur, Peter Jackson's trilogy film treatment of *The Lord of the Rings* fails to capture the true spirit of Tolkien's writing and of his characters, primarily because it ignores character and story in favor of action and visuals.

FOLKLORE AND EPIC

Verlyn Flieger notes in "J.R.R. Tolkien and the Folklore Controversy," that out of Tolkien's desire to "give his own country a mythic (albeit, in his case, entirely fictive) identity of its own" came not only his fiction but his affirmation of "myth's intrinsic value as story" (34). A philologist and medievalist, Tolkien knew and loved the ancient literature and languages of Britain and Northern Europe. He also was a firm believer in the power of fantasy—what he called fairy-stories—to shape reality. As Humphrey Carpenter notes in his seminal biography, Tolkien's desire to create an entire mythology, a mythology for England, had its origins in "his taste for inventing languages" and "his desire to express his most profound feelings in poetry" (89). Tolkien's emphasis on the use of language in the creation of alternate realities underscores what I believe to be one of the fundamental differences between the films and the novel. He makes note of this impulse in his foreword to the revised edition of *The Lord of the Rings* (xvi,xviii; Foreword) and writes in "On Fairy-stories" that:

> To make a Secondary World inside which the green sun will be credible, commanding Secondary Belief, will probably require labour and thought, and will certainly demand a special skill, a kind of elvish craft. Few attempt such difficult tasks. But when they are attempted and in any degree accomplished then we have a rare achievement of Art: indeed narrative art, story-making in its primary and most potent mode. (70)

The Lord of the Rings while not properly an epic—it is in prose and not verse, it was written to be read and not performed orally, it is an authored piece and not a part of traditional (oral) literature—is in the epic tradition and in many ways brings together the disparate traditions that inform the folk literature, the history, the legends, and the language of the peoples of England. Traditional epics, with their stories of warriors and battles, quests and glory, were sung before battles to instill courage and define heroism, to further the primal fight against extinction (Jackson xiii; xvii). Tolkien's story-telling certainly exemplifies the fight against extinction since, if the characters fail, their world will die. As Lin Carter has noted, the dual themes of the epic—war and quest—are at the heart of the novel (96). As Jane Chance demonstrates, *The Lord of the Rings* fits the traditional epic pattern of separation, descent, ascent, and return (*Mythology of Power* 109). Thematically and structurally, then, Tolkien's narratives are grounded in epic and tradition. The novel is founded on the art of the storyteller, be he the bard in the hall or the farmer at the cottage table. They draw on an ancient art form, and the oldest of magic: the power of the spoken word. While some critics do not agree—Roger Sale, for example, finds the narrative voice of *The Hobbit* smug (30) and Jane Chance cites Helms as saying that the narrative voice is patronizing (*Tolkien's Art* 142)—to see the truth of this, one has only to read his novel aloud. *The Hobbit* exhibits a powerful sense of orality, while *The Lord of the Rings*, like the epics and romances it echoes, is filled with the story-teller's art. Characters sing songs, recite poems, and recount legends. They write stories, collect stories, and comment on the process and importance of story-making and story-telling throughout the novel. At moments of despair and self-doubt, the characters comfort themselves with the awareness that they are a part of an ancient on-going story. When Sam asks in *The Two Towers* if the great tales ever end, Frodo replies that they never end as tales, but "the people in them come and go" (697; IV:8). This idea echoes the cyclical pattern of epic identified by Northrop Frye in *Anatomy of Criticism* (317), and perhaps the cyclical nature of life. Tolkien's novel, too, is cyclical. In discussing *The Lord of the Rings* as great read-aloud literature, Ursula K. Le Guin writes of the walking rhythm of its prose, saying that modern "readers have been encouraged to look at a story as a road we're driving, well paved and graded and without detours, on which we go as fast as we possibly can, with no changes of pace and certainly no stops, till we get to—well—to the end, and stop," but that Tolkien takes the reader there and back again (105). The novel ends where it begins in the pastoral Shire after journey and return, discovery and loss, hope and despair, triumph and tragedy, with Sam's simple "Well, I'm back" (1008; VI:9). While Shippey calls this ending and the voyage from the havens "deliberate bathos" ("From Page to Screen" 72), it is actually a fitting conclusion, reflecting as it does several aspects of the heroic pattern of narrative identified by Campbell and others, although the reflection exhibits some interesting variations. In the traditional heroic pattern, the returning hero brings back a reward that restores his world, accepts his place as a leader, and then eventually reconciles himself to death and the final reality (Brown and Rosenberg 301). In the end of *The Lord of the Rings*, while Frodo and his companions restore the world, they do so by losing rather than by gaining a talisman or reward; Frodo must reconcile himself to his loss of that world, but by going into the West rather than through physical death; and Sam, not Frodo, returns to the Shire to lead wisely as mayor, husband, and father.

FANTASY AND REALISM

Epic is an ancient form. Tolkien's sources were ancient works. His love for fantasy lies in part in his interest in the heroic warrior culture of an ancient world, and yet much of the critical attention paid to his writing, particularly the early criticism, seems to be concerned with trying to understand why a modern author would choose to write about anything other than the modern world and why anyone would want to read it anyway, as if there were only one way to address the human condition and only one taste in literature. In essence, this is the same debate that rages between the efficacy of realism and the validity of fantasy in children's literature. Tolkien ably defends fantasy in "On Fairy-stories" as does C. S. Lewis in "Three Ways of Writing for Children." Indeed, they say almost the same thing. Tolkien tells us that we humans, not the fairies, are supernatural, meaning, I believe, that we have a capacity and perhaps an instinct for something beyond the natural world (perhaps something spiritual since in the next breath he mentions that the road to fairyland is not the road to Heaven or to Hell). In contrast, the fairies are a part of the natural world and "Such is their doom" (34). He goes on to assert that what we traditionally call fairy tales are not always about fairies but about Faërie, a magical realm that includes every kind of folklore creature, but also "the seas, the sun, the moon, the sky; and the earth, and all things that are in it" (38). The stories that include fairies, at least the good ones, says Tolkien, are about the perilous visits of humans to fairyland, rare though those be because "Our fates are sundered, and our paths seldom meet. Even upon the borders of Faërie we encounter them only at some chance crossing of the ways" (38). For Tolkien, even though the origins of these tales are lost in antiquity and they are as difficult to unravel as the origins of language (47), they have essential meaning for us for a number of reasons. In the first place, humans are naturally creative beings; we long for a part in the process of creation, to be what Tolkien calls a "sub-creator" (49). Tolkien was neither the first nor the last author to express this view of the role of the writer or the story-teller, though he may have been the first to relate it to fantasy. As we write or tell stories, we make meaning, we create our view of reality, and the act of creation lends credence, authority, essence to what we have seen and presented as truth. The search for truth, the need to find meaning, or more particularly the need to create meaning, is at the core of all folk literature. Myth and legend and tale help us to make sense of nonsense, to give shape to the chaos, to offer justification for the past, reason for the present, and hope for the future. Tolkien says that human beings obtained the color and beauty of nature for the gods (50). As we told the stories about them, we clothed the gods in the colors of perception; by perceiving we created. Because there was thunder, there were stories of thunder, and a god, Thor, to personify thunder. It does not matter, Tolkien says, which came first. All that matters is the realization that if we could go back in time to a reality when there was no story, "there would be just thunder, which no human ear had yet heard" (51). The story-telling impulse, the role of sub-creator, then, is as fundamental as thought or breath or senses.

Tolkien says that fairy tales carry such meaning for us because they are so old, so fundamental, and because they open a door on Other Time for us (56), in essence they take us back to our roots. They also offer us a sense of magic, of wonder, of greater and not lesser possibilities. Tolkien's own early love, as can be surmised from his fiction, was for the languages, forests, and dragons of the North; indeed he "desired dragons with a profound desire" (63-64). Tolkien sees in the fairy-story, and by extrapolation in fantasy literature, essential truth. Fairy-stories help us to see anew (77), putting us in greater touch with the natural world by revealing to us the essence of things, "the potency of the words, and the wonder of the things, such as stone, and wood, and iron; tree and grass; house and fire; bread and wine" (78). Fairy tales also offer hope for the journey. They deal, like fantasy, with the fundamental themes of the human condition, with life and death, triumph and loss, hope and despair. Tolkien says that they offer us the escape from Death (if we are mortal; the tales of the fairies themselves would offer escape from Deathlessness) and the "Consolation of the Happy Ending," the "sudden joyous 'turn'" that Tolkien called *Eucatastrophe* (85-86).

C.S. Lewis said something very similar. For Lewis, the value of fantasy resides in its ability to offer hope and affirmation. Contrasting the school stories of realistic literature with the hero tales of fantasy, he says that it is realistic stories, not fantasies, that give children false impressions. "I never expected the real world to be like the fairy tales. I think that I did expect school to be like the school stories. The fantasies did not deceive me: the school stories did" (Lewis 1078). According to Lewis, fantasy offers children a world that is clearly other, but for our world it also offers the promise that there have been heroes and there will be heroes. He says that in a world of war and atomic bombs and the inhumanity of person to person, these stories allow children (and by extrapolation adults, since Lewis adamantly argues for the value of these stories for the adult world as well) to see courage and to believe in transcendent goodness: "Since it is so likely that they will meet cruel enemies, let them at least have heard of brave knights and heroic courage. Otherwise you are making their destiny not brighter but darker" (1079).

Fantasy, in other words, is timeless and absolutely essential to the creation of and understanding of reality. Dealing as it does with the great conflicts of the human condition—good and evil, life and death, hope and despair—it can often speak to us on a more fundamental level than literature that is slavishly tied to the modern world, or to a realistic one. But fantasy is not for everyone, nor is the voice of fantasy. This conflict between modernity and fantasy seems to be an issue in Tolkien scholarship. While early critics of Tolkien seemed to be bothered that he wrote about an ancient, fantastic world rather than addressing the ills of modern society (a curious echo of the criticism against the *Beowulf* poet that he told too much of monsters and not enough of life in the hall), later writers have come to see that literature doesn't have to be set in modern times to address modern issues. Discussing Tolkien's narrative style in an essay originally published in 1973, Roger Sale feels that the narrative only comes to life when Tolkien is writing of Frodo as the modern hero and utilizing the Hobbits as perceivers, that otherwise his writing is literary and trite (42). Sale locates this flaw in what he sees as Tolkien's withdrawal from the modern world and in an essentially old-fashioned depiction of men and their heroism (48-49). "The old terms for the struggle of good against evil—courage, loyalty, honor, magnificence, fortitude—are mostly irrelevant now" (Sale 53). Three decades later, however, Tom Shippey in *The Road to Middle-earth* argues that Tolkien was not an anomaly but one of a group of modern writers writing fantasy as a means to address the traumatic issues of the modern world (xvii). Similarly, Verlyn Flieger argues that while the form and subject matter of "Tolkien's major fiction clearly derive from the medieval genres of epic, romance, and fairy tale," the characters and "the contexts and situations in which they play a part" were reconfigured to give them a "modern spin" ("Tolkien's Wild Men" 95). For Flieger, Tolkien, though he longed to pass into "Other Time," was a writer of his own time, speaking to the fragmented modern world (*Question of Time* 2-3). She sees Tolkien as a modern thinker "dipping into the past for the stuff of his story but reworking it for the age in which he lived and felt, noting that a story does not "have to have a contemporary setting in order to mirror contemporary thought" (*Question of Time* 8). In the long debate about fantasy vs. realism and ancient vs. modern, the fundamental truth that emerges is that some readers will appreciate and relish the depth and complexity of the fantastic world, seeing its brush with another time and place as heroic and deeply meaningful, while others will seek out the modern and the familiar and simply not understand those things that seem far removed in time and space, nor the longing for them. This longing, however, is at the heart of Tolkien's writing, embodied by the power of heroic narrative. This power is what the films fail to capture, for all the grandeur of their vision and the force of their execution.

PROBLEMS OF ADAPTATION

We tend to use the word epic to refer to works that are grand in scale, whether or not they fit the traditional definition of epic literature. If Tolkien's novel is epic fantasy, Jackson's interpretations of it are epic films. They are grand in vision, in scope, and in implementation. The visual images and impressions captured in the films are monumental. The focus in the films is visual, as befits the medium of film. Another major focus, of course, is action. Almost the whole of the second movie is battle sequences—quite impressive battle sequences. The focus in the novel, however, as befits the story-teller's art, is the narrative and the gradual evolution of character. Both of these elements are largely lost in the films. Changes in the plotlines and in character development contribute significantly to the altered characterization and the loss of narrative focus. Whatever this may do for the average movie-goer, it can't help but weaken the films for the long-time fan of the fiction.

In his review of the films, Tom Shippey implies that the more focused narrative lines of the films improve on the narrative development of the amateur writer Tolkien, even while he suggests that Tolkien's narrative structure was a product of his worldview and could not be duplicated on the screen and that the amateur Tolkien might have "known something that the professionals do not" (71). Amateur or not, Tolkien was a consummate story-teller firmly grounded in the patterns of traditional literature—epic, legend, and folktale—and he had been studying, writing about, and writing this kind of story for his entire adult life.

Many of the changes from text to film are centered in characterization and the shift from narrative to visual art. The characterization is simplified and refocused; the narration is compacted or eliminated. This loss of nuance and depth is noted by several reviewers of the films, in particular Graham Fuller and Charles Noad. The early part of the first film illustrates this shift most dramatically. Apparently in the interest of immediacy and rapid development, the relationships between the various characters are altered significantly, as are their individual qualities. Frodo is much younger than he should be. It is significant in the novel that Frodo is of age to inherit. He and Bilbo are celebrating their common birth date. Bilbo is to be 111, a number of special purport not only in terms of advanced age but also as it represents the tripling of folklore; Frodo will be 33, the age at which Hobbits are considered adult. He is significantly older than the hobbits who are his friends and companions, Merry Brandybuck, Pippin Took, and Samwise Gamgee. This matters since Frodo will become the leader of their company, an authority figure they look up to and follow. In the films all of the hobbits seem to be the same age. While Bilbo's departure and Frodo's consequent inheritance of Bag End occur on this date, Frodo's departure on his own adventure is delayed for a number of years in the novel, until, in fact, he turns 50. This is the age at which Bilbo became an adventurer; both ages (33 and 50) are significant in the novel since it is a story of maturation and personal growth. In the film the flight from Bag End occurs almost immediately. There is no time for planning and preparation, no time to say farewell or gather companions, no time to come to maturity. While it is a given that film is a more immediate medium than the novel and that movie audiences demand quick action, immediacy and movement should not be achieved through the sacrifice of characterization. The result of Frodo's precipitous flight in the movie is that we never have a chance to get to know him or Sam or Merry or Pippin before they are propelled headlong into adventure. Sam is not revealed as a lover of myth and tale devoted to the older Frodo and willing to sacrifice all to follow him into adventure as his protector, servant, and companion. Merry and Pippin become buffoons, tampering with Gandalf's fireworks and being punished by having to wash the dishes from the Birthday Party. They join the trek by accident, and we do not get a chance to appreciate Pippin's simple joy in life or Merry's quiet common sense that has allowed him to know secretly about Bilbo's ring for years, and that makes it possible for him to arrange the expedition from the Shire so thoroughly that Frodo is left with no cares. Everything is so precipitous in fact that common sense is even violated. If it is so urgent that Frodo leave the Shire, there is no sense in Gandalf abandoning him to go to Orthanc. In the film, he knows already that the Black Riders are abroad; he certainly would have traveled with

Frodo to protect him, and, more importantly, to protect the Ring. In order again to move things forward more rapidly, Gandalf gives Frodo much more information, many more cautions, about the Ring and the Riders in the film than he does in the novel. Again, the result is that we don't get a gradual evolution of these details and, in the hobbits' response to them, a gradual development of character. In fact, we never get to know Frodo and his companions very well at all. An even greater loss comes, though, in the limited development of the relationship between Strider and the hobbits. In the film, the scenes in Bree are much compacted. There is no opportunity for a satisfying depiction of the minor characters like Butterbur, and little attention is paid to the developing nuances between the major characters that so inform and enliven the narrative of the novel. The scene in the common room that leads to Frodo's accidental use of the Ring and his conversations with Strider is shortened to a few seconds of clumsy mistakes. The scene that develops Strider's give-and-take with the hobbits regarding his identity and Gandalf's letter providing the first hints as to his importance is gone altogether. We do not learn that he has been expecting the hobbits, or that he has aided Gandalf in their cause. We do not hear the wonderful lines that define his trial and his long burden.

> All that is gold does not glitter,
>   Not all those who wander are lost;
> The old that is strong does not wither,
>   Deep roots are not reached by the frost.
> From the ashes a fire shall be woken,
>   A light from the shadows shall spring;
> Renewed shall be blade that was broken,
>   The crownless again shall be king. (167; I:10)

We do not see his regret at not being trusted for himself, or the poignant moment when he reacts with pain to memories of the Black Riders: "They will come on you in the wild, in some dark place where there is no help. Do you wish them to find you? They are terrible!" (162; I:10). Because the journey through the wild is so compacted, we have no time to experience and appreciate Aragorn's skill as a Ranger; in fact, all scenes of his woodcraft are virtually eliminated from the three movies. Worse, we don't see the developing trust between him and the hobbits that explains their later bond. Lost, too, is the emphasis on Aragorn's skill as a healer that adds such a dimension to his role as king. In the original version of the attack on Weathertop, the hobbits are gathered with Strider around the fire he has set for warmth and protection, listening to his tale of Tinúviel (and discovering along with the reader his skill as a story-teller and his knowledge of the old tales, another dimension to his character) when they are attacked by shadowy figures that only Frodo sees clearly and only because he puts on the Ring. The hobbits are overcome by fear, and only Frodo draws his sword in desperate defiance; Strider fends off the attack with fire. Although Frodo is wounded, there is none of the gasping and wheezing weakness depicted in the movie; he faces the wound bravely and the others hardly realize for quite some time just how serious it is. And Aragorn does not, in the novel, deny his own ability to deal with the wound, as he does in the movie before sending Sam for kingsfoil. Instead, he does what he can to heal Frodo in the wilderness, including performing an incantation over the hilt of the knife before going on a search for the healing plant himself (193; I:12). The attack on Weathertop in the movie becomes one more excuse for an all-out battle, complete with elaborate spectral special effects. So much emphasis, in fact, is placed on fighting in the three movies that the coming-of-age element of the story is lost entirely. In the novel, Pippin and Merry, Sam and Frodo fight reluctantly. They must learn to defend themselves, and each has a moment when he grows into his role of warrior or hero. They are people of peace who fight only when they must, and even then with hesitation. In the films, they draw swords at every opportunity, and fight eagerly. The coming-of-age motif is significant to the epic pattern of the novel and the heroic characterization of the members of the company, as are Aragorn's many skills as a warrior, leader, and king. The culmination of the journey from Weathertop in the film robs Aragorn even of his ability to protect himself and his charges, and Frodo of his fundamental quality of courage. In the novel, the wanderers are discovered and aided by the elf lord Glorfindel, but not before Aragorn is aware of his presence. In the film, Aragorn is surprised by Arwen, taken off guard despite his seasoned skills as a Ranger. It is Arwen who calls the wounded Frodo back from the brink of death and rides with him across the river to safety in Rivendell, defying the Black Riders and even calling up the curse that causes the river to rise against them. In the novel, Frodo, still bravely fighting his wound, rides to the ford on his own, defying the Black Riders before the waters rise in flood at the command of Elrond, not Arwen (218; II:1).

The films' curious emphasis on Arwen seems to be an attempt to justify her relationship with Aragorn, a relationship that, while vital in Aragorn's history, is not a focus of the novel. Their history is discussed in Appendix A of *The Return of the King* (1032-38). There we learn that Arwen rejected Aragorn when they first met because he was too young and untried. Only decades later, meeting him again when he was a proven and seasoned Ranger, an exiled king guarding in obscurity and secrecy his people, did she acknowledge and accept his love. According to the appendix, Aragorn, the last of the line of Isildur and therefore the rightful king of Gondor, was raised in fosterage in the home of Elrond in Rivendell. His father was killed by orcs when Aragorn was only two, and his mother took him to Rivendell for protection. There he was raised in secrecy and not told of his heritage until he was twenty when his foster-father Elrond told him the truth (1032; app. A.I.v). Elrond and Aragorn are distantly related since Aragorn's line is descended through many generations from Elrond's brother Elros who, given the choice of the Half-elven, chose to be of Man-kind (1010; app. A.I.i). Thus, in a distant way, Elrond is Aragorn's uncle. Fostering was a common practice among the Celts whose ancient gods are the models for Tolkien's elves, and the uncle-nephew relationship was a particularly significant one, often closer than father and son. While much is made of the animosity between Elrond and Aragorn in the film, underscored by much discussion of distrust between the races of Middle-Earth, in the appendix to the novel, Elrond and Aragorn part lovingly even though Elrond acknowledges the bitter choice that Aragorn's love for Arwen will force upon them all (1036; app. A.I.v). It is the doom of the children of Elrond to enjoy the lifespan of the elves for as long as he stays in Middle-earth and to go with him to the West when he departs. If they choose to remain when he is gone, as Arwen does, they must accept a mortal life (1036; app. A.I.v). While he does decree that Aragorn cannot marry anyone until he comes into his own as king (1036; app. A.I.v), Elrond never tries to impede the growing bond between Aragorn and Arwen, and it is unlikely that he would object to a union with a mortal since he himself descends from two such unions.

The apparent intent of the films in placing such an emphasis on a relationship that is very much subplot in the novel (though of prime motivation for Aragorn) is at least two-fold. On the one hand, this emphasis serves to highlight the theme of racial discord that becomes of increasing concern in the second and third films; and on the other it serves to characterize Aragorn as a conflicted modern hero. I submit that this is a fundamental misreading of the novel in terms of theme, of characterization, and of genre. While there may be little contact between some of the peoples of Middle-Earth, and downright animosity between elves and dwarves, nothing in the novel prepares the movie-goer for Théoden's angry tirade in the second film against former allies—men and elves—before the battle of Helm's Deep or Elrond's bitter rejection of men as the future hope of Middle-earth in the first movie, including the wholly nonsensical comment that Aragorn had turned from the path of leadership and chosen exile. Later, he confronts Aragorn, who denies ever wanting the kingship, and tells him that he has no choice, as he is the last of the line of kings and there is no other. Throughout the films, Aragorn is conflicted about his role as king and protector of his people. He doubts himself and his ability to fill such a role. In dream sequences and face-to-face meetings, Arwen must constantly reassure him that he will be king and that he is worthy of her love. This reading of Aragorn's character is at odds with his characterization in the novel and with his role as epic hero.

EPIC HERO AND FOLK HERO

While the Aragorn of the novel may occasionally doubt his choices (in particular once the company draws near to Mordor and he has to choose between his duty as leader of the company and his duty as the heir of Isildur and rightful king of Gondor), he is always sure of his fundamental role in life. Indeed, his entire life has been a training ground for the assumption of his throne. He comes out of his crisis of self-confidence able to command loyalty from Legolas and Gimli, and a bit later even from a stranger, Éomer of Rohan (Kocher 139). He is the king, and his destiny will be, must be, to confront the forces of Sauron and reestablish his kingdom. He has endured a long exile and served a hard apprenticeship to come to that place. His life has been one of self-sacrifice and obscurity as he has fought from the shadows to defend his people, and only he can know at what cost to his personal happiness and peace of mind. Aragorn is a true hero; he is in fact an epic hero. His life exemplifies the pattern of the epic hero, including an obscure birth from an extraordinary heritage, being reared in secrecy with no knowledge of his true identity, and his movement through trials and sufferings from obscurity to acknowledgement. There is some validity in Flieger's argument that he is also a type of the medieval hero of romance as exemplified by his possession of a sword with a recognized ancestry, by his role as healer of a diseased society in the tradition of the Fisher King of the Grail legend, and by his attainment of romantic love (Flieger, "Concept" 43-45). However, the emphasis of Tolkien's writing is clearly on the quest of the hero as exemplified in the epic tradition. This hero is personified throughout mythic history by the Everyman figure recognized by Campbell as symbolic of the cycle of existence and the journey of humanity (Campbell 36). As Flieger notes, Frodo exhibits many of the same patterns of the epic hero, but he is in fact the fairy tale hero; his is more of an anti-quest than a quest since he goes not to find something, but to lose something ("Concept" 51-55; 41-42). Frodo is, then, another kind of

Everyman. He is the small hero of folktale who proves that even the weak and helpless can succeed, giving hope for the journey to all those who identify with the disenfranchised and the displaced of society. As he does in so many other ways throughout the novel, Tolkien uses these elements of folklore and tradition to his own ends, giving them a distinct twist that amounts to a reversal. According to Campbell, in the traditional monomythic pattern, "the hero of the fairy tale achieves a domestic, microcosmic triumph, and the hero of myth a world-historical, macrocosmic triumph" (37-38). Yet Frodo, a fairytale hero, saves the world and loses himself. While he and his allies achieve the successful end of the hero's adventure—"the unlocking and release again of the flow of life into the body of the world" (Campbell 40) as symbolized by the defeat of the Dark Lord, the renewal of the White Tree, and the phenomenal spring of the Shire—Frodo himself has suffered too much to profit from or even to be able to endure this grand new world he has initiated. As Flieger notes, Aragorn's is the fairy-tale ending of marriage to the princess and kingship; Frodo's end is the bitter one of the epic hero ("Concept" 42).

Much critical ink has been spent arguing for the identity of the hero in *The Lord of the Rings*. Lin Carter finds the true hero to be Gandalf in his embodiment of the guardian god Odin (192-194); Ann Petty identifies three heroes—Aragorn, Frodo, and Gandalf (47)—and Jane Chance argues for Aragorn, Frodo, and Sam as all being embodiments of the epic hero (*Art* 144). In reality, in addition to Aragorn and Frodo, all of the main characters and many of the minor ones are heroes of one kind or another, to one degree or another, just as people are in real life when faced with life-altering trials. Gandalf's great labor in the long war against Sauron is certainly heroic. Sam's long journey to Mordor and the suffering he endures in the name of love and loyalty places him on a level of heroism seldom equaled in epic or romance. Merry begins his coming of age and growth to maturity when he fights the Uruk-hai at Parth Galen and achieves heroic status at the battle of Pelennor Fields when out of loyalty he dares to strike a deadly Ringwraith to protect Éowyn:

> Éowyn it was, and Dernhelm also. For into Merry's mind flashed the memory of the face that he saw at the riding from Dunharrow: the face of one that goes seeking death, having no hope. Pity filled his heart and great wonder, and suddenly the slow-kindled courage of his race awoke. He clenched his hand. She should not die, so fair, so desperate! At least she should not die alone, unaided. (823; V:6)

And Pippin comes into his own heroic status when he risks everything to save Faramir from Denethor's madness and the fire.

Denethor and Faramir are perhaps the most distorted characters in the films. In another apparent attempt to provide conflict and motivation for the characters, the second film heightens Denethor's preference for Boromir over Faramir as evidenced in a flashback scene wherein Denethor and Boromir know that the ring of power has been found and is the subject of a council in Rivendell to which they have been summoned. Denethor gives the responsibility of the journey to Boromir, precipitating Faramir's guilt over the death of his brother and the strange scene wherein he takes Frodo to Osgiliath with the intention of taking the Ring to Gondor as an offering to his father. In contrast, in the novel, Boromir is not summoned to a council but seeks the explanation of a dream, taking upon himself the journey that more properly belongs to his brother. The Faramir of the novel is far too wise and noble for foolishness or betrayal. He knows of the significance of the Ring without being told because he is not only a captain but a scholar. When he discovers what Frodo is carrying, far from betraying him, he does everything in his power to aid the quest of the Ring-bearer. Unlike his brother, he knows that the Ring cannot be used by anyone other than Sauron. He says, "I would not take this thing, if it lay by the highway" (656; IV:5). Denethor himself is another type of hero. Like his younger son, he is a man of learning and wisdom, but he is also a man of great pride, doomed to be forever a steward and never a king. His pride becomes his downfall as he allows his far-sight that comes from the use of one of the last Seeing Stones to be manipulated into despair by the lies of the Enemy. In the novel, he is cold and distant, but not small, and not un-heroic, far from the gluttonous, petty, and cruel figure of the films who eats greedily in a scene that is vividly intercut with scenes of the near fatal battle for Osgiliath.

Boromir may be the only character who emerges as more heroic in the films than in the novel. Certainly his fall in defense of the young hobbits is moving in *The Two Towers*, coming as it does immediately after his betrayal of Frodo and serving as a penance for that lapse. The scene is even more moving in the film, although it is made so in part by some curious changes in the text. In the novel, although Boromir has not accepted Aragorn's authority as king, Aragorn longs to go to Minas Tirith. He welcomes the passage along the river as delaying the moment of decision, of choice between Gondor and Mordor. In the film, Aragorn is much more assertive about his intent to journey to Mordor, and Boromir encourages him to come to the city, cautioning him against being afraid of his heritage. In the novel, the fight with the Orcs is a stealthy one, since their mission is to kidnap not to attack, but in the film, it is an all-out battle, with everyone, even the hobbits, killing ferociously. In the novel, Frodo leaves the company without knowing they have been attacked; in the film, he runs away and leaves his friends to the mercy of the Orcs, something Frodo would never have done. However, when all the bloodshed is finally over in the film and Boromir lies dying in Aragorn's arms, having sacrificed himself in an attempt to save Merry and Pippin, he swears allegiance to Aragorn, saying, "I would have followed you, my brother, my captain, my king" (*Fellowship*, scene 45: "The Departure of Boromir").

In both the novel and the final film even Gollum becomes a hero of sorts, for it is Gollum after all who destroys the Ring when the fairytale hero Frodo fails in the quest, another interesting twist in Tolkien's re-visioning of traditional narrative patterns and an irony that was important to Tolkien though it may have been lost on the majority of fans (Flieger, *Question* 6). However, again there is a change. In the film, Gollum attacks Frodo on the very edge of the abyss and bites off his finger to get the Ring, dancing around until Frodo attacks him in turn, apparently in an attempt to retrieve the Ring. Their battle pushes Gollum over the edge; together, then, Frodo and Gollum destroy the Ring. In the book, Frodo does not fight back once the Ring has been taken. He falls to his knees, returning to his true character from the madness the Ring has inflicted. Gollum doesn't fall because of Frodo, but because of the Ring itself; a voice from the wheel of fire at Frodo's breast has commanded him to be gone, and warned that if he ever touches it again, he shall be cast "into the Fire of Doom" (922; VI:3).

STORYTELLING AND ACTION/ADVENTURE

Much of the emotive force of the novel comes from Tolkien's ability to move us with his story-telling. The impetus of the novel is verbal and consequently can hardly find a place in the visual medium of film. This is perhaps as it should be, as it must be, but it is a loss nonetheless. As the film demonstrates, the visual images, however rich and evocative, simply can't equal the best of the story-telling. I will attempt to demonstrate this through three passages that resonate with particular power and that fall curiously flat in the films despite their use of sweeping vistas and complex special effects: the journey of the three hunters and their subsequent meeting with the riders of Rohan, the passage of the marshes, and the Paths of the Dead. Each of these sections marks a moment of transition and growth for the characters, a trial that must be endured, and a choice that must be made.

Following the fall of Boromir in *The Two Towers*, Aragorn reads the riddle of the departure of Sam and Frodo and concludes that it would be pointless to follow them into Mordor. His choice at last seems clear; he must follow the orcs who have kidnapped Merry and Pippin and try to rescue the young hobbits.

> "With hope or without hope we will follow the trail of our enemies. And woe to them, if we prove the swifter! We will make such a chase as shall be accounted a marvel among the Three Kindreds: Elves, Dwarves, and Men. Forth the Three Hunters!"
>
> Like a deer he sprang away. Through the trees he sped. On and on he led them, tireless and swift, now that his mind was at last made up. The woods about the lake they left behind. Long slopes they climbed, dark, hard-edged against the sky already red with sunset. Dusk came. They passed away, grey shadows in a stony land. (410; III:1)

This moving passage is the opening of a great journey that takes the determined companions on foot across the plains of Rohan. The narrative follows them as they run tirelessly, depicting Aragorn's skill as a tracker, Legolas's sleepless endurance, and Gimli's stony hardihood. It culminates in their confrontation with the riders of Rohan, rising out of the grass to a ring of spears and the challenge of a warrior society at war, unsure of friend or foe. When Éomer, the Third Marshal of Riddermark, learns of their journey, he is amazed. "Wide wonder came into Éomer's eyes. 'Strider is too poor a name, son of Arathorn,' he said. 'Wingfoot I name you. This deed of the three friends should be sung in many a hall. Forty leagues and five you have measured ere the fourth day is ended! Hardy is the race of Elendil!'" (426; III:2). This entire segment loses much of its force in the second movie, primarily because we are not given a real sense of the passage of time or the distance traveled. We do not see Aragorn's skill in tracking, nor Legolas' grief at delays. The scene between Éomer and Aragorn is so compacted that the instant bond that springs up between them in the novel is forfeit, nor is it ever recovered since Éomer is banished and not given the opportunity to fight beside Aragorn at Helm's Deep. The focus of these scenes becomes the comic characterization foisted upon the proud Gimli as he trots ineffectually in the wake of Aragorn and Legolas, muttering about being a better sprinter than a distance runner. In much the same way, the narrative force of the passage of the marshes and the Paths of the Dead is sacrificed to special effects.

As Sam and Frodo make the difficult journey into Mordor, acquiring against their will a guide in the person of Gollum, they must pass through a seemingly impassable marshland. Only Gollum can help them navigate the noisome pools. The evening of the third day brings them to a particularly difficult patch.

> Presently it grew altogether dark: the air itself seemed black and heavy to breathe. When lights appeared Sam rubbed his eyes: he thought his head was going queer. He first saw one with the corner of his left eye, a wisp of pale sheen that faded away; but others appeared soon after: some like dimly shining smoke, some like misty flames flickering slowly above unseen candles; here and there they twisted like ghostly sheets unfurled by hidden hands. (613; IV:2)

When he asks about the lights, Sam is warned by Gollum to ignore them. "The tricksy lights. Candles of corpses, yes, yes. Don't you heed them! Don't look!" (613; IV:2). Later he trips and falls into the muck:

> There was a faint hiss, a noisome smell went up, the lights flickered and danced and swirled. For a moment the water below him looked like some window, glazed with grimy glass, through which he was peering. Wrenching his hands out of the bog, he sprang back with a cry. "There are dead things, dead faces in the water," he said with horror. "Dead faces!" (613; IV:2)

Frodo, too, has fallen into the bog and seen the dead faces, but Gollum assures his companions that the dead aren't really there; they are just the images of men and elves who died in a great battle there long ago. This very compelling scene gets turned into something out of a horror movie in the second film, with Frodo falling into the water and being snatched back at the last moment by Sam from the grasp of a ghoul who floats up toward him.

The journey on the Paths of the Dead, too, is used as an excuse for elaborate spectral special effects that are in no way as evocative of the fear the original narrative delivered through Gimli's perspective, as he finds himself stumbling along in the dark, last of a column of Dúnedain and their horses who have loyally followed Aragorn where no person has dared pass in countless lives of men.

> Of the time that followed, one hour or many, Gimli remembered little. The others pressed on, but he was ever hindmost, pursued by a groping horror that seemed always

> just about to seize him; and a rumour came after him like the shadow-sound of many feet. He stumbled on until he was crawling like a beast on the ground and felt that he could endure no more: he must either find an ending and escape or run back in madness to meet the following fear. (770; V:2)

This groping horror in the darkness, particularly as experienced by Gimli, a creature of hardihood long familiar with the darkness beneath the earth, is more powerful than a score of spectral images generated through the magic of modern film-making. The following passages that recount the thunderous ride to the Stone of Erech for the honoring of the broken oath by the shades of men long dead is also incredibly powerful. The company rides like the wind with the dead following, and as they pass, the people flee into their homes, escaping Aragorn and his company in his persona as the King of the Dead. This entire sequence serves as Aragorn's journey to the Underworld, a part of the pattern of the epic hero, and it provides one of the final strokes in the master painting of Aragorn's character: elves, men, and dwarf face impossible terror out of love for him, and because he is steady and unfailing, they walk bravely behind him; even their horses face the terror of the long dark because of the courage with which he imbues man and beast. This scene follows on Aragorn exercising his right to look into the *palantír* of Orthanc, and precedes his victory on the fields of Gondor and the subsequent assumption of his title. It marks the final stage of his journey as the epic hero, just as Mount Doom marks the final stage of Frodo's journey as the fairy tale hero. Flieger has said that we identify with Frodo in the modern world because we identify with the little man, that while we admire Aragorn, we don't identify with him ("Concept" 41). I would argue that we identify with both of them, but in different ways. We identify with Frodo as embodying our own limitations, fears, and hopes, though we can never dream of enduring what he endures, or of accomplishing what he achieves. We identify on another level with Aragorn, the epic hero, the warrior and healer, poet and king. We certainly don't want the messy reality, the death and destruction, of war in our own world, but we admire the dedication, the strength, the courage of the warrior with a sword in his hand. We admire skill at tracking and skill at healing and skill at poetry, and if we find all of this present in one man, a sort of ancient-world superhero, the epic hero, we are awed. Yet we also admire Frodo, no hero in his own eyes but simply an ordinary person who against all odds sacrifices himself for others, for his world.

Character is at the center of any great story, and language is the heart of any great story-telling. J.R.R. Tolkien in his *Lord of the Rings* gives us story-telling at its highest, the lofty poetic expression and larger-than-life heroes of epic, and at its most human, the everyday experience and never-say-die determination of the folktale and the folk hero. In his film treatments of this material, Peter Jackson, in contrast, offers the conflicted, modern protagonist, smaller in scope and lesser in nature. Curiously, the effect is not to bring us closer to these characters but to shove us further away. We can't know them with the fundamental recognition that is a part of our primal consciousness, the part of ourselves that reaches out to myth, and folklore, and legend as essential truth, as absolute identity.

Do we want the characters in our fiction and films to look and act just like our next-door neighbors, just like ourselves? Sometimes. But we also at times need them to be larger than life, to validate this great experiment called the human condition. We need them to explain the meaning behind it all, to give us justification for breathing in and out every day. It is this impulse that explains our fundamental drive to create myth and folklore and legend. And epic. Like Tolkien, we desire dragons with a firm desire.

WORKS CITED

Brown, Mary Ellen, and Bruce A. Rosenberg, eds. *Encyclopedia of Folklore and Literature*. Santa Barbara: ABC-CLIO, 1998.

Campbell, Joseph. *The Hero With a Thousand Faces*. New York: MJF, 1949.

Carpenter, Humphrey. *Tolkien: A Biography*. Boston: Houghton Mifflin, 1977.

Carter, Lin. *Tolkien: A Look Behind The Lord of the Rings*. New York: Ballantine, 1969.

Chance, Jane. *The Lord of the Rings: The Mythology of Power*. New York: Twayne, 1992.

—. *Tolkien's Art: A Mythology for England*. Rev. ed. Kentucky: UP, 2001.

Flieger, Verlyn. "Frodo and Aragorn: The Concept of the Hero." *Tolkien: New Critical Perspectives*. Eds. Neil D. Issacs & Rose A. Zimbardo. Kentucky: UP, 1981. 40-62.

—. *A Question of Time: J.R.R. Tolkien's Road to Faerie*. Kent, OH: Kent State UP, 1997.

—. "'There Would Always Be a Fairy-Tale': J.R.R. Tolkien and the Folklore Controversy." *Tolkien the Medievalist*. Ed. Jane Chance. London: Routledge, 2003. 26-35.

—. "Tolkien's Wild Men: From Medieval to Modern." *Tolkien the Medievalist*. Ed. Jane Chance. London: Routledge, 2003. 95-105.

Frye, Northrop. *Anatomy of Criticism*. Princeton: UP, 1957.

Fuller, Graham. "Trimming Tolkien." *Sight and Sound*. (Feb. 2002): 18-20.

Jackson, Guida M. *Traditional Epics*. New York: Oxford UP, 1994.

Kocher, Paul. *Master of Middle-Earth*. New York: Ballantine, 1972.

Le Guin, Ursula K. "Rhythmic Pattern in *The Lord of the Rings*." *Meditations on Middle-Earth*. Ed. Karen Haber. New York: St. Martin's Griffin, 2001. 101-116.

Lewis, C. S. "On Three Ways of Writing for Children." *The Riverside Anthology of Children's Literature*. Boston: Houghton Mifflin, 1985. 1075-1081.

The Lord of the Rings: The Fellowship of the Ring. Special Extended DVD Edition. Screenplay by Peter Jackson, Fran Walsh, and Philippa Boyens. Perf. Elijah Wood et al. Dir. Peter Jackson. United States: New Line Home Entertainment, 2002.

The Lord of the Rings: The Return of the King. Theatrical Release DVD. Screenplay by Peter Jackson, Fran Walsh, and Philippa Boyens. Perf. Elijah Wood et al. Dir. Peter Jackson. United States, New Line Home Entertainment, 2004.

The Lord of the Rings: The Two Towers. Special Extended DVD Edition. Screenplay by Peter Jackson, Fran Walsh, and Philippa Boyens. Perf. Elijah Wood et al. Dir. Peter Jackson. United States: New Line Home Entertainment, 2003.

Noad, Charles. "Jackson's *Fellowship*, Not Tolkien's: A Review of Peter Jackson's *The Lord of the Rings*." *Mallorn* 40 (November 2002): 22-23.

—. "Lost in the Process: A Review of Peter Jackson's *The Two Towers*." *Mallorn* 41 (July 2003): 34-35.

Petty, Ann C. *One Ring to Bind Them All: Tolkien's Mythology*. Alabama: UP, 1979.

Sale, Roger. "Tolkien and Frodo Baggins." *J.R.R. Tolkien*. Ed. Harold Bloom. Philadelphia: Chelsea House, 2000. 27-63.

Shippey, Tom. "From Page to Screen: J.R.R. Tolkien and Peter Jackson." *World Literature Today* 77.2 (July-September 2003): 69-72. 13 Aug. 2004 <http://www.ou.edu/worldlit/onlinemagazine/SA2003/_18-July-Sept03-_Shippey.pdf>.

—. *The Road to Middle-Earth*. Boston: Houghton Mifflin, 2003.

Tolkien, J.R.R. *The Lord of the Rings*. 2nd ed. With Note on the Text by Douglas A. Anderson. Boston: Houghton Mifflin, 1994.

—. *The Letters of J.R.R. Tolkien*. Eds. Humphrey Carpenter and Christopher Tolkien. Boston: Houghton Mifflin, 2000.

—. "On Fairy-stories." *The Tolkien Reader*. New York: Ballantine, 1966. 33-99.

FRODO ON FILM: PETER JACKSON'S PROBLEMATIC PORTRAYAL

DANIEL TIMMONS

Fidelity, while desirable in romantic relationships, may be unneeded, even unwelcome, in film adaptations. Robert Stam in "Beyond Fidelity: The Dialogics of Adaptation" states that the impulse for a strict "faithful" translation of book to film is a "chimera," since the two artistic mediums are inherently distinctive (54). Thus the book lover's feelings of "betrayal" when the film fails to evoke a similar aesthetic response as the written text is a projection of the reader's "desires, hopes, and utopias," rather than the director's insensitivity or disrespect (54). Stam concludes that "[a]bove all, we need to be less concerned with inchoate notions of 'fidelity' and to give more attention to . . . readings, critiques, interpretations, and rewritings of the prior material" and celebrate "the differences among the media" (75-76).

Such an objective response appears most difficult for the passionate readers of J.R.R. Tolkien. Book purists and film lovers continue to debate the pros and cons of Jackson's creative choices.[1] One of their key concerns is the way, whether by design or necessity, screenwriters Philippa Boyens, Fran Walsh, and Peter Jackson have transformed Frodo, the great hobbit hero of Tolkien's text. "Fidelity" is our launching point to analyze the shortcomings of Jackson's film; not for the first time, and certainly not the last, film makers have distilled and weakly presented an author's original vision. Jackson's script is questionable, not simply because it diverges from the letter and spirit of Tolkien's book. The hobbit hero's journey, both physical and psychological, is the heart of Tolkien's

---

1 After a preliminary search of online discussions of the films, I soon became overwhelmed. It would necessitate much slogging through the massive "muck and mire" of commentary to find a few good "gems." Janet Croft kindly drew to my attention to some interesting articles by Patrick Diehl (see http://westbynorthwest.org/artmen/publish/article_676.shtml). Diehl offers some fine perspectives on the books versus the films, using a methodology similar to mine. His scope is broad and succinct, whereas mine is specific and expansive.

masterpiece. Beyond the idea of "faithfulness" to Tolkien's text, Jackson undermines the inner logic and thematic thrust in his portrayal of the hobbit hero. Overall, Jackson does not present his Frodo as the best and only person for the quest, the one divinely designated to carry the Ring.

PART ONE: "I WISH IT NEED NOT HAVE HAPPENED IN MY TIME."

Early on in Tolkien's *The Fellowship of the Ring*, Frodo displays depth and complexity of character. Unlike in Jackson's film, Tolkien's Frodo has no direct speech until he appears at Bag End just after Bilbo has left. Still, Tolkien notes Frodo's distinctive nature with the young hobbit's thoughts at Bilbo's sudden vanishing:

> [Frodo] had difficulty in keeping from laughter at the indignant surprise of the guests. But at the same time he felt deeply troubled: he realized suddenly that he loved the old hobbit dearly. . . . Frodo did not want to have any more to do with the party. . . . he got up and drained his own glass silently to the health of Bilbo, and slipped out of the pavilion. (31; I:1)

In the film, Frodo gleefully parties with the other hobbits and then looks disturbed when Bilbo announces that he is going away. In the book, Frodo had been in the "know" about the plan; in Jackson's film, Frodo only suspects it. Thus, early on, Tolkien signals something special about Frodo. While a hobbit, he stands apart from his carefree and provincial people. This uniqueness is not immediately evident in Jackson's version.

Tolkien's Frodo displays his exceptional character when Gandalf tells him about the threat of the Ring. Curiously, Jackson split these parts of Gandalf's narrative and placed them in different spots. Jackson took some of Tolkien's words from Gandalf in Bag End, where Frodo first learns about the history of the Ring and Gollum's role, and presented them in Moria, after Frodo has survived many perils. The thematic ideas expressed in these lines of Gandalf appear in both versions:

> ∞ "All we have to decide is what to do with the time that is given us." (50; I:2)

> ∞ "Bilbo was *meant* to find the Ring, and *not* by its maker. In which case you also were *meant* to have it. And that may be an encouraging thought." (54-5; I:2)

> ൦ "My heart tells me that he [Gollum] has some part to play yet, for good or ill, before the end; and when that comes, the pity of Bilbo may rule the fate of many—yours not least." (58; I:2)

Some subtle differences exist between the two versions; for example, Tolkien's Gandalf uses "may be encouraging," whereas Jackson's Gandalf says "is." While the thematic essence remains the same, Jackson's change negatively affects Frodo's characterization. At the beginning of Tolkien's book, Frodo is terrified and hostile at Gandalf's words. Yet by Moria, he has acquired some fortitude and wisdom by accepting his fate. In the film, Frodo appears immature in Moria, reflecting hasty anger and stark fear. Jackson's character seems to have learned little from his experiences.

This difference in Frodo's maturity appears in the way the two versions handle Frodo's decision to leave the Shire. Here is one key Frodo speech from the book:

> "I should like to save the Shire, if I could–though there have been times when I thought the inhabitants too stupid and dull for words. . . . I feel that as long as the Shire lies behind, safe and comfortable, I shall find wandering more bearable. . . . "I suppose I must go alone, if I am to do that and save the Shire. But I feel very small, and very uprooted, and well–desperate. The Enemy is so strong and terrible. "(61; I:2)

Naturally, film makers are reluctant to depict such a long speech, and so Jackson portrays this scene much differently. Similar in both versions, Gandalf rejects Frodo's offer for the wizard to the take the Ring. Yet in the film Frodo displays no initiative:

> *[Frodo looks scared and bewildered.]*
> FRODO. But it cannot stay in the Shire!
> *[Gandalf shakes his head gravely.]*
> GANDALF. No, it can't.
> *[Frodo hesitates and then grips the Ring in the palm of his hand.]*
> FRODO. What must I do?
> (*Fellowship*, scene 10: "The Shadow of the Past")

For the rest of the scene, Frodo scrambles to pack, while Gandalf tells him to travel to Bree, leave behind his name of Baggins, and not journey at night. Frodo is told to wait for Gandalf at the Inn of the Prancing Pony. The only confident remark Frodo makes is that he "can cut across country easily enough," when he stands ready to set out.

Given the stark differences in the versions of Tolkien and Jackson, it is difficult to compare them. While Jackson's treatment appears more dynamic and cinematic, something is lost in the pace and intensity. His Frodo seems to be a willing tool of Gandalf. Tolkien's Frodo is reluctant, even resistant to the implications in Gandalf's words, yet still initiates the plan to leave. Jackson turns it around and has Gandalf tell Frodo what to do. True, he agrees to Gandalf's plan and isn't coerced or commanded. But by removing the initiative from Frodo, Jackson undermines the heroism of the hobbit's decision to take on the burden and dangers of the Ring.

Jackson again undercuts Frodo's inner fortitude when he faces his first real test: resisting the temptation to put on the Ring when a Black Rider is hovering close by. Tolkien relates Frodo's inner struggle:

> A sudden unreasoning fear of discovery laid hold of Frodo, and he thought of his Ring. He hardly dared to breathe, and yet the desire to get it out of his pocket became so strong that he began slowly to move his hand. He felt that he had only to slip it on, and then he would be safe. . . . "And I am still in the Shire," he thought, as his hand touched the chain on which it hung. At that moment the rider sat up, and shook the reins. The horse stepped forward, walking slowly at first, and then breaking into a quick trot. (73-4; I:3)

In this moment Frodo's resistance to temptation doesn't appear solid and strong, but it isn't weak and feeble either. Here, and in another encounter a few pages later, Frodo's struggles are halted by outside circumstances: first, the rider's sudden departure, and second, the unexpected appearance of Gildor and his Elven company. In the film, Jackson creates heightened tension and suspense in this scene. But he offers no reason to think that Frodo can *actively* resist temptation, which would make him suitable to bear the Ring:

> [*The Black Rider dismounts near the tree trunk where the hobbits are hiding. Frodo looks startled. The Rider grips the trunk and leans forward. Frodo turns around quickly and gazes at the Rider. The Rider continues to lean against the tree trunk, while the hobbits cower with fear. Slimy bugs start to emerge from the ground and crawl on and near the hobbits. Frodo suddenly looks faint as his eyes roll up behind his lids. He slowly pulls out the Ring and turns it in his fingers. The Rider jerks his head and his horse snuffles. Frodo's eyes are closed and he is sweating, looking ill. The hand holding the Ring edges towards the forefinger of the other hand. Then Sam sees Frodo and hits Frodo's hands. Frodo shakes himself and opens his eyes. He closes his hand around the*

> *Ring. The Rider jerks his head. Merry throws a bag far to their left. The Rider is distracted and darts away.]*
>
>   (*Fellowship*, scene 13: "A Short Cut to Mushrooms")

It's not luck or Frodo's own choice that prevents disaster, but rather Sam's intervention and Merry's distraction. Frodo looks like he falls into a trance and has no will in the matter. Tolkien's Frodo debates inwardly, so the Rider's presence doesn't totally overwhelm him. In the film here, Frodo's facial expressions and body language indicate that he is holding no complex internal debate. Instead, Sam must physically stop Frodo, which enhances his character at the expense of Frodo's! Jackson's elevation of Sam and diminishing of Frodo throughout the three films begins at this moment.

Whenever Frodo faces a difficult decision in Tolkien's book, he reviews the options and chooses the best available path. Some do not work out, but at least he shows some inherent reason and firm determination. Jackson strangely neglects these qualities. In the scene where Frodo is deciding whether to accept Strider as his guide, Tolkien writes:

> There was a long silence. At last Frodo spoke with hesitation. "I believed that you were a friend before the letter came," he said, "or at least I wished to. You have frightened me several times tonight, but never in the way that servants of the Enemy would, or so I imagine. I think one of his spies would—well, seem fairer and feel fouler, if you understand." (168; I:10)

This speech comes at the end of a long consideration of Strider and his true purposes. The last statement is astute: evil can put on a pleasing shape, but if people remain in touch with their inner good sense, they can recognize what is, and is not, evil.

Jackson completely alters this moment, making Strider aggressive and disrespectful, and Frodo overwhelmed and paralyzed:

> [*Strider opens the door to the room and tosses Frodo to the ground.]*
> FRODO. What do you want?
> STRIDER. A little more caution from you; that is no trinket you
>   carry.
> FRODO. I carry nothing.
> STRIDER. Indeed. I can avoid being seen if I wish. But to
>   disappear entirely, that is a rare gift.
> FRODO. Who are you?
> STRIDER. Are you frightened?

FRODO. Yes.

STRIDER. Not nearly frightened enough. I know what it is
   that hunts you.

   *[Strider hears a noise at the door and looks. He draws his sword
   as Sam, Merry, and Pippin burst into the room. Sam raises his
   fists.]*

SAM. Let him go or I'll have you, Longshanks!

   [Strider smiles and re-sheathes his sword.]

STRIDER. You have a stout heart, little hobbit. But that won't
   save you. You can no longer wait for the wizard, Frodo.
   They are coming.

   (Fellowship, scene 15: "At the Sign of the Prancing Pony")

Frodo appears bullied and cowed into accepting Strider as his guide to
Rivendell. In the extended DVD, Jackson added a scene where Frodo does
use Tolkien's words about Strider seeming "fair," though looking "foul."
Still, the above incidents reflect a larger problem with the film: its frenetic
pace and melodramatic approach. Jackson's film lacks the subtle shades of
personality and mood of Tolkien's book. As a result, the characterization
and, indeed, the ennobling of Frodo suffer.

The innate nobility of Tolkien's Frodo, due to his Baggins pedigree
and education in Elvish, appears in his confrontation with the Nazgûl
King at Weathertop. Again, Jackson's transformed Frodo doesn't reflect
such qualities. In both versions, Frodo foolishly puts on the Ring and then
takes it off after being stabbed. Yet in Tolkien's book, Frodo stabs at the
Chief of the Ringwraiths and shouts *"O Elbereth! Gilthoniel"* (191; I:11), an
appeal to Varda, Queen of the stars, which Strider later observes was more
"deadly" (193; I:12) to the Nazgûl than any sword thrust. In the film,
Frodo drops his sword and falls to the ground, stricken with terror. He
puts on the Ring, and his only act of will is that he draws his hand back
when the Nazgûl King reaches for it. After he has been stabbed, Jackson's
Frodo becomes a wailing, convulsing, and almost comatose individual.
Tolkien's Frodo remains lucid, fighting against the physical pain and
psychological torture. Jackson's Frodo displays no strength or resistance
against the effects of the wound from the Morgul blade.

The scene at the Ford of Rivendell may be the worst of Jackson's
alterations of Tolkien's text. One can sympathize with his desire to expand
the role of Arwen. But this is one of the most important moments in the
book, the instance that confirms for Gandalf—and the reader—that Frodo
is the one to bear the Ring. Tolkien presents Frodo's defiance of the
Ringwraiths' call:

> "Go back!" he cried. "Go back to the Land of Mordor and
> follow me no more!" His voice sounded thin and shrill in
> his own ears. . . .
>   "By Elbereth and Lúthien the Fair," said Frodo with a
> last effort, lifting up his sword, "you shall have neither the
> Ring nor me!" (209; I:12)

Even though Frodo is exhausted, wounded, and slipping into the
Ringwraith world, he manages to resist the temptation to evil. And that is
indeed all anyone can be expected to do. Beyond that, as Tom Shippey has
observed when discussing Tolkien's evocation of the Lord's Prayer,
"Temptation is our responsibility, while Evil is outside us" (qtd. in
"Legacy"). We must resist, and if the threat is too strong, we hope for
outside relief, which here is the flood commanded by Elrond.

   Jackson denies Frodo any role in his rescue from the Ringwraiths:

> *[The Dark Riders halt on one side of the river. Arwen, with*
> *Frodo on the horse in front of her, is on the other side.]*
> DARK RIDER . Give up the Halfling, she-elf.
> *[Arwen looks defiant. Frodo is barely conscious.]*
> ARWEN. If you want him, come and claim him.
> *[The Riders start crossing the river. Arwen speaks an elvish*
> *incantation. The water starts to rise up and a huge wave*
> *emerges. The wave of water, with white horse figures at its*
> *head, swoops down and sweeps away the Riders. Then Frodo*
> *starts to convulse and drops to the ground.]*
> ARWEN. No, Frodo. Don't give in. Not now.
> *[Frodo looks like he is on the verge of death.]*
> (*Fellowship*, scene 21: "Flight to the Ford")

Rather than an active hero resisting evil temptation, Jackson's Frodo looks
like a drug-addled addict. Hardly a single moment in the film, from the
time Frodo learns about the Ring to his arrival at Rivendell, proves that he
is suitable to bear the burden. Those movie-goers who hadn't read the
books before would have no reason to accept that Frodo is the one to
destroy the Ring.

   Frodo survives his near-death experience, or dies figuratively and
is "resurrected" by Elrond. Having being brought back from the verge of
becoming a "wraith," Tolkien's Frodo does seem a changed individual.
While recuperating, Frodo *hopes* that his part is over, but he doesn't state
that it has ended. Furthermore, Tolkien gives us Gandalf's inner thoughts
on Frodo: "He is not half through yet, and to what he will come in the end
not even Elrond can foretell" (217; II:1). In contrast, Jackson's Frodo
declares he is ready to go home and is not like his adventurous uncle

Bilbo. Gandalf also appeals to Elrond, saying, "we cannot ask any more of Frodo." If even the wise wizard doesn't believe that Frodo is the one to carry the Ring, why should the audience think so?

Jackson does partially redeem Frodo—and himself in the process—at the Council of Elrond. If the scene at the Ford of Rivendell was one of the worst treatments of Tolkien's text, the moment when Frodo volunteers to bear the Ring to Mordor might be the best. First, here is how Tolkien wrote it:

> Frodo glanced at all the faces, but they were not turned to him. All the Council sat with downcast eyes, as if in deep thought. A great dread fell on him, as if he was awaiting the pronouncement of some doom that he had long foreseen and vainly hoped might after all never be spoken. . . . At last with an effort he spoke, and wondered to hear his own words, as if some other will was using his small voice.
>
> "I will take the Ring," he said, "though I do not know the way." (263-4; II:2)

This brilliant passage highlights both Frodo's character and, in Joseph Pearce's terms, "the mystical interlinking" between freewill and providence (qtd. in "Legacy"). Tolkien offers the dual motivations of Frodo's choice to take the Ring, because no one else seems willing, and of "some other will" using his voice. Both impulses reinforce his suitability to bear the Ring; first, as Gandalf states, Frodo was "meant" to have it; and second, because of his combination of humility and determination, he would resist the Ring's corrupting influence.

Jackson alters the moment in the film, but this time elevates Frodo to the stature that Tolkien has portrayed throughout his book:

> [Gandalf shakes his head as a massive quarrel breaks out among the council members. Frodo looks troubled at the arguing. Gandalf leaves his side and shouts at Boromir. Frodo gazes at the Ring, and the audience sees the reflection of the council arguing. It appears that Frodo hears the Ring reciting the inscription in the language of Mordor. Frodo looks as if he is struggling to block out the Ring's call. He glances quickly at the arguing council members. A look of determination slowly appears in Frodo's face. He stands up.]
> FRODO. I will take it.
> [No one pays any heed to him. He steps closer to the crowd.]
> FRODO. I will take it!
> [Now Gandalf hears him and sighs. As the wizard slowly turns towards Frodo, the council members quiet down. They gaze at

> *Frodo.]*
> FRODO. I will take the Ring to Mordor! Though I do not
>   know the way.
>   (*Fellowship*, scene 27: "The Council of Elrond")

Jackson again chooses a frenetic moment, the council arguing, over Tolkien's, the council in quiet reflection. As well, Jackson might have thought he has enhanced the suspense because previously his Frodo was resolved "to go home." The scene does vividly and effectively display Frodo's momentous decision. We see Frodo's inner struggle, his doubts, his fears, balanced against his sense that he is the right one for the task; he recognizes that his humble and non-aggressive nature make him the best available person to bear this burden. Alas, would that many more such moments existed in Jackson's film.

After the company leaves Rivendell, the film focuses on the action sequences of the remaining chapters of *Fellowship of the Ring*, which offers little time for character development or reflection, often an under-appreciated strength of Tolkien's text. As noted earlier, Jackson curiously took some of Gandalf's words at the beginning of the book and placed them in the Moria sequence. The choice doesn't enhance Frodo's character, but rather makes him seem more indecisive. Tolkien's Frodo bravely attacks and stabs the foot of the cave-troll, thereby helping Boromir (316; II:5). In the film, Frodo doesn't initiate a heroic act and fights rather feebly. After the fall of Gandalf, both Tolkien's and Jackson's Frodos seem lost without their mentors. Their encounters with Galadriel do little to inspire their confidence, though Jackson took a line from Tolkien's Elrond and gave it to the elven queen: "This task was appointed for you [Frodo], and if you do not find a way, no one will." The irony is that Jackson's Frodo has done little to show the audience that he can "find a way."

Frodo's last major decision in *The Fellowship of the Ring*, his choice to journey alone to Mordor, receives a fair, yet flawed, treatment in Jackson's film. Here is Tolkien's text:

> Frodo rose to his feet. A great weariness was on him, but his will was firm and his heart lighter. He spoke aloud to himself. "I will do now what I must," he said. "This at least is plain: the evil of the Ring is already at work even in the Company and the Ring must leave them before it does more harm. . . . I will go alone. At once." (392; II:10)

Again, Tolkien presents Frodo reasoning to a difficult decision. Frodo considers the evil influence of the Ring, his sworn responsibility to destroy it, and his care for his companions. At that moment, he makes the best choice: continue on, alone.

Jackson follows Tolkien's text closely in some respects, yet alters it completely in others. As result, Frodo's inner strength is understated, though perhaps still evident:

> [*After falling from the seat of Amon Hen, Frodo regains his composure. Aragorn suddenly appears.*]
>
> ARAGORN. Frodo?
>
> [*Frodo looks at him anxiously.*]
>
> FRODO. It has taken Boromir.
>
> ARAGORN. Where is the Ring?
>
> [*Aragorn moves towards Frodo, who struggles to his feet and backs away.*]
>
> FRODO. Stay away!
>
> [*Aragorn edges closer. Frodo gazes at him fearfully.*]
>
> ARAGORN. I swore to protect you.
>
> FRODO. Can you protect me from yourself?
>
> [*Aragorn looks startled. Frodo opens his hand and reveals the Ring.*]
>
> FRODO. Would you destroy it?
>
> [*Aragorn gazes at the Ring. We hear it calling to Aragorn, tempting him. Aragorn kneels down and places his hand over Frodo's hand and the Ring. Aragorn closes Frodo's hand.*]
>
> ARAGORN. I would've gone with you to the end. Into the very fires of Mordor.
>
> FRODO. I know. Look after the others, especially Sam. He will not understand.
>
> (*Fellowship*, scene 44: "The Breaking of the Fellowship")

After this scene, Frodo is on the shore of the river and appears to hesitate about whether to follow through on his words to Aragorn. The firm resolve of Tolkien's Frodo is lacking. Jackson does depict Frodo's decision appropriately: Frodo realizes the threat and temptation the Ring poses to the Company, which will endanger the quest, while at the same time, his inner goodness wants to keep his friends from harm. In both versions, Frodo recognizes that Sam's loyalty and companionship are not only welcome, but necessary for any chance of ultimate success.

Tolkien consistently presents Frodo, although at times in doubt, reasoning his way to decisions and displaying courage in many instances. In contrast, Jackson's Frodo, but for one moment at the council of Elrond, appears overwhelmed and constantly afraid. The problem is not that Jackson chose to go "beyond fidelity" and present a different Frodo from Tolkien's. The director gets into trouble because he adopts Tolkien's ideas that the hobbit is "meant to have the Ring" and if he doesn't "find a way, no one will," yet undermines the case in his portrayal of Frodo. For these notions of divine designation to have any power, the character must reveal the presumed qualities. Otherwise, the words about Frodo have no meaning. In Jackson's *The Fellowship of the Ring*, the audience has little reason to feel that Frodo can bear the burden and achieve the quest.

PART 2: " . . . DEFEND YOUR CITY WHILE YOU MAY, AND LET ME GO WHERE MY DOOM TAKES ME."

In *The Two Towers*, Jackson presents, on the whole, a weak-willed, emotionally unstable, and imperceptive Frodo. Such a characterization has nothing to do with the transferring of the written text to the visual medium and other issues of adaptation. Obviously, Jackson must leave out and condense much of Tolkien's text to accommodate the time constraints and pace of film. Yet Jackson cuts almost all of Tolkien's hobbit hero's best lines and inserts moments where Frodo seems psychotic. This choice deliberately transforms Tolkien's Frodo into a different kind of character. No law exists (though some Tolkien purists might wish there were one) to prevent Jackson from making this creative decision. But the director cannot claim that his Frodo appears physically and psychologically suitable to bear the Ring. Thus the artistic consistency and thematic essence of Jackson's vision suffer.

Tolkien's Frodo exhibits a heightened awareness and determined leadership the first time that he speaks in *The Two Towers*. His decision to journey to Mordor without Gandalf or Aragorn seems have strengthened his resolve, even though he remains unclear about the progress of his quest. Sam almost sounds despairing: "[T]hat's just where [i.e. Mordor] we can't get, no how" (589; IV:1). Frodo, however, senses that he is destined to find a way:

> "Mordor!," he muttered under his breath. "If I must go there, I wish I could come there quickly and make an end! . . . perhaps another day will show us a path."
> "Or another and another and another," muttered Sam. "Or maybe no day. We've come the wrong way."
> "I wonder," said Frodo. "It's my doom, I think, to go to that Shadow yonder, so that a way will be found. But will good or evil show it to me? . . . I don't know what is to be done. What food have we got left? (589-90; IV:1)

Throughout their struggles in the Emyn Muil, Sam is discouraged and hesitant, whereas Frodo steadily leads them on and firmly insists that they risk scaling down a cliff face (591-2; IV:1). While Frodo is doubtful and disappointed, he remains assertive and hopeful. Frodo echoes Gandalf's prophetic statement in Rivendell when he says, "It's my doom" to find a way to Mount Doom.

Jackson conceived the above scenes much differently. Consequently, his Frodo looks weak and disconsolate. After adding a brief scene of Frodo dreaming of Gandalf's fall in Moria, Jackson depicts the hobbits' struggles in the hills. In the extended DVD, the director reverses the order of Tolkien's events. Jackson presented the hobbits scaling down the cliff first, adding a comic twist of Sam dropping his salt container. None of the forceful energy of Tolkien's Frodo is evident here. In a parallel scene to the one quoted above, Jackson's Frodo appears on the verge of despair.

> *[Sam and Frodo climb up a rocky hill. They see the glow of Mount Doom in the distance.]*
>
> SAM. Mordor. The one place in Middle-earth that we don't want to get any closer is the one place we want to get to. It's just where we can't get. Let's face it Mr. Frodo, we're lost. *[Frodo looks worried.]* I don't think that Gandalf meant for us to come this way.
>
> FRODO. He didn't mean for a lot of things to happen, Sam. But they did.
>
> *[Frodo gazes at the glow of Mount Doom. We see a flash of the Eye of Sauron. Frodo winces and drops to the ground. Sam looks concerned.]*
>
> SAM. Mr. Frodo? *[Frodo takes deep breaths.]* It's the Ring, isn't it?
>
> FRODO. It's getting heavier.
>
> *[Frodo clutches his chest. Sam sighs and sits down. Frodo takes a drink from his water bottle.]*
>
> FRODO. What food have we got left?
>
> (*Towers*, scene 2: "Elven Rope")

Jackson offers no sense that his Frodo will make it to Mordor. The hobbit already looks dispirited and weakened, and he hasn't even come close to his destination! Tolkien's Frodo declines much more slowly and displays strength of will. Jackson's Frodo looks as if he is ready to give up at any moment.

The scene where Frodo "tames" Gollum is similar in the two versions, though again Tolkien's Frodo appears more firm and decisive than Jackson's character. When Gollum suggests swearing a promise on the "Precious," Tolkien's Frodo speaks harshly:

> "On the Precious? How dare you?" he said. . . .
>
> "No! not on it," said Frodo, looking down at him with stern pity. . . . "Swear by it, if you will." . . .
>
> For a moment it appeared to Sam that his master had grown and Gollum had shrunk: a tall stern shadow, a mighty lord who hid his brightness in a grey cloud, and at his feet a little whining dog. . . .
>
> "Down! down!" said Frodo. "Now speak your promise!"
> . . .
> "Take the rope off, Sam!" said Frodo. (603-4; IV:1)

Earlier, Frodo recalled Gandalf's words about showing pity to Gollum and agrees that the creature deserves it. Yet Frodo, as Sam recognizes, cows and commands Gollum, looking like a strong leader. Jackson's Frodo directly confronts Gollum, but does so in a more kindly way than Tolkien's hobbit.

> GOLLUM. We swears . . . on the Precious! Gollum, gollum.
> FRODO. The Ring is treacherous. It will hold you to your word.
> GOLLUM. Yes. *(Gollum crawls towards Frodo.)* On the Precious.
> SAM. I don't believe you!
> *[Gollum starts to back away and climbs on a boulder.]*
> SAM. Get down! Get down!
> *[Sam yanks back on the rope, choking Gollum as he falls.]*
> FRODO. Sam!
> SAM. He's trying to trick us! If we let him go, he'll throttle us in our sleep!
> *[Gollum gags and coughs, and Frodo looks at him with deep concern. Frodo steps towards him and Gollum looks scared.]*
> FRODO. You know the way to Mordor.
> GOLLUM. Yes.
> FRODO. *[Frodo kneels before him.]* You have been there before.
> GOLLUM. Yes.
> *[Frodo leans forward and takes off the rope. Sam looks disgusted.]*
> FRODO. You will lead us to the Black Gate.
>   (*Towers*, scene 3: "The Taming of Sméagol")

Jackson seems to want to create sympathy for Gollum, and Frodo's soft manner reinforces this. Notice the opposite physical positioning of the parallel scenes. Tolkien has Frodo stand over and order down Gollum, whereas Jackson has Frodo descend to Gollum's level, both physically and figuratively. Both Frodos display "pity," yet Tolkien's character is "stern," while Jackson's is acquiescent.

Both the author and the director develop the evident kinship between Frodo and Gollum during the journey to Mordor. Yet Tolkien presents it in a subtle and gradual way, whereas Jackson makes it obvious and immediate. The distinctive natures of prose and film account for some of the difference. With many pages available, Tolkien can develop some key motifs slowly. The time constraints of film require Jackson to intensify such features. Still, Frodo need not descend so rapidly into Gollum-like characteristics or appear as a zombie or frightened child. Gollum had the Ring for centuries to become what he is. Frodo has only borne it for several months. To be consistent with the idea that Frodo is special, he should maintain self-control at a level far above Gollum.

Tolkien's character displays this mastery, while Jackson's offers none. While in the Dead Marshes, both Frodos are affected by the strange lights and images of rotting corpses. When Sam asks about the faces in the putrid water, Tolkien presents Frodo's response this way:

> "I don't know," said Frodo in a dreamlike voice. "But I have seen them too. In the pools when the candles were lit. They lie in all the pools, pale faces, deep deep under the dark water. I saw them: grim faces and evil, and noble faces and sad. Many faces, proud and fair, and weeds in their silver hair. But all foul, all rotting, all dead. A fell light is in them." Frodo hid his eyes in his hands. "I know not who they are; but I thought I saw there Men and Elves, and Orcs beside them." (614; IV:2)

The spectral images mesmerize Frodo, but they don't anesthetize him. In fact, the tone and cadence of his words parallel Elrond's. Notice the inverted sentence order, "there" coming before "Men and Elves," and lofty word choice, "noble," "proud," and "fell." The entire passage reflects retrospective and melancholy insight, the kind that Elrond offers when he speaks: "I have seen three ages in the West of the world, and many defeats, and many fruitless victories" (237; II:2). Frodo, despite the psychological and physical burden of the Ring, appears to be what Sam had perceived earlier: "A mighty lord who hid his brightness in grey cloud" (604; IV:1).

Jackson, though, choses to silence and immobilize Frodo in this scene. As Frodo stares at one corpse, its eyes suddenly open. Then Frodo acts as if he is suddenly paralyzed: he topples face first into the water, sinks with a look of helpless terror, and is only saved by Gollum pulling him out. Jackson appears to have dramatized the words of Tolkien's Frodo, rather than have the hobbit speak them. In the process of film adaptation, this method is appropriate. However, the cinematic shock value comes at the expense of Frodo's heroic persona. Jackson could have had it both ways: Frodo could have said some of the above lines after he accidentally fell in the water and was rescued. As it is, Frodo merely looks weak and foolish.

Jackson also emphasizes Frodo's weakness in the scene where he caresses the Ring and the Nazgûl flies overhead (*Towers*, scene 14; "The Passage of the Marshes"). Tolkien does depict the effect on Frodo of both the Ring and the Eye, "dragging him earthwards" and "its potency beat upon his brow" (616; IV:2). Also, when the "Wraith [sic] on wings" swoops near them, Frodo, along with Sam and Gollum, falls forward, "grovelling heedlessly on the cold earth" (615; IV:2). But Frodo recovers, mastering his fear and burden: "Nothing remained of it [i.e. his fair dream 'vision'] in his memory, yet because of it he felt glad and lighter of heart" (620; IV:2). Jackson has Frodo pet the Ring lovingly and, to reinforce his kinship with Gollum, the wretched creature pretends that he is caressing his "Precious" at the same time. Then the Nazgûl arrives and all three cower under a bush. But instead of Frodo controlling his impulses, Jackson's character goes into his now familiar trance and clutches at the Ring. Again, Sam's powerful will, not Frodo's, prevents disaster. Sam grips Frodo's hand and stops him from putting on the Ring. Jackson's Frodo offers no sense of the strength and courage of Tolkien's hero.

One of Frodo's finest moments in the books, when he displays the acquired wisdom and intestinal fortitude that prove that he is the one to bear the burden of the Ring, occurs at the Black Gate of Mordor. Tolkien provides almost an entire chapter of Frodo thinking through many conflicting doubts and fears. At last, he decides to turn aside from the direct, and seemingly hopeless, path and go Gollum's "secret way" (312). After Frodo considers what Gandalf would have done, and hears Sam's poem about "the oliphaunt," the hobbit's humble, yet determined, heroism is clear:

> It was an evil fate. But he had taken it on himself in his own
> sitting-room in the far-off spring of another year. (630; IV:3)

> This was an evil choice. Which way should he choose? And if both led to terror and death, what good lay in choice? . . . Frodo stood up. He had laughed in the midst of all his cares . . . and the laugh had released him from hesitation. . . . "Well, Sméagol, the third turn may turn the best. I will come with you." (633; IV:3)

Despite Frodo's choice to follow Gollum, the hobbit doesn't display full trust in his "guide." He simply decides that it is the lesser of two evils. He feels somewhat lighthearted because the obvious despair of the Black Gate can be left behind and a glimmer of hope followed.

Jackson could not dramatize all the workings of Frodo's mind or bring his film to a halt to have a character ruminate for several minutes. But Jackson's hectic sequence minimizes Frodo's reasoning and determination:

> *[As Frodo is about to head for the open Black Gate, Gollum pulls him back again.]*
> GOLLUM. No! There is another way. A secret way, a dark way.
> *[Frodo hesitates. Sam grabs Gollum's shoulder.]*
> SAM. Why haven't you spoken of this before?!?
> GOLLUM. Because Master didn't ask.
> *[Sam pushes him away in disgust.]*
> SAM. He is up to something.
> FRODO. Are you saying there is another way into Mordor?
> GOLLUM. Yes. There's a path. *[Frodo glances anxiously at the ever closing Gate.]* Then some stairs. And then . . . a tunnel. *[Gollum clutches at Frodo. Frodo watches the Gate close. He then sighs in resignation. Gollum sighs in relief and caresses Frodo.]*
> FRODO. He has led us this far, Sam.
> SAM. No, Mr. Frodo, no.
> FRODO. He has been true to his word.
> *[Gollum gazes at Frodo. Sam looks distressed.]*
> SAM. No.
> FRODO. Lead the way, Sméagol.
> GOLLUM. Good Sméagol, always helps.
> *[Sam stares at Frodo in stunned disbelief. Frodo looks back rather feebly. The Black Gate closes.]*
> (*Towers*, scene 18: "The Black Gate is Closed")

In the end, Frodo's decision is made for him, rather than him making it freely. The Gate closes while Frodo hesitates, so even if he chooses to reject Gollum's plea the opportunity is lost. Frodo's anxious demeanor contrasts sharply with Tolkien's character's firm manner. In the book, Sam disagrees with Frodo's precarious trust in Gollum, but has strong faith in his master's judgment. With the film, the audience's reaction might parallel Sam's: bewilderment and disapproval.

The epitome of Jackson's portrayal of Frodo occurs in a scene that doesn't exist in the book (*Towers*, scene 28: "The Forests of Ithilien"). As Gollum flails about in a creek trying to catch a fish, Sam calls him "stinker." Frodo rebukes Sam and defends Gollum. Frodo's key line is "I have to believe he can come back." Jackson conveys the idea that Frodo sees his own possible salvation in Gollum's unlikely rehabilitation. The root of this hope is in Tolkien's text. Frodo's kindness and pity towards Gollum reflects an understanding of the dark side of himself: "Gollum had a claim on him now" (672; IV:6). However, Jackson undercuts Frodo's sagacity when the hobbit turns on his faithful Sam and offers petulant remarks that the Ring is "Mine, my own!" Sam and the audience see Frodo well on his way to sounding, and indeed becoming, Gollum. Jackson emphasizes this Tolkienian motif so intensely, believing it makes good filmic drama, that the noble core of Frodo is neglected or rejected.

Jackson radically alters the Faramir character and subplot, which also impacts Frodo's characterization. Again, the director leaves out the major heroic and humble moments of Tolkien's Frodo. When Faramir questions Frodo, as if the hobbit were on "trial," he answers in a cautious, yet forthright manner:

> "Will you not put aside your doubt of me and let me go? I am weary, and full of grief, and afraid. But I have a deed to do, or to attempt, before I too am slain. And the more need of haste, if we two halflings are all that remain of our fellowship.
> "Go back, Faramir, valiant Captain of Gondor, and defend your city while you may, and let me go where my doom takes me." (653; IV:5)

In the theatrical version of *The Two Towers*, Jackson has Faramir simply bind and lead away Frodo and Sam. In the extended DVD, an added scene presents Frodo protesting briefly: "We are bound to an errand of secrecy. Those that claim to oppose the enemy would do well not to hinder us" (*Towers*, scene 30: "Of Herbs and Stewed Rabbit"). Here, Frodo shows some spirit, though his words don't resonate as wonderfully as those of Tolkien's Frodo. Later, when Jackson's Faramir uses his sword to touch the Ring on the chain around Frodo's neck, the hobbit inexplicably goes into a trance again. Each time before, a Ringwraith's nearby presence causes this swooning in Frodo. The hobbit does regain his composure and defies Faramir, but Frodo's self-control, *as he even admits to Sam*, is in grave doubt. Tolkien's Frodo recognizes his vulnerability and frailty. Still, his determination and fortitude are ever evident.

Perhaps the worst "transgression" that Jackson commits is his invented scene where Frodo almost dons the Ring before the Nazgûl in Osgiliath (*Towers*, scene 57: "The Nazgûl Attack"). Not only does the director make Frodo look like a witless psychotic, but Jackson ignores artistic consistency and presents contrived suspense. First, if Faramir were so determined to bring the Ring to Minas Tirith, why didn't he leave men to guard Frodo and Sam? (Faramir appeared completely resolved on this matter.) Second, even if Frodo is tempted to reveal the Ring, what now compels him to walk, zombie-like, to the Nazgûl and his beast? (He was stricken with terror last time.) Third, why does Sam allow Frodo to leave his side amid danger? (Sam has been overprotective from the very beginning.) Fourth, wouldn't Sauron become aware of the Ring, given his psychic link with his Ringwraiths, when Frodo holds up it for the Nazgûl to see? (Jackson makes no effort to explain this away.) And last, why does Frodo go into a mad rage and threaten to stab Sam? (This didn't happen before when Sam physically prevented Frodo from revealing the Ring.) Of course, there is one simple answer to these questions: cinematic spectacle. If all a director wants is a suspenseful scene, however contrived, then narrative logic isn't necessary.

Furthermore, after Frodo regains some measure of self-control, he makes two statements that should shatter any belief that he is the one most suited to carry the Ring and attempt to destroy it. First, he moans: "I can't do this." These words don't reveal self-doubt or fear, which Tolkien's Frodo often expresses; instead, the statement is defeatist and despairing. Second, after Sam declares they should try and hold on, like the characters in the heroic stories he loves, Frodo responds: "What are we holding on to, Sam?" The reply is obvious: the good of the world is "worth fighting for." Tolkien's Frodo never questions the *value* of his quest; he only doubts and fears his *ability* to achieve it. If Jackson's Frodo can't hold true to the ultimate purpose, the effort to save Middle-earth, then he might as well give the Ring to Sam and stop endangering the mission!

The problem with Jackson's portrayal of Frodo is not that it diverges from Tolkien's text. A director may re-imagine a character in the process of adaptation, and film can't easily present the workings of a character's mind in a way that prose can. And Jackson does emphasize the importance of Gollum's and Sam's roles, in their uniquely opposite ways, in helping Frodo on the journey. However, through facial expressions, body language, and eloquent words, Jackson could visually convince the audience that if Frodo doesn't "find a way, no one will." Jackson's character displays little determination, fortitude, or hope. In the book, when Sam discusses the tale that they are in, Frodo alludes to a metafictional idea: ". . . they never end as tales, . . . But the people in them come, and go when their part's ended" (697; IV:8). In the film, when Sam wonders if they will be remembered in tales, Frodo looks at him strangely and says quizzically: "What?" Once again, Jackson denies Frodo a perceptive and eloquent response. Sam's final words in the second film, although taken from the book, now seem ironic: "Frodo was really courageous, wasn't he dad?" Frodo laughs off the idea and instead praises Sam. The audience may agree with Frodo that no reason exists to admire him.

PART 3: "SO LET US FORGIVE HIM! FOR THE QUEST IS ACHIEVED, AND NOW ALL IS OVER."

The structure of the film *The Return of the King* contrasts sharply with that of Tolkien's book. Jackson diverges so extensively from the source text that comparative analysis is difficult. In some scenes where Tolkien's words still appear, Jackson re-contextualizes them in such a way that the original impact is gone. Since *The Two Towers* film ended with significant events absent, such as the encounter with Shelob, Jackson's *The Return of the King* has to incorporate much material from *The Two Towers* book. Consequently, much of Tolkien's *The Return of the King*, particularly the last third of the book, was cut. Again, this change leaves out many of Frodo's finest moments. And the added Frodo scenes show him weak-minded and disloyal. The purpose of Jackson's transformed characterization isn't easily evident, especially since he accords Frodo a lofty status in the end. His hobbit hero displays few instances where he deserves such honor.

The first Frodo/Sam/Gollum scene in the film only slightly resembles the source text. In Tolkien's book, Sam has been on guard while Frodo sleeps fitfully. When Gollum arrives and urges them to leave, Sam suspiciously wonders about Gollum's eagerness. Gollum shakes Frodo awake and the startled hobbit grabs the wretched creature's arm. Tolkien indicates that both Sam and Frodo questioned Gollum but "nothing more could they get out of him" (685; IV:7). So, with Sam suspicious and Frodo weary, the three continue the journey. Jackson's first such scene presents Frodo in a poor light. First, Sam is sleeping and Frodo is awake, looking as if he is a drug addict in need of a fix. Then, with guilty glances towards

Sam, Frodo pulls out the Ring and fondles it. When Gollum arrives to urge them to go, Frodo hastily tucks the Ring under his shirt. Sam wakes up and is distressed to see that Frodo hasn't been sleeping. For the rest of the scene, Jackson borrows bits from an exchange between Sam and Frodo, many pages earlier in the Dead Marshes, about their low provisions and what they will need after the journey is done. Tolkien's Frodo doubts they will need anything, given their seemingly hopeless quest (610; IV:2). Jackson's Frodo looks doubtful too. However, at least Tolkien's Frodo gives the impression he will struggle on to the bitter end. In the film, Frodo appears erratic, despondent, and listless.

For the film's next Frodo/Sam/Gollum scene, Jackson almost completely abandons Tolkien's text and creates his own situation. This time, Frodo appears idiotic and unfaithful—towards Sam! Gollum has another dual personality dialogue, unintentionally revealing to Sam he plans to see that "the hobbits are dead." When Sam attacks Gollum for his treachery, Frodo pulls Sam away and keeps him from harming Gollum.

> SAM. I heard it from his own mouth. He means to murder us!
> GOLLUM. Never! Sméagol wouldn't hurt a fly! He is a hobbit, a fat hobbit who hates Sméagol and he makes up nasty lies.
> SAM. You miserable little maggot! I'll tear your head off!
> *[Sam tries to grab Gollum, but Frodo restrains him.]*
> FRODO. Sam!
> SAM. Call me a liar? You're a liar!
> *[Gollum cowers away and wails as if in pain.]*
> FRODO. Don't scare him off! We're lost!
> SAM. I don't care! I can't do it, Mr. Frodo. I won't wait around for him to kill us.
> FRODO. I'm not sending him away!
> SAM. You don't see it, do you? He's a villain.
> FRODO. We can't do this by ourselves, Sam. Not without a guide. I need you on my side.
> SAM. I'm on your side, Mr. Frodo.
> FRODO. I know, Sam. I know. *(pause)* Come, Gollum.
> *[Frodo takes Gollum's hand. Sam looks shocked at Frodo's behavior. As Frodo leads Gollum away, Gollum gives Sam a sly look. Sam looks furious.]*
> (*Return*, scene 5: "Gollum's Villainy")

This scene makes little sense. Why would Jackson undermine the suspense by making Gollum's treachery so obvious? Why would Frodo ignore Sam's words and not become suspicious of Gollum himself? And why does Frodo first doubt that Sam is on his side and then state that he knows it? Tolkien's Frodo cares about and trusts Gollum far more than Sam does. But Frodo isn't blind to Gollum's treacherous potential. On the stairs of Cirith Ungol, Frodo states that it is "not unlikely" that Gollum is "up to some wickedness," biding "his time and waiting on chance" (698; IV:8). Jackson's Frodo seems to be dimwitted and disloyal.

By the time the three weary travelers escape the terror of the Minas Morgul entrance (and Frodo's dazed and crazed near-surrender), Jackson's Frodo looks like someone on the breaking point. The director's purpose in this characterization might be evident in the scene where Frodo rejects Sam. Again, Jackson ignores Tolkien's text and artistic consistency in favor of melodrama and contrived suspense. Tolkien provides a literary discussion between Frodo and Sam about the tale they have "fallen into" and a poignant scene with Gollum's near repentance when he sees Frodo and Sam sleeping peacefully (696-9; IV:8). Jackson invents a silly ruse with Gollum putting *lembas* bits on the sleeping Sam's shoulder and then claiming "the fat hobbit" ate all their food. When the enraged Sam attacks his accuser, Frodo accepts Gollum's words at face value and believes that Sam wants the Ring. Jackson's scene parallels Shakespeare's *Othello*: Frodo the deranged Moor, Gollum the cunning Iago, and Sam the hapless Cassio/Desdemona. Sam's innocent offer to "share the load" of the Ring seems to confirm for Frodo Gollum's insidious lie, "the fat hobbit wants it." Frodo's reaction is staggering.

> *[Frodo furiously pushes Sam away.]*
> FRODO. Get away!
> SAM. I don't want to keep it. *[Frodo glares at him*
>   *suspiciously.]* I just want to help.
> GOLLUM. See, see. He wants it for himself.
> SAM. Shut up you! Go away! Get out of here!
> FRODO. No, Sam. It's you. *[Sam looks miserable.]* I'm sorry,
>   Sam.
> SAM. But he's a liar. He has poisoned you against me.
> FRODO. You can't help me anymore.
> SAM. You don't mean that.
> FRODO. Go home.
> *[Sam weeps in distress. Frodo shows no pity towards him and*
> *leaves. Gollum sneers at Sam and follows Frodo. Sam remains*
> *behind.]*
>   (*Return*, scene 19: "The Parting of Sam and Frodo")

Even the most open-minded Tolkien admirer may have cringed at this ridiculous departure from the text. Jackson's defense might be that the

Ring has so twisted Frodo's mind that he would even turn against his dearest friend. The source for this scene might have been in the book where Frodo and Sam are nearing Mount Doom; Sam offers "to carry it a bit for you, Master" and Frodo reacts wildly: "It is mine, I say. Be off!" (916; VI:3). But there, Frodo quickly recovers and apologizes that the Ring has too a strong hold on him. In that context, Frodo's behavior makes sense. It makes no sense in the scene quoted above. Even if the Ring has warped Frodo's reasoning, why would he trust Gollum explicitly? Sam has done nothing threatening to his beloved friend but rather, as Frodo has acknowledged time and time again, supported him unwaveringly. (Tolkien's Frodo knew, from the time when Sam insisted on going to Mordor with his master, "it is plain that we were meant to go together" [397; II:10].) If Frodo should mistrust anyone, it should be the one who once possessed the Ring and desperately desires to reclaim it: Gollum. Jackson seems to think that Frodo's rejection of Sam would make effective filmic drama and heighten the suspense, even though neither version of Sam would leave and start heading "home"! The director doesn't seem to care that his central hero now looks like a fool and a traitor.

After presenting a feeble and weak-willed Frodo throughout most of his three films, Jackson suddenly makes an about-face. Frodo hesitantly enters the spider's tunnel and soon realizes that Gollum has led him into a trap. Now, he transforms into a thoughtful and hardy individual—much like Tolkien's Frodo, in fact. Except for the absence of Sam, Jackson follows Tolkien's text quite closely here. Frodo suddenly remembers the Phial of Galadriel, speaks the elvish incantation, daunts Shelob with its light, slashes free of her webbing, and escapes from her lair. Then Gollum attacks Frodo and the hobbit somehow finds the strength to pin the wretched creature. When Gollum pleads that the Ring made him betray Frodo, the hobbit shows mercy, saying that he has to destroy it for "both our sakes." Frodo's kindness is rewarded with another attack, but Jackson uses a hackneyed film device and has Gollum apparently plunge to his death. Frodo struggles on, sad and regretful about his treatment of Sam. Here Jackson's character displays strength and perceptiveness that he hadn't before.

Then comes a most curious scene: Frodo collapses and seems to wake up in Lórien at the feet of Galadriel. Jackson's inspiration might have been a scene in *The Two Towers* when Frodo calls out the elven queen's name to find courage to face Shelob (705; IV:9). In any case, as if it were a dream vision, Galadriel reminds Frodo—and the audience—of the central theme:

[*Galadriel reaches down to Frodo.*]
GALADRIEL (V.O.). This task was appointed to you, Frodo
   of the Shire. And if you do not find a way, no one will.
   [*Galadriel holds out her hand. Frodo hesitates and then with
   a look of determination, takes her hand, regains his feet, and
   as the vision ends, finds himself back in the pass of Minas
   Morgul.*]
                      (*Return*, scene 29: "Shelob's Lair")

As I have argued all along, Jackson's Frodo has done very little to show that some divine agency has "appointed" the task to him. The irony, which perhaps Jackson intends, is that right after this scene, Shelob attacks and paralyzes Frodo. For the rest of the quest, *Sam finds the way*—despite Frodo's betrayal of him.

With so much emphasis on the battles of *The Return of the King*, Jackson cut much of the Frodo plot from the source text. Leading to the climax in Sammath Naur, Jackson offers some parallel scenes to Tolkien's book: Frodo's rescue and Sam's return of the Ring; Frodo's grim plodding, with such dramatic touches as waving his hand to ward off the gaze of the Eye; Sam's carrying him up the slopes of Mount Doom, Gollum's attack, and Frodo's entry into the Chambers of Fire. Since the journey through Mordor happens so quickly, the audience sees little of Frodo's truly heroic endurance in spite of the physical challenges and psychological torture. Jackson does provide a powerful dramatization of Frodo's heartrending words that he has no memory of "the sound of water" and is "naked in the dark" with "no veil between me and the wheel of fire." This scene may have been Elijah Wood's finest acting moment in the three films (*Return*, scene 49: "'I Can't Carry It for You . . . But I Can Carry You'").

Jackson's altered climax does nothing to enhance Frodo's character, but may not drastically denigrate it either. Clearly, the director felt that Tolkien's rapid and ironic climax, with Gollum slipping into the chasm after biting off the Ring from Frodo's hand, wasn't good enough cinema. So Jackson presents Frodo, sans finger and determined to reclaim the Ring, grappling with Gollum and apparently falling with him into the Cracks of Doom. In another hackneyed film device, Frodo hangs from a precipice; he considers letting go but then, with Sam's help, manages to climb back up and escape the collapsing cavern. The scene between Frodo and Sam, as the lava surrounds them and death appears imminent, is both visually stunning and emotionally moving. Jackson signals Frodo's immediate psychological recovery, also obvious in the book, with his line: "I can see the Shire."

However, the director leaves out Tolkien's key lines that encapsulate the purpose of Frodo's trials:

> "But do you remember Gandalf's words: *Even Gollum may have something yet to do*? But for him, Sam, I could not have destroyed the Ring. The Quest would have been in vain, even at the bitter end. So let us forgive him! For the Quest is achieved, and now all is over." (926; VI:3)

Pity, mercy, forgiveness, and self-sacrifice: the virtues of Frodo, which also complement Divine Grace. But Jackson's character doesn't allude to them. The love Frodo has for Sam, undermined and dismissed since the appearance of Gollum, does resurface after the destruction of the Ring: "I'm glad you're here with me, Samwise Gamgee. Here at the end of all things." Jackson's film fades to black to suggest that the end really has come for his Frodo.

CONCLUSION: ". . . WHEN THINGS ARE IN DANGER: SOMEONE HAS TO GIVE THEM UP, LOSE THEM, SO THAT OTHERS MAY KEEP THEM."

When critics consider film adaptations of great books, they can easily fall into the trap of simply stating "the book is better than the film." That assessment is common, but not very enlightening. We must evaluate the films on their own merits and allow for artistic license because film and print are different media. Books can develop many features, particularly character, in much more detail, given the constraints of time and space of cinema. However, film can sometimes vividly dramatize character, through the skills of the actors, directorial choices, setting, music, and so on. Judged on the basis of their vast popularity and widespread critical acclaim, Jackson's *The Lord of the Rings* films are a fine achievement. With their massive budget and an excellent creative team, these adaptations of Tolkien's masterpiece could have been great. Alas, Jackson took the living and enduring "heart" of the books, the humble and heroic trials of Frodo, and replaced it with a reconstructed and flawed one.

Jackson's reason for diverging so fundamentally from Tolkien's text is not readily apparent, but one may guess: his Frodo has to appeal to the average moviegoer, who is used to frenetic melodrama and staged suspense. Jackson's character is handed a huge responsibility. He has few attributes to bear the burden and has to rely heavily on others, who seem much stronger and more perceptive, to manage on the journey. He often succumbs to the Ring's insidious temptations, augmented by its depraved former possessor, and he betrays his loyal and heroic friend. With no retrospective wisdom and much good luck, he is saved from a fiery death when the Ring is destroyed. He is just a common individual, like most anyone in the audience. If Jackson's film had ended at the marriage of Sam and Rosie, the above assessment would have been complete. But the closing scenes impel us back to Tolkien's great book.

For Jackson desired that poignant and powerful ending, even if for the majority of his films he had divested Tolkien's Frodo of his unique and noble character. Jackson's Frodo, like the book's, appears out of place back home, works on Bilbo's chronicle "The Redbook of Westmarch," retains the wounds (both physical and psychological) from his experience, and receives the honor of sailing to Valinor with the great ones, Elrond, Galadriel, and Gandalf. Frodo recognizes that he "saved the Shire" but not for himself. Sam must "not be torn in two" and remain in mortal lands with "much to do." Jackson, perhaps by necessity, leaves out many key Frodo scenes from the *Return of the King* book, such as his confrontation with Saruman, where his wise nature is evident. But the director clearly loves the Frodo of final pages, although his character throughout the films bears little resemblance to Tolkien's hero.

In the end, both Frodos "were meant" to bear the burden and to "find a way" when no one else could. Thus, *both* the book *and* the film dramatize the themes of divine designation, pity, mercy, forgiveness, and self-sacrifice in the portrayal of Frodo. The difference—and it's a significant one—is that Jackson wants to appeal to a contemporary audience, and so, for the most part, offers a "hero" with whom he thinks "the masses" can relate. On the other hand, Tolkien presents a special character, albeit not a perfect one, whom we can admire and aspire to become. Frodo's doubts, fears, sufferings, and flaws may parallel our own. Yet through steadfast courage, dogged plodding, humility, and faith, we may discover the strength and wisdom to bear our own burdens and to envision our ultimate state of grace: "a far green country under a swift sunrise" (1007; VI:9). Indeed, Frodo's story is a part of the larger "Story" that we all know — and could live.

WORKS CITED

The Legacy of The Lord of the Rings. Documentary. Dir. Daniel Timmons. July 2002. VHS. Toronto: Filmoption International, 2004.

The Lord of the Rings: The Fellowship of the Ring. Special Extended DVD Edition. Screenplay by Peter Jackson, Fran Walsh, and Philippa Boyens. Perf. Elijah Wood et al. Dir. Peter Jackson. United States: New Line Home Entertainment, 2002.

The Lord of the Rings: The Return of the King. Theatrical Release DVD. Screenplay by Peter Jackson, Fran Walsh, and Philippa Boyens. Perf. Elijah Wood et al. Dir. Peter Jackson. United States, New Line Home Entertainment, 2004.

The Lord of the Rings: The Two Towers. Special Extended DVD Edition. Screenplay by Peter Jackson, Fran Walsh, and Philippa Boyens. Perf. Elijah Wood et al. Dir. Peter Jackson. United States: New Line Home Entertainment, 2003.

Stam, Robert. "Beyond Fidelity: The Dialogics of Adaptation." *Film Adaptation*. Ed. James Naremore. Newark: Rutgers UP, 2000. 54-77.

Tolkien, J.R.R. *The Lord of the Rings*. 2nd ed. With Note on the Text by Douglas A. Anderson. Boston: Houghton Mifflin, 1994.

ELISIONS AND ELLIPSES: COUNSEL AND COUNCIL IN TOLKIEN'S AND JACKSON'S *THE LORD OF THE RINGS*

JUDITH KOLLMANN

Throughout his works, J.R.R. Tolkien stresses the importance of wisdom, and through frequent scenes of *council* and *counsel* in his fictional writings, emphasizes that wisdom is most valuable when shared with others, particularly in the forms of counsel between two characters and in councils among several persons. While the word "advice" does appear in *The Lord of the Rings*, Tolkien's word of choice is "counsel." Perhaps it is more elevated in tone than is "advice," but perhaps it is also a less parental and a less arrogant term, as "counsel" suggests a mutual exchange of advice or opinion. "Counsel" abounds in *The Silmarillion* and is common in *The Lord of the Rings*, particularly since Gandalf's primary function is, as a dispenser of wisdom, that of a counselor. As *The Silmarillion* informs us, "all these things [i.e. the destruction of the Ring, the victory over Sauron and the return of the King] were achieved for the most part by the counsel and vigilance of Mithrandir" (*Silmarillion* 278). As a matter of word choice, "counsel" is beloved by Tolkien. Jackson is less enthusiastic about its use, although the term does appear a few times in the films: notably, in *Fellowship*, Saruman uses it when Gandalf comes to Orthanc for "counsel," and Gandalf uses it in *Return* when he arrives at Minas Tirith and offers counsel to Denethor. In neither instance is the counsel accepted by the potential counselee, and consequently the word does not retain the positive and even majestic quality with which Tolkien invested it.

This is not to say that "counsel" in Tolkien's work is invariably good— it can also be lying or devious. If it is lying counsel, it leads inevitably to tragedy if the person counseled accepts and acts on it; if devious, it usually backfires on the character who gave it. Such is the case when Thingol informs Beren that the bride-price for Thingol's daughter, Lúthien, is "a Silmaril from Morgoth's crown" (*Silmarillion* 202); Thingol's wife, Melian, who, as a Maia, is one of the wisest counselors in *The Silmarillion*, informs her husband: "O King, you have devised cunning counsel. But if my eyes have not lost their sight, it is ill for you, whether Beren fail in his errand, or achieve it. For you have doomed either your daughter, or yourself" (203). She is correct; Thingol had doomed himself. If, as is usually the case, the counsel is true, and is accepted by the person counseled, the result will be success. Moreover, the person receiving the counsel thereby makes manifest qualities in him- (or her-) self that are of primary importance in a Tolkienian hero: namely, humility and wisdom. He who rejects sound counsel inevitably manifests serious flaws in his character: pride, stubbornness, impatience, and willfulness figure among them; moreover, he always seals his own fate. Denethor and Isildur are, of course, the preeminent examples in *The Lord of the Rings*. *The Silmarillion* contains a number of characters who listen only to themselves, Aredhel Ar-Feiniel and Fëanor among them.

Closely related to *counsel* is the *council*, a gathering of persons who have been summoned and organized for the purposes of gaining information, taking counsel, deliberating, and, finally, making decisions. There are only three formal councils in *The Silmarillion* and *The Lord of the Rings*. Two are standing, established bodies: the Council of the Valar, and the White Council in Middle-earth. These meet when summoned to do so. The third, the Council of Elrond, meets only once before disbanding. However, because it makes the decision from which all subsequent action in *The Lord of the Rings* ensues, its deliberations become a focal point in both the novel and film versions of *The Fellowship of the Ring*. Less formal councils are frequent. These occur whenever groups of characters assemble, sometimes by (seeming) chance and sometimes by plan; the meetings are informal, but decisions are reached, often by consensus.

Characters who are totally evil, such as Morgoth and Sauron, neither give nor take counsel, and are incapable of functioning in council. They are rather like black holes, which take everything in and give nothing back. In Tolkien's works, divisiveness is a hallmark of evil, while collaboration and concordance are the hope of the good. The pattern for counsel among the evil doers is set by Morgoth:

> Who knows now the counsels of Morgoth? Who can measure the reach of his thought, who had been Melkor, mighty among the Ainur of the Great Song, and sat now, a dark lord upon a dark throne in the North, weighing in his malice all the tidings that came to him, and perceiving more of the deeds and purposes of his enemies than even the wisest of them feared, save only Melian the Queen? (*Silmarillion* 251)

When members of the enemy forces hold council Tolkien always depicts these as a travesty of the ordered councils of Men and Elves; Orc-councils are anti-councils. Notable among these are two examples from *The Two Towers*: the first occurs when the Orcs who have kidnapped Pippin and Merry hold a council on the Plain of Rohan, and the second when Shagrat and Gorbag discuss Frodo's paralysis from Shelob's bite. In each case the "council" ends with the Orcs quarrelling and killing each other (435-7; II:3 and 719-23; IV:10).

As one of my students recently observed, "Practically no one makes snap decisions in this trilogy." Since counsel and council are chief means to wise decisions and subsequent actions, these two terms become a significant theme in Tolkien's work, and are modified in interesting ways in Peter Jackson's films, where they are often abbreviated, enhanced, changed in effect or purpose; they seem to have been simplified, but are in fact rarely simple.

In the text of *The Fellowship of the Ring*, the Council of Elrond is a major nexus that explains what remains to be explained about the One Ring, introduces the as-yet unmet members of the Fellowship, and plans the future. The Council extends for forty-one pages, taking an entire chapter (the longest one in *The Fellowship*). If one is permitted to consider that the council extends beyond the formal Council itself, then the meeting-advisory process continues for another three pages into the subsequent chapter as the hobbits consult, first among themselves and then with Gandalf. Pippin and Merry become increasingly determined to be included in the Nine. In the film, the Council is also a nexus, but is proportionately much briefer. It is, moreover, framed by three scenes found nowhere in the novel. The two versions of the Council are indicative of the directions Tolkien was taking with his characters and themes, and of the divergent purposes of the film.

First, permit me to describe, in some detail, Tolkien's version. On the day of the Council, Frodo awakes, "feeling refreshed and well" (233; II:2). He walks in the garden, meeting Gandalf and Bilbo: a bell rings, summoning them to the meeting. Gathered there are thirteen individuals, twelve of whom have been officially summoned: Elrond, of course; from the Elves, Legolas, Glorfindel, Erestor, and Galdor; of Men, Strider and Boromir; of Hobbits, Frodo, Bilbo and Sam (the uninvited); of Dwarves, Glóin and Gimli; and Gandalf. It is a lengthy and methodical meeting. First there is a summary of current events: Glóin the dwarf reports there is trouble at Lonely Mountain: an emissary from Sauron has come seeking a ring and news of one Baggins; he adds that a delegation has gone to reopen Moria and has not been heard from for years. Elrond observes, "What shall we do with the Ring? . . . That is the purpose for which you are called hither" (236; II:2).

So Elrond summarizes the story of the Ring up to Bilbo's acquisition of it, briefly describing the Last Great Battle, Isildur's appropriation of the Ring, his death, and the realms of men split into the North and South Kingdoms. Boromir informs everyone of Gondor's continuing resistance to Mordor even though it is a steadily losing proposition. He describes his brother Faramir's prophetic dream, instructing him to seek for the Sword that was Broken in Imladris (i.e., Rivendell), and Boromir's subsequent acceptance of this quest for Imladris. Aragorn clarifies who he is by unsheathing Narsil.

At this point, Elrond asks Frodo to display the Ring, which he does, although reluctantly, and Aragorn describes his role as a guardian of the people in the North: "But now the world is changing once again. A new hour comes. Isildur's Bane is found. Battle is at hand. The Sword shall be reforged. I will come to Minas Tirith" (242; II:2). Bilbo tells the story of how he acquired the Ring in the riddle-game, and Frodo concludes the tale of the Ring by describing how it has come to Rivendell.

Galdor asks for Gandalf's story and he also asks why Saruman is not present at the Council. Gandalf responds with the tale of his betrayal and imprisonment by Saruman and his escape from the pinnacle of Orthanc. He summarizes the present situation in Middle-earth: Sauron has risen again and has reinvested Mordor; Saruman had lied about the Ring's survival years ago and Gandalf had believed him; Gandalf watched for Gollum and Aragorn had hunted with Gandalf for him; Gandalf, after much research, particularly among the records in Minas Tirith, had found Isildur's account of taking it from the hand of Sauron, its physical description, and something of its properties as an extension of Sauron's will; Aragorn found Gollum and delivered him to the Wood Elves in Mirkwood for safekeeping. There Gandalf interrogated him and established two things: the identity of Bilbo's Ring and that Sauron knew the Ring had been found. Boromir asks "To what doom did you put him?" (248; II:2), to which Aragorn replies that Gollum remains in prison with the Wood Elves. At this juncture Legolas speaks for the first time, reporting Gollum's escape. Gandalf describes how he was summoned by Saruman to a meeting at which he was given a choice: to ally himself with Saruman and Sauron, or be imprisoned until the end of the war. Upon his rejection of the alliance Saruman's servants had taken Gandalf to the pinnacle from which the Eagle rescued him.

After a silence Elrond picks up various threads of the narratives, observing that the loss of Saruman is a great blow and that he was aware of the Barrow-wights and the Old Forest; he wonders whether Bombadil should have been summoned to the present Council. Gandalf responds: "He would not have come" (258; II:2). This is a significant issue, because Bombadil is the only sentient being in Middle-earth who could hold the Ring as it has no power over him. Therefore he must be eliminated as a possible solution to the dilemma, something Gandalf does handily: "he would not understand the need. And if he were given the Ring, he would soon forget it, or most likely throw it away. Such things have no hold on his mind. He would be a most unsafe guardian . . . " (259; II:2). That, as Glorfindel notes, leaves two options: "to send it over the Sea [to Valinor], or to destroy it" (259; II:2). Elrond narrows these options, pointing out that no craft in Rivendell has the power to destroy it and that the Valar "will not receive it: for good or ill it belongs to Middle-earth; it is for us who still dwell here to deal with it" (259; II:2). Glorfindel suggests dropping it into the deepest seas. Gandalf notes "There are many things in the deep waters; and seas and lands may change. And it is not our part here to take thought only for a season, or for a few lives of Men, or for a passing age of the world. We should seek a final end of this menace, even if we do not hope to make one" (259-60; II:2). Elrond makes the now-obvious conclusion: "We must send the Ring to the Fire" (260; II:2).

There is silence; then Boromir speaks, asking why the good side cannot use the Ring. Elrond explains that the only Lord of that Ring is its maker, Sauron, and that anyone else will be corrupted. He notes that he would not take it to use it, and Gandalf adds that neither would he. Boromir accedes, although "doubtfully" (261; II:2), saying that then Gondor will continue to fight, and adding the jibe, "Mayhap the Sword-that-was-Broken may still stem the tide—if the hand that wields it has inherited not an heirloom only, but the sinews of the Kings of Men." Aragorn responds, "Who can tell? . . . But we will put it to the test one day" (261; II:2).

Elrond observes that Gondor is not the only place or people who are resisting the Dark Lord, and Glóin the Dwarf adds proudly that one reason Balin went to Moria was to seek for the last of the Seven Rings given to the Dwarves. Gandalf, however, has to crush this hope, saying that Thrór, the holder of this last ring, had given it to his son, Thráin, who had been captured and killed in Dol Guldur. Therefore it is in Sauron's possession. Glóin demands to know what the elves are doing with their three rings, which gives Elrond the opportunity to make clear that they were not made by, or ever touched by, Sauron, that "They are not idle,"

153

but that "they were not made as weapons of war or conquest: that is not their power. . . . [instead, they give] understanding, making, and healing, to preserve all things unstained" (262; II:2). So they are not an option for direct help.

Erestor notes that this brings everything back full circle to the issue of destroying the Ring, except that no one has the strength (i.e., military might) to get to the Fire—that is also "the path of despair. Of folly I would say, if the long wisdom of Elrond did not forbid me" (262; II:2). Gandalf, in a prophetic statement strongly reminiscent of Paul's "Here we are, fools for Christ's sake" (1 Cor. 4:10), observes that "as folly it may appear to those who cling to false hope. Well, let folly be our cloak, a veil before the eyes of the Enemy! For he is very wise . . . But the only measure that he knows is desire, desire for power; and so he judges all hearts. Into his heart the thought will not enter that any will refuse it, that having the Ring we may seek to destroy it" (262; II:2). Elrond agrees, adding that "this quest may be attempted by the weak with as much hope as the strong" (262; II:2). Bilbo volunteers to take the Ring to Orodruin. Gandalf advises him that the Ring has passed on, that his job is to be the recorder of history "when they come back" (263; II:2). Bilbo asks: "what do you mean by *they*?" and the response is: "The messengers who are sent with the Ring." Bilbo probably answers for all of us as he exclaims: "Exactly! And who are they to be? That seems to me what this Council has to decide, and all that it has to decide" (263; II:2).

Tolkien has come meticulously to this point of consensus; now, however, Elrond cannot appoint anyone to this task. There have been pauses and silences in the discussion before, but now the silence is lengthy:

> Frodo glanced at all the faces, but they were not turned to him. All the Council sat with downcast eyes, as if in deep thought. A great dread fell on him, as if he was awaiting the pronouncement of some doom that he had long foreseen and vainly hoped might after all never be spoken. An overwhelming longing to rest and remain at peace by Bilbo's side in Rivendell filled all his heart. At last he spoke . . . "I will take the Ring," he said, "though I do not know the way." (263-4; II:2)

Elrond agrees: "I think that this task is appointed for you, Frodo; and that if you do not find a way, no one will" (263; II:2). When he concludes, Sam leaps up and says, "But you won't send him off alone surely, Master?" (264; II:2). Elrond, smiling, responds "No, indeed! You at least shall go with him. It is hardly possible to separate you from him, even when he is summoned to a secret council and you are not." Sam has the last muttering word as the Council disbands: "A nice pickle we have landed ourselves in, Mr. Frodo!" (264; II:2).

This is a brief summary of those forty-one pages. What is notable about this version of the Council is the systematic way in which the agenda is worked through, and, that, although there is often outspokenness and, perhaps, a touch of temper, it is a council conducted with dignity and in peace.

It formally concludes at the end of the chapter, but an informal council consisting of all the hobbits—Merry, Pippin, Frodo, Sam and Bilbo—convenes later in the same day in Bilbo's room, and is joined by Gandalf. Here, Pippin and Merry express their determination to be among the companions chosen for the journey, and Gandalf assures them that he is planning to go along, as well. More business is also taken care of—for example, there is a need to send out scouts to find out what has happened to the Nine Riders and what is going on in the countryside; time must be given for the scouts to gather the information and return. Not only does this meeting make clear that all the hobbits want to go on, but stresses the realistic aspect of great adventures—one does not just start off without one's pocket-handkerchief. This scene also accomplishes one other narrative function: it completes a frame around the Council of Elrond—a frame of hobbits before it and after it.

In Jackson's film, except for the fact that Frodo is healed at Rivendell and reunited with Gandalf and Bilbo, that Boromir, Legolas and Gimli arrive, that the Council of Elrond does take place and that the nine members of the Fellowship are chosen, virtually everything is changed. Yes, Frodo is healed, but Elrond makes clear that although he formally welcomes Frodo, Frodo is not made to feel quite as welcome as he is in the novel—for one thing, there is no celebratory feast for his recovery. The film also notes that both Sam and Frodo are eager to return to the Shire. Sam has the bags packed and waiting. Elrond and Gandalf are almost in a conspiratorial relationship, observing the hobbits unseen. Elrond states that Frodo should be the one to continue the Quest; Gandalf pleads that "It is a burden he [Frodo] should never have had to bear. We cannot ask more of Frodo" (*Fellowship,* scene 24: "The Fate of the Ring"). To do him credit, Elrond does not ask Frodo, but the point is clear. And the Council itself is framed, not by hobbits, but by Aragorn, who has two encounters in a room that appears to be a combined library-museum. The first is with Boromir; the second with Arwen. Aragorn is quietly reading a book when Boromir strolls in, examines a tapestry depicting the broken sword, Narsil, in Isildur's hand at The Last Battle. He becomes aware of Aragorn, who is staring unblinkingly at the intruder. Silent friction is evident. Boromir, nothing daunted, continues to stroll about, and comes upon the shrine on which the shards of the sword Narsil are displayed. He recognizes the sword, and rather arrogantly picks it up by the pommel, running his finger along the broken edge, which cuts his finger. Surprised that after 3,000 years it retains its sharpness, he engages in a short conversation with Aragorn. Boromir makes clear that, while sharp, Narsil is a useless artifact—implying that the men who once wielded it are equally useless. Aragorn gets the point, but chooses to say nothing, and Boromir also appears to discount him; after all, he seems to be just a bookish, slightly scruffy Ranger. He tosses the shard negligently toward the shrine, from which it falls, and leaves without bothering to replace the fragment. Aragorn stands up and reverently replaces the sword as Arwen enters. She has observed part of this, and asks him: "Why do you fear the past? You are Isildur's heir." He replies: "The same blood flows in my veins. The same weakness." She has confidence in him as she says: "Your time will come. You will face the same evil. And you will defeat it." Later, under the stars, they stroll out to the gardens, where Arwen makes clear that she chose him long ago over eternal life: "I would rather share one lifetime with you than all the ages of immortal life. It [my life] is mine to give to whom I will—like my heart" (*Fellowship*, scene 26: "The Evenstar").

The following morning is the Council itself. Elrond, as its convener, introduces it with a characteristically (for the film Elrond, that is) short directive. Gathered here are the representatives of the major sentient species of Middle-earth, and, he tells them, "You will unite, or you will fall." He turns immediately to Frodo and orders him to "Bring forth the Ring." Frodo does so, placing it on a plinth in the center of the Council's outdoor meeting place, a parallel placement of one artifact with another. Boromir, amazed, whispers "So it is true" and immediately starts moving toward the Ring—no explanation of it is necessary. Boromir states that he had a dream—a dream that informed him only that the one Ring had been found. He moves so near it that his hand is inches away from grasping it when Gandalf stops him by proclaiming loudly, in the language of Mordor, the incantation engraved upon the Ring. The reaction of storm and fury startles even Boromir into backing up, as Gandalf states flatly, "The Ring is altogether evil!" However, Boromir pleads eloquently for the use of the Ring to defend Gondor—"Give Gondor the Ring—let us use it against the enemy!" Aragorn quietly but forcefully explains that the Ring has no Master but Sauron, and Boromir, who is contemptuous of this nondescript person, insults him, calling him nothing but a Ranger. Legolas proclaims Aragorn's identity as the heir to the kings of Gondor, to whom

Boromir owes allegiance. Boromir rejects this: "Gondor has no king; Gondor needs no king."

Gimli speaks up for the first time: "What are we waiting for," he says, as he lifts his ax, strikes the Ring for all he is worth, and is flung back, his ax in pieces, proving that indeed no craft known to elves or dwarves can destroy it. Elrond knows, and so states, that the Ring must be taken to Mordor. Boromir is highly skeptical as he describes the approach to Mordor, concluding that "Not with ten thousand men could you do this. It is folly."

At this point argument breaks forth—everyone is shouting angrily, and, as Frodo stares at the Ring he sees, superimposed on it, just where he knows the incantation is engraved, the fighting amongst the Free Peoples that will be their fate if the Ring is not taken to Mount Doom, and he accepts his destiny: "I will take it," he says; "I will take the Ring to Mordor, though I do not know the way." The others stop and silence is finally restored. Gandalf volunteers to help share the burden; Aragorn, Legolas and Gimli offer protection with their weapons; and Boromir, who makes no offer, does make an observation: "You carry all our fates, little one." Sam jumps out of the bushes, and Pippin and Merry slip out from behind columns, each also offering to go. So, on the lighter note that coincides with the novel, Elrond formally accepts and presents "The Fellowship of the Ring" (*Fellowship*, scene 27: "The Council of Elrond").

The sequence is completed by the concluding frame. On the evening of, presumably, the day of the Council, Aragorn visits his mother's grave. As he stands, clearing away the overgrowth, Elrond approaches him, noting that she had brought her child to Rivendell for safety, but that "In her heart your mother knew you would be hunted all your life, that you would never escape your fate. The skill of the elves can reforge the sword of kings, but only you have the power to wield it." Aragorn responds: "I do not want that power. I have never wanted it." Elrond does not plead, but he quietly emphasizes: "You are the last of that bloodline. There is no other" (*Fellowship*, scene 28: "Gilraen's Memorial").

Thus, although Frodo remains important, the sequence as a whole has shifted its emphasis to Aragorn: to his identity, and to his reluctance to strive for the kingdom to which he is heir. To Arwen he has explained why: he shuns power, he fears it because it has destroyed his forefather Isildur. The rest of Jackson's *Lord of the Rings* will, among other elements and themes, show Aragorn gradually assuming this power, growing into it and becoming increasingly aware that he can indeed use it without being corrupted by it. In Moria, Gandalf hands the leadership of the companions to Aragorn before encountering the Balrog, and Aragorn assumes it. But it is not until he goes through the Argonath, the Pillars of the Kings, that he begins to be attracted to the idea. The final honor comes from Boromir, as he is dying, when he acknowledges Aragorn as "My king" and Aragorn accepts the accolade.

Tolkien's *The Two Towers* contains at least thirteen occasions when someone is either counseled by another character or, given the circumstances, must take counsel by himself. One such case occurs when Éomer must decide whether he trusts Aragorn, Gimli and Legolas (421-5; III:2). Perhaps the most notable of these is found in Chapter 10, "The Choices of Master Samwise" (711-25; IV:10), when Sam has to decide whether to leave Frodo's presumably dead body and attempt to take the Ring to Mount Doom by himself. Further, there are occasions when counsel almost becomes council— as, for example, when Aragorn does not know whether to follow Frodo across the Anduin or to attempt to rescue Merry and Pippin from the Orcs (409; III:1); or when Gandalf, Aragorn and Théoden discuss whether or not to ride out to war against Saruman (530-31; III:8). There are three significant councils in the novel: the Entmoot (468-73; III:4), which is a formal, if rustic, affair; and two less formal ones— Gandalf's with Aragorn, Legolas and Gimli in Fangorn Forest (484-89; III:5); and Faramir's with Frodo and Sam (648-78; IV:5-6).

In English history, a "moot" was a meeting of freemen (not therefore, primarily nobility) in a specific, traditional place in order to discuss local affairs. Tolkien doubtless uses the word to connote a meeting less lofty than those held by Elves or Men in splendid buildings— something suitable for tree-men who might be somewhat comic but who have a proud tradition as creatures free of any domination. The other two "councils" are also held in rather unconventional ways—Aragorn and Théoden might be consulting in a king's hall, but on the edge of war they do not stand on excessive ceremony nor take the time to summon the nobles of Rohan. Faramir's "council" may not appear to be one at all, as parts of it include the arrest of Frodo and Samwise, a battle, an interrogation, a remove to a hidden cave, and the capture of Gollum. However, throughout this lengthy sequence of nearly thirty pages Faramir is trying to make up his mind as to what he is going to do with the hobbits; he has the same problem Éomer had when he decided to trust Aragorn and his companions, but his is the more difficult decision. Towards its conclusion, as he is turning in favor of Frodo, he says "I desire your counsel," and at the end he formally announces "I will declare my doom" (675; IV:6). Within the cave, the secret stronghold of Gondor, he has indeed a formal, if rough-hewn, council hall, and he rules therein.

In the novel, Entmoot takes place in Derndingle, where, as Treebeard states, "we have always met" (467; III:4). When the meeting begins, the Ents take their time, but manage to introduce the hobbits to the Ents, to agree they are not orcs, and to insert a new line into the poem "Of the Lore of Living Creatures" (469; III:4). While the Ents deal with additional matters, Pippin and Merry stroll about, drink a draught of Ent-water, recognize that the Ents are more dangerous than they look, and express home-sickness. Then Treebeard brings a younger Ent to them, Quickbeam, who "has already made up his mind and does not need to remain at the Moot" (471; III:4). So the hobbits stay with him until the morning of the third day, when the Ents reach their decision to march on Isengard. This, of course, is very different from the way in which Jackson treats the Ents and Entmoot—which, until the scenes of Saruman's destruction of the southern woods and the Ents' destruction of Isengard, is used mainly to add comedy among the dramatic scenes of the Battle at Helm's Deep. Tolkien brings the Ents into *The Two Towers* three times— first, to introduce the hobbits to Fangorn and for the decision of Entmoot; a second time at Helm's Deep, when the Shepherds of the Trees keep the anger of the Huorns focused on the killing and burial of orcs; and finally when Pippin and Merry recount the story of the destruction of Isengard to Aragorn, Gimli and Legolas, and when Gandalf asks Treebeard to keep Saruman and Gríma incarcerated in the Tower of Isengard. Jackson interfaces Ent-appearances in no less than fourteen scenes; and four of these consist of the Entmoot. In the first, the Ents assemble; in the second, they take all day to say "Good morning," finishing only at nightfall; in the third, they determine that the hobbits are not orcs; and in the fourth they decide "This is not our war." Thus, the first three scenes of Entmoot are used for comedic effect, while the fourth expresses a significant theme in the films—that of peoples who desire to avoid war for parochial reasons. It is not until Fangorn sees Saruman's devastation of the southern forest that he, as well as the other Ents, becomes "hasty." Thus, the Entmoot as a decision-making council is at best only a partial success: it makes the Ents consider war. Their decision is completely opposite to that in the novel, detracting from the wisdom and courage with which Tolkien had imbued them in addition to their comic elements. However, the subsequent scene of the Ents emerging from Fangorn Forest and converging on Isengard helps to restore some of the balance.

Faramir's decision upon taking counsel primarily with himself in the novel is far less conflicted than in the film. In him Tolkien wished to show that the blood of the Númenóreans could flow nearly as pure in Minas Tirith as in the veins of Aragorn, that in the noblest family remaining in Minas Tirith there was someone who had the wisdom not to allow himself to be tempted by the Ring. As he says to Samwise: "I had no lure or desire to do other than I have done" (667; IV:5). As those of us who have watched the commentary to the films are aware, *The Two Towers* was the most difficult section of the trilogy to film. To an audience among whom there were tens of thousands of folks unfamiliar with the novels, the risk of either boredom or confusion was great: there are three story lines that pop back and forth in a complex dance, the introduction of a number of new characters, only one really dramatic incident—the battle at Helm's Deep—and no major deaths, making for heavy going. It is to Jackson's credit that he stayed as true to the novels as he did, and as true to the hobbits' encounter with Faramir as he did, even as he eliminated the Númenórean Faramir and substituted a far more human one who suffers intensely because his father adores Boromir, the man of action, and despises the younger son whom Denethor sees as weaker because he is more introspective. So Faramir is conflicted in a way similar to that of millions of people whose parents prefer one child to the other, and therefore many in the audience will have far greater rapport with this Faramir than they would have had with Tolkien's. When the Ring comes to Jackson's Faramir, his first response is to take it and the hobbits to Minas Tirith and to Denethor in order to prove his fidelity and his "quality" to the man who taunted him about his loyalty and leadership abilities. He is also in greater doubt about Frodo's trustworthiness and thus his "quality" is being tested in two directions. When, in the film, at the conclusion of his decision to free the hobbits Samwise says to Faramir "You took the chance, sir . . . and showed your quality: the very highest" (667; IV:5), his statement carries a double meaning, for Jackson's Denethor had taunted Faramir with these same words. Here Sam bestows them as an accolade; in the novel they demonstrate Sam's cheekiness, though Faramir gravely responds, "The praise of the praiseworthy is above all rewards" (667; IV:5).

There is at least one more council in Jackson's version of *The Two Towers* that is treated very briefly in the novel: the Council of Théoden following the exorcism of Saruman. When, in the novel, Théoden's mind is freed from Wormtongue, Théoden goes right to business: he asks for his own sword, commands that Gríma be brought before him, and then turns to Gandalf, saying, "Now, Gandalf, you said that you had counsel to give, if I would hear it. What is your counsel?" Gandalf responds, "You have yourself already taken it . . . To put your trust in Éomer, rather than in a man of crooked mind. To cast aside regret and fear. To do the deed at hand" (506-07; III:6). So, aware of the need to go to war, he immediately takes the offensive and decides to ride to Helm's Deep, not as a place of shelter, but in order to rescue Erkenbrand. He also welcomes Aragorn and does not perceive him as any threat to his rule over Rohan. Jackson modifies Théoden extensively into a more cautious king who takes all his people to Helm's Deep as a refuge, choosing to take the defensive; in addition, he views Aragorn as a threat to his rule and to his manhood: "When last I looked, Théoden, not Aragorn, was King of Rohan!" (*Towers*, scene 23: "The King's Decision"). During the Battle at Helm's Deep, Jackson has Théoden directing the war from within the keep, while it is Aragorn who has the opportunity to demonstrate his courage, fighting skills and leadership abilities on the ramparts. It is only when he invites Théoden to ride out with him that Théoden recognizes two things: first, that Aragorn is not out to take Rohan from him, but, rather, to work in partnership; but, second, he simultaneously realizes that the real leader of his men has become Aragorn, and this he sees as impugning his own sense of honor. In the novel, the king is unquestionably the leader of the Host of Rohan:

> And with that shout the king came. His horse was white as snow, golden was his shield, and his spear was long. At his right hand was Aragorn, Elendil's heir, behind him rode the lords of the house of Eorl the Young. Light sprang in the sky. Night departed.
> "Forth Eorlingas!" With a cry and a great noise they charged. (528; III:7)

The change was required in order to accomplish several objectives; among them, to begin to build Aragorn into a person the audience can accept as someone with potential for kingly greatness; to foreshadow and intensify Denethor's subsequent jealousy of Aragorn; and to give Théoden his own personal demons to fight, so that he presents a more complex personality.

In both novel and film all things come to crux in *The Return of the King*, which contains much counsel and several councils. Final decisions must be taken and the results of all good or bad counsel, whether taken or rejected, come to their fruition. In the novel, Denethor's ultimate rejection of Gandalf's counsel becomes a significant element of plot and theme, and Tolkien reiterates the word "counsel" as he develops Denethor's character. The word appears as Gandalf and Pippin approach Minas Tirith. They encounter Ingold, the leader of the men repairing the wall of the Pelennor, who uses the word as a blessing: "'Fare you well!' said Ingold; . . . 'May you bring good counsel to Denethor in his need, and to us all, Mithrandir!'" (733; V:1). When Gandalf and Pippin enter the citadel of the kings of Minas Tirith for their initial interview with the Steward, Gandalf salutes him: "Hail, Lord and Steward of Minas Tirith, Denethor son of Ecthelion! I am come with counsel and tidings in this dark hour" (738; V:1). And Denethor begins his fateful rejection of counsel almost immediately. He sees Pippin, asks if he is one of the Halflings who saw Boromir die, adding, "little love do I bear the name, since those accursed words came to trouble our counsels and drew away my son on the wild errand to his death" (738; V:1). Denethor mellows slightly when Pippin gives him his offer of service; however, when Gandalf tries to bring the discussion back to business he suggests that Denethor has been manipulating the situation and deliberately insulting Gandalf by deflecting any real opportunity for counsel: "Do you not think that I do not understand your purpose in questioning for an hour one who knows the least, while I sit by?" (741; V:1). Denethor replies, "Pride would be folly that disdained help and counsel at need; but you deal out such gifts according to your own designs. Yet the Lord of Gondor is not to be made the fool of other men's purposes, however worthy. And to him there is no purpose higher in the world as it now stands than the good of Gondor . . ." (741; V:1).

Thus Denethor makes clear he holds Gandalf's counsel at arm's length since he suspects Gandalf's intentions are not exclusively for the good of Gondor. Gandalf remains calm, but points out that he is also a steward, but his responsibility extends over "all worthy things that are in peril as the world now stands, those are my care" (742; V:1), and leaves Denethor's presence.

Pippin is concerned that he might not have done well. Gandalf reassures him, adding, "you are now sworn to his service. I do not know what put it into your head, or your heart, to do that. But it was well done. I did not hinder it, for generous deed should not be checked by cold counsel" (743; V:1). He adds a little later, "I must go, Pippin. I must go to this lords' council and learn what I can" (743; V:1), for he is already aware that, while he can attend Denethor's councils, he will be able to gather information but not to reciprocate. Information will flow in one direction only—from Denethor to Gandalf.

When we next witness a council of Denethor's, it is in "the private chamber of the Lord of the City. There deep seats were set about a brazier of charcoal; and wine was brought; and there Pippin, hardly noticed, stood behind the chair of Denethor" (793; V:4) while Faramir reports to Denethor of his raid in Ithilien and of the subsequent capture and release of Frodo and Samwise. He asks, "'I hope that I have not done ill?' He looked at his father," who responds,

> "Ill?' cried Denethor, and his eyes flashed suddenly. 'Why do you ask? . . . Your bearing is lowly in my presence, yet it is long now since you turned from your own way at my counsel. . . . [H]ave I not seen your eye fixed on Mithrandir, seeking whether you said well or too much? He has long had your heart in his keeping." (794; V:4)

The discussion continues as Faramir replies, "If what I have done displeases you, my father . . . I wish I had known your counsel before the burden of so weighty a judgment was thrust on me" (794; V:4). As Denethor criticizes him further, Faramir tries to defuse the escalating tensions:

> "Do you wish then . . . that our places had been exchanged?"
>
> "Yes, I wish that indeed," said Denethor. "For Boromir was loyal to me and no wizard's pupil. . . . He would have brought me a mighty gift."
>
> For a moment Faramir's restraint gave way. "I would ask you, my father, to remember why it was that I, not he, was in Ithilien. On one occasion at least your counsel has prevailed, not long ago. It was the Lord of the City that gave the errand to him." (795; V:4)

Thus, Tolkien describes not only the tension between father and son, but also suggests that Denethor has been counseling neither wisely nor well of late. When Gandalf interposes, pointing out that Boromir, increasingly under the influence of the Ring, would not have remained true to his father, Denethor is again abrasive to both men *even as* he lays claim to wisdom: "You are wise, maybe, Mithrandir, yet with all your subtleties you have not all wisdom. Counsels may be found that are neither the webs of wizards nor the haste of fools. I have in this matter more lore and wisdom than you deem " (795; V:4). To lay personal claim to other counsels and to wisdom is a dangerous proceeding in Tolkien's work, especially when we discover that for Denethor this means "If I had this thing now in the deep vaults of this citadel, we should not then shake with dread under this gloom, fearing the worst, and our counsels would be undisturbed. If you do not trust me to endure the test, you do not know me yet" (796; V:4).

Gandalf tries, once more, to impress upon the Steward that the Ring would have overpowered him, that "Were it buried beneath the roots of Mindolluin, still it would burn your mind away . . . " (796; V:4). Denethor is furious, but backs away from the discussion after indicating that he will probably send Faramir back to Osgiliath to resist the first onslaught of Sauron's forces.

I have gone into some detail on this council, in part because the interplay on the word "counsel" demonstrates how very untrustworthy Denethor's state of mind is, and also shows the tension between Denethor on the one side and Gandalf and Faramir on the other. This entire sequence is treated very differently by Jackson: it not only becomes less subtle; it becomes much more brutal.

In the film, when Pippin and Gandalf are about to enter the Citadel for the first time, Gandalf cautions Pippin against saying anything whatever (not just, as in the novel, to say nothing about Boromir or the manner of his death) and to remain silent. Upon approaching Denethor's seat, Gandalf announces, with a hopeful, placatory smile, "I am come with tidings in this dark hour, and with counsel." Denethor immediately rejects the offer. Still, Gandalf reminds Denethor of his duty: "as Steward you are charged with the defense of this city," but this Denethor is reluctant to take charge or lead in any sort of defense; Gandalf must shortly get Pippin to climb the beacon tower in order to light it and call aid from Rohan (*Return*, scene 20: "The Sacrifice of Faramir").

Then, the council of three becomes a discussion between two persons—Denethor and Faramir—from which Gandalf has simply been physically excluded. As Denethor prepares to eat, he maintains that Osgiliath, which has already been taken by the enemy, who have entrenched themselves there, must be retaken. Pippin waits on Denethor and other servants are silently present; however, only Faramir and Denethor are actually in council; the bulk of the vast hall, cathedral-like, is hollowly empty. Into this emptiness Denethor states, "Is there a captain here who cares to do his lord's will?" As Janet Croft has pointed out, this scene is evocative of another moment, in which Henry II of England reputedly said, "Will no one rid me of this meddlesome priest?" and thus sent four of his men to cut down Thomas à Becket in Canterbury Cathedral. The parallel is sketched not only to intensify Faramir's saintliness in the restraint and obedience he shows his father but also in the fact that he is being sent to what is unquestionably martyrdom (*Return*, scene 18: "Allegiance to Denethor").

The scene is intensified by the fact that all this is interspersed with Denethor's preparations for sitting down to a meal to which Faramir has not been invited. The novel contains two occasions when Denethor extends hospitality—the first, when Gandalf and Pippin arrive at the Citadel. Here he commands wine and white cakes be brought for his guests. The second incident occurs at the second council, when "wine is brought" (793; V:4). In neither case does Denethor appear to partake of the refreshments. In the film, however, he never offers hospitality to anyone; instead, a meal consisting of meat and assorted items (among which tomatoes and grapes figure prominently), is brought exclusively for him. While servants spread the meal before him, Pippin attends him as he eats. Before partaking, Denethor commands Faramir to charge the enemy. Then, in one of the most horrific sequences of the film, Denethor begins to eat as the cavalry files through Minas Tirith and the civilian population looks on, strewing the way with flowers, for everyone is aware the men are going to their deaths. Denethor demands that Pippin sing; he chooses a haunting elegy. As the men line up for the charge, Denethor begins to eat —greedily, cracking tomatoes and allowing the juice to run down his chin. As the charge gallops into the arrows of the enemy, and the pig-like orc commander begins to slaver blood that also runs down his chin as he slaughters the men of Minas Tirith, the point is exceedingly clear: Denethor, in his despair, anger and brutality, has become a monster among men (*Return*, scene 20: "The Sacrifice of Faramir").

Tolkien's Denethor, while equally a victim of despair, retains his humanity. He sends Faramir out to Osgiliath on an ill-advised and exceedingly dangerous mission, but the enemy has not yet made the crossing over the river Anduin and has not yet taken Osgiliath. Faramir has been sent to hinder that crossing rather than to engage in a suicidal charge. So there is more hope that some, at least, of the defenders will survive. Still, note how Denethor goes about this:

> In truth Faramir did not go by his own choosing. But the Lord of the City was master of his Council, and he was in no mood that day to bow to others. Early in the morning the Council had been summoned. There all the captains judged that because of the threat in the South their force was too weak to make any stroke of war on their own part, unless perchance the Riders of Rohan yet should come. Meanwhile they must man the walls and wait.
>
> . . . [A]t length Faramir said: "I do not oppose your will, sire. Since you are robbed of Boromir, I will go and do what I can in his stead—if you command it."
>
> "I do so," said Denethor.
>
> "Then farewell!" said Faramir. "But if I should return, think better of me!"
>
> "That depends on the manner of your return," said Denethor. (798; V:4)

He is implacable and, even though here he has a full council (Gandalf as well as all the princes and captains of Gondor who had brought reinforcements the evening before are present) Denethor takes counsel only from himself, despite the collective wisdom of seasoned captains of war. In Tolkienian terms, he is already consumed by hubris, and fated. All that is needed is the catalyst. But he is also a man determined to protect his people. He wears armor that he has worn for many years; he commanded the beacons be lit before Gandalf ever entered Gondor; he has had the walls of the Pelennor and the Rammas Echor reinforced. Thus, even though he is consumed by his personal fears and jealousies, he never quite becomes monstrous. He resembles Agamemnon of *The Iliad*, whereas Jackson's Denethor, simplified and drawn in lurid colors, evokes associations with parental child-killers and devourers such as Chronos, or Jason and Medea, or perhaps Tamora from *Titus Andronicus*. Tolkien's Denethor dies on a funeral pyre, grasping the *palantír* of Minas Tirith; Jackson's, a ball of flame, throws himself off the "knee" of Mount Mindolluin, his long fall symbolic of his personal fall from humanity.

Another council in *The Return of the King* that has significant implications is the one called "The Last Debate" in both book and film. This occurs after the victory of the Pelennor Fields. In the novel, Aragorn and Gandalf, along with other captains of war decide their next move. Prince Imrahil initiates this council:

> When the Prince Imrahil had parted from Legolas and Gimli, he at once sent for Éomer; and he went down with him from the City, and they came to the tents of Aragorn that were set up on the field not far from the place where King Théoden had fallen. And there they took counsel together with Gandalf and Aragorn and the sons of Elrond (860; V:9)

Although Prince Imrahil convenes it, however, it is Gandalf who leads throughout the council. It is he who points out that Denethor had been correct when he had pointed out that *"against the Power that has now arisen there is no victory."* Yet, maintains Gandalf, "You have only a choice of evils; and prudence would counsel you to strengthen such strong places as you have, and there await the onset . . . " (860; V:9).

Imrahil indicates the lack of maturity in such a course: "Then you would have us retreat to Minas Tirith, or Dol Amroth, or to Dunharrow, and there sit like children on sand-castles when the tide is flowing?" (860; V:9).

Gandalf responds: "That would be no new counsel. . . . But no! . . . I do not counsel prudence." Instead, he advises they take the offensive by taking the war to the Black Gates of Mordor:

> "This, then, is my counsel. . . . We cannot achieve victory by arms, but by arms we can give the Ring-bearer his only chance, frail though it be.
>
> "As Aragorn has begun, so we must go on. We must push Sauron to his last throw. . . . We must march out to meet him at once. We must make ourselves the bait, though his jaws should close on us." (862; V:9)

Aragorn responds first: "Let none now reject the counsels of Gandalf, whose long labours against Sauron come at last to their test"; then Elrohir states: "From the North we came with this purpose, and from Elrond our father we brought this very counsel. We will not turn back" (862; V:9). Éomer declares he trusts, and follows, Aragorn as his ally; Prince Imrahil, now functioning as Steward *pro tem* of Gondor, declares that as far as he is concerned, Aragorn is his liege-lord and that he therefore owes obedience to his king; however, as Steward, he expresses concern for leaving Minas Tirith undefended. Gandalf responds: "I do not counsel you to leave the City all unmanned" (863; V:92), for he has already considered how many men were needed to guard the City and still put a respectable force into the field. Swiftly the Council reaches consensus to march upon Mordor. Therefore, although this Council also decides on what appears to be a suicide mission, the decision is not the result of one unadvised will imposed upon others; it is a parallel, yet distinctly antithetical decision to Denethor's fatal command, based on the good counsel not only of Gandalf but also Elrond.

The film makes a number of insignificant modifications to The Last Debate but at least one all-important change. For simplicity's sake and for dramatic effect Jackson eliminated the feudal principalities of Gondor, so the military forces are only those of Minas Tirith and Rohan. Consequently the participants in The Last Debate consist of Aragorn, Gandalf, Éomer, Legolas and Gimli, and the place where the council is held is the Great Hall within the Citadel. So it becomes a gathering of friends, and the atmosphere is casual (Gimli sits in Denethor's seat, smokes, and interjects his usual sardonic comments). The only step to a greater formality is that Aragorn's hair is combed and his clothing is richer in color and quality than it has been. Gandalf begins by expressing a deep worry for Frodo, who "has passed beyond my sight. The darkness is deep." Aragorn tries to be reassuring: "If Sauron had the Ring, we would know it," but Gandalf is not comforted: "It's only a matter of time," he replies; "He has suffered a defeat, yes, but behind the walls of Mordor our enemy is regrouping." Gandalf sees the problem; but here, he does *not* see the solution—or, at least, he appears not to; his expression is anxious—but is he anxious for Frodo, or is he anxious for Aragorn? This is left deliberately ambiguous: is the ultimate counselor without advice, or is he waiting, hoping, that Aragorn will pick up the reins of leadership?

And Aragorn does. He takes the initiative, stating: " . . . There's still hope for Frodo. He needs time, and safe passage across the plains of Gorgoroth. We can give him that." Gimli coughs, presumably in astonishment at this foolhardy concept. Gandalf offers no military insights; instead, it is Éomer, and he merely expresses his doubts about any military success: "We cannot achieve victory through strength of arms." It is at this moment that Aragorn steps in with breadth of vision: "Not for ourselves, but we can give Frodo a chance if we keep Sauron's eye fixed upon us—keep him blind to all else that moves." In Aragorn's two statements we see Jackson's change of real significance: this scene is not Gandalf's finest hour, his best counsel; instead, it belongs to Aragorn. While each character has something to say, the group is led, and inspired, by Aragorn. Jackson has, throughout *The Return*, been developing Aragorn's kingly qualities, a process that has been escalating from the moment he accepted Narsil from Elrond's hands and when he determined to find, and command, the Army of the Dead. It now culminates in a two-part movement: part one occurs here, in The Last Debate, where he manifests the kind of breadth of understanding that few have had throughout *The Lord of the Rings* (*Return,* scene 46: "The Last Debate").

The second movement is the demonstration of his ability to inspire men to follow him in battle, even, indeed, as Éowyn had told him —"to death." This of course is demonstrated in his speech before the Black Gates:

> Hold your ground! Hold your ground! Sons of Gondor, of Rohan! My brothers! I see in your eyes the same fear that would take the heart of me! A day may come when the courage of men fails, when we forsake our friends and break all bonds of fellowship. But it is not this day. An hour of wolves and shattered shields, when the age of men comes crashing down. But it is not this day! This day we fight! By all that you hold dear on this good Earth, I bid you stand, Men of the West!
>
> (*Return,* scene 48: "The Black Gate Opens")

Not by accident does this echo another famous speech, also spoken by a man who was reluctant to become king, but, having accepted the responsibility, determined to be a good one, and who went to a war in which he found himself fighting a battle against overwhelming odds. But he fought it, won it, and, with his victory, won a country, a princess, and the respect of his people:

> We few, we happy few, we band of brothers;
> For he to-day that sheds his blood with me
> Shall be my brother.
>
> (*Henry V* 4.3.60-2)

In the film, Denethor not only rejects counsel but rejects all help and shrivels his real concerns into entirely selfish ones: his sons, his stewardship, his dynasty. He, and the Ents (charming though they might be) care only for what is theirs. Théoden is initially like this as well; bitter that Gondor had not come to his aid against Saruman, he also expresses reluctance to help Gondor, but overcomes this when he sees the beacons, and although he listens to counsel is often testy about accepting it. Of all the leaders, Aragorn always sees the whole spectrum and all the implications. His is not a question of pride but, perhaps, of excessive humility. It is this humility that makes him listen to good counsel; and in these two scenes, he proves he has become a man of both action and counsel himself: he has developed his own insight along with the confidence with which to act on his perceptions and decisions. Tolkien's Aragorn does not go through this process: he is the heir of Elendil from start to finish, having no doubts about his right, or ability, to rule, should he ever achieve the opportunity to do so. Jackson's Aragorn does not want the responsibility because he is afraid he might be Isildur's heir rather than Elendil's, and that he might succumb to the same weaknesses of pride and lust for power that Isildur did. He is never in any doubt that he has the qualities of a hero: he knows he has courage and that he can fight very well. But being a hero is one thing; being a king is another. He gradually proves his own motives to himself. When Elrond brings him Narsil reforged as Andúril, Aragorn accepts it only when he becomes convinced that, first, Arwen will die if Sauron is not defeated, and second, that Sauron's defeat is impossible without the help of the Dead, who will follow only the heir of Elendil, and the only way to prove his credentials is by means of the sword. When he accepts the weapon, Aragorn knows that he has accepted the destiny that goes along with the weapon—but he also knows he has done so for selfless reasons. He had given Arwen up so that she would be free to leave Middle-earth. She has instead chosen to stay, and only he can help her stay alive. From this point, Aragorn begins to take charge. Both Gandalf and Elrond have advised him to take the Paths of the Dead. Now he does so, and dominates the King of the Dead; he is no longer a captain of Rohan but the leader of an army, and, as the leader in counsel and council, the initiator of a strategic and highly dangerous "diversion" in which, as uncrowned monarch, he inspires his troops indeed to follow him, even to death. He has always been a man of courage and intelligence; now he is inspired as a leader in council and in action. Jackson suggests these are the qualities of a great king, of one who is, indeed, the heir of Elendil and not of Isildur.

In "The Feminine Principle in Tolkien" Melanie Rawls argued that "Tolkien believes that *gender* and *sex* are not one and the same" (5). Rawls deals primarily with *The Silmarillion*, and in so doing lays the groundwork for *The Lord of the Rings*, in which the Jungian principles Rawls wants to discuss are not so readily perceivable. She points out that the Feminine is concerned with understanding, and among the positive elements of understanding are love, counsel, intuition (insight and foresight), mercy, and compassion. The Masculine is concerned with power, and its positive elements encompass law, action, reason and justice (6). Rawls's discussion deals mainly with establishing that Tolkien respected and understood not only the Feminine but also the difference between Masculine and Feminine. What I also found interesting in her analysis is the fact that very few of Tolkien's male characters are able to keep a perfect, equal balance between the Masculine and the Feminine within themselves: Elrond, according to Rawls, is mainly Feminine; I suggest Tolkien's Aragorn is mainly Masculine. Perhaps only Gandalf is perfectly poised between the two: as a Steward for the Valar, his role is primarily that of understanding, and his notable function is that of counselor. Yet, as Wizard, he is empowered to act, and does so without hesitation when necessary. I suggest that, by the conclusion of *The Return of the King*, Jackson has shifted this: it is Aragorn who is perfectly poised between the Feminine and the Masculine. In *The Silmarillion* the males who achieve real happiness are those who have consorts who offer them balance: Thingol and Melian, Beren and Lúthien, for example. In Tolkien's *Return* Gandalf offers this balance to a Masculine Aragorn who continues to need, among other things, counsel: therefore it is Gandalf who leads him up the heights of Mount Mindolluin to find the sapling White Tree and who, while there, advises him always to plant any seed the tree might bring to full development. But in Jackson's version Aragorn is perfectly balanced within himself: he may *want* Arwen to fill his personal life with joy, but he does not *need* Arwen to provide qualities lacking in himself — the feminine qualities of intuition, understanding, love, counsel, mercy or compassion—he contains them along with the ability to act with power. Arwen appears almost as an after-thought at the coronation—as a friend of mine has observed, it is as if "and, behind the third door—the Fairy Princess!" She, and her son, will fill the emotional gap, the isolation a ruler must inevitably face, and there is no doubt that Aragorn will always listen to her: he always listens to good counsel. Hers is not a weak personality; nor does she lack wisdom. Still, one has the distinct impression that Jackson's Aragorn, even if he lived with a silent sadness, would have ruled successfully without her; as a king, he has become self-sufficient.

WORKS CITED

The Lord of the Rings: The Fellowship of the Ring. Special Extended DVD Edition. Screenplay by Peter Jackson, Fran Walsh, and Philippa Boyens. Perf. Elijah Wood et al. Dir. Peter Jackson. United States: New Line Home Entertainment, 2002.

The Lord of the Rings: The Return of the King. Theatrical Release DVD. Screenplay by Peter Jackson, Fran Walsh, and Philippa Boyens. Perf. Elijah Wood et al. Dir. Peter Jackson. United States, New Line Home Entertainment, 2004.

The Lord of the Rings: The Two Towers. Special Extended DVD Edition. Screenplay by Peter Jackson, Fran Walsh, and Philippa Boyens. Perf. Elijah Wood et al. Dir. Peter Jackson. United States: New Line Home Entertainment, 2003.

Rawls, Melanie. "The Feminine Principle in Tolkien." *Mythlore* 38 (1984): 3-13.

Tolkien, J.R.R. *The Lord of the Rings.* 2nd ed. With Note on the Text by Douglas A. Anderson. Boston: Houghton Mifflin, 1994.

—. *The Silmarillion.* 1st American ed. Boston: Houghton Mifflin, 1977.

PART IV:

A WOMAN'S PART

TOLKIEN'S WOMEN (AND MEN):
THE FILMS AND THE BOOK

JANE CHANCE

J.R.R. Tolkien's epic fantasy, *The Lord of the Rings*, is now beginning to be accepted by the academic world as canonical in the literature of the twentieth century, in part because of the BBC/Waterstone Bookstore's book poll in Britain in the nineties (Shippey, *Author of the Century xxi*), but more importantly because of the three recent films by New Zealand director Peter Jackson for New Line Cinema, in 2001, 2002, and 2003. The films' popularity has prompted Tolkien fans, readers, and scholars to ask how clearly and well Jackson has adapted to film medium this important modern classic, and what in particular he has left out or changed (and to what purpose).

These questions bear a certain importance for scholars, in particular, who know something about the medieval genre of *The Lord of the Rings*—epic and romance—given Tolkien's own postmodern understanding in his book, of epic as "anti-epic." Certainly Oxford medievalist Tolkien, stirred by the heroic exploits of *Beowulf* and *The Battle of Maldon,* Old Norse sagas, Welsh romances, and the Finnish epic, *Kalevala,* re-created his own version of the Middle Ages in the world of Middle-earth (Chance, *Tolkien's Art; Tolkien the Medievalist*; and *Tolkien and the Invention of Myth*). However, wounded spiritually by his own participation in the Battle of the Somme during World War I—a battle in which he lost important school friends (Garth)—Tolkien recast the medieval hero in this world in new, unlikely, and multiple forms. These forms include small Hobbits, suspiciously dark Rangers like Strider, sisters and sister-daughters (nieces) like Éowyn, sister of Éomer and niece to King Théoden, and second sons like Faramir, younger brother of Boromir.[1]

---

[1] Éowyn is niece to Théoden, brother of her mother, Théodwyn. In the medieval romance the quest-hero frequently appears as the nephew to the king—the son of the king's sister, or "sister-son"—as was Gawain, nephew to King Arthur in the fourteenth-century *Gawain and the Green Knight* and son of Morgan la Fay and her half-brother, Arthur, in the

Tolkien chose as the heroic adversary not the Vikings or a monster like Grendel or the dragon, but the antiheroic and formless tyrant Sauron, a fallen tyrannical Maia who longs for power. Most importantly, Tolkien changed the nature of the epic quest from a journey to join in the war of nations to an *anti*-quest, a *non*-battle, and a lonely trip to run an errand—to throw something away—across the margins of the battlefield.

What has Jackson done to Tolkien's anti-epic? First and most obviously, he returns it to the film genre of the Hollywood epic by transforming *The Lord of the Rings* into a high-tech Computer-Generated Imagery (CGI) adventure. The never-ending scenes with Goblins, Orcs, the Cave Troll, and the winged Balrog, or with Wargs, Oliphaunts, Orcs, Ents, Men, and Nazgûl, flash by so indiscriminately that the eye cannot focus on a single unifying thread, although in Tolkien's book such battling occurs offstage and in relatively little narrative space. Most unaccountably, there are few quiet moments in these films, despite Tolkien's penchant for the moving intimate exchange between two characters or for dramatic inner revelation. Even in the few scenes of anger, love, and grief, Jackson pushes the envelope.[2]

Such rewriting is not wholly unexpected on the part of horror-film-specialist Jackson. The dead bodies and severed heads littering the floor of the Mines of Moria constitute the same kind of Jacksonian grotesquerie found in his film *The Frighteners* (1996). But this is an inexplicable step backward from his fine, critically acclaimed film, *Heavenly Creatures* (1994), which dealt with the murder of a mother by her fourteen-year-old daughter and her daughter's best friend, Juliet Hulme (later to earn fame as Anne Perry, detective-story writer). The sensitivity shown in this film would have enhanced his treatment of the quieter scenes in *The Lord of the Rings*.

If Jackson's film adaptation of Tolkien may more precisely be designated as just one interpretation, or "translation"—to borrow a term from some of the Oxford don's most important scholarly articles about the necessity for literal accuracy in any scholarly rendition of a work in a

---

fifteenth-century Sir Thomas Malory's *Morte Darthur*. To my knowledge no woman has played this role in a medieval romance or epic.

[2] For example, in *The Fellowship of the Ring*, when Jackson's Gimli, who has imagined that Dwarf hospitality would be extended to the Fellowship by his kinsman Balin as a respite from the rigors of the journey (although Dwarves are not known for their hospitality elsewhere in Tolkien's work), finally finds the tomb of Balin, he sobs horribly in a most un-Tolkienian moment of grief. In Tolkien's text Gimli merely "cast his hood over his face" (312; II:4).

different language[3]—then how has Jackson interpreted Tolkien? What has Jackson omitted from, added to, and changed in Tolkien's text in a way that distorts the meaning of epic (or anti-epic)?

To answer these questions it is necessary to explain, first, the screenwriter's tight focus on selected, representative incidents and his or her omission of the didactic and non-dramatic—non-visual—portions of a text. Jackson has had to reduce *The Lord of the Rings* to three relatively spare action films. This demand results from the nature of the medium: if in a screenplay one page counts as one minute of film time, the screenplay for each four-hour film must be about 240 pages long—but Tolkien's single-spaced, crammed pages in *The Fellowship of the Ring* alone amount to 479 pages, or the equivalent of about 960 double-spaced screenplay pages. Further, each film is not divided into two consecutive books, as are *The Fellowship of the Ring, The Two Towers,* and *The Return of the King.* The first half of *The Fellowship of the Ring* film—the first twenty-seven scenes of the extended version—is equivalent to the twelve chapters of the first book, which ends with the Flight to the Ford. In the second half—another twenty-one scenes—the film compresses ten chapters. Deleted from the first film are central episodes primarily from the first book, such as Tom Bombadil's rescue of the Hobbits from the Old Forest and the Barrow-downs. Although these omitted episodes may not seem so crucial to the dramatic narrative, they (and others that precede them) constitute about seven of the twelve chapters in the first book of *The Fellowship of the Ring* alone.

By changing the focus from Frodo's hero-journey in the book to the love story of Arwen and Aragorn in the films, Jackson subordinates and devalues (or at least defers) Tolkien's key theme of the ennoblement of the ordinary to the more ordinary marriage of the nobility. In the first film, in the "Flight to the Ford," Jackson substitutes Arwen (Liv Tyler), daughter of Elrond (Hugo Weaving), for Frodo's rescuer, the Elf-lord Glorfindel on his horse, Asfaloth (*Fellowship*, scene 21: "Flight to the Ford"). Although Jackson makes other changes to Tolkien's text in all of the films, the emphasis on Arwen as a feminized Amazon/Valkyrie warrior astride her own white horse, along with what might be termed an infantilization of Frodo and the Hobbits, represents his most egregious

---

[3] See my discussion of Tolkien's various comments about the translator's obligation to provide a faithful rendering of the text in Chance, *Tolkien's Art,* 26-28, which assimilates comments from the preface to Tolkien and E. V. Gordon's *Gawain* edition; the preface to Tolkien's translation of *Sir Gawain, Pearl,* and *Sir Orfeo;* and the 1940 prefatory remarks to the John Clark-Hall translation of *Beowulf,* among other works which Tolkien taught and of which he was fond.

refiguration of Tolkien's epic. In the first film, Jackson dilutes the heroic development of Frodo and the other Hobbits, just as he similarly weakens the role of Aragorn to bolster Arwen. In the second film, under the director's even freer hand, Aragorn becomes stronger and more decisive, while a fight seems to be shaping up on his account between Arwen and Éowyn. The Hobbits are lost in the narrative amid the thunderous battles, despite moments of heroism by Merry and Pippin and Frodo and Sam. In the third film, Arwen finally chooses her own destiny because of a vision of her future child, and in the end marries Aragorn, while the Hobbits, whose heroism saves the day in many ways, accomplish much of their action through unseemly violence against adversaries and companions. At the same time, the Hobbits' loyalty and love for one another contrast starkly with the murder of Déagol by Sméagol after he finds the Ring, in a scene that Jackson pulls from the first volume and inserts as an overarching theme at the beginning of the third film. Why has Jackson infantilized Frodo and the Hobbits, reduced the manliness of Aragorn, and enhanced the power of Arwen in all three films?

What Tolkien has to say about the role of Arwen and Aragorn and the journey of the Hobbits, in a draft of a letter to Michael Straight written in January or February 1956, is most significant for understanding Tolkien's postmodern anti-epic of *The Lord of the Rings*:

> I regard the role of Arwen and Aragorn as the most important of the Appendices; it is part of the essential story, and is only placed so, because it could not be worked into the main narrative without destroying its structure: which is planned to be "hobbito-centric," that is, primarily a study of the ennoblement (or sanctification) of the humble. (*Letters*, 237)

Tolkien speaks, surprisingly, about the importance of Arwen and Aragorn to the story. But it is a story he has for the most part placed, not in the narrative of the epic (or anti-epic) fantasy, where his primary concern is to ennoble the Hobbits, but in the back, in the appendices.

Truly, this theme of ennoblement of the humble is the heart of the narrative in Tolkien's book. *The Lord of the Rings* is not about large battles and the killing of the enemy by the aristocracy of Middle-earth, be they regal Men or reigning Elves and Wizards. Instead, this anti-epic is about the way that the humble—the Hobbits—come to be ennobled, empowered as heroes, and how they earn their place in an epic narrative in which the background of the battle scenes and the clash of metal on metal have become, strangely, the foreground. What is lacking in the films is depth of characterization, and therefore the acting is offset by the fellowship of the ensemble. However, just as the first film presents Frodo, Merry, Pippin, and Sam as childish Hobbits, and the Rightful King, Aragorn, as passive, the second and third films compensate by tracing their growing maturation.

Having criticized Jackson's treatment as unreflective of Tolkien's intentions, I will seem to contradict myself by now suggesting that Jackson's changes are truer to Tolkien's overarching drama, the story of Middle-earth and its four ages, in which *The Lord of the Rings* portrays the transition from the Third Age, of Elves, to the Fourth Age, of Man. Jackson's most important changes in all three films, which generally appear to give women—in particular, Arwen—a greater role than that found in Tolkien's anti-epic, are actually intrinsic to Tolkien's larger contextualizing mythology, which features Arwen's great sacrifice of her Elven immortality. Less justifiably in Jackson's version, a puerile Frodo and Sam demonstrate the effect of the Ring through violence, at least in the third film, which exaggerates the heroic change in their characters at the end by means of dramatic contrast, as does the establishing shot in the third film, in which a more Hobbit-like Sméagol murders Déagol because of the Ring. I will first examine Jackson's changes in the Hobbits before returning to his emphasis on the story of Arwen and Aragorn.

Of the changes most important in the first film, the infantilization of the Hobbits (in part to appeal to the nineteen-to-twenty-six-year-old male youth market) stands out most glaringly.[4] Frodo diminishes from a fifty-year-old Hobbit to the boyish (even childlike) Elijah Wood in the central role as he begins the quest. Even if it is argued that Frodo, at thirty-three, is in fact just coming out of his "tweens" at his coming-of-age party in the text of *The Fellowship of the Ring*—a "Long Expected Party" like

---

[4] Aspects of the respite in Lothlórien are also changed or omitted in the first film, but in line with the general patterns we have detected. Only Frodo, not Sam, looks into Galadriel's mirror. Gifts from Galadriel are not given out to all four Hobbits (except in the extended version) (*Fellowship*, scene 41: "Farewell to Lórien"). Nor does Jackson return us to the Shire to see it scoured, as it is at the end of book 6 of *The Lord of the Rings*. Galadriel—played admirably by Cate Blanchett as simultaneously regal and ethereal—does not explain any of her history: why she might be expected to want the Ring (which we learn in the chapter on Galadriel in *Unfinished Tales*) and why Galadriel's refusal means she has, in fact, won while seemingly losing power and being diminished (which means, that is, she must cross over to the West and give up rule of Lórien). Her mate, Celeborn, seems to have been erased in importance completely, although intermarriage of different branches of the Elf family (Telerin, Noldorin, Sindarin), as in the marriage of Celeborn and Galadriel—or of different kindreds, Maia and Elf, Elf and Man—looms throughout Tolkien's mythology as an important theme. In the extended version of the film, in this same scene, Celeborn does address Aragorn as the heir to the throne.

179

Bilbo's own birthday party in the text—he does not leave on the quest for some fifteen to twenty years after that party, at a "sober" age that Tolkien describes as "significant": "So it went on, until his forties were running out, and his fiftieth birthday was drawing near; fifty was a number that he felt was somehow significant (or ominous); it was at any rate at that age that adventure had suddenly befallen Bilbo" (42; I:2). Tolkien himself would have been nearing fifty in the late 1930s when he began *The Lord of the Rings,* and he was into his sixties at the time that it was first published, in 1953. It seems unlikely that Tolkien intended Frodo to resemble a teenager, especially taking into consideration Tolkien's remark to Deborah Webster, in Letter 213, that "I am myself a Hobbit" (*Letters,* 288). Further, the films' logic about the reason for the Hobbit's youthfulness is inconsistent. Although Frodo appears young because of Elijah Wood's own youth during this period of passage while Bilbo still possesses the Ring—which according to Tolkien's text preserves youthfulness—Bilbo (as portrayed by Ian Holm) always appears extremely old, even at the moment he gives up the Ring to Gandalf.

That literal childishness we see in Frodo is characteristic of all the Hobbits of the Fellowship and not just the Ringbearer. For example, in the first film, when Merry (Dominic Monaghan) and Pippin (Billy Boyd) burst forth exuberantly from the cornfield with some carrots and other vegetables stolen from Farmer Maggot's garden, they literally bump into Frodo and Sam (Sean Astin). This encounter conflates episodes from the book's Farmer Maggot chapter (I:4, "A Short Cut to Mushrooms"), in which it was Frodo in particular who as a child used to steal mushrooms from the farmer. And in the film at the Inn of the Prancing Pony, the Hobbits, like typical university students, all want a pint of beer (*Fellowship,* scene 15: "At the Sign of the Prancing Pony"). In the film Pippin is criticized by Gandalf at the Mines of Moria when he terms the Hobbit's deed of knocking a dead man into the well "stupidity" ("Fool of a Took!" is the wizard's response to this "nuisance" in the book [305; II:4]). Certainly it is stupid, for in the film Pippin thereby awakens malice in the persons of the Orcs; simple Pippin, also always hungry, elsewhere in Tolkien's book and in the film wants second breakfasts, elevenses, lunch, tea, *and* dinner. But in the text, it is not a Hobbit alone who awakens the Orcs or the Balrog: it is the Man Boromir whose stone first causes trouble before they enter Moria by alerting the Watcher in the Water—and there are no dead Orcs or Dwarves perched on the well (299, 305; II:4).

Jackson deemphasizes the Hobbits and Aragorn in the first film so that he can empower and ennoble them in the later films. In support, Jackson emphasizes male bonding at the end of the first film in an understanding of Tolkien's own interest throughout his life and works in male camaraderie and heroic friendship and service: mainly through showing Aragorn (Viggo Mortensen), Gimli (John Rhys-Davies), and Legolas (Orlando Bloom)—as Man, Dwarf, and Elf—committing themselves to the pursuit of the captured Merry and Pippin. Accompanying this male camaraderie in the film is Boromir's redemptive confession to Aragorn at the moment of his death and his formal submission as guardian of Gondor to his king, just as Sam is also rescued from drowning by his master, Frodo, in the boat and expresses his love for him (*Fellowship*, scenes 45 and 46: "The Departure of Boromir" and "The Road Goes Ever On"). These are all rich, masculinized, Tolkienian moments, true to the text in a figurative sense.

As Frodo and the other Hobbits diminish into naughty children in the film of *The Fellowship of the Ring*, so also is Arwen made into a hero, chiefly in the Flight to the Ford scene (*Fellowship*, scene 21). Arwen's beefed-up role in the film creates a female presence where there was none in Tolkien's text. In the film the Black Riders pursue Arwen, who carries Frodo protectively on her white horse like a mother clutching her baby. Arwen has ignored Aragorn's overprotective patronization and holds Frodo herself because she can ride faster than Aragorn—a characterization wholly missing in Tolkien's book. In fact, when Arwen first appears in the scene, she has been out looking for Aragorn, as Glorfindel was looking for Frodo in the book. She herself carries Frodo to Rivendell on her white horse rather than permitting him to ride Asfaloth alone and bravely confront the Black Riders at the Ford.

Second, in the film Arwen tells Aragorn she will forsake immortality (in a scene that jumps ahead to the third volume of the novel)—reminding us of her role in and importance to Tolkien's mythology as revealed in the appendices and *The Silmarillion*, which depends upon her uniting Elf with Man to bring about the peaceful transition to the Fourth Age, of Man.

Third, in the film, at the Ford itself, Arwen rescues Frodo from the Black Riders, as an overpowering maternal *dea ex machina* in the guise of an Amazonian warrior, an event unprecedented in Tolkien's *Fellowship of the Ring* (or in either of the other two volumes, for that matter). "If you want him, come and claim him" is the challenge she hurls at them, while the passive and drooling Frodo gazes blankly into the sky. Jackson, by stripping Tolkien's text of early episodes in which the Hobbits play key roles, reduces Frodo to a two-dimensional hero whose supposed courage as a Hobbit is only rather suddenly and abruptly acknowledged by Elrond at Rivendell.

In the text of *The Fellowship of the Ring*, in contrast to its visualization, Frodo demonstrates his heroism through his bold oath to Varda and Lúthien: "'By Elbereth and Lúthien the Fair,' said Frodo with a last effort, lifting up his sword, 'You shall have neither the Ring nor me!'" (209; I:12). With this action Tolkien provides the climax of Frodo's physical evolution as a hero in the first book of *The Fellowship*: the Hobbit is torn, on the one hand, between the Ring demanding that he put it on as the nine Black Riders call him back and, on the other, the goal of reaching safety at Elrond's Rivendell house on the opposite side (representing Elven goodness and security and power). Further, Elrond, not Arwen, commands the flood, and Gandalf, through the encouragement of Glorfindel—as we learn later—adds to its tumultuous power the marvelous white water horses (218; II:1).

In contrast to the dominant Valkyrie Arwen, in the first film Aragorn is strangely deflated in some ways, in other ways pumped up. In scene 25, "The Sword That was Broken," as if in symbolic agreement with his missing virility, the blade that cut off the Ring lies broken, its shards posed as if a relic passively stored in a museum. In the book the sword is reforged and presented to Aragorn after the Council of Elrond, before the Fellowship departs. At the end of the first film a regretful Aragorn appears, to tell Frodo, "I would have gone with you to the end—to the very fires of Mordor," he says to the Hobbit, then tells him to "Run!" (*Fellowship*, scene 43: "Parth Galen"). Indeed, it is Boromir and not the sentimental Aragorn who shines most brightly at the end of the first film: Boromir seems to be picking up firewood and not deliberately following Frodo (as he is in Tolkien's book) when he makes his grab for the Ring (*Fellowship*, scene 43: "Parth Galen"). When Jackson's Boromir later compensates for his deed by bravely protecting Merry and Pippin, the Man from Gondor is slain in a very long death scene in which he is pierced by many arrows (*Fellowship*, scene 44: "The Breaking of the Fellowship"). Further, Boromir also quite movingly confesses his guilt and, after Aragorn refers to "our people," pledges his support to Aragorn and then dies (*Fellowship*, scene 45: "The Departure of Boromir"). It is curious that Jackson has tacked on here the beginning of book 3, perhaps with an eye to a "happy ending" that will satisfy viewers and impel them to see the second installment. Jackson will similarly defer the unhappy ending of *The Two Towers*—the encounter with Shelob—until the third film, *The Return of the King*.

The second film also changes central features of Tolkien's epic, adds material not found in the text of *The Lord of the Rings,* and omits other material.[5] In one of the most important additions, as we shall see in returning to Jackson's emphasis on Arwen and Aragorn, Éowyn, sister-daughter (niece) of the king of Rohan, epitomizes the female stereotype of caretaker for the children and aged of the kingdom and the eroticized object of Gríma's desire. Note that she is perceived as "fair and cold" when he attempts to intimidate her over the dead body of King Théoden's son Théodred (*Towers*, scene 20: "The King of the Golden Hall").

Éowyn's role in Tolkien's *Two Towers*, however, is fuller and more balanced in terms of her social and political role as shieldmaiden, leader, and future ruler. There she also assists her uncle, King Théoden, at the meeting with Gandalf and the company, and, though "stern as steel" and the "daughter of kings," appears to Aragorn incomplete, or at least immature—"like a morning of pale spring that is not yet come to womanhood" (504; III:6). Like the Old English queen Wealhtheow in *Beowulf*, wife of Danish king Hrothgar, Éowyn in Tolkien's text passes the cup at a hall ceremony to knit up peace after feasting in a joyful gift-giving—specifically, the shining mail and round shields bestowed upon Aragorn and Legolas and the cap of iron and leather chosen by Gimli from the king's hoard. In Tolkien's text, "The king now rose, and at once Éowyn came forward bearing wine. '*Ferthu Théoden hál!*' she said. 'Receive now this cup and drink in happy hour. Health be with thee at thy going and coming!'" (511; III:6). The Rohirrim (modeled on Old English) means "Fare well [hale] Théoden!"[6] In the text she also passes the cup to Aragorn (but trembles as she does so to show her infatuation).

Although in the text of *Two Towers* Théoden names Éomer as his heir, upon the suggestion of Háma the hall-guardian (who has released Éomer from prison) it is to Éowyn that Théoden entrusts his people—no mean responsibility—when he and the Company depart for battle. In the film, in contrast, Éomer is banished by Gríma-Wormtongue (*Towers*, scene 8: "The Banishment of Éomer") and Éowyn appears to be primarily a

---

[5] For example, one of the most crucial changes—and a distortion of Tolkien's text—is the continuing notion (picked up from the first film) that Saruman and Sauron are in league together: Saruman says, close to the beginning of the film version of *Two Towers*, "Together we shall rule Middle-earth" (*Towers*, scene 4: "The Uruk-Hai"). At no time, however, does Sauron in Tolkien's book imagine he needs Saruman as an ally, although the Dark Lord uses those times when Saruman peers into the *palantír* to obtain information and thereby help subvert him. Certainly Saruman never imagines that he is using Sauron—in fact, he breeds a new species of Orc that can function during the day in order to wrest power from Sauron.

[6] See T. Northcote Toller, *An Anglo-Saxon Dictionary*, s.v.

nurturing caregiver to her uncle (and king) and her people (*Towers*, scenes 27 and 35: "Exodus from Edoras" and "Helm's Deep"). In Tolkien's book, Théoden is not thinking of Éowyn when he asks Háma for someone in whom "my people trust." For Théoden, Éomer is he whom he is unable to spare or leave behind, "the last of that House" (of Eorl). Háma corrects him: "I said not Éomer. . . . And he is not the last. There is Éowyn, daughter of Éomund, his sister. She is fearless and high-hearted. All love her. Let her be as lord to the Eorlingas, while we are gone" (512; III:6). In Théoden's absence, *as lord* she will lead the folk of the Golden Hall. Thus, in the text, as the splinter Fellowship departs, Éowyn stands dressed in mail and lays her hands upon the hilt of a sword. We will not see her again until the third volume. But in the film, she seems to be herding her people in an exodus to Helm's Deep—in advance of their flight in volume three. And in the film, like the shieldmaiden she will become only in the third volume of the text, she attempts swordplay with Aragorn, who offers in defense a knife—a scene of sexual symbolism nowhere found in Tolkien's text—and speaks of her caretaking role as a "cage" (*Towers*, scene 26: "A Daughter of Kings").

In the second (and third) films the figure we see more of than in Tolkien's narrative is, of course, Arwen, Elven beloved of Aragorn and symbol of wisdom, who will be, apparently, lost to Men after the passing of the Elves. Initially, her importance in the film of *The Two Towers* is not entirely clear. Her providential role is underscored in Aragorn's two dreams. First, after Aragorn smokes, she materializes before him to tell him to sleep, that this is a dream, and to kiss him; she also instructs him to follow the path, not to falter (*Towers*, scene 33: "The Evenstar"). Second, Arwen appears in a scene that does not exist in the narrative of *The Lord of the Rings* but instead only in the appendices: she is told by her father, Elrond, that her time on Middle-earth is ending and that she must sail with her kin to the Undying Lands—although she will ultimately decide to stay with Aragorn (*Towers*, scene 38: "Arwen's Fate"). In fact, in the text, at the end of the trilogy, it is Galadriel and her Elves and not Arwen who must depart for the Undying Lands when the Third Age melds into the Fourth; Arwen gives away her passage to Frodo (952-53; VI:6). This departure, earned by Galadriel's rejection of Frodo's proffered Ring, represents forgiveness for Galadriel's own role as half-niece to Fëanor and participant in the revolt of the Noldor (described in *The Silmarillion*). Because of her disobedience, she was banned from joining the other Elves in Valinor for long years.[7] This fact's importance for Tolkien, if not for *The Two Towers* or even *The Lord of the Rings*, cannot be underestimated, for the harmony that will exist at the beginning of the Fourth Age, of Man, following the ending of the bellicose Third Age, of Elves, will be symbolized by the marriage between the Man Aragorn and Half-elf Arwen.

The endpoint toward which much of the film narrative of *The Lord of the Rings* has been moving rests upon Arwen's decision to stay behind in Middle-earth with Aragorn and thereby sacrifice her immortality out of love for a human. This final decision of Arwen is anticipated in the film (but not the book) of *The Two Towers*, when Aragorn is injured in a battle with Wargs prior to the battle of Helm's Deep and floats away. Aragorn seems to be nearing his own end although he is watched over by natural and supernatural forces—for example, a visionary Arwen kisses him while his horse awakens him and kneels for him to mount (*Towers*, scene 35: "The Grace of the Valar"). Indeed, to the choice that Arwen's father, Elrond, offers Arwen—death with Aragorn or life in the Undying Lands—Arwen replies, "You have my love, father," and is shown departing Middle-earth with the other Elves of Rivendell (*Towers*, scene 38: "Arwen's Fate"). As if this ominous sign were not enough, Galadriel offers Legolas an analogous choice when she notes that "the time of the Elves is over. Do we leave Middle-earth to its fate?" (*Towers*, scene 39: "The Story Foreseen from Lórien"). Clearly Men are in danger: Galadriel declares prophetically in the film that "Sauron will try to destroy Rohan. The Eye turns to Gondor, the last free city of men," and she predicts that the Quest will claim the Ringbearer's life and that "the Ring is close to achieving its goal." The end of the second film, however, leaves the audience with the impression that Arwen and Aragorn will never marry, in spite of her promise to relinquish her immortality for Aragorn's sake in the first film.

In the third film, two scenes at the beginning serve as establishing shots—frames for the final film that help to unify it thematically as well as mark its importance as the endpoint in the trilogy. The first reveals Sméagol's murder of his cousin Déagol in order to obtain the Ring that the latter has found on Sméagol's birthday, a scene that should have been part of Gandalf's explanation to Frodo of the history of the Ring in *The Fellowship of the Ring*, as that is where it is found in Tolkien's book. The second offers a vision of the child Arwen ought to have had with Aragorn

---

[7] See the different unused texts that appear in J. R. R. Tolkien, *Unfinished Tales*, ed. Christopher Tolkien.

and her confrontation with her father, Elrond: in a moment of transcendent love for a being of different kindred she says to him, "You saw my son—it is not lost. Some things are certain—if I leave him, I will regret it forever. . . . Reforge the sword!" (*Return*, scene 7: "Arwen's Vision"). This latter theme unifies all three films and explains all the individual films' emphases, on Hobbits as Halflings, on diminished Men, and, most importantly, on Arwen as a Half-elf.

The first establishing shot in *The Return of the King*, the kin-killing by Sméagol, signifies in Halfling fashion the equivalent of Fëanor's Kinslaying in *The Silmarillion* and is similarly followed with consequences grim and terrible. Sméagol's physical degeneration into Gollum, a being set apart from his kind both physically and spiritually, provides obvious evidence of his descent into evil. As a theme it anticipates the division, discord, and disloyalty that arise between Frodo and Sam, as the Ring's influence becomes more pronounced as they near Mount Doom. The theme also anticipates the self-division and discord within Gollum himself, as he debates the pros and cons of whether he should betray his master, Frodo, to win the Ring (a more powerful master still). In general, the increasing violence by Frodo and Sam in the film graphically represents the effects of greed and pride on the Hobbits.

In the text, of course, neither Hobbit displays the physical violence exhibited in the film. In the film Sam attacks Gollum just as Gollum—Narcissus-like looking into a pool—debates whether he should let Shelob have Frodo; Sam's actions tip the balance toward Shelob. In the text, Gollum shows concern and love for his sleeping master by almost touching his knee, which Sam mistakes for a threat. Sam's chastisement for Gollum's one kind gesture unfortunately compels Gollum's betrayal of them to Shelob. But Jackson adds Gollum's unlikely staged set-up of Sam as a greedy thief of *lembas*: the degenerate Hobbit sprinkles crumbs on Sam. This malicious sprinkling leads in the film to Sam's attack on Gollum and Frodo's suspicions of Sam, suspicions sufficiently keen to arouse Frodo's demand that his friend and servant go home. Later in the film, Gollum himself will attack Frodo in a manner very un-Tolkienian in nature: in the text, Tolkien clearly marks Gollum's faithfulness to his master by having Frodo make him swear a feudal oath of fealty to "Master," a rite ambiguous in nature because it is unclear whether it is Frodo to whom he is swearing or to the Ring (603-04; IV:1). Further, in the film Sam is never seen taking up the bearing of the Ring and suffering his temptation, as he does in the text when he thinks his master, Frodo, is dead and the mission must continue.

Jackson, in his preference for graphic violence, may ignore the subtleties of the master-servant/knight-squire relationship that Tolkien has so carefully developed in *The Return of the King*. Nevertheless, in the third film, by means of several visual markers of separation and connection, Jackson truly renders the bond of friendship and caring between Frodo and Sam and among the three Hobbits whom Frodo leaves behind in the Shire at the end. These visual markers contrast with the unlikely violence that has continued to take center stage in all three films in a way not present in the anti-epic. In the film of *The Return of the King*, just as Gandalf beats up Denethor and then participates vigorously in battle, including the attack of the Nazgûl, Sam kills Orcs, Sam fights Gollum, the Eagles fight the Nazgûl, and Frodo battles Gollum. The visual markers that Jackson provides to counter the violence are equally stunning. In Jackson's depiction, Frodo perilously hangs from the edge of Mount Doom as Sam, like Michelangelo's God touching Adam's finger at the moment of creation in the fresco at the Sistine Chapel, reaches out to grasp him and thereby return Frodo to Middle-earth and safety. Literally, Sam saves Frodo; figuratively, love and friendship and loyalty—the glue of Middle-earth—save the Hobbit hero. Later, Arwen joins Aragorn in a scene of spring blossoms and song to usher in the Fourth Age, of Man—and the end of the Third Age, with the departure of the Elves, the Three Rings, and Arwen's father and their people. Finally, Frodo and the Elves accompany the decrepit Bilbo to the boat to ferry him over to Valinor; the other Hobbits have to bid goodbye to their beloved Frodo in a wrenching end-scene—that finishes, curiously, with Frodo's smile of acceptance. If the opening scene of Sméagol's murder of his cousin in the film of *The Return of the King* provides a clear definition of evil as greed, pride, and selfishness at the expense of the Other, then at the end the rectification of that crime is the love that binds the Fellowship.

What Jackson sees in the heroism and loyalty of the Hobbits in this third film is linked to the loving union between the Valkyrie-like Arwen, Half-elf, and Aragorn, Man, the theme that for Jackson unifies all three films—clarified by what I have called the second establishing shot in *The Return of the King*, "Arwen's Vision." It seems equally clear in the film that Jackson's invented scenes concerning Aragorn and Arwen are meant to mirror the pattern of the quest of their ancestors Beren and Lúthien. This love story of two kindreds in *The Lord of the Rings* echoes that told in *The Silmarillion* (and in the appendices to the novel) of the Man Beren and the half Elf / half Maia Lúthien. Aragorn and Arwen must overcome the obstacle set by Elrond that Aragorn must be worthy of marrying his daughter, which he does by being crowned king. Beren and Lúthien are essentially prohibited from marriage by her father, Thingol, when he demands an extraordinary boon of Beren in return for his daughter's hand—the retrieval of one of Fëanor's captured jewels, the Silmarils, from Morgoth's crown.

In *The Silmarillion*, during Beren's quest for the Silmaril, Lúthien, like Jackson's Arwen, functions as hero equally with her male lover, in fact transcending him in her artistic and heroic roles (*Silmarillion* chapter 19). For example, Rapunzel-like, Lúthien escapes imprisonment by her father by braiding her hair into a rope; further, her singing has a power that stuns her enamored adversaries. Indeed, through her efforts and those of her shape-changing hound, Huan, she escapes capture by Celegorm, conquers Sauron (whose form she wrests from him), and rescues Beren from imprisonment. Further, like Elrond to his daughter, Arwen, in the film, loyal Lúthien offers Beren the choice either of relinquishing the quest and wandering the earth or of challenging the power of darkness, although she promises that "on either road I shall go with you, and our doom shall be alike" (*Silmarillion* 214). Lúthien matches in knowledge or artistry whatever Beren accomplishes in brave feats: for example, when Curufin, brother of Celegorm, tries to shoot her with an arrow, Beren steps in front and is himself wounded—but then Lúthien heals him. She sings for Morgoth, blinding him, so that Beren can steal the Silmaril. Lúthien sucks out the venom from Beren after the wolf Carcharoth has bitten off Beren's hand holding the Silmaril (*Silmarillion* 182). Although Beren also dies upon the successful completion of the quest, Lúthien sings to him and they meet again "beyond the Western Sea," where she is offered the choice of mortal life with Beren without certainty of joy, which she accepts.

But Beren and Lúthien are not only romantic paradigms and antecedents for Aragorn and Arwen; they are also their ancestors. Significant in this respect is the ennoblement of the Man Aragorn through his Elven-Maian blood and also the fact that he is related as cousin to Half-elf Arwen, who herself mixes the blood of different branches of Elves. Aragorn descends ultimately from Elros, the brother of Arwen's father, Elrond; both of these Elves are the children of Eärendil and Elwing and—not surprisingly—the great-grandchildren of Lúthien and Beren. Arwen is the daughter of Celebrían and Elrond and granddaughter of Galadriel and Celeborn (a connection that explains why the filmic Arwen might meet for advice with her grandmother Galadriel in Lothlórien). Certainly in the appendices to *The Lord of the Rings* Arwen is described as having spent time in Lothlórien both before she meets Aragorn and then after he dies and leaves her behind.

The family backgrounds of Arwen, Galadriel, and Lúthien are important to Tolkien's mythology and also explain Jackson's filmic emphasis on the Arwen-Aragorn story. All three family lines mix the blood of different kindreds or tribes, symbolic of Tolkien's appropriation of the ideal of peace-weaving pursued by Anglo-Saxon noble women[8] and the utopian goal of the unification of differing cultures. Arwen is Half-elf and granddaughter of Galadriel, who herself unites the Noldorin-Vanyarin Elves with the Teleri through her mother, Eärwen, daughter of the Teleri's Olwë of Alqualondë. That is, through Galadriel's father, Finarfin, the half brother of the important *Silmarillion* anti-hero Fëanor, Arwen is connected to both the Noldor and the Vanyar. Finarfin's mother, Indis of the Vanyar, was the second wife of the Noldo Finwë.

But Lúthien's ancestry is even more impressive in its symbolic uniting of differing peoples: Lúthien's mother was Melian the Maia (servant to the Valar), and her father was Thingol (or Elwë), the brother of Olwë of the Teleri. The linking of all families of Elves with the progeny of different kindreds, Maia, Elf, and Man, for Tolkien suggests the harmonious reconciliation of all social differences through peace and harmony in marriage. Modeling these intermarriages and mixed-blood progeny on the classical prototype of the hero as half god, half human, Tolkien finds his ideal union in the coupling of Beren and Lúthien, ancestors of Aragorn and Arwen. Their union is mirrored in that of Aragorn and Arwen, the ideal character of which is only hinted at in the third volume (and film) of *The Lord of the Rings*.

In the appendices Tolkien explains that only three such unions of Eldar and Edain have existed in the history of Middle-earth—Beren and Lúthien, Tuor and Idril, and Aragorn and Arwen. All three couples, but especially Aragorn and Arwen, are important because of their symbolic role in unifying alienated, diverse, or separated peoples: "By the last the long-sundered branches of the Half-elven were reunited and their line was restored" (1010; app. A:I:i). The long history of the Elves dramatizes the division of the three branches, the Noldor (joined by Men), the Teleri, and the Vanyar, at various times alienated or geographically separated from each other. Specifically, in *The Silmarillion* the Noldor, headed by Fëanor,

---

[8] See the discussion of Anglo-Saxon gender roles in Chance Nitzsche, "The Structural Unity of *Beowulf*: The Problem of Grendel's Mother," 287-303, and also "Peace-Weaver, Peace Pledge: The Conventional Queen and *Ides*," chapter 1 of Chance, *Woman as Hero in Old English Literature*, 1-12. Tolkien was familiar with *Beowulf* and with the symbolic importance of the monsters and the failure of heroes: see his important essay: J.R.R. Tolkien. "Beowulf: The Monsters and the Critics," *Proceedings of the British Academy* 245-95; reprinted in *The Monsters and the Critics and Other Essays*, ed. Christopher Tolkien, 5-34.

are exiled from the Blessed Realm because of the Kinslaying; from them and their alliance with the Edain—Men of the Three Houses of the Elf-friends who came to the West because they were attracted to the light and joined the Eldar against Morgoth—descends Tolkien's ultimate hero, Eärendil the Mariner. As the son of the Man Tuor and the Elf Idril (the third important union in Tolkien's mythology), Eärendil the Mariner represents both the Elves and the Men.[9] From him spring the Half-elven sons Elros and Elrond—father of Arwen.

The unification of Man, Elf (all the branches), and Maia through the marriage of Aragorn and Arwen comes about only through the sacrifice and suffering of the lovers, chiefly because of the Doom of Men (Tolkien's euphemism for death, also called a "Gift"). In the appendices (1032; app. A:I:v)—which form a part of the tale of Aragorn and Arwen—after the death of his own father, Arathorn, the mother of two-year-old Aragorn takes him to live in the House of Elrond, where he is called Estel, "Hope," to disguise his true identity from the Enemy. On the very next day after Aragorn's foster father, Elrond, reveals Aragorn's true identity as the Heir of Isildur—when he turns twenty—Aragorn first sees Arwen (who has been living in Lothlórien with her mother's kin) and, thinking she is Tinúviel (Lúthien), falls in love with her. He does so even though his mother, Gilraen, warns him that "it is not fit that mortal should wed with the Elf-kin" (1034; app. A:I:v) and, additionally, even though Elrond informs Aragorn that he will not have any bride until he is found worthy (Aragorn will be over eighty years old when he earns that honor) (1034-35; app. A:I;v). In these relatively mild twin obstacles we can see a parallel to those to the marriage of Beren and Lúthien. Further, there is an additional "doom" laid upon Elrond and Arwen (exile, because of the Kinslaying) to remain with the youth of the Eldar until Elrond must depart, when Arwen can choose to accompany him or not. Although Arwen accepts human mortality in order to marry Aragorn, she must also accept parting from her father and her people—and, along with that parting, the eventual demise of Aragorn before her.

Thus, while Jackson does not finally follow the literal line of Tolkien's narrative in his films, the director appears to be establishing this

---

[9] Idril, an Elda and daughter of Turgon, king of Gondolin, marries Tuor, human son of Huor of the House of Hador (Third House of the Edain) and gives birth to Eärendil the Mariner. Through this special position of mariner, ideal hero Eärendil sails to the Uttermost West as "ambassador of both Elves and Men" to obtain the help that will defeat Morgoth. He and his ship are thereafter transformed into a star to provide hope to voyagers (1010; App. A:I:i).

central concern of the overarching mythology through Tolkien's focus on the relationship between Aragorn and Arwen that appears in the appendices. For this mythological reason also, Jackson brings into the forefront the epic battles in the War of the Ring that Tolkien, for the most part, uses only as background to the drama of the ennoblement of the Hobbits, through their Quest to return the Ring to its source. Within a filmic context, both of these mythological events—the union of Aragorn and Arwen and the War of the Ring—as dramatic narratives may be visually superior to that of the psychological journey of the Company—and the Halflings in particular—and their salvation of Middle-earth.

But these are not the themes Tolkien chose to emphasize in his anti-epic. Within the literary masterpiece and the medium of print, the journey and the knitting together of a peaceful end are of paramount importance to Tolkien. It is at the expense of Frodo, who, unlike Arwen, does cross over to Valinor, that the aims of the film are achieved. Because Tolkien the medievalist lived through two World Wars in a small country where many felt insignificant and helpless against the strength of the German superpower and its allies, we must remember that Frodo's dilemmas, not Aragorn's or Arwen's, are most important in the story Tolkien told and provide a paradigm in the text for the ennoblement of the ordinary, today and always.

NOTE

Portions of this essay were originally published in Jane Chance's film review, "Is There a Text in this Hobbit? Peter Jackson's *Fellowship of the Ring*," for *Literature/Film Quarterly* 30, no. 2 (2002): 79-85, and are reproduced here by permission of the editor. Portions of this essay were previously also presented as part of various invited lectures: "Peter Jackson's 'Hobbito-Centric' *Fellowship of the Ring*?," for the Rice University Alumni Group, Denver, CO, April 29, 2002; "Filming an Epic: Peter Jackson's Interpretation of *Fellowship of the Ring*," for the Rice University Alumni Group, Austin, TX, October 10, 2002; "Tolkien and Middle-earth," for the Rice University Society of Women, St. Paul's Methodist Church, Houston, TX, November 11, 2002; "Tolkien's Women: The Film and the Book," at Houston Baptist University, Houston, TX, January 14, 2003; and "Tolkien and the Re-making of the Middle Ages: The Epic and the Book," in the Medieval Fact and Fiction Track, for the Rice University Alumni College, Rice University,

Houston, TX, March 1, 2003. With the same title as this essay, this essay was delivered as a featured lecture at the Tolkien Society Oxonmoot ("Bilbo's 111th Birthday"), St. Hugh's College, Oxford, UK, September 20, 2003; and as guest lectures at the English Department, Pázmány Péter Catholic University, Piliscsaba, Hungary, April 26; the English Department, Károli Gáspár Protestant University, Budapest, Hungary, April 27, 2004; and in a seminar on "Reading Tolkien and Living the Virtues" (a month-long seminar funded by the Lilly Foundation and directed by Professor Ralph Wood of the English Department), at Baylor University, Waco, TX, June 23, 2004.

I am grateful to have had the benefit of the audiences' questions and points in revising this essay for publication. My thanks also go to Theresa Munisteri, editorial assistant for the Rice English Department, for advice on styling this essay for publication.

WORKS CITED

Chance (Nitzsche), Jane. "The Structural Unity of *Beowulf*: The Problem of Grendel's Mother." *Texas Studies in Literature and Language* 22 (1980): 287-303.

—. ed. *Tolkien and the Invention of Myth: A Reader*. Lexington: University of Kentucky Press, 2004.

—. *Tolkien's Art: A Mythology for England*. 1979. Reprint, Lexington and London: University of Kentucky Press, 2001.

—. ed. *Tolkien the Medievalist*. London: Routledge Ltd., 2002; New York: Routledge, Inc., 2003.

—. *Woman as Hero in Old English Literature* (Syracuse and London: Syracuse University Press, 1986).

Garth, John. *Tolkien and the Great War: The Threshold of Middle-earth*. London: HarperCollins, 2003.

Jackson, Peter, dir. *The Frighteners*. 35 mm. 1996.

—. *Heavenly Creatures*. 35 mm. 1994.

—. *The Lord of the Rings: The Fellowship of the Ring*. Special Extended DVD Edition. Screenplay by Peter Jackson, Fran Walsh, and Philippa Boyens. Perf. Elijah Wood et al. Dir. Peter Jackson. United States: New Line Home Entertainment, 2002.

—. *The Lord of the Rings: The Return of the King*. Theatrical Release DVD. Screenplay by Peter Jackson, Fran Walsh, and Philippa Boyens. Perf. Elijah Wood et al. Dir. Peter Jackson. United States, New Line Home Entertainment, 2004.

—. *The Lord of the Rings: The Two Towers*. Special Extended DVD Edition. Screenplay by Peter Jackson, Fran Walsh, and Philippa Boyens. Perf. Elijah Wood et al. Dir. Peter Jackson. United States: New Line Home Entertainment, 2003.

Shippey, Tom. *J.R.R. Tolkien: Author of the Century*. London: HarperCollins, 2000.

Tolkien, J.R.R. "Beowulf: The Monsters and the Critics." *Proceedings of the British Academy* 22 (1936): 245-95. Reprinted in *The Monsters and the Critics and Other Essays*, ed. Christopher Tolkien, 5-34. London: George Allen and Unwin, 1980.

—. *The Letters*. Selected and edited by Humphrey Carpenter, with the assistance of Christopher Tolkien. London: Allen, 1980; Boston: Houghton, 1981.

—. *The Lord of the Rings*. 2nd ed. With Note on the Text by Douglas A. Anderson. Boston: Houghton Mifflin, 1994..

—. *The Silmarillion*. Edited by Christopher Tolkien. 1976; 2nd ed., London: Harper, 1999; Boston: Houghton, 2001.

—. *Unfinished Tales of Númenor and Middle-earth*. Edited by Christopher Tolkien. London: Allen and Unwin, 1979; Boston: Houghton Mifflin, 1980.

Toller, T. Northcote. *An Anglo-Saxon Dictionary Based on the Manuscript Collections of the Late Joseph Bosworth*. Supplement. London: Oxford University Press, 1921.

FAIRY PRINCESS OR TRAGIC HEROINE?
THE METAMORPHOSIS OF ARWEN UNDÓMIEL
IN PETER JACKSON'S
THE LORD OF THE RINGS FILMS

CATHY AKERS-JORDAN

Casual readers of J.R.R. Tolkien's *The Lord of the Rings* might see Arwen Undómiel as either a fairy princess (a prize for Aragorn's successful completion of his quest) or a tragic heroine (who dies in despair after the death of her beloved). Peter Jackson avoids these simplistic extremes in his depiction of Elrond's daughter and Aragorn's Elvish fiancée. Instead Jackson attempts to portray her as a true descendant of her heroic ancestors, such as Lúthien, Eärendil and Galadriel. In doing so he remains loyal to the spirit of Tolkien's books, especially in terms of Arwen's influence on Aragorn's life and fate, and makes her more appealing to a modern audience. Jackson also uses Arwen to represent the past, present, and future of the Elves in Middle-earth, with strong overtones of Tennyson's Lady of Shalott.

Like all film-makers Jackson faced the challenge of changing a story from one medium to another. What works in books does not always work on film, and Jackson first had to sell a studio on the idea of filming *The Lord of the Rings*; that included changing Arwen's role in all three films. As screenwriter Philippa Boyens explains in "From Book to Script: Finding the Story":

> Arwen had to be, because she was the love of Aragorn's life, much more participatory in the story. You just figure studio executives who are going to be reading this script, you can't have her three hundred miles away from the hero. You know, you try pitching the idea of a psychic connection between two lovers and they'll just tell you to get out of there. (*Towers*, app.: "From Book to Script")

In the books, Arwen's influence and her importance in Aragorn's life are subtle. In fact, she appears only briefly in *The Fellowship of the Ring*, does not appear in *The Two Towers* at all, and does not show up in *The Return of the King* until after Aragorn's coronation. Most of her important actions are recounted in Appendix A (1032-38; app. A:I:v). Jackson's challenge was to transform Arwen for the screen, to make her role more active and obvious to viewers who had not read the books, but without alienating fans of the books. In some ways Jackson's depiction of Arwen significantly differs from the books, but in others follows the books closely. How well this combination succeeded can only be judged by comparing her appearances on page and on screen.

THE FELLOWSHIP OF THE RING

Arwen appears only briefly in the book *The Fellowship of the Ring*, in two scenes in Rivendell and twice indirectly when Aragorn is thinking of her, but these glimpses and their implications provide the basis of Jackson's portrayal of her on film. They provide most of what the reader knows about Arwen outside of Appendix A.

The first reference to Arwen is when Aragorn tells the hobbits the tale of Lúthien Tinúviel as they travel from Bree to Rivendell. Although he does not mention Arwen by name he is clearly thinking of her because of her similarity to Lúthien, her great-great-grandmother. Lúthien was the daughter of Thingol, the Elven King of Doriath in the First Age, and Melian, a Maia (one of the lesser angelic beings). This unusual heritage made her "the fairest maiden that has ever been among the children of this world." This story has great meaning for Aragorn, for Lúthien chose to become mortal for the sake of the Man she loved and "so it is that Lúthien Tinúviel alone of the Elf-Kindred has died indeed and left the world, and they have lost her whom they most loved" (189; I:11). Elves and wise Men believe that Lúthien's line shall never fail; her descendants include Elrond, Arwen, and Aragorn. Lúthien's influence shows in all of them, but especially Arwen, who is the very likeness of Lúthien. Although the Hobbits don't realize the significance of the tale, Aragorn is undoubtedly thinking of Lúthien's choice of mortality, which has been echoed by her granddaughter.

The reader's first glimpse of Arwen is at the feast in Rivendell. Frodo notices:

> . . . a lady fair to look upon, and so like was she in form of
> womanhood to Elrond that Frodo guessed that she was one
> of his close kindred. Young she was and yet not so. The
> braids of her dark hair were touched by no frost; her white

> arms and clear face were flawless and smooth, and the light
> of stars was in her bright eyes, grey as a cloudless night; yet
> queenly she looked, and thought and knowledge were in
> her glance, as of one who has known many things that the
> years bring. Above her brow her head was covered with a
> cap of silver lace netted with small gems, glittering white;
> but her soft grey raiment had no ornament save a girdle of
> leaves wrought in silver.
>
> So it was that Frodo saw her whom few mortals had yet
> seen; Arwen daughter of Elrond, in whom it was said that
> the likeness of Lúthien had come on earth again; and she
> was called Undómiel, for she was the Evenstar of her
> people. (221; II:1)

This brief portrait of Arwen is important because it captures some of the characteristics Jackson portrays on film: her Elven wisdom, beauty, and nobility. It is also the first mention of her name, Undómiel, which means "twilight maiden"; it is a fitting name for the most beautiful of all the Eldar in the fading years of the Third Age. Evenstar has a similar meaning but also links Arwen to her ancestor Eärendil, who was set in the sky with a Silmaril on his brow to become the Morning and Evening Star and to bring hope to all who are oppressed by evil. While Eärendil brings hope to all, Arwen brings hope to Aragorn in particular; Aragorn, named Estel ("Hope") by his mother and known as such in his youth, in turn represents Eärendil on earth and brings hope to Men. Arwen's belief in him keeps him going, even when he doubts himself, a theme Jackson plays up in the films.

The second appearance of Arwen in the book is when Frodo sees her speaking with Aragorn in the Hall of Fire in Rivendell, and although her dialog with him is not important enough to include in the text, her influence on Aragorn is clear. "To his surprise Frodo saw that Aragorn stood beside her; his dark cloak was thrown back, and he seemed to be clad in elven-mail, and a star shown on his breast. They spoke together, and then suddenly it seemed to Frodo that Arwen turned towards him, and the light of her eyes fell on him from afar and pierced his heart" (232; II:1). This is not only an example of the near divine impression Elves make on other races, but also an indication of Arwen's influence. In her presence Aragorn's nobility, which is usually disguised, shines through. Part of this is Aragorn's heritage as The Dúnadan and a descendant of Lúthien, but part is from his association with Elves, like his ancestors in the First and Second Ages, who were ennobled by their friendship with the Eldar. According to Appendix A, there were three marriages between Eldar and Edain (Lúthien and Beren, Idril and Tuor, and Aragorn and Arwen). In each of these marriages, like that of Thingol Elven King of Doriath and Melian the Maia, the woman is of a nobler race and her spouse is ennobled by association. In Aragorn and Arwen's case their union also reunites the branches of the Half-elven (the descendants of Elros and Elrond) and restores and ennobles their family line. This is more than mere medieval courtly love, in which a knight is ennobled by the inspiration of his adored lady; this is the influence of the Elder Children of Ilúvatar.

The final reference to Arwen in the book is when Aragorn remembers her in Lórien at Cerin Amroth:

> At the hill's foot Frodo found Aragorn, standing still and silent as a tree; but in his hand was a small golden bloom of *elanor*, and a light was in his eyes. He was wrapped in some fair memory: and as Frodo looked at him he knew that he beheld things as they once had been in this same place. For the grim years were removed from the face of Aragorn, and he seemed clothed in white, a young lord tall and fair; and he spoke words in the Elvish tongue to one whom Frodo could not see. *Arwen vanimelda, narmarië!* he said, and then he drew a breath, and returning out of his thought he looked at Frodo and smiled.
>
> "Here is the heart of Elvendom on earth," he said, "and here my heart dwells ever, unless there be a light beyond the dark roads that we must still tread, you and I. Come with me!" And taking Frodo's hand, he left the hill of Cerin Amroth and came there never again as living man. (343; II:6)

Frodo can see that the mere memory of Arwen ennobles Aragorn in this place where they plighted their troth to one another. The hope of reuniting with her is "a light beyond the dark roads that we must still tread," yet the scene foreshadows Arwen's eventual death. This is where she will return to die after Aragorn passes away.

Because Arwen actually does little in the first book, most of her role in the first film is composed of actions taken by several different characters in the book, including Glorfindel, Elrond, and Gandalf. By attributing these actions, especially those of other Elves, to Arwen, Jackson makes the logical assumption that she is just as brave, wise, and capable in battle as a male Elf. One has only to look at *The Silmarillion* to see that female Elves in Middle-earth are equal to their male counterparts in wisdom, and Jackson apparently assumes they are also equal in strength and martial ability. Arwen's actions in the film *The Fellowship of the Ring* are strongly reminiscent of her Elven ancestors in *The Silmarillion* when

Elves were at the height of their power in Middle-earth, so in this sense Arwen represents the past power and glory of the Elves.

In the film, the viewer first meets Arwen in a scene that is not based on the book, when Aragorn is looking for *athelas* to heal Frodo after the Ringwraiths attack him on Weathertop. Aragorn stops looking for the plant when he suddenly finds a sword at his throat and Arwen says "What's this? A ranger caught off his guard?" (*Fellowship*, scene 21: "Flight to the Ford"). Despite the seriousness of the situation (she knows the Ringwraiths are hunting Aragorn and the Hobbits) her tone is playful; this is a side of Arwen the reader never sees in the books. Perhaps it is a hint of the days in Lothlórien when Aragorn and Arwen first fell in love. Jackson filmed such a flashback but later decided not to use it (*Towers*, scene 33: "The Evenstar," commentary).

The first time the viewer sees Arwen is through Frodo's eyes, glowing with the light of the Eldar as she dismounts her horse and walks toward him, calling him back to the light. She looks much as Glorfindel is described in the book: "to Frodo it appeared that a white light was shining through the form and raiment of the rider, as if through a thin veil" (204; I:12). Given her angelic appearance and her use of elven "magic" to try to save Frodo from the evil of the Morgul blade which has injured him, it's not surprising the Hobbits are in awe of her.

When Arwen is unable to heal Frodo, she argues with Aragorn that they must get Frodo to her father, Elrond. Aragorn is reluctant to let her take Frodo ahead on Asfaloth, knowing there are at least five Ringwraiths chasing Frodo. She convinces him that she is most qualified for the task because she is a faster rider than he and because she does not fear the Ringwraiths. In the book it is Glorfindel who tries to heal Frodo and sends him across the Bruinin on Asfaloth. Having Arwen do so in the film is logical not only because she is just as capable as Glorfindel, but it allows Jackson to avoid the problem of introducing another character (Glorfindel) only to have him disappear after Frodo reaches Rivendell.

Arwen takes Frodo and races all nine Ringwraiths to the Ford of Bruinin. When she crosses the river, the wraiths halt at the water's edge, reluctant to enter the water. They taunt her and Arwen defies them, drawing her sword, saying "If you want him, come and claim him!" (*Fellowship*, scene 21: "Flight to the Ford").

In the book it is Frodo who draws his sword and defies the Ringwraiths, but when Arwen does so in the film readers are reminded of her great-great grandmother Lúthien who stood up to both Morgoth and Sauron ("Beren and Lúthien" in *The Silmarillion* 162-187). Careful viewers will also recognize that Arwen's sword is the same sword used by Elrond in battle with Sauron at the end of the Second Age (*Fellowship*, scene 1: "One Ring to Rule Them All").

Jackson uses the sword to extend Arwen's connection even to her more remote ancestors. As a subtle treat for fans of the books, all weapons in the films are engraved with inscriptions, including Arwen's sword:

> *Aen estar Hadhafang i chathol hen,*
> *thand arod dan i thang an i arwen.*
>
> Translation: (It) is called Throng-cleaver this broadsword-blade, (a) defence noble against the (enemy) throng for (a) noble-lady.
>
> This last line was dropped from the inscription due to lack of space:
> *Idril i hel en aran Gond Dolen*
> Translation: Idril, daughter of the king (of the) Hidden Rock (i.e., Gondolin).
>
> (Derdzinski, "Sword Inscriptions" 4)

The word *Hadhafang* comes from "The Etymologies" in Tolkien's *The Lost Road* ("Syad" 434). According to Ryzsard Derdzinski's *Tolkien's Language in the Lord of the Rings Movie* page, part of a web site devoted to Tolkien's many languages, "Tolkien devised this Sindarin name for a sword but never used it in any of the tales; David Salo [a language consultant for the films] suggested employing it here" (Derdzinski, "Sword Inscriptions" 4). In the film, Hadhafang is not only a visual connection to her father, Elrond, but a spiritual connection to Arwen's heroic female ancestors, especially her great-grandmother Idril Celebrindal for whom the sword was made. The lovely pun, of course, is the inclusion of Arwen's name (which means noble-lady) in the inscription. The even subtler reference is the reminder that Idril chose to marry a mortal, as will Arwen.

As the Ringwraiths step into the water at the ford, Arwen uses her Elven "magic" to call forth the waters of the Bruinin to wash away the wraiths. In the book it is Elrond who calls forth the waters and Gandalf who gives the waves the shape of white horses. To have Arwen do so in the film shows that her "Elven magic" is a force to be reckoned with, which is appropriate for the daughter of Elrond and granddaughter of Galadriel.

After the Ringwraiths are washed away, Frodo grows weaker and collapses. Arwen lowers him to the ground and cradles him, crying. Her prayer is heard in a voice over: "What grace is given me, let it pass to him, let him be spared, save him" (*Fellowship*, scene 21: "Flight to the Ford").

200

Although it was not included in the film, for the reader familiar with the text, this prayer is beautifully evocative of the moment in *The Return of the King* when Arwen gives Frodo her place in the white ship to the Undying Lands where he can at last find peace and healing:

> A gift I will give you. For I am the daughter of Elrond. I shall not go with him now when he departs to the Havens; for mine is the choice of Lúthien, and as she so have I chosen, both the sweet and the bitter. But in my stead you shall go, Ring-bearer, when the time comes, and if you then desire it. If your hurts grieve you still and the memory of your burden is heavy, then you may pass into the West, until all your wounds and weariness are healed. (952-53; VI:6)

While Frodo rests in Rivendell, Aragorn struggles with his self-doubt; the Council of Elrond is framed by it. Although he shows no lack of confidence during the Council, Arwen encourages him before the council and Elrond after it. While Elrond reminds him of his destiny and duty, Arwen encourages him by reminding him of her faith in him. Of the two, Arwen's encouragement is most effective. "Why do you fear the past?" she asks him. "You are Isildur's heir, not Isildur himself. You are not bound to his fate." "The same blood flows in my veins . . . The same weakness" he replies. "Your time will come," she tells him. "You will face the same evil, and you will defeat it. The Shadow does not hold sway yet, not over you and not over me" (*Fellowship*, scene 25: "The Sword That Was Broken"). This scene sets up a theme that runs through all three films: Aragorn's doubt and Arwen's steadfast love and faith in him, which inspires him even when the foresight of the Dúnadan fails and he cannot see his future.

Unlike in the book, Arwen and Aragorn plight their troth at this time. Readers know from Appendix A that this happened in Lórien at Cerin Amroth years before the events in *The Fellowship of the Ring*, but Jackson uses it as an opportunity for Arwen to give Aragorn a visual reminder of her love that he will carry through all three films: the Evenstar pendant. In the book she gives to Frodo, along with her place in the ship, "a white gem like a star" to comfort him "When the memory of the fear and the darkness troubles you . . . this will bring you aid" (953; VI:6). The pendant serves a similar purpose in the film for Aragorn and provides viewers with a constant reminder of Arwen's love and faith. Their betrothal dialog also ties Arwen's choice of mortality to the pendant. Arwen recalls what she told him when they first met, that she would bind herself to him, forsaking the immortal life of her people. "And to that I hold," she reminds him. "I would rather share one lifetime with you than face all the ages of this world alone." She then gives him the Evenstar pendant. When he protests she reminds him that "It is mine to give to whom I will . . . like my heart" (*Fellowship*, scene 25: "The Sword That Was Broken").

Arwen is last seen in the film when the Fellowship departs from Rivendell. Although she has no dialog, she is clearly sad at Aragorn's departure and exchanges a last long look with him (*Fellowship*, scene 30: "The Departure of the Fellowship"), which is explained in the second film.

The last reference to Arwen in the first film is when the Fellowship takes its leave of Galadriel and Celeborn in Lórien. Galadriel tells Aragorn "I have nothing greater to give, than the gift you already bear," as she touches the Evenstar pendant, referring to Arwen's love. She is troubled by her granddaughter's choice, for she tells Aragorn, "For her love, I fear the grace of Arwen Evenstar will diminish." By choosing mortality Arwen will not only diminish, lose her Elven "magic," but like Lúthien she will die and leave the circles of the world, forever lost to her Elven kin who are bound to Arda. Again Aragorn protests Arwen's choice, but Galadriel reminds him that "That choice is yet before her," reminding him (and the viewer) that choice is Arwen's, not his (*Fellowship*, scene 41: "Farewell to Lórien").

Although Arwen's role in the first film is unlike her role in the book, Jackson succeeds in capturing the spirit of the books. While some subtleties like the inscription on Hadhafang are lost on most viewers, Arwen's role is a logical extrapolation based on the actions of other Elven characters, a reflection of the past power of the Eldar in Middle-earth.

THE TWO TOWERS

Arwen does not appear in Tolkien's *The Two Towers* at all; there is not even a passing reference to her. This was a problem for Peter Jackson, who needed to keep her active in all three films in order to maintain her connection to Aragorn for the film audience. When Jackson first approached Miramax with a two-script proposal for *The Lord of the Rings* films, he had significantly altered Arwen's role and included her in the battle of Helm's Deep. Even after New Line accepted Jackson's proposal and expanded it from two films to three, the Arwen-at-Helm's-Deep plot remained. As Jackson explained in the documentary "From Book to Script: Finding the Story," the real problem with Aragorn and Arwen was geography: "They were in two completely different places in Middle-earth. So how on earth can you keep a romantic story going when you can't actually have the two people connecting?" Producers were not likely to approve of the psychic connection between the characters as a substitute for having them together, so Jackson kept Arwen at Helm's Deep. Co-Producer Rick Porras explained that seemed like a good idea because Arwen is such a strong character: "The way it was written, she actually was this incredibly gifted and courageous and ruthless fighter, like all Elves are capable of being" (*Towers*, app.: "From Book to Script"). This fit well with the role established for Arwen in the first film.

When word of this change leaked on the Internet, many fans objected to it. Liv Tyler, the actress who plays Arwen in the films, read some of the comments and was so upset with the negative reactions she cried. "And I cried so hard afterwards because they were calling me, like, 'Liv Tyler, Xena Warrior'" (*Towers*, app.: "From Book to Script"). Jackson's solution was to return to Appendix A of *The Lord of the Rings*, which includes the tale of Aragorn and Arwen, and to incorporate that story into the main plot through a series of flashbacks.

Everyone involved with the decision was much happier with the result, including Liv Tyler: "And what we came to realize was that you don't have to put a sword in her hands to make her strong. And where we've come to now is all these true elements of who Arwen is. I mean, this is an incredibly powerful and fearless woman . . . filled with so much hope and belief. And that is strong enough." Executive Producer Mark Oredsky agreed that the flashbacks are "far more powerful material for Arwen" than having her fight at Helm's Deep (*Towers*, app.: "From Book to Script").

Despite minor changes, the portrayal of Arwen in *The Two Towers* is most faithful to the books. In these flashbacks Arwen is less physically active but still very influential in Aragorn's life. Her role is more passive, reflecting the fading powers of Elves in the present times of Middle-earth. Although they are still a force to be reckoned with, the Elves realize their time is nearly over and the time for the dominion of Man is drawing near.

The first flashback in the film is based on a theme of Appendix A, Arwen's faith in Aragorn. It occurs when Aragorn is resting and smoking, thinking of Arwen. "The light of the Evenstar does not wax and wane. It is mine to give to whom I will . . . like my heart," Arwen says in a voiceover, reminding him of her steadfast belief in him. "Go to sleep," she wills him and the scene shifts to Rivendell, the night before the departure of the Fellowship. "I am asleep. This is a dream," Aragorn says and closes his eyes, but when he opens them the dream flows into a flashback. Aragorn is uncertain of the path his future will take. Arwen reassures him that his place is with Frodo and tells him, "This is not the end . . . it is the beginning. If you trust nothing else, trust this, trust us" as she touches the Evenstar pendant around his neck to remind him and the audience what it represents. Her message is subtly reinforced as her words are repeated in the Sindarin lyrics in the background: "*Ú i vethed nâ i onnad. Ae u-esteliach nad, estelio han, estelio ammen*" (Derdzinski, "Soundtrack" 22). The Evenstar pendant is also a segue from flashback to present as Éowyn asks Aragorn, "Where is she? The woman who gave you that jewel?" (*Towers*, scene 33: "The Evenstar").

Before Aragorn can answer her he recalls Elrond urging him to let Arwen go:

> ELROND. Our time here is ending. Arwen's time is ending. Let her go. Let her take the ship into the West. Let her bear away her love for you to the Undying Lands. There it will be evergreen.
> ARAGORN. But never more than a memory.
> ELROND. I will not leave my daughter here to die.
> ARAGORN. She stays because she still has hope.
> ELROND. She stays for YOU! She belongs with her people!
> (*Towers*, scene 33: "The Evenstar")

While this scene does not appear in the book, it strongly echoes one from Appendix A, when Elrond learns of the love between his daughter and Aragorn, whom he loves as a son. Elrond cannot be certain of the future, that Aragorn can overthrow Sauron and reunite the kingdoms of Gondor and Arnor. He tells Aragorn, "though I love you, I say to you: Arwen Undómiel shall not diminish her life's grace for less cause. She shall not be the bride of any Man less than the King of both Gondor and Arnor" (1036, app. A:I:v). Aragorn and Arwen agree to these terms, not because Arwen is a fairy princess and a prize for successful completion of Aragorn's quest, but because of their belief in "authority, propriety, and law" which will serve them well as King and Queen of the Reunited Kingdom (Kocher 136). Perhaps Aragorn also hopes that if he does fail, Arwen can still sail West, preserving her immortality.

The flashback continues as Aragorn tries to return the Evenstar to Arwen just before the Fellowship leaves Lórien. "You have a chance for another life. Away from war . . . grief . . . despair. . . . I am a mortal. You are elf kind. It was a dream, Arwen, nothing more," he says. She doesn't believe him, even when he tries to give back the pendant. "It was a gift. Keep it," she tells him decisively, folding his hand over the pendant (*Towers*, scene 33: "The Evenstar"). This is not in the book, but it adds tension to the film, and gives Arwen a chance to demonstrate her strength and resolve. It apparently does not convince Aragorn, however, for when he finally answers Éowyn's question about the woman who gave him the jewel he tells her, "She is sailing to the Undying Lands with all that is left of her kin" (*Towers* scene 33). Aragorn seems certain that despite her love for him, Arwen will obey her father's wishes and sail into the West.

The next scene with Arwen is not a flashback, but her continuing presence in Aragorn's life. On the way to Helm's Deep Aragorn is wounded in a skirmish with Orcs and Wargs. He falls over a cliff, into a river, and floats unconscious to the shore. Arwen is shown lying on her bed, then her image appears over Aragorn, kissing him, as her voiceover says "May the grace of the Valar protect you" (*Towers*, scene 37: "The Grace of the Valar"). This scene is probably based on a line in Appendix A: "Arwen remained in Rivendell, and when Aragorn was abroad, from afar she watched over him in thought" (1036; app. A:I:v). Jackson's representation of this description is a logical extrapolation based on Arwen's Elven powers as the daughter of Elrond and granddaughter of Galadriel, and a beautiful depiction of the spiritual bond between Aragorn and Arwen.

Elrond finally confronts his daughter about her decision. He tells her there is no hope for her in Middle-earth, only death. Even if Aragorn defeats Sauron, as a mortal he will eventually die. Elrond describes Arwen's fate as a mortal after Aragorn's death:

> There will be no comfort for you. No comfort to ease the pain of his passing. He will come to death. An image of the splendor of the Kings of Men in glory undimmed before the breaking of the world. But you, my daughter, you will linger on in darkness and in doubt as nightfall in winter that comes without a star. Here you will dwell, bound to your grief, under the fading trees until all the world is changed and the long years of your life are utterly spent. Arwen . . . There is nothing for you here, only death. Do I not also have your love?
>
> (*Towers*, scene 38: "Arwen's Fate")

Elrond's description, based on Tolkien's prose, coupled with images of Aragorn's tomb and Arwen's sorrow are heartbreaking. Arwen's words to Aragorn, "This is not the end . . . it is the beginning. If you trust nothing else, trust this, trust us," again echo in the background in Sindarin, connecting this scene to the one in Rivendell, adding to the sorrow (Derdzinski, "Soundtrack" 22). Elrond cannot see the future with certainty and fears losing his daughter forever. He is trying to protect her from the grief of Aragorn's eventual death and the bitterness of mortality which she cannot yet understand. He is also forcing her to choose between immortality spent with her father or mortality and death with Aragorn. Weeping, perhaps considering for the first time what death really means, Arwen replies, "You have my love, father" (*Towers*, scene 38: "Arwen's Fate").

The last view of Arwen in this film is her departure from Rivendell with the other Elves leaving for the Havens. She looks sorrowfully over her shoulder at Elrond, who looks troubled (*Towers* scene 38). Clearly father and daughter are sad to be parted, even temporarily, and both know there is a chance Elrond may not make it to the Havens if the war with Sauron spreads. These scenes between Elrond and Arwen show the father's and daughter's deep love much more effectively than Tolkien's passing comment that "she loved her father dearly," giving the viewer a better understanding of the difficulty of Arwen's decision (1036; app. A:I:v). Like Aragorn, the viewer is left with the impression that Arwen has changed her mind and left Aragorn to face his fate alone in Middle-earth.

THE RETURN OF THE KING

Although there are three passing references to her (when Halbarad brings Aragorn the banner of the King of Gondor, when Aragorn tells Éowyn his heart dwells in Rivendell, and when the banner of the King is unfurled during the Battle of the Pelennor Field), Arwen appears in *The Return of the King* only after Aragorn's Coronation. After their many years of trial and waiting, their wedding on Midsummer's Day merits only one paragraph. After that the only actions she takes are giving Frodo the jewel to comfort him in his pain, and riding with everyone else to take King Théoden's body to Rohan for burial. As the others ride towards Rivendell, she remains in Rohan where "she said farewell to her brethren" and to her father Elrond. Of that Tolkien only says "None saw her last meeting with her father, for they went up into the hills and there spoke long together, and bitter was their parting that should endure beyond the ends of the world" (956; VI:6). One can only assume that Tolkien glossed over these important events in the lives of Aragorn and Arwen because they were not important to the main plotlines of the story. Readers who want more of their story must rely on Appendix A, which is slightly more developed.

Lack of material for Arwen was a problem for Peter Jackson. Of the three films, Arwen's role in *The Return of the King* is least like the book.

He had already used most of the material in Appendix A in *The Two Towers*, so to expand Arwen's role in the third film and her importance to the plot, Jackson adds elements that are not in the books. Some are clear while others are much more subtle, so subtle one can't help but wonder how they strike viewers who have not read the books.

Arwen is first seen in this film riding with the other Elves towards the Grey Havens. She has a vision of a boy running to Aragorn. Father and son embrace joyfully and when the boy turns to make eye contact with her, Arwen sees that he is wearing her Evenstar pendant. Overcome by this vision of her future, she closes her eyes and begins to cry (*Return*, scene 7: "Arwen's Vision"). In the background the sad Sindarin lyrics (by Philippa Boyens) called "Twilight and Shadow" reflect Arwen's vision:

> I saw a star rise high in the
> Evening sky,
> It hung like a jewel,
> Softly shining.
>
> I saw a star fade in the
> Evening sky,
> The dark was too deep and so light died,
> Softly pining.
>
> For what might have been,
> For what never was.
> For a life, long lived
> For a love half given.
> (Derdzinski "Soundtrack" 34)

The very words "Twilight and Shadow" are a reference to Aragorn and Arwen's betrothal in Appendix A. They stood on the mound of Cerin Amroth in Lothlórien, between the shadow of Sauron to the east and the Twilight of the Undying Lands to the west, and choose to reject both (1035-36; app. A:I:v). Cerin Amroth is a fitting place for such a decision because, as Haldir tells Frodo during his visit, from there one can see the struggle between Sauron and Galadriel, between light and dark (343; II:6). It is to this place which symbolizes their decision that Arwen will come to die alone after Aragorn's death. The title of the song and the lyrics are reminder of the difficulty of Arwen's decision and her fate.

When Arwen closes her eyes on the vision of her son, she hears her father saying "There is nothing for you here. Only death"; when she opens her eyes the vision is gone (*Return*, scene 7: "Arwen's Vision"). Without hesitating, she turns her horse back to Rivendell where she confronts Elrond about this vision of the future. He tells her that that future is almost gone and nothing is certain. Arwen tells him, "Some things are certain. If I leave him how, I will regret it forever. It is time" (*Return*, scene 8: "The Reforging of Narsil"). Elrond looks grief-stricken as he realizes she has already made her decision, and he will lose his daughter forever. Although these scenes are not taken from the books, they continue to develop the theme of Arwen's decision to become mortal, like Lúthien, and be forever parted from her Elven kin by death. Jackson shows the immensity of this decision and its implications, which Tolkien chose to downplay.

Jackson visually connects Arwen's return to the re-forging of Narsil. A careful viewer will notice that time passes between Arwen's return and the line of dialog where she urges Elrond to re-forge the sword. Presumably the scenes between Elrond and Arwen hinted at in *The Return of the King* trailer will be added here, scenes which likely will include Elrond's initial anger and eventual acceptance of his daughter's decision. The important thing is that only by Arwen's return and urging does Elrond have the sword re-forged, and the juxtaposition of images in scene 8 ("The Reforging of Narsil") tie Arwen's mortality to the sword. Instead of the banner of the King of Gondor, Andúril becomes the symbol of Arwen's love and Aragorn's acceptance of his role as King. After Arwen tells Elrond to reforge the sword, the scene cuts to Arwen in her room reading, where, looking somewhat dismayed, she drops her book. Elrond picks it up and takes her hands. "Your hands are cold. The life of the Eldar is leaving you," he says, grief-stricken. "It is my choice. *Ada* [Father]. Whether by your will or not, there is no ship now which can bear me hence," she replies (scene 8). It is at this moment that she becomes mortal. Elrond continues to look grieved as he watches the sword re-forged.

It should be noted that although Jackson ties Arwen's mortality to her return to Rivendell, something which did not happen in the books until after Aragorn's death, it makes Arwen more important to the overall plot of the film. She starts a chain of events which will save Minas Tirith and which at last sets Aragorn on the path he has been resisting out of self doubt. It is only by her urging that Narsil is reforged. Without it Aragorn can not convince the dead to follow him and without them he cannot save Minis Tirith so, indirectly, Arwen is responsible for his success at the Battle of the Pelennor Field. By accepting the sword, Aragorn also finally accepts his destiny as Elendil's heir: to become King of Gondor. Unlike the other characters who choose to die fighting side by side with a friend, Arwen makes the much scarier choice to die alone, sacrificing herself for Aragorn's success. While this shows great strength of character and makes her as important to the plot as other characters without upstaging Éowyn on the battlefield, it is such a diversion from the book that its subtlety may be lost on the audience.

Although there are hints in *The Return of the King* trailer, scenes of Elrond and Arwen's reconciliation and parting before he takes the reforged Andúril to Aragorn are not in the theatrical version of the film. Instead, Jackson presents a series of images which reinforce the link between Aragorn and Arwen's fates, images which echo Tennyson's Lady of Shalott. This series of images begins as Aragorn tosses restlessly in his sleep at Dunharrow. Next, Arwen is seen lying on her bed looking pale and weak. With her dark hair spread over the pillow, the vivid blue and red of her dress, and the cut of her gown, she becomes an image strongly reminiscent of the many Pre-Raphaelite paintings of the Lady of Shalott in her boat. The leaves, which were vivid autumn colors during the Council of Elrond, are dry and crumbling as they blow into her room while Arwen dies and the power of the Elves fades (*Return*, scene 22: "Andúril – Flame of the West").

This is a fitting image because, like Tennyson's Lady of Shalott whose fate is sealed the moment she sees Lancelot, Arwen's fate is sealed the moment she first meets Aragorn. In Appendix A, Tolkien tells us that as a young man, Aragorn sees her walking in the shadows under the trees of Rivendell while he sings part of the Lay of Lúthien and calls her Tinúviel, for she is the very image of Lúthien. "Yet her name is not mine," Arwen tells Aragorn. "Though maybe my doom will be not unlike hers" (1033; app. A:I:v). Although Aragorn does not yet realize it, Arwen has already foreseen that her fate is like Lúthien's: to fall in love with a Man and give up her immortality for him.

After the Lady of Shalott image in the film the scene switches quickly several times, from a close-up of Arwen growing weaker, to a sweeping view of the entrance to the Paths of the Dead, to Aragorn sleeping more quietly as Arwen's voice over says "I choose a mortal life." When the image cuts back to Arwen lying in her bed looking paler and weaker as a tear trickles down her cheek. "I wish I could have seen him, one last time," she laments (*Return*, scene 22: "Andúril–Flame of the West"). Because she is now mortal she can no longer watch over him from afar. As Arwen closes her eyes, apparently dying, Aragorn dreams that the Evenstar pendant falls and shatters. He wakes in horror and is summoned to Théoden's tent where he is surprised to find Elrond. This sequence reminds the audience of the spiritual bond between Aragorn and Arwen (he already knows something is horribly wrong) and foreshadows her lonely death on Cerin Amroth in Appendix A.

209

The meeting between Elrond and Aragorn is painful for them both. "I come on behalf of one whom I love," Elrond tells Aragorn. Both look worried. "Arwen is dying. She will not long survive the Evil that now spreads from Mordor. The light of the Evenstar is failing. As Sauron's power grows her strength wanes. Arwen's life is now tied to the fate of the Ring. A shadow is upon us, Aragorn. The end is come" (*Return*, scene 22: "Andúril–Flame of the West"). Arwen's increasing weakness as Sauron's power grows is not even hinted at in the books, but Jackson foreshadowed it in *The Fellowship of the Ring*. In the Council of Elrond the Elves, especially Elrond and Legolas, react as if to physical pain when Gandalf uses Black Speech, a not-so-subtle indication of the effect of Sauron's power (*Fellowship*, scene 27: "The Council of Elrond"). By tying Arwen's fate to the Ring, Jackson gives Aragorn personal as well as altruistic reasons for his quest to defeat Sauron. This is a great deviation from the book, but perhaps he is using Arwen to represent the future of the Elves of Middle-earth. If Sauron wins they will be unable to escape to the Undying Lands and will be destroyed by Sauron's evil. Even if the Ring is destroyed, the time of the Elves is nearly over. Those who remain in Middle-earth will "dwindle to a rustic folk of dell and cave, slowly to forget and to be forgotten," as Galadriel explains to Frodo in Lórien (356; II:7).

Elrond warns Aragorn that he rides "to war, but not to victory" because of Sauron's treacherous plan to attack with unexpected forces from the river. Aragorn's only hope is more men, and the only place to get them is to call on the murderers and traitors who haunt the mountain. "You would call upon them to fight? They believe in nothing. They answer to no one," Aragorn says. "They will answer to the king of Gondor!" Elrond replies and reveals the reforged sword (*Return*, scene 22: "Andúril–Flame of the West"). He explains that the man who can wield the sword can summon the most deadly army on earth and urges him, "Put aside the Ranger. Become who you were born to be. Take the Dimholt road." It is not surprising that Aragorn seems uncertain. As he admitted to Arwen in Rivendell he cannot foresee his path and now, knowing that Arwen is dying, he has no hope for himself. "*Ónen i-Estel Edain*. [I give Hope to Men]" Elrond encourages him. "*Ú-chebin Estel anim*. [I keep none for myself]" Aragorn replies (scene 22). This not only suits Aragorn's feelings, it is the Elvish poem carved on his mother's grave in Rivendell, the site of his previous conversations with Elrond, and another reminder of his duty and destiny. Readers will recognize that these were Gilraen's last words to Aragorn; she had no hope for herself, though her son would bring hope to the Dúnedain (1036; app. A:I:v). Aragorn resigns himself to a future without personal hope, though he continues to bring hope to others.

Although Arwen is not physically present when Aragorn enters the Paths of the Dead, he carries two symbols of her devotion: the Evenstar pendant and Andúril. Both are the only objects in these scenes which emit light, a suitable symbolism for the light of the Evenstar herself.

Arwen is not mentioned or seen again until Aragorn's Coronation. He endures the ceremony, looking serious but sad on what should be a joyous occasion. He has brought victory and peace to his people, but he believes Arwen is dead, and without her he has no hope of personal joy. To use Tolkien's term, her surprise appearance is a "eucatastrophe," a sudden joyous turn providing "a fleeting glimpse of Joy" (Tolkien, "On Fairy-stories" 86). Like their wedding in the book, her appearance at the Coronation is brief and joyous, but lacking in dialog. Unlike the book, the feelings the images evoke are so strong that dialog is not necessary. Aragorn and Arwen's joy is clear, as is Elrond's sorrowful acceptance of her decision. Jackson ends his version of the tale of Aragorn and Arwen with the new King and Queen kneeling in gratitude before the Hobbits who "bow to no one" (*Return*, scene 57: "The Return of the King").

By ending on a happy note for Aragorn and Arwen Jackson avoids the tragedy of Arwen's death, which he hinted at in *The Two Towers*. In Appendix A Tolkien describes Aragorn and Arwen's long happy life together which ends as Aragorn finally grows old and prepares to die. When Elrond left Middle-earth Arwen "became as a mortal woman, and yet it was not her lot to die until all that she had gained was lost . . . She was not yet weary of her days, and thus she tasted the bitterness of the mortality she had taken upon her" (1037; app. A:I:v). By this Tolkien seems to be implying that Arwen remained immortal until Aragorn's death. It is only as she faces her own death that she finally comprehends what it means: an unknown fate. Elves return to the Undying Lands but the fate of Men is unknown, even to the Eldar. All they know is that after death Men leave the circles of the world, while the Eldar are bound to it until the end of time. Arwen realizes she has not only lost Aragorn, but she has separated herself from her Elven kin and has no idea what fate awaits her after death.

Aragorn seems to see some kind of afterlife, for he tries to comfort Arwen: "In sorrow we must go, but not in despair. Behold! we are not bound for ever to the circles of the world, and beyond them is more than memory." But Arwen, lacking Aragorn's foresight, is not comforted. Tolkien tells us that after his death "the light of her eyes was quenched, and it seemed to her people that she had become as cold and grey as nightfall in winter that comes without a star" (1038: app. A:I:v). Tolkien's choice of words is intriguing. Throughout *The Lord of the Rings* the Elves are repeatedly described as having "a light like the light of the stars" in their eyes (221; II:1). Taken in this context, "the light of her eyes was quenched" could mean that that was the moment she lost her immortality. The rest of the sentence, "she had become as cold and grey as nightfall in winter that comes without a star," evokes the imagery of Eärendil, Arwen's grandfather who is also the morning and evening star whose light brings hope to those in Middle-earth. For Arwen, whose very name–Evenstar–ties her to Eärendil, to be without a star, hope, evokes an image of a long night of despair. Without Aragorn, who personifies Eärendil on earth, Arwen loses hope. The great tragedy of Arwen's fate is that after inspiring Aragorn to impossible victory and inspiring him to bring hope to others, she dies alone, and in despair.

To make Arwen's death even more tragic is the possibility that she might have had the chance to sail to the Undying Lands, even after Aragorn's death. Arwen thinks she has no choice, but on his deathbed Aragorn tells her "The uttermost decision is before you: to repent and go to the Havens and bear away into the West the memory of our days together that shall there be evergreen but never more than memory; or else to abide by the Doom of Men" (1037: app. A:I:v). This dialog, used in a different scene by Jackson, seems to imply Arwen still has a choice and is supported by a careful examination of Appendices A and B. According to Appendix B (The Tale of Years) Aragorn dies in March 1541, then Legolas builds a ship and he and Gimli sail for the Undying Lands (1072; app. B). Appendix A says Arwen dies in the winter after Aragorn's death that spring (1038; app. A:I:v). Careful readers can't help but wonder if Legolas and Gimli left before or after Arwen died. Tolkien doesn't say. If they left before she died, that means she truly did not have a second chance at immortality, and was trapped in a death of despair. If they left after her death, there is a possibility that she could have gone with them but chose to die and be with Aragorn in the afterlife of Men (whatever that is) instead of returning to immortality. That implies the possibility that she died in hope of being reunited with Aragorn instead of in despair. Perhaps this subtle possibility is the basis of Jackson's happy ending for Aragorn and Arwen in the films.

Overall, Jackson succeeds in his depiction of Arwen. Despite some changes, some of them quite drastic, he remains true to the spirit of the books. Since hope is one of the overall themes of *The Lord of the Rings*, Jackson's treatment of Aragorn and Arwen's tale is more fitting and satisfying. Although he hints at Arwen's tragic fate in *The Two Towers*, he avoids Elrond and Arwen's bitter parting and ends Aragorn and Arwen's story with a joyous reunion.

WORKS CITED

Derdzinski, Ryzsard. "Dialogs: a Linguistic Survey." *Tolkien's Language in the Lord of the Rings Movie.* 13 August 2004 < http://www.elvish.org/gwaith /movie.htm>.

—. "Soundtrack: a Linguistic Survey." *Tolkien's Language in the Lord of the Rings Movie.* 13 August 2004 < http://www.elvish.org/gwaith/movie.htm>.

—. "Sword Inscriptions: a Linguistic Survey." *Tolkien's Language in the Lord of the Rings Movie.* 13 August 2004 < http://www.elvish.org/gwaith/movie.htm>.

Kocher, Paul H. *Master of Middle-earth: the Fiction of J.R.R. Tolkien.* New York, Ballantine, 1972.

The Lord of the Rings: The Fellowship of the Ring. Special Extended DVD Edition. Screenplay by Peter Jackson, Fran Walsh, and Philippa Boyens. Perf. Elijah Wood et al. Dir. Peter Jackson. United States: New Line Home Entertainment, 2002.

The Lord of the Rings: The Return of the King. Theatrical Release DVD. Screenplay by Peter Jackson, Fran Walsh, and Philippa Boyens. Perf. Elijah Wood et al. Dir. Peter Jackson. United States, New Line Home Entertainment, 2004.

The Lord of the Rings: The Two Towers. Special Extended DVD Edition. Screenplay by Peter Jackson, Fran Walsh, and Philippa Boyens. Perf. Elijah Wood et al. Dir. Peter Jackson. United States: New Line Home Entertainment, 2003.

Tennyson, Alfred Lord. "The Lady of Shalott." *Arthur Charon home page, Southern Florida State University: The Tennyson Page.* 13 August 2004 <http://charon.sfsu.edu/TENNYSON/TENNLADY.HTMLl>.

Tolkien, J.R.R. *The Lord of the Rings.* 2nd ed. With Note on the Text by Douglas A. Anderson. Boston: Houghton Mifflin, 1994.

—. *The Silmarillion.* 2nd edition. Edited by Christopher Tolkien. New York: Houghton Mifflin Company, 1999.

—. *The Lost Road and other Writings: The History of Middle-earth.* Edited by Christopher Tolkien. New York: Ballantine, 1996.

—. *The Tolkien Reader.* New York: Ballantine, 1966.

"CRIMES AGAINST THE BOOK"?
THE TRANSFORMATION OF TOLKIEN'S ARWEN
FROM PAGE TO SCREEN AND
THE ABANDONMENT OF THE PSYCHE ARCHETYPE

VICTORIA GAYDOSIK

In the director's and writers' commentary for the Special Extended Edition DVD of *The Two Towers*, Philippa Boyens jokingly observes that "we could . . . do courses in criminal screenwriting," to which Fran Walsh adds, "Crimes against the book!" and Boyens replies with "Crimes Against the Books 101!" (*Towers,* scene 57: "The Nazgûl Attack," commentary). Their comments indicate their awareness of the dissatisfaction among some devoted readers of J.R.R. Tolkien's *The Lord of the Rings* upon seeing the liberties that Peter Jackson took in bringing the classic fantasy epic to movie theaters. Jackson's own attitude is suggested by his response to harsh criticism of the cooking of tomatoes on Weathertop: "I find it all a bit ludicrous to worry about that sort of thing: when you're dealing with Middle-earth and Balrogs and Cave Trolls, what is the problem with a tomato?" (*Fellowship,* scene 19: "A Knife in the Dark," commentary). The challenge of adapting a creative work from one artistic medium to another, like the problem of translating poetry from one language to another, requires the adapter to make hard choices. Inevitably, not everyone will be happy with the choices made. However, if we put aside issues of the degree of personal satisfaction produced in particular individuals who experience both works, the comparison of the original work and its derivative adaptation can shed light on the world we live in.

The seed that eventually grew into this essay was planted in December of 2001 when I went to see *The Lord of the Rings: The Fellowship of the Ring*. I had read the trilogy long ago at the end of high school, when it had become a cult phenomenon. As I watched the movie, which was then in the early stages of becoming a global phenomenon, I was dismayed to discover how little of the text I still remembered: the Shire, Bilbo and Frodo, Gandalf's fall in Moria, and the treachery of Saruman were about it. My first assumption was that the adapters had radically transformed this

215

text; however, since I couldn't actually produce a memory of an alternative "real" story line, I decided I had better go back to the drawing board and read the book again. More importantly, however, as I re-read the book after about a thirty-year lapse, and only a week or so after seeing the film adaptation of its first volume, I was struck by the ways the film varied from the book and by the light that such variances shed on shifts in cultural values that have occurred, at least in some circles, within living memory.

In particular, I was struck by the contrast between J.R.R. Tolkien's creation of an Arwen patterned on the Psyche archetype and Peter Jackson's creation of an Arwen patterned more closely on, although not identical to, what I have come to think of as the "James Cameron archetype": pumped-up, butt-kicking fearless heroines who are masters of machinery, weapons, battle tactics, physical hardship, and emotional adversity, but who can also still nurture a child and experience romantic attachment for a significant other. Perhaps you've met the representatives of this new heroine: Ripley from *Aliens*, portrayed by Sigourney Weaver; Sarah from *The Terminator*, portrayed by Linda Hamilton; Lindsey from *The Abyss*, portrayed by Mary Elizabeth Mastrantonio; and Max from Fox's *Dark Angel*, portrayed by Jessica Alba. In my own lifetime, I have seen the expectation of what women are supposed to *do* and to *be* transformed, or perhaps diversified and multiplied, from Psyche's model of patient passivity, clearly and explicitly and repeatedly articulated to me by my parents during my childhood (and by an entire wagonload of cultural baggage during the rest of the time), to Ripley's model of courageous power that does not sacrifice love in its many forms. Through the adaptation of Tolkien's epic to the movie screen, two versions of Arwen now exist, and the differences between them point to changing perceptions of and expectations about women.

My interest in Psyche was first aroused in a course on Greek mythology through one of my textbooks, Joseph Campbell's *The Hero with a Thousand Faces*. The course focused on the gods and heroes of the classical world, reviving the adventures of the members of the pantheon of the Olympian gods, such as Zeus, Ares, Hermes, Apollo, Dionysius, Hephaestus, and Eros. Additionally, there were the adventures of semi-divine and merely mortal creatures such as Perseus, Hercules, Jason, Theseus, Achilles, and Odysseus. Campbell's book expanded these particular instantiations of heroic stories into an overarching concept of the mythic archetype. The pattern of the archetypal hero was clear: auspicious signs at his birth, evidence of greatness in infancy or youth, the receiving of a summons to adventure, the acquisition of a helper or guide, the journey into the underworld, the winning of a boon for humankind, and the return to the world of the living with this prize.

Curiously, Campbell's book does not have a corresponding companion text called *The* Heroine *with a Thousand Faces*; for the most part, in the hero's story women are either in the background, in some helping or waiting capacity, or they are victims such as Io, Antigone, Philomela, the Trojan women. Powerful women such as Medea do exist, but they are to be feared: the intensity of their love (or hatred) overwhelms their respect for human life and law. Positive womanly models in the hero's story include Penelope, patiently waiting and weaving in Ithaca while Odysseus goes on a twenty-year adventure, or helpful Ariadne, who has the foresight to provide a ball of string to Theseus as he enters the labyrinth of the Minotaur (only to find herself discarded—to have her strings cut, so to speak—when he no longer needs her). The title of Sarah Pomeroy's book on the lives of women during the classical era summed up the options: goddesses, whores, wives and slaves. "Heroine" does not enter into the roles available to women until later in literary history.

However, in addition to these more usual paragons of domestic passivity and victims of masculine violence, the classical world also preserved a few rare stories of warrior women who embraced lives of activity and who eschewed the company of men other than to propagate the species. The hero's challenge, in dealing with such opponents as Amazons, was clear: powerful women devoid of Medea's evil were to be conquered and then married (i.e., *totally* conquered through domestication), just as Theseus conquered Hippolyta and then constrained her to marry him. Differing versions of Hippolyta's story suggest shifts in cultural attitudes toward women. Apparently some degree of change in the perceived status of such women was already underway by the time of Shakespeare, since he makes his Theseus say of Hippolyta, in *A Midsummer Night's Dream*, that her conqueror has won her heart as well as her arms (1.1.16-17). Clearly, a woman's consent has increased in value at least somewhat by the time of the Renaissance for Shakespeare to find such a statement significant to his audience. With or without her consent, however, the hero's story places the warrior woman in the domestic sphere of marriage and family.

Other examples of the manly warrior woman are available from around the world and include the Asian tale of Mulan, the biblical story of Judith and Holofernes, and the French legendary heroine Joan of Arc. They are marked out from other women by their wearing of armor, their wielding of weapons, their assumption of masculine responsibilities such as leadership or warfare, and especially by their entry into the sphere of action. These are not stories of girl meets boy, but of girl *becomes* boy, at least for a while. But surely this kind of masquerade is not the story of the archetypal heroine; instead, these are stories of the atypical girl forced to deal with adversity in extreme circumstances.

The Psyche archetype stands at the opposite end of the spectrum of action to both the Medeas and the Hippolytas of mythology: her attributes are not passion, courage, martial arts, and violence, but beauty, obedience, and patience marred by curiosity. In the story of "Cupid and Psyche" related by Apuleius, and created much later in the mythic tradition than most of the classical stories, Psyche's beauty rivals that of Venus herself. The vain goddess sends her son Cupid to humble Psyche by making her fall in love with some despicable object. Cupid, however, seeing her beauty, falls in love with her himself. He arranges to marry her secretly and keeps his identity from her so that his mother can't find out what he's done. But when Psyche's curiosity, egged on by her envious sisters, reveals her husband's true identity, his cover is blown. Psyche accidentally drips hot oil from her lamp onto Cupid's shoulder, and he flies home to his mama to be solaced and nursed back to health. Venus sets Psyche a series of tasks that she must complete in order to prove herself worthy of forgiveness. As she faces each task, Psyche is in despair, and nature, egged on by Cupid, sends some salvation to her aid: the ants sort the vast piles of grain, the reeds tell her to gather the golden wool from thorn bushes, and Persephone gives her the box of beauty Venus has demanded. When Psyche's curiosity gets the best of her a second time, and the beauty in the tempting little box turns out to be a Stygian sleep, Cupid himself rescues her and takes her before Jupiter to plead their case. Through Jupiter's intercession, Venus is appeased, Psyche is made immortal, and she and Cupid bring forth a daughter, Joy. The moral: soul joined to bodily love gives rise to enjoyment. And the corollary: soul deprived of bodily love falls into despair and would die without nature's intervention.

This model of obedient passivity is common in the western literary tradition, with varying degrees of corrupting curiosity mixed into the story: the Virgin Mary fits the model, passively accepting her fate at the Annunciation (Warner 177), as do Sleeping Beauty, Cinderella, Snow White, the Lady of the courtly love tradition, the Victorian Angel of the House, and many others. Along the way, the passive feminine love object is rewarded with a pedestal that simultaneously elevates her in relation to her suitor/supplicant and removes her even further from the sphere of action, re-emphasizing the passive nature of her identity. Clearly, Tolkien's Arwen fits the Psyche model of feminine deportment, although without the marring effect of curiosity. Like Penelope, she waits and weaves, and like Ariadne, she helps the hero by sending to him the finished product of her weaving to help him claim his birthright among the dead warriors of the underworld.

It is a serenely beautiful and traditionally feminine image of passivity that Tolkien presents in his original creation of Arwen. In the main text, she is barely present, sitting at her father's side at a banquet in Rivendell before the Fellowship of the Ring sets out (221; II:1), weaving Aragorn's banner at a safe distance from the action (758; V:2), and arriving for her wedding after the fighting is done and the battles are won (951; VI:5). Her choice of a mortal life is the strongest action she takes, since it is contrary to her father's wishes, but it is a mental act rather than a physical one, and it is related in the Appendix rather than in the body of the narrative (1036; app. A:I:v). Tolkien seems to have recognized that the connection between Arwen and Aragorn was too sketchily presented in *The Lord of the Rings*, since after the initial publication he provided an appendix in which the relationship is fleshed out and placed in the context of other mortal-elven matrimonial unions. This emendation seems to be characteristic of Tolkien's ongoing construction of the entire history of Middle-Earth: Galadriel, for example, also underwent some re-thinking before being settled into the form of the Marian benefactress of the Fellowship.

Peter Jackson clearly recognized this "work-in-progress" quality in the published novel of *The Lord of the Rings*. In his commentary for the extended DVD edition of *The Two Towers*, he says

> Arwen's story line was a problem for the obvious reason that it doesn't exist in the books, other than the *concept* exists that an immortal Elf loves a mortal Man. And we—we—wanted to create a story for Arwen—and we just thought, well, you know, why don't we crank up the tension by having Arwen sort of ordered to take the ship as well. There's no way you can create a greater conflict between Aragorn and Arwen than to have them permanently separated. (*Towers*, scene 38: "Arwen's Fate," commentary)

As he observes in the following scene, the changes to Arwen were the result of a desire "to have a sense of drama and dramatic reversal." In spite of Tolkien's ongoing construction of Middle-earth, his ultimate goal was undoubtedly something beyond dramatic reversal.

Between the time when Tolkien constructed Arwen, however, and the time when Peter Jackson re-constructed her for a visual rather than a print medium, the world had changed. Many of us already could "feel it in the water . . . feel it in the earth . . . smell it in the air" (*Fellowship,* scene 1: "Prologue"). Some had begun to suspect that perhaps father did *not* know best after all, or at least not in every case. Divorce rates, educational opportunities, and underpaid employment outlets for women had multiplied. The domestic pre-occupations of the post-World-War-II era gave way to the great consciousness-raising of the sixties and seventies, and women were making their voices heard. *The Mary Tyler Moore Show* held out the promise that women could be happily single, meaningfully employed, and personally fulfilled all at the same time.

By the 1960s and 1970s, women were joining reading groups and analyzing novels and non-fiction that explored the very unromantic reality in which many of them lived. In this story, chronicled, for example, in Marilyn French's *The Women's Room,* Psyche tries to follow the archetypal model set before her; instead of being rewarded, however, she is punished. She gets Cupid reluctantly to tie the knot after no small struggle, sometimes under the impending doom of fatherhood, and then proceeds to get worn to a stunted frazzle by the "shit and string beans," in the phrase of French's protagonist, of ordinary domesticity. Cupid, meanwhile, remains in a sphere of action increasingly populated by young women having to, or desiring to, make their own way in the world. Psyche doesn't become immortal; she gets older, less beautiful, and less desirable, until eventually she is discharged from her duties in divorce court and dumped into the sphere of action, sometimes with her children still clinging to her newly impoverished skirts. For a while the Superwoman model held out a certain enticement: surely women can be effective executives, efficient mothers, and loving wives all at the same time?

The practical response to the Superwoman model was a resounding rejection. Oddly, however, in the eighties and nineties, the Superwoman model has been displaced by the super-super-*super*-Superwoman model: the James Cameron archetype. In this story, Psyche retains her youth and beauty, but not her passivity. She earns her bread by the sweat of her *own* brow, sometimes as a waitress in a diner, and sometimes as the designer of underwater oil-drilling platforms. She is quick-witted and courageous: she doesn't seek out danger, but when it presents itself she proves herself worthy of the challenge. Although she may at first be unskilled in the use of arms and the strategies of the battlefield, she quickly shows herself to be a regular Athena, but without giving up the sexual allure of an Aphrodite. In her, Cupid (if present) does not find his dependent—he meets his match. Through their partnership, they then proceed to kick the universe's ass and maybe create offspring.

This Psyche is also good with kids (if present). And they live happily ever after—or, if Cupid doesn't make it, Psyche's up to the task of soldiering on without him.

I have deliberately caricatured the new super-super-*super*-Superwoman; however, I have to admit that every time I've seen her, I've enjoyed the experience tremendously. Although she is hardly universal, her presence can be detected in a wide range of popular cultural venues, from *Power Rangers* to *Buffy the Vampire Slayer* to Dana Scully in *The X-Files* to Trinity in *The Matrix* to Dr. Samantha Carter in the television version of *Stargate*—these last two providing particularly brainy instantiations of the type—to Rene Russo's character in the third and fourth editions of *Lethal Weapon* to the doomed *Daredevil* love interest, Elektra—the list could go on for a very long time, so common has this replacement for Psyche become. Rose, in Cameron's *Titanic*, is a New Psyche in training: she begins as a young woman passively accepting her marital fate, but Jack teaches her to abandon passivity and embrace the adventures and challenges that life has to offer, even if he can't be there to share them with her. So it is perhaps not at all surprising that when Peter Jackson, Philippa Boyens, and Fran Walsh re-conceived Arwen, she at first acquired a kinship, although not a twin-ship, to Ripley. And alas, since these changes are not achieved without sacrifice, Glorfindel had to die, or at least be exiled from the story, so that the new Arwen might have something to *do* to make her more than a passive lady in waiting for the hero's return.

In the Jackson-Boyens-Walsh "fan fiction" version, as some have termed it, Arwen not only finds Aragorn and the hobbits in the wilderness, she also asserts her superiority to Aragorn in equestrian skills and fearlessness in the face of the Nazgûl. She rescues Frodo in the race to the ford, draws her sword—the one her father carried in the Battle of the Last Alliance of Elves and Men—to entice her pursuers into closer confrontation, and summons nature to her aid—rather than waiting in despair, as the original Psyche would have done—when she calls forth the flood that sweeps away the enemy. She then seems to pray that some part of her powers will pass to Frodo to keep him alive just a little longer. Later, she plays a *nice* Lady Macbeth to Aragorn's waffling ambition. This woman is not modeled on the Psyche archetype, despite her soulfulness.

This transformation of Arwen was a hot topic of debate on fan web sites after the movie was released, but it seemed to me to be no surprise at all; instead, it was thoroughly consistent with the reinterpretation of the role of women that has been going on in literature since—well, since the beginning of literature (it's just been going on much faster and more dramatically since the invention of the movie as a story-telling form). Passivity has, in many cases, given way to active involvement in the complication and resolution of the plot; the medium demands action characters, and female characters are being reconfigured to serve these demands. Peter Jackson shows greater loyalty to this historical process than to Tolkien's original text in the way he presents Arwen in his version of *The Fellowship of the Rings*.

In the director's and writers' commentary on the extended DVD edition of *The Fellowship of the Ring*, Peter Jackson comments on the problem of bringing Arwen to the screen (transcribed and punctuated to the best of my ability):

> Obviously, one of the major changes to the book was the fact we replaced Glorfindel with the character of Arwen, but, um, you know, there were really logical reasons to do that. One of the problems with *The Lord of the Rings*—there are so many characters, and to introduce an Elf called Glorfindel in this scene and then to have Glorfindel drop out of the story, um, a few minutes later and to have to then introduce Arwen at Rivendell—it just seemed like it would be introduction upon introduction, and there's so many that we—we felt we needed to somehow condense characters, uh, reduce them and condense them.

Fran Walsh then adds "And additionally increase Arwen's role, because it was so small," to which Jackson replies

> Yeah. Yeah. So we, you know, we took a chance here at— at—at doing this, and um—you know; but the character of Arwen essentially is still very much within the spirit of the character in the books. I know there was a lot of criticism— a lot of concern early on that we were going to do things to Arwen that would have made her a very different character but, um, but ultimately I think we've ended up with somebody who does feel pretty much like they belong in the books. (*Fellowship*, scene 21: "Flight to the Ford," commentary)

Jackson's comments highlight a crucial difference between the options available to the novelist and those open to the filmmaker: the expense of movie making and the tradition of the short (two-to-three hour) finished product experienced in theaters all in one sitting mitigate against the complexity, the subtlety, and the length a writer can indulge in. Most filmmakers have to answer to corporate supervisors who keep one eye on the bottom line and the other on the clock. Novelists still have the option of answering to their muse.

But in addition to the merely practical concerns about reducing the number of characters and therefore the number of introductions that Tolkien originally created, it makes sense to ask why the film adaptation features a woman undertaking the action role traditionally associated with men. After all, Jackson could have remained true to Tolkien's image of Frodo riding Asfaloth across the Bruinen all by himself, with the river under a spell to rise against the evil presence of the Black Riders, as Tolkien has Gandalf explain to Frodo in Rivendell. Jackson could have merely omitted Glorfindel rather than deciding to replace him with Arwen, and still had a coherent story at least as consistent with the original text as one which omitted Tom Bombadil. I suggest that advent of the New Psyche—the woman who rejects passivity, who rises above fear, helplessness, and despair, and who solves problems herself—provided a ready-made alternative. Arwen's first appearance in the film avoided the whole issue of introducing her and providing exposition of her back-story with Aragorn since this connection is implied in the way he immediately trusts her and in the way she takes precedence over him without an affront to his pride.

Ironically, Jackson seems to have reconsidered his strategy for presenting Arwen in *The Two Towers*, perhaps explaining his comment that "we've ended up with somebody who does . . . belong in the books." I saw a photograph on the web of Arwen in full armor wielding her father's sword at Helm's Deep, but the film version presented in theaters did not include this "slight departure" (Philippa Boyens's tongue-in-cheek phrase) from the original text. In *The Two Towers*, Arwen is once again much more of a passively feminine figure, remaining a distant and perhaps unachievable ideal to Aragorn. The scenes in which she appears are dream visions—inventions that step beyond Tolkien's original text, but that are actually more in keeping with his depiction of Arwen.

In Tolkien's novel, Arwen does not appear in *The Two Towers*. Between the scene in Rivendell in which the Fellowship is formed and the one in Gondor when the fair company arrives for the wedding of King Elessar and his beloved, Arwen makes no personal appearance in the story. Additionally, she is mentioned only a couple of times during this long interlude, and then only in connection to the banner she weaves for Aragorn and sends to him when her brothers go to join his fight against Sauron. The banner influences the dead warriors who betrayed Aragorn's ancestor to follow his summons, and in this way Arwen assists the hero to achieve the boon he seeks in the underworld. Later, it proclaims Aragorn's arrival in Gondor and implies his defeat of the enemy forces whose ships he has appropriated.

223

Tolkien's appendix tells the persevering reader that Aragorn and Arwen had already promised themselves to each other in Lothlórien many years earlier, and that Elrond had placed on Aragorn the requirement of succeeding to the kingship and reuniting the two kingdoms of Arnor and Gondor before claiming Arwen as his bride. The Aragorn of the novel calmly and confidently pursues this double goal with full knowledge of the reward that will follow upon his coronation. He does not doubt himself, and he does not live under the false belief that Arwen will leave Middle-earth for Valinor. In fact, as a character, Aragorn in the novel undergoes very little development, remaining the same noble hero from beginning to end. In E.M. Forster's descriptive term, he is a flat character—filled with admirable virtues, but lacking the evidence of how he acquired them.

In contrast, Peter Jackson attempts to adapt Aragorn for film by making him a round character. Just as Jackson, Walsh, and Boyens initially strengthened Arwen for the film adaptation, they weakened Aragorn in order to show the growth and development of the qualities the character already possesses in full measure in Tolkien's initial creation. The film Aragorn suffers from a diffident self-doubt, and a key signifier of his self-doubt is the fact that he tells Arwen to take the ship to Valinor: he knows that she has a chance for happiness there, but in offering this possibility as a reason in favor of her going there he implies that he doubts she will come to the same condition by staying with him in Middle-earth. This change in Jackson's version has the added benefit of clarifying Aragorn's purpose in saving Gondor and Middle-earth from Sauron: in Tolkien's version, winning the kingdom and winning the girl are two tasks inextricably bound together so that Aragorn's motivation to achieve one goal cannot be separated from his desire to achieve the other. In Jackson's version, Aragorn believes he will never see Arwen again, and so he carries on the fight because it is the right thing to do, and not because doing so will secure for him the woman he desires as a wife. His ability to carry on the fight without her support helps demonstrate his increasing confidence in himself and in his cause. Jackson then muddies this clarity of purpose somewhat in the theatrical version of *The Return of the King* when Elrond tells Aragorn that Arwen's life has become bound to the fate of the Ring. By the end of the film epic Aragorn is fighting not to win Arwen's hand, but to save her life.

Arwen's complete absence from the original novel of *The Two Towers*, especially for a series of films separated by a year from one installment to the next, would have flattened the effect of the lovers' reunion in *The Return of the King*. Jackson uses a non-linear narrative to place the story of the parting of the lovers out of its chronological position: it belongs in *The Fellowship of the Ring* since it occurs within the sequence of that story's action, but it appears in *The Two Towers*. The choice of a dream vision to bring Arwen into the film version of *The Two Towers* is apt, since the dream vision is a particularly medieval narrative device, and Tolkien's writing has a particularly medieval affinity. In the director's commentary for the film's extended edition, Jackson makes no mention of a conscious decision to use a dream vision, referring instead to the necessity of using a flashback:

> It's tricky because our big problem, obviously, with Aragorn and Arwen is, um—well, one, she doesn't appear in the book of *The Two Towers* at all—but, even keeping her in the story, how do you have the two of them together, because there's no way that you can actually have them physically together, so the only way we could do it was to have flashbacks to an earlier time period. (*Towers*, scene 33: "The Evenstar," commentary)

But Aragorn's meditative stance at the beginning of the flashback combines with the soft-edged visual quality of the scene he sees in his mind's eye to suggest a dream vision—to suggest something happening *to* the character rather than *with* the narrative.

Fran Walsh confesses that the conception of Arwen underwent a sea change before the release of *The Two Towers*. Primed by the rumors on fan web sites, some movie viewers may have anticipated—or dreaded—that Arwen would wield a sword in battle in the second film of the series. But in the commentary for the extended edition of the DVD, she says:

> One of the, uh, things that became apparent with us working with Liv was that we needed to bring the character back to the books—that we had to somehow make her bigger than the books and make her more actively involved in the story and in the plot of the story. And the more we did that, the more it moved away from being the true center of *The Lord of the Rings*. And so it was Liv that pointed that out to us: in the trilogy she remains true to her, um, her essence and to the world of the Elves rather than the world of the fellowship, if you like. (*Towers*, scene 37: "The Grace of the Valar," commentary)

In Jackson's film version of the second novel, Arwen is evocatively ethereal rather than actively physical. The quality of her character for this adaptation to film is more harmonious to the quality with which Tolkien endowed her for the novel, even though the scene of parting at Rivendell is constructed out of whole cloth.

By the time that *The Return of the King* appeared in theaters, Arwen had moved to a death-like passivity. Elrond's explanation to Aragorn implies that her choice of a mortal life has bound her vitality to the fate of the Ring. She makes that choice in another scene invented for the film version: the moment when she experiences "the sight" and sees a future vision of the child—the son—born of her marriage to Aragorn. It's impossible to know at this point whether this maternal moment had been planned as an integral part of the story or whether it arose out of the necessity of retaining narrative continuity with earlier choices the screenwriters had made. Here again, novelists have a freer hand in revising a written text, since all that is lost is the paper upon which it's written and the time the writer has invested in producing it. Filmmakers bear a different yoke: throwing away a completed piece of the story may be the equivalent of throwing away a fortune and may require the elision of other artists' work from the finished film. Fran Walsh explains:

> There were decisions that we had made with *The Two Towers* that we'd made two or three years prior to finishing the film. And some of them were quite radical decisions, like the Elves arriving at Helm's Deep—that was not a decision we could reverse . . . we were locked into it. (*Return*, scene 57: "The Return of the King," commentary)

Arwen's abandonment of the journey to Valinor, and the device the adapters chose to bring about that result, may have more to do with the financial constraints of filmmaking as a creative medium than it does with narrative strategies and adaptive preferences.

In any case, Arwen returns to Rivendell and almost immediately begins to fade into immobile passivity. She no longer rides a horse or bears a sword or stirs a step, although she still retains her unearthly beauty as she fades. She has moved as far away from the "James Cameron archetype" she seemed originally to be destined to become in the film version as she possibly could.

And why shouldn't this be the case when Tolkien himself has obligingly provided the New Psyche character of Éowyn in the second volume of *The Lord of the Rings*? Had Peter Jackson stuck to the action-heroine version of Arwen he started with in *The Fellowship of the Ring*, and had he brought her to Helm's Deep to fight alongside Aragorn, he would have had two battling females in one fortress, both in love with the same man. This is not a picture of the New Woman; it's a recipe for a catfight.

And the situation would have been doubly confusing because the woman who has overtly chosen the warrior's training and ethos—Éowyn—was sequestered in the Glittering Caves with the ordinary domesticated women and their children. How could the end of the middle movie play out with Éowyn emerging into the dawning daylight to find Aragorn embracing a mail-clad Arwen? How could she have gone on to destroy the Witch-king of Angmar after seeing the immortal Arwen as a warrior woman? Her own ability to "run with the wolves" would have been annihilated.

And here is part of the problem with the New Psyche: she continues to exist primarily in relation to men rather than in relation to the world, the human race, herself, or another outside standard of reference. The super-super-*super*-Superwoman model kicks giant insect butt, kicks criminal butt, kicks vampire butt, kicks gluteal Terminator II butt; however, her relationship to other New Pyches has yet to be imagined, plotted, developed, and fleshed out on either the page or the screen (although the frames of comic books, positioned kind of half-way between novel and film, might contain useful examples such as Wonder Woman and Promethea). It would seem that artists are still mulling over just how it might happen that strong, active women will interact in an entire world of strong, active women. But mythology did imagine it: the race of women warriors known as Amazons were all strong and active, but their world had no permanent place in it for men. Have human beings come far enough in the intervening millennia to resolve this issue?

Long ago in that course in Greek Mythology, my teacher, Dr. Diane Westbrook, threw out a challenge to her students. Joseph Campbell fills in the outlines of the archetypal hero's story, she said; the Psyche myth presents one version of feminine identity that can be summed up in the single term "passivity." But what about the *journey* of the heroine? The birth, growth, development, challenges, and resolutions that provide an alternative to the passive story? Does anyone know what that is? Has this archetype been theorized—does it even exist? An understanding of the two Arwens, I think, points us in the direction of some of the answers to her questions.

With respect to the relationship between the work on the page and the work on the screen, Fran Walsh's closing comments for *The Fellowship of the Ring* and *The Two Towers* make an interesting contrast. After completing the extended version of the DVD for the first film in the trilogy, but while work was still underway—including shooting of new material—for *The Two Towers* and *The Return of the King*, she said:

It was a hugely daunting task to be taking on these books, and in a way we felt we had to give ourselves as much permission to deviate and as much creative latitude as possible, and so that was our starting-off point: don't be afraid to make changes, and we made a lot of changes in our first passes; we thought, well, what do we need to do in order to get this functioning as a—a screen story. And then, having done that on, you know, a few drafts, we started to feel secure enough to start to adjust the screenplays back to the book. It was like once we had a really firm sense of how the stories could play, it was like, okay, now—now retrieve it; make it the story that everybody knows and loves. And that—that was not a sort of conscious path that we plotted, it was just the way it organically happened—that we really wanted to give the fans of the book something that they would love and a story that—that would reflect the book in a truthful way. And there's always a tension between doing that and also creating something which is cinematically satisfying. So we started off regarding the needs of cinema and then came back to the needs of the people who love this book and hopefully we found some sort of balance. (*Fellowship*, scene 47: "Credits," commentary)

A year later, in the commentary for *The Two Towers*, she notes that:

All cinema story telling, to a degree, is shallow [laugh]—I mean, that's the nature of the medium. You've got two or three hours to present a world and a dense story with a hundred themes, and a ton of back-story in this instance, um, and twenty-two characters. So you—you can only really have the—the—veneer of depth. You really can't have anything that comes close to the depth of the books or the experience of the books. So I think what we attempted to do was to use the language of the books where we could and to certainly invoke them—the iconic images—where we could, but to keep the story telling very much—to modernize it, if you like—in terms of cinema language. . . . You can't hope to really satisfy people who adore this book with the movie. You can only ever give them the sense of what might have been. That's all a film can do. I—I—I think in that sense, films—I mean, they're entertainments. They're just not going to give you the pleasure that a book can give you. (*Towers*, scene 67: "End Credits," commentary)

Clearly, the filmmakers experienced their own journey of discovery and transformation in the course of completing their adaptation of Tolkien's work. They drew deeply from that very deep well, but they also drew on cultural currents that have surged since Tolkien finished his epic—or in any case since he was prevented by death from carrying his exploration of it any farther.

In my opinion, when we evaluate the success of the film with reference to the book, a judgment that focuses more fully on how well the final cinematic work turned out is closer to capturing their real relative merits than one that emphasizes the discrepancies between them to the disadvantage of either. As Peter Jackson noted in his commentary for the extended DVD edition of *The Two Towers*, "really there's no definitive *Lord of the Rings*" (*Towers*, scene 33: "The Evenstar," commentary). In the private space of each person's mind, we all receive our very own version of the story, whether from the page or from the screen. Most of us will also misinterpret and misremember it in our own unique ways, and some of us will deliberately re-craft it for our own purposes. It has often been noted that Tolkien wanted to create an original mythology, and to the extent that myths are the stories that keep being told and retold and adapted to new techniques of telling, I think that Peter Jackson's adaptation of Tolkien's masterwork stands as a testimony to the novel's enduring value while also helping to guarantee its survival and extending its influence to new generations of enthusiasts.

WORKS CITED

The Abyss. Dir. James Cameron. Perf. Ed Harris, Mary-Elizabeth Mastrantonio, and Michael Biehn. 1989. Videocassette. Twentieth-Century Fox, 1996.

Aliens. Dir. James Cameron. Perf. Sigourney Weaver, Carrie Henn, Michael Biehn, and Lance Hendrickson. 1986. Videocassette. Fox Home Entertainment, 2003.

Apuleius. *The Golden Ass*. Trans. Jack Lindsay. Bloomington: Indiana University Press, 1962. 110-142.

Campbell, Joseph. *The Hero with a Thousand Faces*. Bollingen Series XVII. Princeton: Princeton University Press, 1949.

Estés, Clarissa Pinkola. *Women Who Run with the Wolves: Myths and Stories of the Wild Woman Archetype*. New York: Ballantine Books, 1992.

Forster, E.M. *Aspects of the Novel*. New York: Harcourt, Brace, and Company, 1927.

Frazer, Sir James George. *The Golden Bough: A Study in Magic and Religion*. 1922. Abridged ed. New York: Collier Books-Macmillan Publishing Company, 1950.

French, Marilyn. *The Women's Room*. New York: Summit Books, 1977.

Frye, Northrop. *The Anatomy of Criticism: Four Essays*. New York: Atheneum, 1970.

The Lord of the Rings: The Fellowship of the Ring. Special Extended DVD Edition. Screenplay by Peter Jackson, Fran Walsh, and Philippa Boyens. Perf. Elijah Wood et al. Dir. Peter Jackson. United States: New Line Home Entertainment, 2002.

The Lord of the Rings: The Return of the King. Theatrical Release DVD. Screenplay by Peter Jackson, Fran Walsh, and Philippa Boyens. Perf. Elijah Wood et al. Dir. Peter Jackson. United States, New Line Home Entertainment, 2004.

The Lord of the Rings: The Two Towers. Special Extended DVD Edition. Screenplay by Peter Jackson, Fran Walsh, and Philippa Boyens. Perf. Elijah Wood et al. Dir. Peter Jackson. United States: New Line Home Entertainment, 2003.

Phillips, John A. *Eve: The History of an Idea*. San Francisco: Harper & Row, 1984.

Pomeroy, Sarah. *Goddesses, Whores, Wives, and Slaves: Women in Classical Antiquity*. New York: Schocken Books, 1975.

Shakespeare, William. *A Midsummer Night's Dream. The Riverside Shakespeare*. Ed. G. Blakemore Evans. Boston: Houghton Mifflin Company, 1974.

The Terminator. Dir. James Cameron. Perf. Arnold Schwartzenegger, Michael Biehn, and Linda Hamilton. 1984. Videocassette. Artisan Entertainment, 2000.

Titanic. Dir. James Cameron. Perf. Leonardo DiCaprio and Kate Winslet. 1997. Videocassette. Paramount Studio, 2003.

Tolkien, J.R.R. *The Lord of the Rings*. 2nd ed. With Note on the Text by Douglas A. Anderson. Boston: Houghton Mifflin, 1994.

Warner, Marina. *Alone of All Her Sex: The Myth and the Cult of the Virgin Mary*. New York: Vintage Books-Random House, 1976.

The X-Files: Fight the Future. Dir. Rob Bowman. Perf. David Duchovney and Gillian Anderson. 1998. Videocassette. Twentieth-Century Fox, 2001.

THE "SUB-SUBCREATION" OF GALADRIEL, ARWEN, AND ÉOWYN: WOMEN OF POWER IN TOLKIEN'S AND JACKSON'S *THE LORD OF THE RINGS*

MAUREEN THUM

In "Tree and Leaf," J.R.R. Tolkien refers to the writer and teller of fairy tales as "sub-creator" (56-57) whose stories "open the door on Other Time" and allow us to "stand . . . outside time itself" (56). The sub-creator is capable of evoking a secondary world filled with wonder, strangeness and enchantment (60). However, Tolkien also denies the possibility of representing this world "visibly and audibly" (70). It must forever remain a world of the imagination only. In Tolkien's words, "Fantastic forms are not to be counterfeited" (70).

Tolkien had never met film director Peter Jackson. Jackson and his production team have surely succeeded in making a "sub-creation" of Tolkien's work, a sub-creation that achieves the goal of successfully imaging Tolkien's alternate reality. While doing so, Jackson recognizes that the medium of film requires not merely a translation but a transmutation of Tolkien's enchanted world from words into filmic images. I believe that he has succeeded in this task.[1]

In the film trilogy, Jackson's role as sub-creator is tellingly evident in the portraits of three women: Galadriel, the Lady of Lórien and Queen of the Woodland Elves (*Silmarillion* 358); Arwen Evenstar, daughter of the half-Elven Elrond; and Éowyn, Shieldmaiden of Rohan. The changes appear in some instances to be so radical that viewers familiar with Tolkien's text might even argue that Jackson went beyond transmutation, taking considerable license in his translation from text to film.

I wish, however, to make the case that Jackson's sub-creation of Galadriel, Arwen, and Éowyn as positive and powerful figures by no means represents a falsification or distortion of Tolkien's attitudes toward

---

[1] Reviewers frequently decry Jackson's effort arguing that he has re-created the novel and omitted much of the text. See for example Jane Chance's review of the film. For a contrasting view, see Elvis Mitchell's review of *The Two Towers*.

women as some critics have argued.[2] Indeed, Tolkien's vision of women is far more complex than many critics have allowed, and Jackson's portraits reflect and comment on that complexity.

Throughout his works, from *The Lord of the Rings* to *The Silmarillion* and the *Unfinished Tales*, and *The Shaping of Middle-earth*, Tolkien consistently portrays women in powerful and positive roles. With few exceptions, he reverses many of the stereotypical expectations traditionally attached to women of power. In his mythical creation stories, he even goes so far as to reverse the biblical account of the Fall, so that man, not woman, is responsible for the destruction of paradise. In presenting Galadriel, Arwen, and Éowyn as stronger and more fully developed figures than we might at first expect from Tolkien's text, Jackson accurately represents the positive view of unconventional and powerful women throughout Tolkien's writings.

In order to make my case, I will first discuss Tolkien's view of women in *The Shaping of Middle-earth*, *The Silmarillion*, and the *Unfinished Tales*, where Yavanna, Varda, and Lúthien play pivotal roles. Even a brief overview of these figures will serve to counter charges that Tolkien's writings are anti-feminist. I will then discuss Galadriel, Arwen, and Éowyn, demonstrating how their presence permeates *The Lord of the Rings*, extending their significance far beyond their relatively brief appearances in the novel. In each case, I will discuss Jackson's sub-creation of these figures. Far from distorting Tolkien's view of women, Jackson's invented scenes and images allow the significance Tolkien implies to emerge fully and vividly. Despite sometimes radical alterations in the text, then, Jackson's re-creation remains true to the spirit of Tolkien's writings.

WOMEN OF POWER IN THE LEGENDARIUM

Basing their arguments in part on the relatively small number of women characters in his writings, critics have charged that Tolkien is an anti-feminist who subscribes to traditional views of gender roles. Thus, Brenda Partridge states that Tolkien's women are "conceived along traditional lines" (183), while Candice Frederick and Sam McBride see Tolkien as proposing the "natural subordination" of women and limiting their roles accordingly (114). Tolkien, like his fellow Inklings, is therefore

---

[2] See Jane Chance, who argues the characters in Jackson's first film have little resonance or depth, and that Arwen in particular is no more than the caricature of a "feminized Amazon Warrior."

unable to escape the label of "misogynist" (Frederick and McBride 160). Catharine Stimpson dismisses Tolkien's female characters on the ground that they are "the most hackneyed of stereotypes" (18).[3] However, I wish to argue with Leslie Donovan, Helen Armstrong, and Lisa Hopkins[4] that the significance of Tolkien's women has been underestimated and even overlooked. Tolkien is by no means an anti-feminist. Indeed, he subverts and undermines traditional views of men's and women's roles throughout his works.[5] Furthermore, although they are few in comparison to the numerous male characters in *The Lord of the Rings*, women are of key importance to the text.

A brief overview of gender stereotypes will help to provide a point of departure for my argument concerning Tolkien's view of women. According to traditional binary constructions of gender, men and women fall into diametrically and mutually exclusive categories. Men are ideally strong, active, and adventuresome; they are heroic, rational, and in charge. Women, by contrast, are viewed as weak, passive, dependent, and powerless. While men are active in the wider, public and political world, women's lower intelligence and lack of political acumen restrict them to the domestic sphere. While men are destined to take the initiative as leaders, women are viewed as naturally submissive followers. Men make history; women walk obediently in their footsteps.[6] Traditionalists from

---

[3] As Leslie Donovan notes, "many readers have considered the paucity of female characters [in *The Lord of the Rings*] . . . as a serious flaw in his work" (106). Critics such as Edith Crowe, who defend Tolkien's lack of women characters, do so primarily by referring to the anti-feminism inherent in many of his medieval sources. In Crowe's words, "He was only reflecting his sources and his times" (272).

[4] I would argue with Hopkins that the importance of women in *The Lord of the Rings* is "remarkably disproportionate to their numbers" (365). For an excellent overview of previous criticism arguing for both views, see Donovan (106-7). Donovan notes that such critics as Mac Fenwick and Peter Goslin "support readings of Tolkien's women as strong, authoritative characters with pivotal narrative importance" by reading them "in the context of classical epics, Christian typology, psychological archetypes, or contemporary gender constructs" (107).

[5] Lisa Hopkins makes the case that Tolkien is exceptional among his circle of friends in presenting "a vision of women . . . unhampered by that crippling fear of femininity which besets the world of his fellow Inklings" (366).

[6] These binary views of gender roles can be found throughout the history of western civilization, in the writings of such key figures as Aristotle and Rousseau. Rousseau's highly influential *Emile; or, On Education* (Book Five) states that men and women have delineated and opposing roles. According to Rousseau, women should be "shut up in their houses" so that they restrict all their activities "to their households and their families. Such is the way of life that nature and reason prescribe for the fair sex" (366). See the excellent discussion of

Aristotle and Thomas Aquinas to Darwin and Freud believe that the higher reaches of the mind and intellect are closed to women; thus, they can never reach the level of intelligence and knowledge enjoyed by men. As Darwin states, "The chief distinction in the intellectual powers of the two sexes is shewn [sic] by man's attaining to a higher eminence in whatever he takes up, than can a woman—whether requiring deep thought, reason, or imagination, or merely the use of senses and hands" (260). And in the words of Friedrich Nietzsche, "Superficiality is the character of woman, a moving, tempestuous membrane on shallow water" while "the soul of the man is deep; . . . Woman guesses his power but is unable to understand it" (269).

Traditionally, both men and women have been censured for transgressing the restrictive boundaries of their gender roles. Passive, non-heroic and submissive men are frequently the subject of derision, and seen as effeminate, a word that continues to carry negative connotations even in the twenty-first century. By the same token, active, powerful women who step outside the limitations of their accepted roles are viewed as man-like, aggressive and domineering. Castigated for violating their own divinely ordained nature, and usurping roles that rightfully belong to men, such independent female figures have been portrayed throughout the centuries as perverse and demonic creatures who must be imprisoned, banished, or killed. As Nietzsche's Zarathustra states, "Do you go to women? Do not forget the whip" (269). [7]

---

gender roles in the collection of articles entitled *Nature, Culture and Gender*, edited by Carol MacCormack and Marilyn Strathern. See also the discussion of the male-female binary roles in Mary O'Brien's essay.

[7] A long history of anti-feminist writing decrying the evil of the woman who usurps men's roles is represented by John Knox's attack on Queen Mary of England, "The First Blast of the Trumpet Against the Monstrous Regiment of Women" (1558). This document was penned during the Renaissance, but whatever the justice or injustice of its specific historical context, it fairly stands for the angry reaction to power in women both in the centuries before and after Knox's diatribe. See the collection of texts in Rosemary Agonito's *History of Ideas on Women* for an excellent cross-section of feminist and anti-feminist texts from Plato and Aristotle through the twentieth century. The killing of wicked women and "witches," was, of course, not limited to fairy tales, but was carried out in the burning of witches from medieval times until the seventeenth century. See Diane Purkiss' *The Witch in History*. See also the well-known medieval document, *The Witches' Hammer* written by Heinrich Kramer and James Sprenger, first published in 1484. When it was republished in 1928 and 1948, the introductions to the translation into English registered strong approval of the document's contents. The 1928 introduction begins approvingly with the statement that we have recognized "from the very earliest times" that "witchcraft is an evil thing, an enemy to light, and ally of the powers of darkness" (xi), while the 1948 edition praises the document for its

Contrary to those who see Tolkien as an anti-feminist writer, I wish to argue that Tolkien by no means underwrites the binary views of gender construction outlined above. He is no feminist. Nevertheless, he subverts traditional views of gender roles throughout his writings. To offer a point of comparison, let us pause briefly to look at his contemporary and long time-friend, C.S. Lewis. In Lewis's Narnia series, young girls play unconventional roles. But in his choice of the representatives of Good and Evil in the magical land of Narnia, Lewis has remained conventional. Evil is frequently represented by a demonic woman, in particular an actively evil witch. We have, for example, The White Witch of *The Lion, the Witch, and the Wardrobe* and the green Queen of Underland in *The Silver Chair*. The highest Good on the other hand is represented throughout the series by a venerable and powerful male figure, by a Lion – one would assume, a British lion—named Aslan.

Tolkien, by contrast, almost invariably portrays powerful women positively and seldom portrays such figures as evil and in need of punishment or death. We see such positive and unconventional portraits in the creation myths of *The Silmarillion* and *The Shaping of Middle-earth*. In the tales of the Valar, two divine women, Yavanna and Varda, reverse the tale of Eve, whose weakness, passivity, and inability to resist temptation led to the Fall and ejection from the garden of Paradise. In Tolkien's tales, the destruction of Paradise is not brought about by a woman, but by a male figure, Melkor or Morgoth, Demon of the Dark. Formerly one of the Valar, Morgoth has turned to evil and treachery. After rebelling against the chief of the Valar, he "overthrows the lamps set up to illumine the world" (*Shaping* 12), then flees and fortifies dungeons in the north (*Shaping* 12; *Silmarillion* 29). The Valar move to the West, to Valinor, where they "gather all light and beautiful things, and build their mansions, gardens, and city" (*Shaping* 12). Instead of playing a negative role, Yavanna and Varda are creators and givers of light and life.

In contrast to Eve, whose deed casts all subsequent generations out of Eden, Yavanna becomes the gardener in the mythical realm of Valinor and restores the Edenic world that Morgoth attempted to destroy. In place of the extinguished lamps, she plants two blessed trees: "Under her songs the saplings grew . . . and thus there awoke in the world the Two Trees of Valinor" (*Silmarillion* 31). Telperion, the eldest of the two, produces a "dew of silver light," while Laurelin, the younger, has yellow

---

"edification" which has provided "seemingly inexhaustible wells of wisdom" for subsequent readers (ix).

blossoms which produce "heat and blazing light" (*Shaping* 12). "Each tree waxes for seven hours to full glory, and then wanes for seven; twice a day therefore comes a time of softer light" (*Shaping* 12). In other words, Yavanna's trees provide the light by which the Valar live. When Morgoth destroys the trees, Yavanna, using her powers, causes Telperion to bring forth "one last great silver bloom" and Laurelin "one great golden fruit" (*Shaping* 21). The silver bloom becomes the moon, and the golden fruit becomes the sun. They light up Middle-earth, and bring about the awakening of men, "the younger children of the earth" (*Shaping* 22).

A second powerful figure, Varda, portrayed as the creator of the stars, ranks first among the Valier or female Valar. While Yavanna's blessed trees still live, Varda, Queen of the Stars, gathers their light "in great vats like shining lakes" (*Silmarillion* 32). Taking the hoarded light from the two trees, she creates new and brighter stars. When she has completed this "greatest of all the works of the Valar" (*Silmarillion* 44), the elves awaken and "their eyes [behold] first of all things the stars of heaven" (45). Henceforth, the elves revere Varda, whom they call upon for protection, using her Sindarin name, Elbereth (*Silmarillion* 34). Varda and Yavanna are not isolated figures limited to the creations myths of *The Silmarillion*. Their influence is continually evident throughout *The Lord of the Rings*. Yavanna is felt in two ways. First, she is present in the continuing efficacy of the light shed by the two blessed trees, which has been captured in the Silmarils. In *The Lord of the Rings*, Tolkien refers frequently to the Silmarils and their power. Captured in Galadriel's star glass, the light from the Silmaril on Eärendil's brow continues to ward off evil. As Galadriel explains to Frodo when she gives him the gift of the star glass, "In this phial . . . is caught the light of Eärendil's star, set amid the waters of my fountain" (367; II:8). Thus, Yavanna's two trees continue their beneficent work after they are long gone. Her influence is also suggested in The White Tree of Gondor which has a strong symbolic value throughout the novel. As Gandalf informs us, the white tree is a descendent of Telperion, the "Eldest of Trees" that Yavanna had planted (950; VI:5), and it shares some of its ancestor's magical qualities.

Like the fruit of the tree, which remained dormant in the mountains until the coming of Aragorn (950: VI:5), Yavanna appears to lie sleeping and unheard in Middle-earth, and yet her influence has awakened and helps to change the course of events that lead to Sauron's fall. Without the light from her trees, caught in the phial of Galadriel, neither Sam nor Frodo could have survived the onslaught of Shelob. Sam could not have passed the watchers at Minas Morgul to rescue Frodo (882; VI:1), and both Sam and Frodo would have been trapped in Minas Morgul without the power of the elven glass to subdue the watchers who barred their escape (894; VI:1).

Varda/Elbereth's presence is frequently evident in *The Lord of the Rings*. She not only appears numerous times in the text but she also palpably influences the outcome of Frodo's quest.[8] Elbereth is the guide to the elves and the protector of Frodo to whom he calls in his need. When the Ringwraith threatens Frodo in the forest at the beginning of his quest, the creature immediately retreats after the elves sing "Gilthoniel! O Elbereth" (77; I:3). One of the elves, Gildor Inglorion, blesses Frodo on his journey, invoking her name: "May Elbereth protect you" (83; I:3), and she does intervene at crucial points. At Weathertop, when the Ringwraiths attack, they are not fended off by Frodo's knife, which merely strikes their leader's cloak. Instead, as Aragorn notes, they retreated upon hearing Frodo invoke Elbereth's name: "More deadly to [the Ringwraith] was the name of Elbereth [than Frodo's blade]" (193; I:12). Later, at the Ford of the Bruinen, as the Ringwraiths close in on Frodo, he swears "By Elbereth and Lúthien the Fair . . . you shall have neither the Ring nor me" (209; I:12), just before the rushing waters sweep the enemy away. Near the falls of Rauros, Legolas calls upon her powers before successfully shooting down the winged steed of a Ringwraith (378; II:9). Like Yavanna, her presence is also felt in Galadriel's star glass. Her connection with the phial is through Eärendil, on whose ship she put the Silmaril as a lantern light This Silmaril provides the source for the mysterious light in the elven glass (367; II:8). The reader is reminded of this connection when Sam uses the glass in Shelob's lair. The phial "kindled to a silver flame . . . as though Eärendil himself had come down from the high sunset paths with the last Silmaril on his brow" (704; IV:9). When Sam finally overcomes Shelob, the star glass strikes the final blow, blasting her sight with "intolerable light," and an invocation to Elbereth galvanizes Sam's spirit to action (712-13; IV:10). Thus, the power of Elbereth, like that of Yavanna, is felt each time Galadriel's phial shines to ward off evil in the darkness.

A third powerful woman in *The Silmarillion*, Lúthien the Fair, the ancestor of Arwen Evenstar, is an independent and courageous heroine. She not only rescues her lover, Beren, from the prison of Sauron, but outfaces Morgoth in a daring and successful attempt to recapture one of the stolen Silmarils from his iron crown. None of the male elves had attempted that feat. The elves state in astonishment upon hearing of the

---

[8] Frederick and McBride dismiss Elbereth as unimportant. In their words, "she does not have enough direct involvement in the plot to be considered a character" (113). However, the constant references clearly indicate not only her strong presence, but also her intervention in the events of the quest.

deed: "a maiden had dared that which the sons of Fëanor had not dared to do" (*Silmarillion* 206). As in the case of both Yavanna and Varda/Elbereth, the reader of *The Lord of the Rings* is constantly reminded of Lúthien. Her tale is told by Aragorn more than once, and is invoked in his reference to Arwen as "Tinúviel" the name Beren had given to Lúthien many ages before. The reader is also told that Lúthien appears to have been reborn in the figure of Arwen, so that Arwen literally embodies this earlier heroine, and reminds the reader of her great exploits. Remarkably, in all of the tales and novels, Tolkien portrays only two actively evil female creatures: Ungoliant, the accomplice of Morgoth, who takes the form of a great spider, and who sucks the light out of the two blessed trees (*Shaping* 17); and her wicked daughter, Shelob, whom Frodo and Samwise encounter in their attempt to enter Mordor, and who is designated as "the last child of Ungoliant to trouble the unhappy world" (707; IV:9). The fact that Tolkien portrays powerful women almost invariably as positive givers of life and light is truly unusual, breaking with accepted conventions of female roles. In legends and fairy tales, active women are most frequently evil stepmothers or wicked witches who must be destroyed.

As these brief examples demonstrate, although women make few overt appearances in Tolkien's works, their role is both positive and significant. The presence of Elbereth, Yavanna, and Lúthien permeates the entire spiritual fabric of *The Lord of the Rings*. These three women are representative of Tolkien's consistently positive portrait of powerful women throughout his works. Galadriel, Arwen, and Éowyn are no exception. All three look backward to *The Silmarillion* for their history, their female precedents, and their parallels, and all three play heroic roles in their own right.

GALADRIEL: THE POWER OF WISDOM

Let us begin by considering Galadriel, first as she appears in Tolkien's novel and then as she is translated by Jackson. In *The Lord of the Rings*, Tolkien portrays her as strong, wise, and gifted woman who is only considered a witch by those who know nothing of her real nature. In the *Unfinished Tales*, Tolkien presents her as the greatest of Elven women, and indeed the greatest of all the Noldor "except Fëanor . . . though she was wiser than he and her wisdom increased with the long years" (*Unfinished* 229). Galadriel's greatness thus sets her beyond all women and most men. She has the accomplishments associated with men, for she is "strong of body, mind, and will, a match for both the loremasters and the athletes of the Eldar" (*Unfinished* 229). As the keeper of Nenya, one of the three Elven rings, she wields great power and is able to protect Lothlórien from evil.

In numerous traditional tales, such women are portrayed as inherently wicked and demonic. Wicked witches and wicked sorceresses abound in the world of fairy tale.[9] Almost invariably, these active and gifted women wreak havoc, and must be punished or killed in order to rid the world of their evil presence. Galadriel breaks the stereotype. Although wise and active, she is neither demonic nor dangerous. Unlike Eve, who cannot resist evil, Galadriel is able to withstand a temptation that many strong men, including Boromir, Saruman, and Denethor, find irresistible. All of them succumb to the lure of the Ring. By contrast, when Frodo freely offers the Ring to Galadriel, she refuses its temptation and resists its power even though she knows that, henceforth, she will diminish and that her time on the Middle-earth will now inevitably draw to its close.

Galadriel's beneficent influence extends far beyond her relatively brief appearances in *The Lord of the Rings*. The reader is reminded of her presence especially through the powerful gifts she gives to the members of the Fellowship. The elven cloaks, made by her own hands, protect them from detection; the phial, which captures the light of Eärendil's Silmaril, protects them from harm; the elven rope responds to her name and unties itself; the lembas or waybread of the elves feeds the Fellowship in times of hunger; her words, sent through Gandalf, provide guidance to the fellowship members; her gift of earth from her garden causes the devastated landscape of the Shire to blossom and grow fruitful again.

She also plays a positive role both politically and personally, intervening at crucial junctures to organize the defense against the Sauron, to provide help and healing, and to summon aid when it is needed. It is she who first calls the White Council to counter the growing power of Sauron (348; II:7); it is she who heals Gandalf after his deadly combat with the Balrog (491; III:5); and it is she who summons the Dúnedain from the north to help Aragorn (759; V:2). Contrary to Frederick and McBride's assertion (112), she is not to be dismissed as an unimportant character who has little influence on Tolkien's tale.

Let us now look at her transformation in Peter Jackson's films. Jackson clearly views her as a central rather than peripheral character. In *The Fellowship*, the director has chosen to emphasize Galadriel's power by featuring her not only in the Lothlórien segment, but also in the film's

---

[9] The images are well known. One need merely mention the wicked witch in the Grimm Brothers' "Hansel and Gretel" or the wicked stepmother turned witch in "Snow White," to indicate only the most famous of these reprehensible and demonic creatures.

invented prologue, where her voice-over tells the tale of the Ring. Galadriel plays the role of the historian, the powerful tale-teller who understands the history and wider implications of the Ring's story and who transmits this history to the audience. In the medievalized context of Middle-earth, Galadriel takes the traditionally male role of the scop. During the prologue, Galadriel guides the viewer through a series of pictorial reenactments of the events she describes, showing the three ages of Middle-earth, as well as the significance and continuing power of the Ring. Tellingly, Jackson's prologue shows that Galadriel, a woman, knows more than any of the other characters portrayed in the film, whether male or female. Boromir is puzzled and never understands history except as it pertains to Gondor; Gandalf must discover this information in the library at Minas Tirith; the Hobbits are blissfully unaware of any history outside their own. Even Bilbo, who has possessed the Ring for many years, knows only of his own previous journey and has no knowledge of the Ring's significance and power. As Galadriel's historical account comes to a close, the final shot shifts to Bilbo's study in the Shire, where Bilbo, the male narrator, takes over. In the film, he is given the limited role of describing only the circumscribed world of the Hobbits. In the opening of the film, these two narrators, Galadriel and Bilbo, demonstrate a reversal of roles which we will see frequently in Jackson's films. Galadriel, a woman, recognizes and understands the wider historical, political, and cultural context of the Ring as a threat to the peoples of Middle-earth, while Bilbo, a male hobbit, is restricted to the domestic concerns of the Shire, and, as we will later discover, sees the Ring mainly as a fascinating toy.

Jackson dramatizes Galadriel's appearance in Lothlórien through lighting, slow motion, special effects, and digitization. During her first encounter with the Fellowship, although she stands side by side with Celeborn, her husband, the viewer's attention focuses on her. Backlighting and fill light provide a halo-like aura about her figure. Digital enhancement alters subtly the color tones of her face, giving it an unearthly pearlescent cast (*Fellowship*, app: "From Book to Vision"). The faces of the Fellowship members have been digitally highlighted, so that they appear to reflect the light of her presence. Her gaze is shown to have the power and control traditionally associated with men. Close-ups of her face and eyes, as she looks intently at each of the Fellowship members, alternate with shots of their faces, reacting to her gaze, each with a different emotion. Jackson uses both her spoken voice and a voice-over to show that she communicates both in the ordinary sense, in spoken words, and by projecting her thoughts and probing the mind of each member of the Fellowship.

In the garden scene, when Frodo looks into her mirror, and offers her the Ring of power, Jackson continues to emphasize her otherworldly power by subtle technical manipulation of sound, light and movement. Her figure, standing out against the relative darkness of the backdrop, appears to emit light, creating the sense of a visible aura. When she glides through the night to meet Frodo, Jackson slows her movements almost imperceptibly by increasing the number of frames per second (*Fellowship*, app.: "From Book to Vision").[10] During the temptation scene, Jackson, following Tolkien's cue, does not present Galadriel as the traditional feminine ideal of ignorant innocence, untainted by knowledge of evil. Instead, he demonstrates that Galadriel understands the temptation of power and recognizes its frightening and dangerous implications. When Frodo offers her the Ring, through special effects, the beautiful, wise Galadriel is transformed into a demonic and frightening creature, not unlike the Ringwraiths. This transmogrification illustrates visually her knowledge of the horror that she could unleash as the new Master of the Ring.

In *The Two Towers*, Galadriel reappears, almost mid-point in the film, once again playing the role of the scop who narrates the continuing history of the Ring. An extreme close-up only of Galadriel's eyes emphasizes the power of her vision. As in the prologue to *The Fellowship*, her historical overview and analysis of the present situation is illustrated by a series of scenes through which she guides the viewer. Close-ups of Galadriel's face are intercut with close-ups of Elrond, who can hear her from afar. Again roles are reversed. The female historian, Galadriel, instructs the male leader who silently and attentively listens (*Towers*, scene 39: "The Story Foreseen from Lórien").

In *The Two Towers* and *The Return of the King*, Jackson, like Tolkien, also suggests Galadriel's continued presence and influence through her gifts to members of the Fellowship. In the extended version of *The Fellowship*, we see her bestow those gifts. In the two later films, as in Tolkien's text, the phial, the elven rope, and the cloaks are featured constantly, giving special protection to the user and wearer. Jackson even portrays Galadriel as appearing to Frodo in a vision after he falls unconscious to the ground outside Shelob's lair (*Return*, scene 29: "Shelob's Lair"). In Galadriel, then, Jackson presents the viewer with a figure who images the positive view of female power implied by Tolkien's

---

[10] See the description of techniques used to slow the movements, deepen the voice and provide Galadriel with an other-worldly appearance in the section concerning Galadriel in *The Appendices Part One* of the extended version of *The Fellowship*.

portrait in *The Lord of the Rings.* Unlike the demonic witches of traditional fairy tales, Galadriel is not trapped by an inherently evil nature; she is not seduced to do evil, and she is not punished by a terrible death for her active role. She is therefore no "hackneyed stereotype." On the contrary, active, powerful, and wise, yet kind, compassionate, and nurturing, she defies the traditional binaries, and steps outside the limited role allotted to women in a patriarchal society.

ARWEN: THE POWER OF LOVE

In the case of Galadriel, Peter Jackson has not altered Tolkien's essentially unconventional portrait except through a greater emphasis on the power Tolkien himself attributes to her throughout his writings. In the case of Arwen, by contrast, Jackson makes what appear to be radical changes. In the novel, we only catch a brief glimpse of Arwen, who does not appear until Frodo and the members of the fellowship arrive at Elrond's elven haven of Rivendell. There Frodo first sees her at the table with the Elf Lords. "Such loveliness in living thing Frodo had never seen before or imagined" (221; II:1). Later he catches a glimpse of her with Aragorn: "Arwen turned towards him, and the light of her eyes fell on him from afar and pierced his heart" (232; II:1). As with Galadriel, she is a positive and powerful figure with gifts and abilities beyond those of mortal beings. But we are given only a few tantalizing glimpses of her past history, her long relationship with Aragorn, and her willingness to sacrifice immortality for the sake of love.

Tolkien, however, implies far more than he states. Thus he introduces Arwen initially through the parallel to Lúthien, whose tale is told in *The Fellowship* by Aragorn (187-89; I:11), as well as in *The Silmarillion.* As Tolkien stresses in a letter to the editor,[11] the tale of Arwen, "in whom it was said that the likeness of Lúthien had come on earth again" (221; II:1), is to be understood against the backdrop of Lúthien's tale. Lúthien was a strong heroine who braved the terrors of Sauron to rescue Beren, who restored him to life twice after he was mortally wounded, and who overcame even the dreaded Morgoth. These intertextual references to Tolkien's own pre-histories and to his

---

[11] Tolkien made clear in a letter to the editor that *The Silmarillion* was indispensable to a full understanding of *The Lord of the Rings.* Specifically the tale of Beren and Lúthien provides a "fundamental link in the cycle," and it is "deprived of its full significance" if it is not taken into account when reading *The Lord of the Rings (Silmarillion* "Preface" xxi).

appendices provide Arwen with a far greater depth and dimension than might otherwise be surmised if one were to look only at the text of *The Lord of the Rings* itself.[12] Furthermore, as Leslie Donovan has compellingly argued, like Galadriel and Éowyn, Arwen is one of the "narrative agents charged with authority of distinct heroic women figures from Old Norse mythology and literature called the valkyries" (108). As Donovan demonstrates, Arwen shares many of the characteristics of these fiercely independent figures. She has a "valkyrie-like radiance" which is "identified with starlight" (Donovan 127). Like the valkyrie, she bestows important gifts "of inspiration and reward with illuminative properties to heroes" (Donovan 127). These include Aragorn's banner, which is a "potent, radiantly shining, heroic standard" and Frodo's necklace, which is both a "heroic reward" and a comfort when he is troubled (Donovan 128). Seen in this light, Tolkien's Arwen has unplumbed depths that are only evident if we take into account what Tolkien suggests beyond the text itself.

In the film, Jackson plumbs those depths by inventing several sequences in which Arwen plays a leading role. We see her courageously venturing forth from Rivendell to rescue Frodo; we view her encouraging Aragorn when he is uncertain of his path; we observe her rescuing him and awakening him with her kiss; and we witness her commanding the reforging of Narsil, the sword that was broken. I will examine three scenes which exemplify the kinds of changes Jackson has made. They are the rescue of Frodo, and the two parallel scenes showing real and visionary kisses which Arwen and Aragorn share.

Jackson radically alters the rescue of Frodo. In the novel, a male figure, Glorfindel, a powerful Elf Lord, rides out to seek the Fellowship as they make their way toward Rivendell. In *The Fellowship*, by contrast, Jackson attributes the rescue to Arwen, thus linking her to her ancestor, Lúthien, who carried out similar exploits of bravery and heroism. Jackson uses the rescue sequence outside Rivendell to present the many facets of Arwen's character as a knight, as a woman with special skills and powers, and as a compassionate healer and nurturer. He uses lighting and slow motion, as well as multiple camera perspectives and digitization, to dramatize his portrait. Arwen is introduced in a striking scene. It is night. The members of the Fellowship have recognized that Frodo is failing fast from the deadly knife wound received at Weathertop, and have spread out

---

[12] Frederick and McBride's conclusion that Arwen is unimportant because she "makes only the briefest of appearances in the narrative" (110) does not take into account the clues and suggestions throughout the text pointing to her power and significance.

in the woods in search the healing herb, kingsfoil. The camera focuses on Aragorn who is down on his knees, gathering kingsfoil. Not only is he in a submissive posture, but he also assums the role of healer and herb gatherer, roles traditionally assigned to women. Suddenly, from the upper right corner of the frame, a sword blade is thrust into the picture, and held against Aragorn's throat. We do not see the perpetrator. Aragorn looks around and upward to see who is holding the blade. The viewer expects to hear the voice of the enemy. Instead, off-screen, Arwen speaks, chiding Aragorn for his failure to notice her approach: "What's this? A ranger caught off his guard?" she asks in a playfully mocking tone. Only with the next shot of Arwen as a knight on horseback do we recognize that Jackson has intentionally imaged a reversal of the traditional fairy tale roles of powerful knight and vulnerable woman. Aragorn is not only on his knees before her, but helplessly in her power (*Fellowship*, scene 21: "Flight to the Ford").

We now see Arwen from the point of view of the half-conscious Frodo as she gallops toward him. Backlighting outlines her figure with a halo-like effect, while soft fill-light allows us to see her features as she moves in slow motion. The slow motion emphasizes the dramatic effect, but also suggests the dream-like quality of her appearance, as well as the mixture of power, beauty and lyricism in this iconic figure. She dismounts, and approaches slowly. The backlighting fades so that she appears less dream-like, yet still ethereal, as she calls Frodo in Elvish to come back to the light. The lighting and special effects change as Jackson cuts to a shot of Aragorn and Arwen bending over Frodo. Arwen is no longer suffused with otherworldly light, appearing as a mortal being rather than a vision. A compassionate yet skilled healer, she quickly assesses the gravity of the situation and decides that Frodo must be taken immediately to Rivendell.

Jackson now portrays the heroism of her rescue against the backdrop of protesting men who believe that a woman should not undertake such an errand. Aragorn objects that the ride is "too dangerous" for a woman, and should be entrusted to him, a man. Arwen overrides his objections: "I am the faster rider," she states. Then, referring to the Ringwraiths, Arwen asserts, proudly and firmly, "I do not fear them . . . The power of my people will protect [Frodo]." In the novel, Frodo rides on Glorfindel's magical steed, escaping the pursuing Ringwraiths. In the film, by contrast, Jackson portrays Arwen as undertaking a daring rescue and out-riding her deadly pursuers.

The flight to the ford is dramatized by alternating close-ups of Arwen holding Frodo, aerial shots following the riders from above, medium action shots of the Ringwraiths closing in, reaching out hands to grasp Frodo, and long shots of the horses wheeling through the trees. The dangerous and suspenseful ride emphasizes her skill, her heroism, her determination, and her sheer will to outride her pursuers. At the river ford, her horse rears up as she whirls to face the nine riders who have stopped at the other side of the river—Tolkienists know that Ringwraiths as servants of the Dark Lord shun water (*Silmarillion* 138), probably since "the spirit of Ulmo [one of the Valar] runs through the veins [waterways] of the world" (*Silmarillion* 17). Unsheathing her sword in a swift movement, she holds it aloft, challenging the Ringwraiths in a voice Jackson has deepened for effect, "If you want him, come and claim him." In the text, we discover that Gandalf and Elrond are responsible for the flood that now overwhelms the pursuers. But Jackson uses this occasion to demonstrate Arwen's special powers, showing her to be similar to Lúthien, who could cast a spell on Sauron, and who was even able to subdue Morgoth. Arwen speaks an incantation that calls forth the magic horses of the river. Just visible in the approaching foam, the white horses sweep over her pursuers.

Her enemies vanquished, her expression softens to pity. Now the compassionate healer and wise woman, she folds Frodo into her arms, weeping as she prays, "What grace is given me, let it pass to him." The scene dissolves into light suffusing a chamber in Rivendell, focusing finally on Frodo convalescing, suggesting that much of the healing was due to Arwen's rescue and intervention. During the above sequences, Arwen undergoes a series of transformations which point to the complexity of her unconventional female role. She appears as warrior, as divine other, as healer, as woman and mother, roles that are only suggested in Tolkien's text (*Fellowship*, scene 21: "Flight to the Ford").

Although she remains in Rivendell, Jackson makes her presence and significance felt throughout *The Two Towers* and *The Return of the King* in a series of flashbacks, dreams, and visions. Two scenes involve a kiss and a role reversal. The first is Aragorn's flashback on the road to Helm's Deep, just before the attack of the Warg Riders. The scene is Rivendell. Arwen is standing, while Aragorn, reclining on a couch, expresses his doubts that "This is a dream." In a reversal of the fairy tale motif of the Sleeping Beauty, Arwen leans over to kiss him and to awaken him from his dream to the reality of their shared love (*Towers*, scene 33: "The Evenstar"). We see a similar reversal after the attack of the Warg Riders. Flung over a cliff during the attack, Aragorn has been left for dead. He is floating in the river, eyes closed and unconscious. The scene dissolves into rippling water with dancing reflections of sunlight in soft focus, giving a surreal, visionary quality to the picture. The scene shifts to Arwen,

245

reclining on a couch in Rivendell before dissolving once again to Aragorn's face, seen in profile, floating as if superimposed on the dancing ripples of the water. Arwen's face, also viewed in profile, descends into the picture from above. As in the Rivendell flashback, she seems to be bending over to kiss him. Her lips touch his. She whispers softly in a voice-over: "May the grace of the Valar protect you." Again the viewer is reminded of the Sleeping Beauty awakened to life and consciousness, and as in the previous scene, the roles are reversed. Aragorn suddenly opens his eyes and looks into hers before visibly taking a breath. Arwen's face begins to withdraw, then fades from the vision (*Towers*, scene 37: "The Grace of the Valar"). The scene is hauntingly accompanied by a song in Elvish entitled "The Breath of Life," sung in a dark, exotic register by Sheila Chandra (*Towers,* Appendix One). The music provides a rich, lyrical accompaniment to the scene, suggesting the mysteriousness of a shared vision. This sequence is not pure invention. In the Appendix Tolkien states, "Arwen remained in Rivendell, and when Aragorn was abroad, from afar she watched over him in thought" (1036; app. A:I:v), possibly suggesting the scenario Jackson provides. Furthermore, the scene sequence echoes the tale of Lúthien, who twice restored Beren to life, healing his mortal wound "by her arts and by her love" (*Silmarillion* 210). Thus Jackson incorporates both the tale in the Appendix, and the echoes of an earlier history into the story world of the film. The scene now shifts to a shot of Aragorn, lying half-conscious on the river bank, restored and perhaps even given the "breath of life," by Arwen's kiss.

Several additional scenes, including flashbacks, scenes with her father, Elrond, and a sequence during which she commands the reforging of the broken sword, keep Arwen before the viewer's eyes during *Two Towers* and *The Return of the King*. Although the sequences are invented by Jackson, they reflect the significance and the wider implications that Tolkien himself attaches to the figure of Arwen in his pre-history, and his frequent references to her as the reincarnation of Lúthien.

ÉOWYN: THE POWER OF COURAGE

Neither Galadriel nor Arwen are stereotypical figures who remain within the confines of traditional women's roles. The same may be said for Éowyn, the Shieldmaiden of Rohan. Tolkien does not present Éowyn in traditional terms as a robust, intelligent woman who must be silenced, and punished or killed for transgressing the patriarchal codes that govern her society. Instead, Tolkien undermines the traditional binaries by showing how Éowyn defies the limits of her mythic/historical context and becomes one of the most important figures in the siege of Minas Tirith. Far from containing and silencing Éowyn, Tolkien allows her to unfold her talents and to demonstrate her heroism. Instead of being punished, Éowyn is not only praised, but recognized and rewarded for stepping outside her expected role

When we first meet Éowyn, she is simply "a woman clad in white" standing behind the chair of her uncle, King Théoden (501; III:6). Nevertheless, the narrator is quick to point out her distance from the degraded king. She supports the king, but looks at him with "cool pity in her eyes" (504; III:6). Although Théoden has been overpowered by the spell of Gríma Wormtongue, Saruman's emissary, Éowyn resists his poisoned words and retains her independence of mind. She is both womanly and powerful: "slender and tall she was . . . but strong she seemed and stern as steel, a daughter of kings" (504; III:6). The men of Rohan admire and respect her. Háma suggests that she be given a man's role as Lord of the Eorlingas while the men are at war: "She is fearless and high hearted. All love her" (512; III:6).

In a court and a society dominated by men, Éowyn resists the "cage" of women's roles when she speaks out. She argues with Aragorn about the wisdom of his planned course of action, even going so far as to suggest, "Lord, you are astray," and to protest, "This is madness," when he states that he will take the Paths of the Dead (766; V:2). She is proud of her courage and skill: "I can ride and wield blade, and I do not fear either pain or death" (767; V:2), and she expresses impatience with the limitations of a woman's role in her traditionalist society.

Much like the powerful women in medieval romances and in Shakespeare's comedies, she finds strategies to break the bonds that imprison her. Forbidden to go to battle with the men, and ordered to remain at home, she disguises herself as a soldier, Dernhelm, and goes to war. To avoid the censure of the more conservative of his readers, Tolkien does not at first reveal her identity. Instead, he hides the fact that she fought along side the king during the worst of the battle until after the king is brought down by the Witch-king. When the Witch-king descends to attack his helpless prey, only Dernhelm—Éowyn—remains on the battlefield beside the dying king. When all men flee, Tolkien shows a woman standing her ground. Only at this point does Tolkien reveal her identity and show how Éowyn is able to reverse the conventional role of the legendary male hero who slays a dragon. Not a man, but a maid, is the hero who slays the Witch-king and his dragon beast. She thus saves her people and the people of Gondor.

Tolkien is careful to show that she is not simply a virago, a manly woman who was dismissed in patriarchal societies as a mere anomaly, or even a perversity of nature. Instead, she is clearly both woman and hero, retaining her womanly beauty while demonstrating her undaunted courage:

> . . . her bright hair, released from its bonds, gleamed with
> pale gold upon her shoulders. Her eyes grey as the sea were
> hard and fell, and yet tears were on her cheek. A sword was
> in her hand, and she raised her shield . . . (823; V:6)

As the winged beast falls down upon her, "shrieking, striking with beak and claw," she remains courageous. At the same time, Tolkien stresses that she is both beautiful and distinctly feminine: "Still she did not blench: Maiden of the Rohirrim, child of kings, slender but as a steel blade, fair yet terrible" (823; V:6).[13]

If she were a stereotypical figure in a traditional tale, she would be punished for her transgression, and castigated for taking a man's role, an act that was considered no less than a perversity, or even an abomination of nature. But Tolkien does not show her as being punished. Quite to the contrary, she is received with praise, sympathy, and understanding by all of the main male characters including Aragorn, Éomer, Théoden, Gandalf, Faramir, and Merry, who in fact fought with her. Gandalf sympathetically sets forth her dilemma and her suffering as a woman with heroic qualities who has been born into a man's world: "[Éomer] had horses, and deeds of arms, and the free fields; but she, born in the body of a maid, had a spirit and courage at least the match of [his]." And yet, Gandalf continues, she was doomed to watch the degradation of her king, and suffer the advances of Wormtongue (848-49; V:8). While Gandalf sympathetically analyzes the problematic role of women in the patriarchal society of *The Lord of the Rings*, Aragorn openly expresses his admiration for her unconventionality and her heroism: "Her deeds have set her among the queens of great renown" (849; V:8). After hearing from the eyewitness, Merry, the story of her deeds on the battlefield, Faramir explains why he loves her in terms one would expect to be addressed to a man: "For you are a lady high and valiant and have yourself won renown that shall not be forgotten" (943; VI:5). Instead of being castigated for her transgressions, as one would expect, she is praised and treated with both sympathy and understanding.

---

[13] Jackson accomplishes a similar combination of heroism and femininity in the lyrical portrait of Arwen as she rides toward the suffering Frodo in slow motion, with back lighting haloing her in otherworldly light.

Leslie Donovan has convincingly demonstrated that Éowyn, like Galadriel and Arwen, resembles the heroic valkyrie maidens of old Norse mythology and literature. However, unlike the valkyrie, Éowyn is allowed a heroic completion, finding a new vocation and marrying a partner worthy of her love. After demonstrating that she has the power, the will, and the courage to kill the most feared of the enemy, she recognizes that the needs of society have changed and she joins those who help to rebuild civilization. Tolkien thus portrays her as finding a new path in life. As she states to Faramir, she will no longer "take joy only in the songs of slaying" as she had previously, but "will be a healer and love all things that grow and are not barren" (943; VI:5). By so doing, she is following in the footsteps of one of the most powerful women in Tolkien's fiction, namely Yavanna, who planted and nurtured the two blessed trees. As Tolkien shows throughout *The Lord of the Rings,* the light of these trees, captured in the Silmarils, continues to have beneficent effects long after the trees themselves have been destroyed.

Tolkien also shows that Éowyn is emotionally fulfilled when she chooses as her husband Faramir, a hero who is both worthy of her love and who reciprocates her sdmiration and deep respect. Taking all these aspects of Tolkien's portrait of Éowyn into consideration, I cannot agree with those who decry his portraits of women as cardboard figures conceived along traditional lines.

Instead of presenting a hackneyed stereotype, as some have charged, Peter Jackson's film captures the significance, the unconventionality, and the heroism of Éowyn in memorable and convincing images. Jackson stresses what Tolkien implies by providing a back-story for Éowyn, by fleshing out her relationship with Aragorn, and by focusing at length not only on her killing of the Witch-king, the Lord of the Nazgûl, but also on her prowess in battle.

In the novel, we first catch a glimpse of her behind Théoden's throne and we discover her "back-story" only later. Her love for Aragorn is caught in her gaze, the trembling of her hand as it touches his, and in a few brief images: Éowyn as cup-bearer, handing the cup to Aragorn; Éowyn as Lord of the Eorlingas, standing alone before the silent halls of Edoras, her mail-clad body shining like silver in the sun; Éowyn as Dernhelm, the mysterious rider and heroic slayer of the Witch-king; and finally Éowyn as the woman who turns from death to healing and marriage with a partner who is her equal.

Jackson focuses on each of these brief events, demonstrating their significance by expanding them into a series of telling images. Brief scenes, often without words, give her a powerful presence on screen. We catch a brief glimpse of Éowyn running in from the ramparts to see the dying Théodred, son of King Théoden. As she leans over his body and observes his mortal wound, her face shows deep emotion but she does not lose her strong control. We see her whispering to Théoden, "Your son is dead," while holding his distorted, discolored hands in her own. We watch her standing on the ramparts, the wind blowing her golden hair and white gown, as if trying to escape for a moment from the oppression of the palace and the atmosphere of death. We observe her gazing from a distance at Éomer and Wormtongue as her brother states the words (spoken by Gandalf in the text): "too long have you watched my sister" (*Towers*, scene 8: "The Banishment of Éomer"). These filmic images provide the background for her loneliness and her sudden passion for Aragorn, a hero who enters a palace bereft of heroism and shrouded in despair.

We already noted the power of Galadriel's gaze which causes Boromir to weep, and each of the members of the Fellowship to react with strong emotions to the steady looks and probing thoughts of the Lady of Lothlórien. In his portrait of Éowyn, Jackson also focuses on the power of her gaze, a power generally attributed to men. In a close-up of Éowyn's face, she stares unflinchingly at Wormtongue, knowing his desire for her and hearing words expressing his insight into her solitude and despair. She says nothing, but a series of emotions are registered on her face as he attempts to overcome her will just as he had overthrown the mind of Théoden. After closing her eyes for a brief moment to gather her forces, she reopens them and watches his face, steadily, before casting off the mesmerizing spell of his words: "Your words are poison," she exclaims, her face filled with disgust and anger as she wrenches herself away (*Towers*, scene 20: "The King of the Golden Hall"). Jackson uses numerous close-ups of her expressive face and its play of emotions as a powerful strategy to show her significance, her passion, and her proud self-control even when she speaks no words. In *The Return of the King,* Éowyn gazes at Aragorn, smiling, over the cup she has handed to him. When the men are strategizing, her thoughtful gaze holds the camera time after time. Although silent, she is no less a power among the leaders of the Rohirrim. Only twice does Jackson portray her allowing her pain and passion visibly to break through. During the scene at the encampment, when Aragorn rejects her love, he states, "I cannot give you what you seek." A close-up of her face as she backs away from Aragorn reveals her unspoken pain as tears start into her eyes, but do not fall (*Return*, scene 23: Aragorn Takes the Paths of the Dead"). During the battle with the Witch-king her face shows fear and courage, but no tears. Only after Théoden's death do the tears well up in her eyes and finally fall, as she weeps openly in grief over her loss (*Return*, scene 43: "The Passing of Théoden"). More than any other character in Jackson's film, Éowyn's gaze dominates our impression of this heroine. Significantly, Jackson depicts silence not as a negative trait associated with weakness and powerlessness, but in the case of Éowyn as the expression of pride, strength, and passion rather than humility, weakness, and impassivity.

Two representative scenes further demonstrate Éowyn's level of empowerment in Jackson's film: her lament at Théodred's funeral, and her battle with the Witch-king. In the extended version of *The Two Towers*, she plays a powerful role when she sings the lament for Théodred, taking the place of the male scop, who would normally have fulfilled this task in a medieval world. The Old English words have been adapted by David Solo from the language and meter of *Beowulf* (*Towers*, app.: "The Battle for Middle-earth Begins").[14] The Old English language and the implied reference to *Beowulf* provides a context which heightens the unconventionality of her role.

Jackson also uses a subtle interplay of diagetic and non-diagetic sounds (that is, sounds within [diagetic] and sounds outside [non-diagetic] the story world of the film) in order to underline Éowyn's ambiguous position as a powerful woman attempting to break out of the confines of a patriarchal society. Although the lament is bracketed by chorale and orchestral music on the soundtrack outside the story world of the film, Éowyn sings the lament, unaccompanied at first, as part of the diagetic sound within the story world itself. However, toward the end of the lament, chords of non-diagetic music from the soundtrack blend subtly with her voice. She is thus placed in a paradoxical position: she remains within the story world as she sings the dirge, and yet she transcends that world as her voice joins sounds from the non-diagetic space outside her world. Éowyn's anomalous position is also emphasized through lighting effects. As she sings, we see a close-up of her face brightly lit, flanked by two elderly women of Rohan whose faces remain in shadow. The lighting dramatizes the way Éowyn stands out against the backdrop of a medieval society. Through the lighting, Jackson stresses the fact that the other women play traditional roles, and stand in the shadow whereas Éowyn emerges into the light as a leader and woman of power. Through the

---

[14] His translation is based on the following words, as indicated in the Appendices to *The Two Towers*: "An evil death has set forth the noble warrior/ A song shall sing sorrowing minstrels/ In Meduseld."

blending of diagetic and non-diagetic sound, he shows how she transcends her world (*Towers*, scene 21: "The Funeral of Théodred").

In *The Lord of the Rings*, during the siege of Minas Tirith, Tolkien implies that Éowyn has fought beside her king through the thick of the battle (822; V:6). Jackson renders Tolkien's implications in vivid images. In a spectacular scene, rivaling the exploits of the men, Éowyn uses her wits to overcome a mighty Oliphaunt or Mûmak who is among the beasts charging toward the men of Rohan. Shouting to Merry, "Take the reins," she raises two swords into the air as she gallops between the legs of the Mûmakil, cutting their tendons so that the monsters topple to the earth. Her agility and skill in overcoming brute force prepares us for the final encounter with the Witch-king, while the cutting of the tendons adumbrates Merry's role in bringing him down (*Return*, scene 37: "The Battle of the Pelennor Fields").

Jackson has prepared the viewer for the battle between two great opponents, Éowyn and the Witch-king, by portraying the former as a strong, able warrior and the latter as a terrifying, seemingly invincible adversary. The Witch-king first appears at Weathertop, where he stabs Frodo. This we discover only much later, through Gandalf. Gandalf also tells us, "No man can kill him." Jackson presents several shots of the Lord of the Nazgûl, riding his monstrous dragon steed at Minas Morgul, wheeling above the orc troops, and later, after the fall of Osgiliath, sitting on the ramparts, boasting to the captain of the orcs that he will "break" the white wizard, Gandalf. Significantly, instead of feminizing evil, Tolkien masculinized the word "witch" by portraying the Lord of the Nazgûl in traditional masculine terms. Taking his cue from Tolkien, Jackson depicts the Witch-king as a large, muscular figure, who speaks in a deep baritone voice. His geometrically shaped armor, his great iron-clad hands, and his iron mask are all traditionally associated with powerful men of war.

Jackson pictures a dramatic prelude to the encounter between Éowyn and the Witch-king, showing the mesmerized and horrified face of Théoden as he watches the great monster and its deadly rider swooping down upon him from the sky. The dragon seizes Théoden's horse, Snowmane, and flings it aside like a plaything. Théoden, now pinned under his horse, lies dying. The dragon beast and its dreadful master land. The king watches, helplessly, as the huge neck and jaws of the dragon moving threateningly toward him and the Witch-king commands the beast in ghastly tones, "Feast on his flesh."

Suddenly Éowyn, a tiny yet undaunted figure, sword in hand, leaps between King Théoden and his monstrous predator. She challenges: "I will kill you if you touch him." The Witch-king threatens in turn, "Do not come between the Nazgûl and his prey." The dragon strikes out at her. With two great sword strokes she chops through its neck, and the head rolls away. Grabbing a shield, Éowyn takes a defensive posture as the Witch-king dismounts from the shuddering corpse of the giant dragon. In a shot from behind and to the left of the Witch-king, we see Éowyn, fearful yet undaunted and in the defensive posture of a warrior. She is silhouetted and seems contained by the dread outline of the Lord of the Nazgûl, his dark ragged cloak framing her on one side, and the great arm and spiked ball and chain on the other as he towers over her. Éowyn dodges the spiked iron ball with agility until finally her shield is shattered, and she drops her sword. The Lord of the Nazgûl closes in for the kill (*Return*, scene 39: "The Nazgûl and His Prey").

The next close-up of Éowyn shows her frightened face as the Witch-king's great, iron-clad hand closes about her throat. In a deep, hollow voice he gloats, "Fool, no man can kill me. Die now." Merry, who has recovered from being thrown from his horse, shakes the dust off himself, and strikes the Witch-king's leg behind the knee, severing the tendon. The towering figure crashes to his knees. The Lord of the Nazgûl has literally been cut down to Éowyn's size. A close-up of Éowyn's face shows her ripping off her helmet, loosening her golden hair onto her shoulders. In a triumphant voice, she declares, "I am no man." The next shot frames the two figures, Éowyn standing, the Witch-king on his knees before her. With a warrior's yell, she thrusts her sword into the gaping hole of his iron mask. A shriek emerges from the creature, then the Witch-king's clothing crumples as he shrivels into nothingness, defeated at the hands of a woman (*Return*, scene 41: "Shieldmaiden of Rohan").

In Tolkien's text, Théoden never discovers that Éowyn was by his side in the battle. Ironically, when Éowyn's unconscious body is discovered, the men of Rohan voice their regret that Éowyn came disguised to battle: "We knew naught of her riding until this hour, and greatly we rue it," they lament (827; V:6). They clearly do not know that only *she*, a woman, could have saved them from the dreaded foe whom no man could kill. Such irony highlighting the unconscious marginalization of the true hero of the battle field is too subtle for the screen. Jackson substitutes an imagistically effective death scene in which Théoden recognizes Éowyn, understands her deed, and praises her for saving him from shame and dishonor: "I go to my fathers in whose mighty company I shall not now feel ashamed." With his dying breath, Théoden then speaks her name. In the theatrical version, Jackson ends Éowyn's tale with this scene (*Return*, scene 43: "The Passing of Théoden"). He shows only a glimpse of the Shieldmaiden transformed into a lover and healer. During the crowning of Aragorn, the camera twice, and very briefly, focuses on Éowyn and Faramir standing side by side. First they are smiling at each other, then they smile at Aragorn and Arwen who have finally been reunited.

CONCLUSION

As Jackson states in his commentary, the three films provide only a relatively shallow rendering of Tolkien's complex novel. However, the images and translation techniques Jackson chose for his re-creation of Tolkien's vision present a vivid picture of the women in *The Lord of the Rings.* Jackson gives them a visual importance in the film that matches their unusually high significance in a novel that only seems to be dominated entirely by men. Although his transmutation of Galadriel, Arwen, and Éowyn involve often radical departures from the text, Jackson accurately represents Tolkien's views of women as they are expressed throughout his writings. Women for Tolkien are positive figures whose influence extends far beyond their often brief appearances in the pages of his writings, and Jackson's film reflects that fact.

WORKS CITED

Agonito, Rosemary, ed. *History of Ideas on Woman: A Source Book.* New York: G.P. Putnam, 1977.

Chance, Jane. "Is there a Text in this Hobbit? Peter Jackson's *Fellowship of the Ring.*" *Literature/Film Quarterly* 30.2 (2002): 79-85.

Crowe, Edith. "Power in Arda. Sources, Uses, and Misuses." *Proceedings of the J.R.R. Tolkien Centenary Conference, Keble College, Oxford, 1992.* Ed. Patricia Reynolds and Glen GoodKnight. Combined Issue of *Mytholore* 80; *Mallorn* 30. Mythopoeic Press, 1995. 272-77.

Darwin, Charles. "The Origin of Sexual Differences." *The Descent of Man.* 1871. Rpt. in *History of Ideas on Woman: A Source Book.* Ed. Rosemary Agonito. New York: G.P. Putnam, 1977. 251-63.

Donovan, Leslie. "The Valkyrie Reflex in J.R.R. Tolkien's *The Lord of the Rings*: Galadriel, Shelob, Éowyn, and Arwen." *Tolkien the Medievalist.* Ed. Jane Chance. London and New York: Routledge, 2003. 106-132.

Frederick, Candice and Sam McBride. *Women among the Inklings*: Westport Ct.: Greenwood Press, 2001.

Guiley, Rosemary. *An Encyclopedia of Witches and Witchcraft*. New York: Facts on File, Inc., 1989.

Hopkins, Lisa, "Female Authority Figures in the Works of Tolkien, C.S. Lewis and Charles Williams." *Proceedings of the J.R.R. Tolkien Centenary Conference, Keble College, Oxford, 1992*. Ed. Patricia Reynolds and Glen GoodKnight. Combined Issue of *Mytholore* 80; *Mallorn* 30. Mythopoeic Press, 1995. 364-66.

Knox, John. "The First Blast of the Trumpet against the Monstrous Regiment of Women." 1558. *Renaissance Woman: A Sourcebook: Constructions of Femininity in England*. Ed. Kate Aughterson. London: Routledge, 1995. 138-9.

Kramer, Heinrich, and James Sprenger. *Malleus Maleficarum* (*The Witches' Hammer*). 1484. Transl. Montague Summers. New York: Dover Publications, 1971.

The Lord of the Rings: The Fellowship of the Ring. Special Extended DVD Edition. Screenplay by Peter Jackson, Fran Walsh, and Philippa Boyens. Perf. Elijah Wood et al. Dir. Peter Jackson. United States: New Line Home Entertainment, 2002.

The Lord of the Rings: The Return of the King. Theatrical Release DVD. Screenplay by Peter Jackson, Fran Walsh, and Philippa Boyens. Perf. Elijah Wood et al. Dir. Peter Jackson. United States, New Line Home Entertainment, 2004.

The Lord of the Rings: The Two Towers. Special Extended DVD Edition. Screenplay by Peter Jackson, Fran Walsh, and Philippa Boyens. Perf. Elijah Wood et al. Dir. Peter Jackson. United States: New Line Home Entertainment, 2003.

MacCormack, Carol and Marilyn Strathern. *Nature, Culture, and Gender*. London: Cambridge University Press, 1980.

Mitchell, Elvis. "Soldiering On in Epic Pursuit of Purity." *The New York Times*. (18 December 2002): E1.

Lewis, C.S. *The Lion, the Witch, and the Wardrobe*. New York: Collier Books, 1970.

—.*The Silver Chair*. New York: Collier Books, 1970.

Nietzsche, Friedrich. "Woman as a Dangerous Plaything." *Thus Spake Zarathustra*. 1896-7. Rpt. in *History of Ideas on Woman: A Source Book*. Ed. Rosemary Agonito. New York: G.P. Putnam, 1977. 267-9.

O'Brien, Mary. "Feminist Theory and Dialectical Logic." *Feminist Theory: A Critique of Ideology*. Ed. Nannarl Keohane et al. Chicago: University of Chicago Press, 1981. 99-112.

O'Neil, Timothy. *The Individuated Hobbit. Jung, Tolkien, and the Archetypes of Middle-Earth*. Boston: Houghton and Mifflin, 1979.

Partridge, Brenda. "No Sex Please–We're Hobbits: The Construction of Female Sexuality in *The Lord of the Rings*." *J.R.R. Tolkien: This Far Land*. Ed. Robert Giddings. London: Barnes and Noble, 1983.

Purkiss, Diane. *The Witch in History: Early Modern and Twentieth-Century Representations*. London and New York: Routledge, 1996.

Rousseau, Jean-Jacques. *Emile; or, On Education*. 1762. Ed. and Trans. Allan Bloom. New York: Basic Books, 1979.

Stimpson, Catharine R. *J.R.R. Tolkien*. New York: Columbia UP, 1969

Tolkien, J.R.R. *The Hobbit: Or There and Back Again*. New York: Ballantine Press, 1980.

—. *The Lord of the Rings*. 2nd ed. With Note on the Text by Douglas A. Anderson. Boston: Houghton Mifflin, 1994.

—. *The Shaping of the Middle-Earth: The History of Middle-Earth*. New York: Ballantine Books, 1986.

—. *The Silmarillion*. Ed. Christopher Tolkien. New York: Ballantine Books, 1999.

—. "Tree and Leaf." *The Tolkien Reader*. New York: Ballantine Books, 1966. 29-120.

—. *Unfinished Tales of Numenor and Middle-Earth*. Ed. Christopher Tolkien. Boston: Houghton Mifflin, 1980.

PART V:

FAN
FICTION

TALES AROUND THE INTERNET CAMPFIRE: FAN FICTION IN TOLKIEN'S UNIVERSE

SUSAN BOOKER

INTRODUCTORY REMARKS, OR WHAT IS THIS ALL ABOUT AND WHY DO WE CARE?

This essay provides an overview of the twisting and turning paths of the world of fan fiction on the Internet, with fan fiction in Tolkien's universe of particular interest. We will explore a few interesting side trails along the way, asking many questions about how we got here and where we might be going next. Consider this essay both a passport and a guide to this new literary world. The comments made here can be taken to apply to much of fan fiction; there is a surprising homogeny of authors' habits across universes in the fan fiction world.

Peter Jackson's recently released trilogy of movies based on *The Lord of the Rings* saga has inspired many fans to write fan fiction and post it on the Internet, using Tolkien's characters and landscapes. This growing body of literature is rising up from its misty electronic birthplace and making itself noticed as a recognizable entity. Counting searches on the Internet reveal sky-rocketing numbers of fan fiction sites, and we will explore possible reasons why these types of sites have increased in number. While we will study these numbers a bit later in this essay, note here that a basic Internet search for fan fiction in March 2004 revealed there were 3,560,000 web sites available at that time, and nearly 10% of these were stories set in Tolkien's universe—certainly a phenomenon worth some attention.

We will find that, despite the fact that the world of fan fiction is ephemeral, and housed in the shifting world of the electronic Internet, it is not a free-wheeling, amorphous entity after all, but one that surprisingly exerts a formative guidance upon itself from within. Information and ideas that are generally accepted by the fan fiction community will be reviewed here in an effort to preserve commonly accepted Internet fiction concepts in something of a more durable format. We'll also slog through issues of social context, both in the outside world and within the fan fiction community, and wrap up with commentary specific to fan fiction in Tolkien's universe.

The study of a literature that is ephemeral and non-permanent in nature, written by mostly anonymous authors, poses many problems for the scholar. These stories are veritable "messages in bottles" that are cast adrift on electronic seas, and they wash up on the shores of our computer screens. The very nature of fan fiction demands an open-minded and forgiving attitude not only on the part of the researcher, but also from fan fiction readers and writers as well. While documenting various aspects of this literature can prove difficult, my personal experiences as a fan fiction reader and writer give me some "hands-on" data to work with. I have received e-mail feedback from readers in Manila, Canada, Prague, South America, the U.S., and various other unknown places. Some letters were supportive, some critical, some sought help for their own writing projects; some even offered ideas, the fans being too shy to write the stories themselves. Many hosting web sites have a formula at the beginning of each story that contains the title, the author's name or their pseudonym, a rating system or comment on the nature of the text, and often an invitation to the readers for feedback. Some readers were not shy pen-pals, writing several times, others offered a short comment and never wrote again.

Most of my contacts have been with the loosely identified majority in the fan fiction universe, females. It is generally accepted that the fan fiction universe is composed mostly of the female sex, yet usually very little substantiating evidence is presented to support this theory. In my little corner of the fan fiction universe, however, the writers and readers were mostly women, judging from fan letters to which they signed their own names. If we postulate that the fan fiction community includes a large number of educated, intelligent women who secretly express their inner desires for action-adventures though fan fiction, should we now review the fiction with an eye open for an Amazonian aspect in the work?

My intuition is that the shorter versions of fan fiction might be penned by males, and those with some storyline development might reflect a female author, though this generalization may reflect broad gender stereotypes that continue outside the world of fan fiction. Typically the fan letters I receive politely ask for clarification on a few points in a story, or suggest a new storyline for me to adopt, or indicate their favorite aspects of a particular story, and these letters are generally supportive in nature. The only lambasting, ranting and thoroughly intolerant letter I got was from a male reader. My response to him was what I counsel in this essay: "Click on by it if you don't like it."

THE PERILS OF FAN FICTION SCHOLARSHIP:
YOU ARE DOING WHAT? WITH WHOM? AND WHERE? –
OR PERILS ALONG THE FAN FICTION PATHWAYS

Some colleagues cringe when they find out that I study fan fiction, and few ever learn I write it as well. But, after all, could one honestly study alligators without going near treacherous bayous? Actually the experience of being a fan fiction author is very much like the experience of seeking the eye of the hurricane in a small airplane: an adventure that is foolhardy, generally informative, and mostly satisfying, if you survive the flight. But explorers can't make discoveries if they don't bravely step out into the new territories.

Nowhere is there a list of rules imposed upon new authors in fan fiction, yet good ideas, ones that prove useful, are rapidly taken up and become part of the commonly shared environment. Fan fiction authors can receive immediate reader feedback to their stories, and this feedback can influence the development of further tales in particular story-line. The practice of requesting feedback from readers, for example, is one of these interesting aspects of fan fiction. Ratings systems and disclaimers were ideas that rapidly became the norm, and we will revisit them further along in this study. Some readers are supportive in their comments to authors, and some are vicious, and yet the intercommunication strengthens the bond between readers and writers, and furthers the ties among the fan fiction community. The community feeds itself, and self-determines, to some extent, what might be produced next, regardless of how the authors respond to the remarks of their readers.

The fan fiction Internet universe is both shaped from without, via the Internet and the electronic environment in which it exists, and from within, where the writers feed readers and the readers feed responses back to the authors, working with literary ideas which generally suit the community. Does the notion that most of this community is made up of middle class, educated females affect the extent to which suggestion and criticism molds the group? We need a sociologist for that study, not a librarian such as myself.

Peter Jackson's three recent films interpreting J.R.R. Tolkien's *The Lord of the Rings* have reawakened legions of dormant long-time fans, and created armies of new ones. Many who became fans of the story shortly after the release of the novel in three parts in the late 1950's, or who found the tales during the intervening years, have either read and reread the novel, or they have simply held the characters and locations dear to their hearts, like absent friends and beloved memories. These fans had personal interpretations of Middle-earth with them as they crossed Jackson's cinematic threshold. The new generations of fans created by the movies come in two varieties: first, those who have been entranced by Tolkien's magical world solely though Jackson's outstanding visual presentations, and second, those who, enraptured by the scenic vistas and strong characterizations in the films, have carried these images with them as they turned to the novel for more information.

Stepping back we can see a spiraling scenario, one where a literary work has moved to a visual format, which in turn may drive fans back to read the original novel, or send them upwards and out, where they produce fan fiction which further reinterprets characters and plotlines. Members of all these camps of fans have engaged in the production of fan fiction based in Tolkien's universe, as evidenced by the dramatic increase of posted fiction in this area, and the levels of understanding and change seen in the stories.

These literary responses by Tolkien's fans also lead us to explore just how we continue to meet the ancient human need for a good story filled with heroes, that we can pass on and embellish, and how we manage our storytelling today within the Internet environment. To understand the importance and persistence of this ancient cultural thread through western societies, simply consider King Arthur. His stories, rising through ancient mists about someone who was possibly a flesh and blood tribal leader, have been embellished through time and passed on from generation to generation, his character changing to meet the demands of that particular audience, and he continues to live with us today in various aspects in movies and on television. We will revisit King Arthur, and his symbolism as a timeless hero, later in this essay.

Around the turn of the last century, Sir Arthur Conan Doyle faced a similar situation when Sherlock Holmes fans, cherishing his gripping stories and familiar hero, took their grievances directly to the author. He was met with overwhelming cries of "More, More!" when he left his detective Sherlock Holmes supposedly dead at the Reichenbach Falls. So many reacted so negativley that the popular detective made a surprise reappearance to quell the demand for more stories.[1] The contemporary

---

[1] Arthur Conan Doyle, *The Original Illustrated Sherlock Holmes* (Edison NJ: Castle, 1976) This volume contains facsimiles of the stories and illustrations as they appeared originally in *The Strand Magazine* from July 1891 through January 1905. Holmes dies at the Riechenbach Falls, in "The Adventure of the Final Problem" 327-339. Holmes makes his comeback in "The Adventure of the Empty House," 449-462.

need and desire by fan authors to "fill in the blanks" in the original storyline and the characters' lives will be examined as well. It is not enough for fans to simply be satisfied and enjoy the exploits of a popular character, either in text or on film. They want to know more. What did Merry and Pippin, or Strider, or Frodo, do yesterday, and the day before, and last week? Where did they go and what did they see? Who were their grandparents and great-grandparents? Who were they with, what did they eat, and perhaps even, whom did they have sex with?

While we have seen that the need to know more on the part of fans is not a completely modern desire, we might guess that television, a technology nearing fifty years old, with its magical portal into the living rooms and bedrooms of sit-com and dramatic characters, has encouraged this desire for extreme familiarity. We look over the shoulders of our favorite television fathers, mothers, singles and teenaged stars, and we ask ourselves why can't we know more about our favorite literary or movie characters as well? Why can't Rosie, who works in a pub in the movies, or Arwen, an immortal Elf maiden, share their escapades with us like our familiar iconic buddies do in *Cheers*, *Frasier*, *Friends* or *Sex in the City*? They can, and do, in the world of fan fiction.

In Tolkien's universe, if the readers can't find this desired additional information in the canon of the novels, or the lengthy back story provided by Tolkien in appendices, or *The Silmarillion*, or in the twelve volumes of *The History of Middle-earth* edited and published by Tolkien's son Christopher, then someone will be writing about it soon, and posting that tale on the Internet. As extensive as Tolkien's descriptions of Middle-earth are, and as much as he delved into the histories of his peoples and their lands, there are still uncounted days, hinted-at participants, and enough barely mentioned events to fuel the imaginations of armies of follow-up authors—as indeed has been the case. This desire by fans for more knowledge is the impetus for sequels in novels and movies, and helps to explain the burgeoning Internet literary forum that evolved to meet this desire for more, and yet more, details in a popular culture area.

Fan fiction. The words bring cringes to the faces of purists, or sly smiles to those readers in the know. Why do some in the academic world care about a few stories on the Internet? I personally find myself straddling the fence of so-called scholarly pursuits on one side and the study of popular culture topics on the other. In the academic environment, when asked what my research as a professional librarian concerns, I respond: "It is a study of fan fiction, and why society needs this outlet." The common response I get to this remark is glazed eyes and a sigh, or an impatient wag of the head. Tsk tsk, they think (or remark), it is a waste of time to study this drivel; it is not nearly as serious as *real* literary criticism. Yet, to a librarian, whose work is intimately and inextricably tied to the written word, whether on a computer screen or on a printed page, this new phenomenon of hundreds of amateur authors posting volumes of text in cyberspace is a legitimate interest, and it is worthy of attention. And the study of the mere 9% of fan fiction web sites that deal with the characters and worlds of J.R.R. Tolkien covers enough of a subset and microcosm to keep one busy— very busy. The 354,000 Tolkien-based fan fiction web sites available at this particular time provide more than enough information to navigate, and try to digest.

Again here we face the ephemeral nature of Internet sites, where what we might read one day could very well be gone tomorrow, and for a variety of reasons. New material often replaces the old, copyright challenges remove some sites, or the hosts do not have the data storage space to archive stories written over lengthy periods of time. Some fan fiction sites do try to preserve their materials, but as time passes, host sites will be filled to their maximum storage limits, or pressed beyond their abilities to cope with the large amount of information pouring in daily. Scholars and librarians both lament the lack of consistent archiving of information posted on the Internet. Their concerns about the disadvantages of electronic format postings apply not only to news reports or academic studies; the rapid disappearance of information in the popular culture sphere is particularly difficult in this fledgling area of study. Hence "state of the art" reports such as this one can document a moment in time, even as the genre continues to change and evolve in cyberspace.

Studies such as this one also help identify and categorize this genre of fiction. We are finding that just as ancient bards told rousing and heroic stories to village audiences gathered around a crackling campfire, fan fiction authors are captivating and thrilling readers around the world today via fan fiction host sites on the Internet. If we view the electronically connected world as a new tribe of humanity, then the Internet is the heart of its societal culture, an electronic campfire for a global village.

Over the last ten years librarians have been concerned with the possible loss of readers and library users due to the new electronic environment, yet here we actually find readers, and writers, flourishing in cyberspace. And these new forms of literature are driving some of the readers to further research and reading, and some of it is done in libraries. In a world of computer "haves and have-nots," libraries are also serving as access points to the globally linked new world tribe though the provision of public terminals. So, we can put those institutional fears to rest for now; libraries are finding a new niche in the electronic environment, and continuing to provide informational support and entertainment, as they have always done.

Fan fiction is what it is. Some readers and writers accept the open environment available to them; some people who are Tolkien purists reject these secondary stories nurtured in the absolute freedom of expression that feeds further efforts. The denizens of the electronic environment of the contemporary "connected" world are generally sophisticated, and worldly, and those who are "newly stumbled" into the environment of electronic fan fiction either get that way fast, or get out. My only advice to readers is to say that the fan fiction reader must be selective in respect to quality vs. quantity; the Internet is an open forum for amateur authors, and typographical errors, bad grammar, and descriptions of graphic sex acts are out there just waiting for the indiscriminate reader. Just as with materials found on the television, or the Internet, simply be ready to click on past what you don't want to see, and get on with your life.

Whether you support the versions of Middle-earth found in Peter Jackson's movies, or are critical of them, he gave credible visual presence to beloved literary locations and characters as no previous animated attempt has been able to do. Cinematic technology rose to the challenge of placing flying dragons in the air and depicting massive armies ranged across vast plains. Jackson's use of New Zealand's unique and unspoiled beauty places the viewers in a land that time truly forgot. The creature Gollum came to life for viewers through the dramatic skills of actor Andy Serkis and motion tracking electronic wizardry. Bringing the novel to virtual reality through cinematic efforts was a risky and titanic task, when the story and environment had been so well established by the author, and the characters so firmly entrenched in the minds of readers. By all accounts Jackson has pulled it off.

As for the scenario of literary characters moving from the printed page to the movie screen, we can again look to literary precedents. Just as the written descriptions of Sherlock Holmes, and the accompanying illustrations by Sidney Paget in *The Strand Magazine* issues of 1890 through 1905 established the classic profile with pipe in mouth, early Holmes detective movies presented on film that same profile, establishing it in the minds of viewers who had not read Conan Doyle's stories or seen *The Strand Magazine* illustrations. In this case a literary character was created, embellished, and passed on into a visual context. We see this as well in the way *The Lord of the Ring's* literary characters and landscapes have moved out of the novel and onto the movie screen, and then into the minds of fans who have never read the novel. Jackson's movies, and New Zealand's varied landscapes, have presented new generations of fans of Middle-earth with powerful images in support of most of the original storyline. Fan fiction authors are taking Tolkien's stories and back stories, or Jackson's slightly reworked characters, a little further in the timeless story-telling model, sharing this progress via countless Internet fan fiction sites.

The movie trilogy has won critical acknowledgement and awards around the world.[2] With experts in the field rewarding Jackson and his company's efforts, is there any wonder that fans have been so inspired by the movie trilogy that they pick up pens, or grab keyboards most likely, and write more adventures for these heroes? Don't we still find imitation to be the most sincere form of flattery? Again the desire to know more about these beloved characters drives us to explore the newly written pathways of fan fiction.

Some who read or study fan fiction assume it is more understood and better known generally than it may truly be. While the world of fan fiction is just recently coming under formal study, it is now being identified as a separate genre of writing, with rules, an established lexicon, accepted formatting and a ratings system, with commonly posted disclaimers and other aspects of an established entity. Yet it also remains

---

[2] Academy of Motion Pictures Arts and Sciences, available from http://www. oscars.org/74academyawards/nomswins.html, http://www.oscars.org/75academyawards/no mswins.html, http://www.oscars.org/76academy awards/nomswins.html, for the pages for the 74th, 75th and 76th years of awards, which covers the awards for 2001, 2002 and 2003. Accessed March 24, 2004, information from the Academy of Motion Picture Arts and Sciences web site posted these American awards: In 2001 *The Lord of the Rings: The Fellowship of the Ring* won awards for Cinematography, Achievement in make-up, Achievement in Music, and Achievement in Visual Effects. In 2002, *The Lord of the Rings: The Two Towers* won for Achievement in Film Editing, Achievement in Sound Editing, and Achievement in Visual Effects. In 2003 *The Lord of the Rings: The Return of the King* won awards for Art Direction, Costume Design, Directing, Film Editing, Make-up, Original Song, Sound Mixing, Visual Effects, Adapted Screenplay, and Best Picture.

Among other rewards we might mention are: The American Golden Globe Awards for best Motion Picture-Drama, Best Director, Best Original Score, and Best Original Song for *The Lord of the Rings: The Return of the King;* the Costume Designers Guild Award for Excellence in Film, Period/Fantasy to Ngila Dickson for *The Lord of the Rings: The Return of the King;* The Empire Magazine Awards for Best Film of the Year; The Sony Ericcson Scene of the Year for "The Ride of the Rohirrim"; and the Best British Actor award for Andy Serkis in *The Lord of the Rings: The Return of the King.* A true child of popular culture, MTV, acknowledged *The Lord of the Rings: The Two Towers* with awards for Best Movie, Best Action Sequence for the scene at Helm's Deep, Best Duo for Elijah Wood and Sean Astin, and Best Virtual Performance for the character of Gollum. These awards are also listed on the Official Lord of the Rings web site, online, available from http://www.lordoftherings.net/index_105 _fi_news.html.

wildly independent, and it is growing at a remarkable rate.[3] The circle of fan fiction readers and writers is still relatively small, a tiny subset of the vast electronic universe of the Internet, and the area of Tolkien based fan fiction a mere percentage of that. Yet, the self-imposed infrastructure of fan fiction appears to provide a stable base for its own explosive growth, and more readers stumble into this brave new universe daily.

One way to gain a palpable overview of the slippery and elusive Internet fan fiction experience is to track the number of fan fiction sites on the Internet. The large number of sites seems to add a cloak of respectability to the study of this outlaw practice ("outlaw" because most fan fiction sites do actually violate strict copyright interpretations, despite posted disclaimers). Speaking to a mostly literary and purist audience at a Popular Culture conference in 2003, I found the audience "politely" listened to my presentation on fan fiction in Tolkien's universe, until I shared numbers of Internet sites and participants with them. The audience sat up and listened with a bit more interest afterwards; the fact that there were 89,700 Internet sites dealing with fan fiction in Tolkien's universe (at that time) was indeed worthy of some attention, even from this skeptical audience.

The sheer number of fan fiction writers and host sites on the Internet was attention-grabbing then, and it has reached jaw-dropping proportions today. While we will discuss numbers further in a bit, let it suffice to say here that a basic *Google* Internet search in March 2004 indicated that there were 3,560,000 web sites devoted to all forms of fan fiction. Within this number we find 354,000 sites featuring characters from Tolkien's universe. Anyone must admit these numbers and their rapid growth are the staggering revelations of a ground swell phenomenon, a global mass movement of extreme popularity, aided and abetted by increasingly easy access to the Internet and the global tribe of interested readers and writers.

Considering that the body of fan fiction authors includes very busy professionals, college students, and parents, the number of web sites reflects an astounding number of hours spent typing fan fiction stories

---

[3] Fan fiction studies, still a new area for research, are appearing in article format, in such works as the article by Anne Kustritz, "Slashing the Romance Narrative," appearing in the *Journal of American Culture* 26.3 (Sept. 2003) 371-85. In this article Kustritz outlines general aspects of fan fiction, and supplies terms used within the genre. Works featuring studies of popular culture and the impact of cyberspace on modern societies include Henry Jenkins, *Textual Poachers: Television Fans and Participatory Culture* (London: Routledge, 2003), and Marshall W. Fishwick's two studies, *Popular Culture: Cavespace to Cyberspace* (New York: The Haworth Press, 1999), and *Popular Culture in New Age* (New York: The Haworth Press, 2002).

while burning the midnight oil. This does not take into account the equally numerous hours spent managing these stories by web site hosts, most of whom are deluged with literary submissions. We have to ask, what drives these busy people to rebuild various popular culture locations, people them with new stories, and to manipulate the characters in new and often bizarre fashions?

How can we understand this activity in today's business-oriented, intelligent, over-worked global community? Does the manipulation of familiar characters give us a sense of control and order? Does working with established characters remove annoying developmental aspects of the story, and let us get straight to the good parts (whatever those "good parts" might be)? All of these questions and answers provoke more thought, and create more questions.

DANGEROUS CURVES, FALLING ROCKS, AND GRAPHIC SEX RATINGS: SIGNPOSTS FOR TRAVELERS IN THE REALM OF FAN FICTION

Beyond cyberspace reviews of fan fiction, there are now published articles available as well, so we might say we are entering a secondary stage of understanding this type of fiction. Before we go further in this particular explorative study, a brief review of the various identifiable aspects of fan fiction is necessary, and a rehash of the definitions accepted by the community itself will provide some signposts for travelers trying to comprehend the nebulous world of fan fiction. We now run the risk of repetition in defining fan fiction terms, but the studies of this area are still so new that a generally understood way of talking about fan fiction is still being formally laid down in published works such as the essays in this book, as well as continuing on numerous help sites on the Internet.

Those who are knowledgeable to some extent in this area will recognize the terms that have been accepted by the fan fiction community, and that are used globally in the defining of this new environment. Readers new to this area might be amazed to discover that fan fiction authors, site hosts and readers have so rapidly and readily established this lexicon for use among themselves. Useful terms, granting a working knowledge of how to rapidly surf the fan fiction universe, are handy tools indeed considering the eclectic vastness of its cyberspace existence.

Fan fiction stories, or *fanfic*, are literary inventions by fan authors, using already established characters and universes commonly found on television shows or in the movies. Comic book characters and literary heroes also find their way into these spin-off stories. Fan fiction authors then add new twists, such as interesting pairings of characters, or they add entirely new characters, and exciting, often dangerous, further adventures. *Fanzines*, early examples of magazines prepared by fans to host these stories, were available at conventions, or *cons,* or by mail once you had the author's address. Fanzines burst onto the scene in the 1970's accompanying the *Star Trek* phenomenon of excited fans hungry for more information, and the resultant rapidly growing society of Sci-Fi fandom. I myself, like many others, come to the study of fan fiction today after a thirty-year hiatus. I remember awaiting the next installment of a mimeographed fanzine in the mail in the 1970's. The electronic environment makes these types of stories accessible now at a quick keystroke, available as rapidly as the host site managers or authors can post them.

Host-sites are web addresses where editors have provided gathering places for authors to post their stories. Some sites are dedicated to one universe of fan fiction, *The Lord of the Rings,* or *Buffy the Vampire Slayer,* or the *X-files* for example. Within these localized groups, some sites specialize in one variety of fan fiction, PG rated stories only, for example. Thus we find a self-cataloging system existing within the world of fan fiction, one that came into place early in the electronic phenomenon, and one that has continued to grow as the postings increase. Often host sites have some sort of formatted header for each story, an idea readily adopted by the posting authors, wherein descriptions of the stories are listed as reader's guides. These headers include such information as the story's title; the author's name, mostly likely a pen name (making the stories somewhat anonymous); information about whether the story fits into a continuing series by that author or stands alone (and there are many who write extended series within their own sub-worlds); the rating of the story based on its violence or sexual content; and various other descriptive pointers. The e-mail address of the author is often posted to accommodate feedback from readers.

Cross-over fan fiction introduces one set of established characters into another established universe. For example: the crew of the Enterprise might beam across time and space into Rivendell. Merry confusion, drama, romance and adventure always results in these stories built on multiple realities and locations. These stories draw on the reader's broad foundation of knowledge of the various popular culture universes.

Mary Sue stories are another fan fiction sub-genre, wherein one of the newly introduced, commonly female, characters is intelligent, capable, agile, loveable or sexy, or all of the above, and for the most part perfect. The Mary Sue character is commonly thought to represent the author, or someone he or she knows. Again we can ask ourselves, are these now stereotypical characters a reflection of the psyches of the mostly female authors of fan fiction? There has been a considerable negative backlash in the fan fiction universe against Mary Sue stories and there are even lists found online of characteristics to use to identify a Mary Sue character, and taken at face value these lists of a character's attributes are pretty humorous.

We find, moreover, that the characters identified as "Mary-Sues" are invariably female. I have to imagine that if I read critically and specifically across the board for this type of character a few male versions would slip into the statistics. The *Star Trek* character Wesley Crusher might be called a Marty Stu type character for example. Again we need our missing sociologist to step back and look for gender-specific aspects of fan fiction escapades. If we accept the premise that most of the readers and writers in the fan fiction community are women, we might be surprised at the widespread rejection of Mary Sue characters, since they do seem to exemplify a feminine ideal.

The way that the nebulous fan fiction community can be so very extreme in its identification and censure of a type of fan fiction story is interesting in itself. Acknowledging that the authors have already borrowed someone else's universe of characters and landscapes, do readers really have a right to be bitterly critical if the authors have inserted themselves into the storylines? I'd advise a reality check here, but we are in a multi-verse of divergent literature. Pornographic stories are acknowledged and overlooked to some extent as just another aspect of the fan fiction world, yet let an author slip in a somewhat recognizable Mary Sue character and the community's critical wolves gather for a literary kill.

However, one could also say the author was writing about what he or she knew (or dreamed of) and the introduction of characters that represent the everyday variety of individual are not uncommon literary and cinematic devices, used to help draw the reader or the viewer into the story. For example, consider the various everyday folks who found themselves suddenly, and sometimes unwillingly, explorers on the TARDIS, in the television show *Dr. Who*. For a literary example, consider that Holmes and Watson aided not only members of royalty, but everyday typists as well. [4] Perhaps the *frequency* with which Mary Sue characters appear, and the nascent writing skills of amateur authors, are to blame

---

[4] Doyle, *Complete Illustrated Works*, "A Case of Identity" pp.41-52. Mary Sutherland was a typist interviewed by Holmes, and he determined her trade though careful observation of marks in the plush fabric of her sleeves.

here. Why would we care about the stories if we couldn't relate to the characters, both the established ones and the new ones? Not many of us in the fan fiction readership are in reality princesses, witches, sorcerers, pirates, or starship captains or officers, regardless of whatever electronic gaming habits we may indulge. We often need the introduction of common folks in fantastic stories to carry us along the storyline.

Actually most of us participating in the fan fiction world find ourselves comfortably ensconced in mundane lives, well fed, educated and bored. When Frodo and Samwise gather up victuals and cloaks, and leave their comfortable existences to innocently set out on unimagined adventures, then we are drawn into the story along right alongside them. They take a few friends along with them, and we can relate to that idea as well. On their journey they come across some characters that help them willingly, or unwillingly, and some met along the way give them good advice, while others deceive them. Tolkien's literary skill in developing characters in a variety of situations provides a broad and sturdy platform for us to relate to, and for other authors to build on.

Frodo and Samwise, as well as Merry and Pippin, start out living everyday existences that are ones we can relate to, and we build a gradual understanding of their changing world upon experiencing their increasingly intense adventures, just as they do. Their need for food, sleep, and safety, demonstrated in both the novel, and in the movies, grounds them firmly in a reality we can accept. The rough life they faced on their journeys was described in the novels, but who failed to note the grubby faces and hands, and dirty fingernails, and the increasingly ragged appearances of the intrepid band as they trekked across the giant movie screens?

And just as we hear daily of the ups and downs of our co-workers in the next cubicle, or down the hall, or in line at the copy machine, we also want to know the minutiae of the lives of Frodo and his friends as well. Tolkien's world is made into something we can understand through the character's hunger, fear and amazement at new things. If these details differ dramatically from our own lives because they include dragons, Elves and wizards, then it is so much the better to serve as escapist fare.

Another important signpost for wanderers along fan fiction roads is the rating system. Fan fiction authors have adopted the ratings system commonly used by American motion pictures for the rating of their stories. Thus we find Internet sites not only hosting, but labeling works as

G, PG, PG-13, R, and NC-17. [5] In the natures of the stories, fan fiction runs the gamut from hand-holding friendship stories, through angst ridden drama, to down-and-dirty adult themes of every permutation. Many stories featuring these ratings are also labeled *het*, or heterosexual in nature, or *slash*, homosexual in nature. Don't confuse the term slash as a rating for violence; it commonly just refers to the sexual orientations of the characters in that particular story.

The diagonal slash originally found between the letters K/S, for Kirk and Spock stories, or later found in M/M, F/F, giving a gender clue, lend this genre its name. Slash fiction stories are generally of an adult nature, usually between members of the same sex. Commonly thought to have originated with fan fiction stories featuring the *Star Trek* characters Kirk and Spock, slash fiction remains a popular sub genre in many fictional universes. Group sexual activities can figure in either het or slash stories.

Arguments for and against slash are viewed within the fanfic community as somewhat old fashioned now. This sort of string is often started by some unsuspecting reader who stumbled across a slash site, and never recovered from the shock. The short history of Internet fan fiction slash sites has revealed that if you hate it you hate it, if you read it you read it, and others don't care and don't want to hear about it. Again, like television shows and web sites of a sexual nature, just click on by if you don't want to see it. Reader comments are sometimes welcomed by an author; unbridled ranting is not.

Some slash stories are fairly tame, and actually PG in nature in regard to the sexual expressiveness of the stories. While some are simple tales of longing, others are painfully no-holds-barred. (Oh yes, there are also S/M, or sadomasochistic, stories out there.) Host site managers, and usually the authors, are generally very careful to define the literature they present, the signposts along the Internet highway so to speak, not to censor the materials, but to warn the unwary reader. If you don't want to read graphic sex stories between Merry and Pippin, check the highway signposts, and don't take that side road!

Sometimes a reader runs across the overall descriptions *AU* and *RP*. AU refers to an alternate universe situation where the details can differ from the established canon considerably, and RP refers to real people being included in the story, either living or dead. *OOC* indicates

---

[5] The Motion Picture Association of American ratings can be found on their homepage at http://www.mpaa.org/movieratings/. Accessed 03-30-2004. Ratings systems for other countries can be reviewed at the Wikipedia Free encyclopedia web site at http://en.wikipedia.org/wiki/Motion_picture_rating_systems. Accessed 03-30-2004.

that the characters act "Out Of Character" in this particular tale. Other generally descriptive terms include *UST* for unresolved sexual tension, and *H/C*, for hurt/comfort situations. H/C situations can also be UST, or finally resolved by a sexual encounter.

Another descriptive clue can be found in *PWP*, for Plot? What Plot? This is usually applied to stories that revolve around getting the characters into a sexual situation ASAP, involving very little scenario or dialog. After all—if we are gossiping about characters we already know intimately, there is no need for extensive plot development, is there? Now, if you come across a fanfic on a slash site that is rated PG-17, and includes S/M, H/C and UST, you should have a clue about exactly what you are getting yourself into.

Participants in the online world of fan fiction, by adopting and adapting these terms, have been not only reading and writing fan fiction, but they have been observant of their new culture from within as it developed. Not only has the body of fan fiction readers and authors been observant, but they have been analytical as well, developing this lexicon to describe the works within this universe. While the world of Internet fan fiction appears on the surface to be a liberal free-for-all, there actually are aspects of self-governance from within, and the posting of signposts for travelers is an unusually mature and organized characteristic for such a new entity. While we might imagine that authors come from every age group, and many walks of life, this organizational principle has appealed to most, and has become somewhat standard across the fan fiction universes.

Well-armed with these definitions as a compass, you might consider yourself geared-up for exploration of the twisting, uneven, and sometimes quite dark, roads of fan fiction. Regardless of the worlds you select to venture into, be prepared to find some fair stories, some pretty darn good stories, and a few just awful ones. And most importantly, you should be prepared to just click on to the next offering if the current one goes sour.

HEROES AND HEROISM: WE ARE TECHNOLOGICALLY ADVANCED AND COMFORTABLY ENSCONCED IN THE MODERN WORLD—WHO NEEDS HEROES?

As we speak of heroes and their supporters today, for the purpose of this essay we will refer to literary heroes only. Not to slight all the real-world heroes, like firemen or surgeons, or all the ordinary people who perform heroic feats when called upon to do so, but here we explore a new literary world that has arisen to meet a need where even more heroism than is available in reality is called for to sustain us.

Literary heroes make personal sacrifices, take arduous journeys, fight uncommonly dangerous beasts of various types, often discover lost treasures, and change history though their acts of selfless courage and bravery. Tolkien's heroes meet these criteria, and we find that many fan fiction heroes do as well. Most myths and heroic tales follow the formula of departure, initiation, and return; in essence these tales are stories of enlightenment and passage from one stage to the next in life. The one-page fan fiction stories where "character A and character B jump directly into bed" might be considered to follow a much abbreviated heroic tale format, especially considering the parties involved and the activities that ensue, but we digress.

As a member of western civilization today, I enjoy a world of readily available groceries, and a variety of restaurants to choose from. I have disposable cash (well, a little at any rate) and mostly reliable health care is available to me. I am an observer of popular culture when I get a chance, and I have noticed the overwhelming popularity of action adventure movies released in recent decades. More films in the *Star Wars* series are filling in back story, *The Mummy* and *The Mummy Returns* draw on that perennially favorite archaeologist/adventurer film genre, as well as nodding to the Indiana Jones character, and *The Lord of the Rings* film trilogy won Oscar awards and box-office rewards.

Fans vote for their favorites these days with ticket purchases. We watch Harry Potter pack for school at Hogwarts, and wonder what evil might befall him while there. The aging James Bond character continues to reinvent himself, and push forward in time with ever more outré spy devices at his disposal. Our lives are filled with the escapades of basically indestructible popular characters in television and in the movies. These days we click past the 6:00 news filled with violent images telecast from the Middle East, or Northern Ireland, to settle in and cheer our heroes on as they navigate chase scenes down crowded highways, or rappel down yet one more skyscraper, or we sit on the edge of our seats as heroes such as Harry Potter and his friends, or Frodo and his companions, do battle with a gigantic cave-troll.

These images inform our daily lives. As we ponder the cultural and social implications of the global village and Internet connection, we can pause here to reflect on our 20th century loss of innocence in the United States, and our increased need for heroes. Does the creation and consumption of fan fiction in Tolkien's universe give us chances to escape our boring or troubled lives, and travel into their fearsome and troubled worlds? What aspects of our lives have made us so open to fan fiction and its heroes?

Many of us are members of the cohorts of babies born during the post-WWII baby boom. We grew up alongside television. We most likely ate dinner every night though the sixties to televised newscasts with scenes from the Vietnam War. Tolkien's novel, originally released in three volumes in 1954-55, became widely popular in the 1960's with an audience who embraced the noble struggle of the common man (or hobbit) against overwhelming odds and uncontrollable social changes. The unsettled times of the Vietnam War years created an environment in the United States that was ripe for folk heroes, and the psychedelic youth culture was all too ready to embrace flying dragons, elegant Elves, and everyday fellows like the Hobbits, who were trying to enjoy a good ale and mind their own business as the rest of world crumbled around them. The flower power generation, embracing peace and nature, could empathize readily with the simple lives of the agrarian Hobbits. Lapel buttons proclaiming "Frodo Lives" were common accessories. The horrors of war, engraved upon Tolkien's mind through his experiences in World War I, and expressed in his novel, were readily apparent to a new generation of readers suffering social upheavals and the effects of the distant war in Vietnam.

We grew up further, still tied to our televisions, and saw images of violence from Belfast and Beirut on the evening news. We were saddened by the crash of Pan Am flight 103 in 1988 near Lockerbie, Scotland, with rumors of terrorist action involved. A sad story, yet still physically far away and removed from most of us.

Growing up in the heartland, my fears centered on tornados suddenly forming and sweeping across the plains, but never on possible terrorist attacks. I remember walking past my television one morning in 1995, with the sound obscured by the vacuum sweeper, and noting the images of a bombed-out building. Perhaps it was some professional implosion of an unwanted building, or another bombed out building in Beirut. As I came around on another pass of the room, the continuing coverage caught my attention and I paused to listen. This shattered edifice was the nine story Oklahoma City Murrah Federal Building, half blown away; papers fluttering in the breeze, sagging floors gaping open to the morning light. I had been in that building before. That building was twenty-one miles from my front door. This event happened practically in my own backyard. The violent horrors found in other places were suddenly occurring in my little part of the world.

A somewhat sympathetic friend in England contacted me to see if I was affected in any way. Her ending remark was, "How does it feel to have terrorists in your own patch?" A friend from Ireland remarked that it was considered cool back home to be the last person to have been in a bombed business before it blew. It is interesting how we cope with these radical interruptions in our modern and progressive civilized lives.

The hypnotizing images of the jet flying into the World Trade Center on September 11, 2001, that were broadcast over and over again, held me in a horrified trance. After hours of this I had to turn the television off. And I left it off to digest what I had learned. This was no movie; this was not a special effect. Real people died. Real destruction rained down upon the streets. Even raised on action adventure movies as I had been, I was not immune to this reality. One wonders if younger generations, who have added dramatic and often extremely violent electronic games to their daily lives, could comprehend what had really happened. It was Pearl Harbor all over again; someone had dared to provoke the sleeping giant of the United States. Our naïve sense of safety was dashed again.

While we in the United States continue moving forward with our lives, a bit wiser, a bit more in tune with the rest of the world, and now wary of terrorists, we appreciate the real heroes, and continue to seek the larger-than-life heroes as well. We carry on the tradition of telling and retelling folk tales, today mostly on the cinematic screens around the world, and more familiarly at home with the handy DVD player. In these fantasy worlds, somehow the superheroes overcome all obstacles, beat the bad guys and prevail in the end. Just like Odysseus, Sherlock Holmes, Indiana Jones, Luke Skywalker and Frodo Baggins, the good guys always win. In the turbulent and unsettled modern world, we continue to seek fictional and idealistic heroes, and we continue to celebrate both ancient and modern heroes today.

Ancient Troy is rising from history's ashes in a forthcoming movie, bringing classical and well-known characters to realization for modern audiences. With popular actors Brad Pitt and Orlando Bloom as bait, new generations of fans may become hooked on the classic story, and find themselves running to the libraries of the world for more information on this ancient story. Love, a desire for power and territory, and revenge, drive this timeless tale. These remain emotions that we can experience and understand today.

And what of tales of King Arthur? Arthur, a character whose origins are lost in time, lives on magically not only in misty Avalon, but on our movie and television screens as well. As his legend promises, he returns in time of need for his people, and indeed he has returned for us again and again across pages of text and movie screens. His movie incarnations keep him firmly in the minds of passing generations. Due for release in theaters in July 2004 is *King Arthur*, a new retelling of his tale, one geared to the sensibilities of viewers today. We have seen Arthur reappear on the movie screen in recent decades in *Camelot* (1967), *Monty Python and the Holy Grail* (1975), *Excalibur* (1981), *First Knight* (1995), *Merlin* (1998), and *The Mists of Avalon* (2001).

These movies draw on a rich literary heritage starting with recorded tales by Geoffrey of Monmouth and Chrétien de Troyes. The characters were later enhanced in Sir Thomas Malory's *Le Morte Darthur*, reinterpreted by Alfred Lord Tennyson in his *Idylls of the King*, and continued in the wry four-novel retelling by T. H. White, *The Once and Future King*. Arthur, who is of common upbringing and who is only a teenager when he is discovered to be the true king, seeks justice and order for his kingdom, creates the noble Round Table of knights, and, tragically, is finally betrayed and killed by his illegitimate son. This character, with his vision and flaws, desires and frailties, is someone any generation can call hero. His trials and grief are human trials and grief. Can we say that the popular stories of King Arthur paved the way for Tolkien's tales, or do we see that the current popularity of Tolkien's sword-waving heroes has paved the way for another return of the king, Arthur in this case? Is this scenario just one more twist in the evolution of heroes celebrated through storytelling, and preserved and passed onwards through the ages?

Medical advances, space exploration, increasing mobility and increasingly sophisticated technological achievements do not remove us from the need for heroes; they only change the environment in which we share their tales. The visual images we gather from movies and television reinforce literary characters and landscapes in our minds. The modern day "campfire" around which we gather to hear inspiring tales of challenge and achievement, spans the earth; there is now an electronic hearth around which to share the stories of heroic deeds. And around this electronic hearth are gathered the denizens of the Internet fan fiction community, and they embrace and continue to embellish these heroes as at no other time in our history. Not only do we cheer for Frodo and Sam, we dust off our ancient cultural heroes as well and send them out to champion our spirits in the face of modern uncertainties.

FAN FICTION?
"BAH-HUMBUG" SAY THE PURISTS, "WRITE MORE!" SAY THE FANS

We have seen in these examples that those who embrace popular heroic tales throughout human history, and certainly fans in the past century or so, have admired their fictional heroes and embellished these stories in the retelling. The two world wars shocked humanity by presenting previously unheard of dangers, such as mustard gas, atomic bombs, and unimaginable death tolls, dashing the feelings of security and invincibility that characterized the Age of Innocence. We still know war, and rumors of war, today. Are we really that far removed from the threats of invading Vikings, or Mongol hordes? Can't we intuitively feel the fear of those ranked across the battlements of Helm's Deep as they prepare for war against overwhelming odds? Could we have stood there? Would we have stepped up to the call? Fan fiction authors can take us to that wall, and put us in that place, armed and wet from the rain, awaiting our doom. They can force us to look deep within ourselves for untapped wells of courage.

Once again we live in perilous times, and we continue to identify with our fictional heroes as a way to escape from the daily grind. Fan fiction, carried around the globe via the Internet, through the magic of uplinks and other modern miracles, ties the international fan fiction community together. While few of the new Internet authors rate with Homer in storytelling skills, some literature in this new genre is actually good enough to keep a reader "turning the pages," so to speak. Fan fiction authors, especially in Tolkien's universe, have fertile grounds to build on, add to, and change, as we see in the increasing fan fiction sites devoted to fan fiction in general, and to Tolkien's universe especially.

The trials and struggles of Tolkien's characters evoke both sympathetic, and empathetic, responses in modern audiences. The overwhelming odds, the titanic battles, the breadth of the story and its subplots, all combine to lift modern viewers out of the mundane, out of office cubicle seats, and away from everyday familial demands. The trivial worries of everyday life (that undone homework, what to prepare for dinner, or the drudgery of facing evening traffic) fade away at the sound of the hoof beats of the black rider's horses, the skitter of Shelob in her lair, or the blare of battle horns sounding the charge.

Regardless of whether you chose to grumble about the missing character Tom Bombadil, or some other detail you have imagined differently, Jackson's films will carry forth the dynamic characters in their heroic struggles in such a fashion as to make the films modern classics.

These movies will continue to serve as visual doorways to Tolkien's rich literary world. Fan authors will fill in the rest of the details.

Inspired by the novels, or sometimes just the movies, fan fiction authors are sharing their tales of the further exploits of Tolkien's characters internationally, through hosting Internet websites. We find a multi-national gathering of readers and storytellers linked via the Internet and personal computers. The Internet is serving, in essence, as an international campfire, with focus groups in every conceivable subject area gathered and interlinked via electronic modern marvels. The human desire to share a good story with others has not changed or been lost; it has expanded and grown to an unimagined extent.

In 2003, when I began exploring this genre with some semblance of order, I found the following numbers of Internet sites. On February 2, 2003, a basic *Google* search revealed: Fan fiction web sites in general: 1,440,000, *Lord of the Rings* fan fiction web sites: 89,700, and *Lord of the Rings* slash sites: 7,040. Shortly thereafter, on February 11, 2003, I found that numbers for fan fiction web sites had increased to 1,450,000. On this date there were also: *Lord of the Rings* fan fiction sites: 88,000 a drop it seems) and *Lord of the Rings* slash sites: 24,600. I also began to search for a few new categories. *Lord of the Rings* fan fiction sites with archives of material: 39,400, and *Lord of the Rings* fan fiction sites with cross-over stories: 8,160, *Lord of the Rings* fan fiction sites rated PG: 5,370. There were also 259,000 web sites with information for fan fiction writers available. You see now what I mean by these numbers being worthy of attention.

Why are these numbers important? We can use these figures as benchmarks to determine the growth, and track increases or decreases of these types of web sites. One could simply monitor this growth and chart its ups and downs and never read a single story, but that coolly observational method lacks excitement and depth of exposure.

At the time this essay was completed in early 2004, a quick *Google* search revealed these increases: Fan fiction sites in general: 3,560,000 (*jaw-dropping* is still a good description of this number), *Lord of the Rings* fan fiction: 354,000, *Lord of the Rings* slash fiction: 9,410, *Lord of the Rings* PG sites: 20,800, and *Lord of the Rings* cross-over sites: 9,440. While we must reasonably argue that the effects of Peter Jackson's movies upon fans have fueled the dramatic increases of fan fiction in Tolkien's universe, we have to wonder how sustained this outpouring of fan fiction will be as time goes by. Continued numerical tracking of numbers of *Lord of the Rings* fan fiction web sites will answer this question. We see in these dramatically increased numbers of fan fiction sites that the readers have asked for more, and they are getting it.

While movie makers can use fictional characters such as King Arthur or Achilles with little concern for modern copyright issues, ensuring a continuing thread of their stories into modern days, only with much negotiating around legal issues and other contemporary pitfalls for movie makers, will we see any continuation of the adventures of Tolkien's characters on the big screen. Is making *The Hobbit* anywhere on Jackson's agenda? Who knows? Can the forebears of Middle-earth's heroes rise up from the back story and live on the screen? Probably not; however, they do live on in fan fiction.

By violating strict copyrights, fan fiction writers further the online feeding frenzy for more, more, more about Frodo, Strider, and Gandalf. The back story in the *Silmarillion* provides early histories for the cultures of Middle-earth; in the case of the long–lived Elves, it gives details about what they were doing 3-6,000 years ago. Elrond's youthful adventures alone could keep amateur authors busy at their keyboards for years, and the movie's delicately portrayed Galadriel actually kicked some serious booty in her literary younger days.

Christopher Tolkien's multi-volume histories tell us what the grandmothers and grandfathers of our beloved characters were doing, and explain to some extent how things got the way they got later. Just how did those pesky rings get here? The movies don't really tell us the whole story on that question. What was the origin of those nasty orcs? In the movie they just exist, though hints were given that they were "created" in the conversation between Gandalf and Elrond, when they discuss the cross-breeding of orcs and Goblin men. Rich fodder like the back stories information could keep fan fiction authors in Tolkien's universe going for decades, with audiences ready to log in and read away.

Concluding Remarks—or "Are We There Yet?"

Fan fiction in Tolkien's universe covers a wide range of topics, and then some. We can find het fiction of a GP nature, slash fiction of a fairly graphic, adult nature, a cross-over story where Buffy and Angel fall down a sewer tunnel and tumble out into the Bruinen River near Rivendell, or anything else you could possibly want. Lost loves are returned, battles take a different turn, and comrades become lovers. Sometimes fan fiction authors get really revved up and continue their divergent storylines across a whole series of tales. One slash web site provided an aid to aspiring authors with a "random pairing generator," which provided various pairings of characters and challenged authors to write a story around that relationship. This device is sure to send the reader out of their chair and onto the floor, either in extreme pain and denial or in uncontrollable laughter. The fact that Bill the pony was included is just an indication that a wry sense of humor is the most valuable tool one can bring along on these expeditions. Truly, some fan fiction is not to everyone's taste, so just click on by and go to the next one; you have still 353,999 stories left to review.

We have seen that fans who embrace their fictional heroes and wish to know more about them exist not only in the 20th century, but probably exerted their considerable influence on humanity's first storytellers and their tales of wonder. We have argued that fan fiction writers in general, and in Tolkien's universe specifically, continue the ancient thread of storytelling that marks us as human. Today we not only adore our fictional heroes, but we want to know everything about them. The contemporary invasive interfaces provided by television and the movies have created an intimate environment between the fan and the characters, and fan fiction is busy filling in the blanks.

Tolkien's characters, whether preserved in the minds of literary purists, or embraced by newly created fans of the movies, or in the expanding world of fan fiction literature, live on and live with us today. Chances are they will be here tomorrow and the next day as well. The books preserve Tolkien's thoughts and ideas, the histories fill in the blanks of the storylines, and the movies will preserve Jackson's vision for future generations. The powerful visuals of the movie trilogy will impress viewers in the future as they do now. And with this entrancing exposure to a mystical world, future generations will most likely continue to add new elements, and embellish the story yet again.

The Internet is truly the electronic campfire for the global village, and fan fiction writers and readers gather around its familiar glow to share and pass on heroic tales in a timeless cycle. Frodo and Sam will down an ale and swing a sword in many fan fiction incarnations yet to be, and readers will be waiting to read and rate the stories as soon as they are posted. On this journey into cyberspace, taking the highway marked "Fan Fiction-Middle-earth," we can ask, Are we there yet?

No, we have not arrived at this journey's end, and with the ever increasing numbers of fan fiction writers posting new stories every day, it will be a good long time before we are "there."

WORKS CITED

Academy of Motion Pictures Arts and Sciences. "74th Academy Awards Nominees and Winners." 31 March 2004 <http://www.oscars.org/74academy awards/nomswins.html >

Academy of Motion Pictures Arts and Sciences. "75th Academy Awards Nominees and Winners." 31 March 2004 < http://www.oscars.org/75academy awards/nomswins.html >

Academy of Motion Pictures Arts and Sciences. "76th Academy Awards Nominees and Winners." 31 March 2004 < http://www.oscars.org/76academy awards/nomswins.html >

Doyle, Arthur Conan. The Original Illustrated Sherlock Holmes. Edison, NJ: Castle Press, 1976.

Fishwick, Marshall W. Popular Culture: Cavespace to Cyberspace. New York: The Haworth Press, 1999

Fishwick, Marshall W. Popular Culture in a New Age. New York: The Haworth Press, 2002.

Jenkins, Henry. Textual Poachers: Television Fans and Participatory Culture. London: Routledge, 2003.

Kustritz, Anne. "Slashing the Romance Narrative." Journal of American Culture 26 (Sept. 2003): 371-385.

The Motion Picture Association of America. "Movie Ratings." 31 March 2004 <http://www.mpaa.org/movieratings/>

Official Lord of the Rings News. "The Lord of the Rings Receives 11 Academy Awards!" 1 March 2004. 13 Aug. 2004 <http://www.lordoftherings.net /index_105_fi_news.html>

Tolkien, J.R.R. The History of Middle-earth. Ed. Christopher Tolkien. 12 volumes. Boston: Houghton Mifflin Co., various dates.

Tolkien, J.R.R. Tolkien. The Silmarillion. 2nd ed. Ed. Christopher Tolkien. Boston: Houghton Mifflin Co., 2001.

Wikipedia Free Encyclopedia. "Motion Picture Rating Systems." 10 Aug. 2004. 13 Aug. 2004 <http://en.wikipedia.org/wiki/Motion_picture_rating_systems>

MAKE MINE "MOVIEVERSE": HOW THE TOLKIEN FAN FICTION COMMUNITY LEARNED TO STOP WORRYING AND LOVE PETER JACKSON

AMY H. STURGIS

"I do hereby witness that J.R.R. Tolkien is God and Peter Jackson is his prophet."
--Preface to "Saddle Sore: a Legolas/Éomer story" by Emma Keigh

INTRODUCTION: THE *OTHER* "OTHER MINDS AND HANDS"

In a letter to Milton Waldeman probably written in 1951, J.R.R. Tolkien describes the dream he had held "once upon a time" for his Middle-earth fiction, that "body of more or less connected legend": "I would draw some of the great tales in fullness, and leave many only placed in scheme, and sketched. The cycles should be linked to a majestic whole, and yet leave scope for other minds and hands, wielding paint and music and drama" (*Letters* 144-45). Tolkien became convinced such grand designs for an epic, inspiring, and ultimately multi-authored myth were "absurd" (145), but the decades that followed proved him wrong. Tolkien's Middle-earth has indeed captured the imagination of painters and musicians and dramatists from around the globe. But still further artistic enthusiasm and creative involvement has arrived in a form Tolkien did not anticipate: fan fiction.

Fan fiction itself is far from new, of course; one could say that the medieval authors who embellished and explored preexisting Arthurian legends were early, if not the earliest, fan fiction producers. Contemporary fan fiction has been dated from the publication of the first *Star Trek* fanzine, *Spockanalia*, in 1967, and ably analyzed and documented by scholars such as Henry Jenkins, Camille Bacon-Smith, Joan Marie Verba, Constance Penley, Cheryl Harris, Alison Alexander, and Matt Hills, among others. Tolkien fan fiction likewise has a notable history. One need only to glance over past publications from The Tolkien Society, The American Tolkien Society, and The American Hobbit Association, to name but a few groups, to recognize the ongoing literary impulse to contribute to the landscape of Middle-earth.

It took the 2001 debut of Peter Jackson's *The Lord of the Rings: The Fellowship of the Ring* film, however, to launch an unprecedented explosion in a distinctively twenty-first century incarnation of Tolkien literary fandom: the online production, dissemination, and critique of fan fiction. It seems safe to say that when Tolkien imagined an expanding body of interrelated Middle-earth legend, he did not think forward to the yet-unborn World Wide Web at all, much less of the Internet as a conduit for publication of fictional works written to satisfy the tastes of self-proclaimed Pervy Hobbit Fanciers or Legomance Addicts. Nevertheless, a new cyberculture has evolved around just such writing. Now that *The Lord of the Rings: Return of the King* has moved from silver screen to DVD, the online phenomenon of Tolkien fan fiction not only promises vitality and longevity, but also remains significant in three key ways.

First, it is big. At the time of this writing, the fan fiction clearinghouse website *Fanfiction.net* alone houses 29,500 individual *The Lord of the Rings* stories and 1,117 *Silmarillion* tales, many with multiple chapters. Specialized archives for Tolkien fan fiction number in the dozens and range in size from broader sites like *Henneth Annûn*, which boasts 1,061 stories based on Tolkien's various works, to narrower ones like *Emyn Arnen*, which includes 54 stories focusing specifically on the characters of Éowyn and Faramir. The popular *Yahoo! Groups* forum includes 274 different lists devoted solely to Tolkien fan fiction. Among the largest of these groups is "Aragorn and Legolas: The Mellon Chronicles" with 1,159 members, "Henneth Annûn" with 1,152 members, "Legolas and Aragorn Slash" with 1,069 members, and "Bitter Chains" with 969 members. Fan presses such as SpiderWeb Press, Battlefields Press, SkyFire Press, and Blackfly Presses, though publishing collections of fan fiction in traditional, hard-copy fanzine format, are using the Internet to publicize and distribute their new and forthcoming Tolkien-related offerings.

Second, it is diverse. Traditional fan fiction outlets and by-products such as conventions, printed fanzines, and fiction awards continue to thrive, but the Web allows online fan fiction archives, discussion boards, lists, blogs, live journals, RPGs (role-playing games), and MUSHs (multi-user shared hallucinations) to flourish, as well. These channels greatly expand the opportunities for experiencing fan fiction at every stage of its production. For instance, collaborators can "act out" scenes in virtual venues before committing them to the page. Writers can post works in progress for friends' eyes only, to gain critical feedback during the revision process. Readers can list and link to stories that they recommend to others. Unlike older fan fiction communities such as the often-studied *Man From U.N.C.L.E.* or *Blake's 7* groups who have had to make the transition from a pre-Internet fan fiction culture, this post-Peter Jackson *The Lord of the Rings* fandom quite literally was born online.

Third, it is unusual. For instance, one variety of fan fiction producers concentrates on franchises such as *Star Trek* and therefore draws inspiration from one central text. Even though the original *Star Trek* series has blossomed into several independent spin-offs—*The Animated Series*, *The Next Generation*, *Deep Space Nine*, *Voyager*, *Enterprise*, and multiple films—a single medium, directed by a united team, offers the "canonical" storyline. Associated professional novels do not compete with this tale, but rather appear secondarily as supplementary resources to reemphasize the primary narrative.

In contrast, another variety of fan fiction participants has a dual heritage in novels and films, such as the *Harry Potter* series, but those fans also have the luxury of knowing that the rapidly-following cinematic interpretations of the books they love have the tacit, and often active, approval of the original author. For example, *Harry Potter* enthusiasts can feel secure using actors Robbie Coltrane and Maggie Smith as the models for characters Rubeus Hagrid and Minerva McGonagall because they knew such casting reflects J.K. Rowling's expressed desires ("Smith, Coltrane Confirmed"). In a sense, the films work together with the books to offer very coherent, if not exactly identical, windows into the same story.

Those individuals drawn into the post-Jackson world of online Tolkien fan fiction find themselves in a different situation altogether. Peter Jackson's *The Lord of the Rings* film trilogy appeared half a century after the fiction on which it was based, behind multiple radio and cinematic dramatizations that had offered still different interpretations of the tale; moreover, Jackson's trilogy diverges at times quite widely from Tolkien's original text, and direct response from the late author about these changes is, obviously, impossible. Fans are left to draw inspiration from unresolved narratives that differ from each other in both fundamental outline and specific detail, sometimes to the point of outright contradiction. To make matters more complicated, members approach the Tolkien fan fiction community from dissimilar backgrounds and educations in the texts, stretching along a spectrum from "purists," who resist exposure to any secondary interpretations of the original novels, to "newbies," who feel they know Middle-earth despite never having read a word of Tolkien's books.

When writing new works set in Tolkien's world, then, fan authors must decide whether to center their plots and characterizations on his descriptions or Jackson's imagery—or, perhaps most interesting of all, to negotiate a space in between, blending the most compelling aspects of each while attempting to reconcile the points where they diverge. Meanwhile, other fan fiction writers choose to take Jackson's artistic license with *The Lord of the Rings* as an invitation to produce their own "alternate universe" realities, based on Tolkien's work, yet free to stray from its storyline in original, unexplored directions. But even as Jackson's films allow for this diversification of fan fiction, they also offer an opportunity for unification, as well, by providing all fans with a vocabulary of terminology and visual images by which to speak to one another. In short, Tolkien's premise opens the door for the "other minds and hands" of this online fan phenomenon, but it is Peter Jackson's vision that gives a common language to its many voices.

THE COMMON JACKSON LANGUAGE
PART I: WITH WORDS

The Tolkien fan fiction writers known as "The Protectors of the Plot Continuum" include the following disclaimer on their online archives homepage: "We do not own *The Lord of the Rings*, bookverse *or* movieverse. If we did, we wouldn't have to put this site on a free-home-page thingy. We do not own Boromir or Elrond; they own us." The Protectors—or the PPC, as they call themselves—feel no need to explain their meaning, nor should they. The fan community of which the PPC are a part has inherited an evolved and extensive language for introducing, labeling, and classifying individual works of fan fiction, and to this language they have added new terminology specifically relevant to Peter Jackson's films.

For example, the PPC's use of the terms "bookverse" and "movieverse" refer to the distinct Middle-earth universes created by Tolkien through his words and Jackson through his images, respectively. When applied to fan fiction, the names indicate either novel-inspired or film-inspired tales. A bookverse story about Frodo's quest would begin with a rounded, middle-aged Hobbit bachelor as described by Tolkien in his books. A movieverse story about Frodo's quest, however, would begin with a slender, youthful, wide-eyed Hobbit patterned on the performance provided by Elijah Wood for director Peter Jackson. Likewise, a bookverse story about the battle of Helm's Deep would focus primarily on Men, specifically the Rohirrim, while a movieverse story about that same battle would include the force of Elves led by Haldir of Lórien. As *The Fanfiction Glossary General Version 3.0* indicates, the general labels of bookverse and movieverse have become so popular with post-Jackson Tolkien fan fiction writers that these fans now are identified directly with the terms.

Over the years since the first online fan fiction appeared, etiquette and protocols have developed for labeling fan fiction works once they are completed and ready to be shared with an audience. Whether they are housed in archives, posted on discussion lists or live journals, or simply showcased in authors' websites, individual pieces often open with introductory classifications using common terms shared by and accessible to the larger fan fiction community. For instance, an author might identify his or her story as "slash" (either emotionally or sexually homoerotic), "gen" (appropriate for general audiences, without sexual content), "h/c" (exploring the hurt of at least one character with comfort afterwards), and/or "drabble" (a vignette of 100 words) ("Fanfic/dom Terms"). Other label options are more specifically Tolkien-related. For instance, "Silmfic" refers to stories set in or based on Tolkien's work *The Silmarillion* (Brobeck).

Just as Peter Jackson's films have popularized the distinction between bookverse and movieverse Tolkien fan fiction, they have also introduced altogether new language to the Tolkien fan community. Certainly the recent development of the "Legomance"—a romance starring Legolas Greenleaf as the male lead—owes much to the popularity of actor Orlando Bloom (*Legomance Rex*). The most notable examples of this terminology refer to fiction that explores the perceived sexual chemistry between actors in Peter Jackson's *The Lord of the Rings* trilogy. "RPS" ("real-people slash") and "lotrips" or "Lo-trips" ("*Lord of the Rings* real-people slash") are recent additions to the broader fan fiction lexicon ("Fanfic/dom Terms"). *The Library of Moria: RPS Archive* is one of many sites that houses stories falling under this heading. There one can find, among other things, fiction positing a same-sex romance between Viggo Mortensen and Sean Bean, who appear as Aragorn and Boromir, respectively, in the films. Titles such as "The King's New Clothes" and "Still Playing Roles" draw an obvious connection between the actors and the characters they portray in Jackson's trilogy.

A still newer label is "DomLijah," which denotes a subset of RPS, namely fan fiction devoted to the relationship between Dominic Monaghan and Elijah Wood, or Merry and Frodo in the *Lord of the Rings* trilogy. The popular support needed to coin such new terminology and give it purchase among fans is significant: the "DomLijah Lovers" Live Journal Community, established on January 5, 2003, to date boasts 586 members and another 463 watchers, and includes 1,145 different journal entries. *The Original DomLijah Archive* houses an even 50 works, while 54 different authors have contributed to *The DomLijah dot Com RPS FanFiction Archive*. Fan fiction in this category often focuses on the actors' experience of filming and promoting the *Lord of the Rings* trilogy, and may also conflate narratives about the actors and the characters they portray in the films. Neither DomLijah in particular nor RPS in general is universally accepted by online community members, but one thing is certain: this young and frequently controversial subset of Tolkien fan fiction owes its life and language to Jackson's cinema event.

THE COMMON JACKSON LANGUAGE
PART II: WITH IMAGES

Of course, not all Tolkien fan fiction is set in Jackson's movieverse or concerned with actors from his trilogy. Yet Jackson's influence is felt even in the more book-based regions of the online community, because he provides fans a common vocabulary of imagery that complements the works of even the most "purist" authors. Two accomplished fan fiction writers, each a recipient of multiple peer-chosen fan fiction awards, provide useful examples.

The first, Baylor, writes Hobbit-centered stories and archives her work at her personal site, *A Short Cut To Mushrooms: Lord of the Rings Fanfiction by Baylor*. Her tales spring from her careful consideration of Tolkien's *The Lord of the Rings* text. Stories such as "We Three Together" and "The Road and the End," for instance, display her familiarity with Appendix B's section "Later Events Concerning the Members of the Fellowship of the Ring" and all of Appendix C's "Family Trees." Baylor anticipates that her readers are similarly well read, and thus takes pains to explain her rationale for certain characterizations and plot devices. Her eleven-chaptered piece "I Always Know You," for example, rests on the premise of Pippin's frail health prior to the events in *The Lord of the Rings*. Since Tolkien does not overtly discuss such a concept in his fiction, Baylor provides notes explaining the textual clues she followed to draw this conclusion:

> There is nothing from Tolkien that supports the health
> history I have given Pippin, but his descriptions of Pippin
> in the books were the seed of the idea. . . . Specifically, there
> were several references to Pippin lagging behind, and to
> him being smaller than the other hobbits. Also, he had the
> most difficulty at the Redhorn Pass. He may not have been
> of age, but certainly was a full-grown hobbit physically, so
> if anything, he should have had more energy and stamina
> than his older hobbit companions. (Have any of you tried to
> keep up with a teen-ager on an outing lately? If you have,
> you know what I'm talking about.) ("Baylor's Notes" to "I
> Always Know You")

In this explanation Baylor's intention is clear: she wants to expand on
Tolkien's narrative while seeking harmony with the specifics of his text. In
other words, her work is original but dedicated to preserving the integrity
of the bookverse.

Many of her stories take place before or after the events depicted
in Peter Jackson's trilogy. Where the two differ, however, Baylor sides
with Tolkien's written word. Her tale "Take Them As Was Willing"
remains faithful to the book description of the conspiracy involving Sam,
Merry, Pippin, and Fredegar Bolger to help Frodo leave the Shire and
achieve his quest. This not only opposes Peter Jackson's suggestion in *The
Lord of the Rings: The Fellowship of the Ring* that Merry and Pippin joined
Frodo and Sam due to an accidental encounter in Farmer Maggot's
cornfield, but also rescues the character of Fatty Bolger, whom Jackson
eliminates completely. Yet again, Baylor's loyalty to the bookverse seems
clear.

Even this close adherence to Tolkien's fiction, however, does not
keep Baylor from using Peter Jackson's films to draw on a common
language shared by other fans. Centered on her main *A Short Cut to
Mushrooms* introductory page is the now-famous silhouette of the nine
Fellowship characters from Jackson's *The Lord of the Rings: The Fellowship of
the Ring*. In Baylor's fan fiction archive, each of the individual stories set
during the timeline of Tolkien's *The Lord of the Rings* opens with an image
from one of Jackson's films. For instance, "Take Them As Was Willing"
sports a publicity still of the four actors who portray the Fellowship
Hobbits, and "The Care and Feeding of Hobbits" opens with an action
shot of Sean Bean as Boromir. Her piece "Elf-Envy" remains faithful to
Tolkien's text to the point of rescuing another canonical character lost in
the films, Glorfindel; however, Baylor admits in her notes that she wrote it
with movie fans in mind, including inside jokes about a *Premiere* magazine

article featuring Hobbit actors Elijah Wood, Sean Astin, Billy Boyd, and Dominic Monaghan. The story, then, acts as a blessing of sorts for Jackson's trilogy, suggesting that bookverse fan fiction writers and readers not only can enjoy the films, but also can employ the movies to further their understanding and appreciation of Middle-earth.

Baylor does not explain the origin or identity of the film pictures she uses; she expects her readers instantly to recognize the images, and to view the emotions and associations they elicit as prefaces to her stories. Fan author Thevina, at her personal website *Thrihyrne: Thevina's Mountainous Fanfiction Archive*, speaks the language of Jackson's imagery with equal fluency. Baylor takes her website's name from the fourth chapter title in *The Lord of the Rings*, and thereby shows her love both of Tolkien's text in general and of Hobbits in particular. Thevina likewise says much with her website's name, revealing her intimate knowledge of Tolkien's work and her special interest in the culture of the Rohirrim, since Thrihyrne refers to three mountain peaks of the Ered Nimrais chain that stand behind the Hornburg in Middle-earth (Foster 486). Writing in both Rohirric and Sindarin mode Elvish further distinguishes Thevina's site as the home of a serious student of Tolkien's texts.

Thevina's archive displays wider range than Baylor's in terms of style and content. Her Tolkien-related works vary from short poetry and character sketches to novellas and research articles. Her fan fiction follows standard paths from *The Lord of the Rings*—unlikely friendships, such as those between Éowyn and Merry, and Gimli and Legolas, for example— but also far less traveled territory, such as the relationship of Tuor and Ulmo from *The Silmarillion*, and the star-watching habits of Tar-Meneldur Elentirmo as mentioned in *Unfinished Tales of Númenor and Middle-earth*. Her commentary notes explain the origins of her pieces: "Boar and Steward" sprang from inspiration found in appendix notes to "Cirion and Eorl" in *Unfinished Tales*, and "One Who Ran" from three provocative sentences in *The Lord of the Rings*.

Her story "A House Divided" explores the union of Thengel, 16th King of the Riddermark, and Morwen of Lassarnach. In her "Author's Notes" that follow the tale, Thevina refers to reading Anglo-Saxon poetry and other Tolkien fan fiction above and beyond Tolkien's texts in preparation for this project:

> "Well-wrought this wall: Weirds broke it. The stronghold burst . . . " and the torrent of words creating this story rushed forth. Morwen and Thengel appear only in Appendix A of *Lord of the Rings*, though Gandalf occasionally invokes him when addressing Théoden as "son

of Thengel." . . . The quote at the top is from *The Ruin*, a
piece of "anonymous" 8th-century Anglo-Saxon poetry, as
translated by Michael Alexander. It reflects how I felt after
reading Altariel's story, "A Game of Chess," whose
beautifully-written narrative was the inspiration for this
story. ("Author's Notes" to "A House Divided")

Thevina thus secures her bookverse credentials as a productive member of
the Tolkien fan fiction community: she reads Tolkien's works, including
his more obscure texts, as well as the literature Tolkien himself read and
drew upon, and furthermore she is familiar with her fellow fans' writings.
All of these texts inform her fiction. She credits Peter Jackson as an
influence for only one of her twenty-six Tolkien-related pieces, however;
otherwise, her author's notes make no mention of Jackson's films as
inspiration for her work.

Clearly, though, the films are. Thevina tells us so visually. She
introduces the "Rohirrim" section of her archive with an image of the
doors to Théoden's Golden Hall in Edoras as shown in *The Lord of the
Rings: The Two Towers* film. The "Éowyn and Merry" stories sit beside a
screen capture of Miranda Otto portraying Éowyn, as the "Gimli and
Legolas" tales share space with a picture of John Rhys-Davies in complete
Gimli costume and makeup. Even the cropped map of Middle-earth is
recognizable as the green map used in New Line Cinema's marketing of
Jackson's trilogy. Aside from one set of Dwarvish runes and one portrait
of a dragon, all of the visuals on the archive page relate to Jackson's films.

The implications of these choices are twofold. First, Thevina
expects that the smiling face of Miranda Otto as Éowyn, for instance, will
instantly speak to fellow fans, putting them intellectually and emotionally
"in the mood" for further explorations of the character and her
relationships. Thevina does not label the picture as a depiction of Éowyn,
because she can assume this is already known, and that the image serves
as a form of shorthand to evoke in the audience a wealth of thoughts and
feelings about the character, her setting, her time, and her symbolic power.
Second, by tapping into the common language of Jackson's imagery,
Thevina embraces the film trilogy as a worthy accompaniment to, though
not a substitute for, Tolkien's literature. Just like Baylor, Thevina gives
Jackson her blessing by adopting and sharing his visual interpretation of
Tolkien's myth. Seeing Middle-earth through Jackson's eyes, she implies,
can be a step toward a deep and satisfying exploration of Tolkien's myth.

THE COMMON JACKSON LANGUAGE
PART III: WITH LAUGHTER

Baylor's and Thevina's fan fiction archives are examples of a trend seen on many Tolkien websites, the use of movieverse illustrations for bookverse literature. When Baylor and Thevina employ Jackson's images on their sites, they bring attention to the places where Jackson's films and Tolkien's words intersect smoothly. Other fan fiction writers use descriptions of Jackson's imagery, coupled with the genre of parody, to bring attention to the places where Jackson's movies and Tolkien's words most greatly diverge. These authors are not attacking the film trilogy in anger; on the contrary, they intend not to divide but to unify their readers by filling the space between Tolkien and Jackson with popular culture references and, ultimately, laughter.

The epitome of Tolkien fan fiction parody is Cassandra Claire's *The Very Secret Diaries* series. This phenomenon began humbly enough. Claire wrote an online Live Journal entry on December 30, 2001 in reaction to viewing Peter Jackson's *The Lord of the Rings: The Fellowship of the Ring*, which had debuted in theaters only days earlier (*The Original Pervy Hobbit Fancier's Journal*). That single tongue-in-cheek post, "The Secret Diary of Aragorn," eventually grew into an eighteen-chapter parody, however. Fan reaction was immediate and enthusiastic, and the series' popularity spawned t-shirts, mugs, and mousepads, spin-off fan fiction series written by admiring authors, and an organized effort by readers to attend promotional public appearances by the film actors and present them with copies of the work (*The Original Pervy Hobbit Fancier's Journal*, *The Very Secret Diaries*).

Claire sets *The Very Secret Diaries* series directly in Peter Jackson's movieverse. Claire's characters at times are even self-aware about their existence on screen: at one point in the first chapter, for instance, Aragorn asks, "My God, is everyone in this movie gay but me?" ("The Very Secret Diary of Aragorn, Son of Arathorn"). In her loving send-up of the films, Claire shows an appreciation for Tolkien's books as well as an understanding of how Jackson's imagery at times conflicts with Tolkien's original vision. For example, in the eleventh chapter, "The Very Secret Diary of Ringwraith No. 5," Claire recalls *The Fellowship of the Ring* film's Weathertop sequence. She does not describe the scene in great detail; she expects her audience to remember Jackson's portrayal of the Ringwraiths' attack and Frodo's reaction as he drops his sword, falls to the ground, and stares up at the Witch-king in horror. The entry she writes alludes to this visual moment, as the Dark Rider notes: "Suspect Gandalf chose

Ringbearer on account of big blue eyes and pouty lower lip, rather than possession of heroic-type fortitude" ("The Very Secret Diary of Ringwraith No. 5"). Here "Gandalf chose Ringbearer" stands in for "Peter Jackson chose Elijah Wood," noting that the actor's appearance and performance could be attributed more to a filmmaking mentality than a close attention to Tolkien's text.

Other entries mock the casting and costuming of the film trilogy and what new character insights follow from them. In "The Very Secret Diary of Arwen Undómiel," Claire pokes fun at Orlando Bloom's appearance as Legolas: "Legolas got all shirty when I accused him of trying on my dresses. He says I have impugned his masculinity. What masculinity?" Likewise, Claire brings attention to Jackson's depiction of King Théoden's decline under the influence of Gríma Wormtongue. In "The Very Secret Diary of Théoden," she writes, "New makeover gone horribly awry. Do not look fresh and youthful, instead resemble albino dwarf after two years pickling in the Dead Marshes. . . . Why has no one noticed I now resemble a weevil?" With each reference, Claire assumes her readers will recall the images that inspire her humor.

Molly J. Ringwraith's Condensed series—including "The Condensed Parody Version of the FOTR Script," "The Ten-Minute *Two Towers*," and "*The Return of the King*: Condensed"—also began life in the author's online Live Journal as reactions to viewing Jackson's movies. On her website *Lemon, Lay of the Nitrice*, under the heading "Other books I highly recommend," Molly states her loyalties both to Jackson and to Tolkien, crediting the filmmaker with leading her to the author:

> I curse myself for listening, all those years, to the people who said this trilogy was boring. It took the fabulous new movie of *The Fellowship of the Ring* to convince me to start thinking otherwise. I am ashamed to have taken this long to find the brilliance and beauty of little Frodo's journey. Go ahead, read other fantasy novels instead, if you want. Or you could read this one, which all other fantasy novels ripped off. Up to you, of course. ("Literature")

Insofar as her series parodies aspects of Jackson's films, then, her jokes are lovingly meant. Written in script format, her works, like Cassandra Claire's, include characters who are aware they are in the movies. To this formula she adds audience members who actively participate in the dialogue. Her treatment of the Helm's Deep sequences in "The Ten-Minute *Two Towers*" illustrates this dual emphasis on the movieverse.

Molly's Aragorn criticizes Jackson's choice to focus so much attention on the battle:

> ARAGORN. This siege is lasting forever. These poor people
>
> . . .
>
> LEGOLAS. We will fight to the death. We will not fail you.
> ARAGORN. Oh, not you guys--I meant the audience.

And as the action unfolds, the viewers note Jackson's deviations from Tolkien's narrative:

> ROHIRRIM GUARD. Sire, there are some really femmy people at the gate. They have bows.
> ARAGORN. Those are Elves. Let them in.
> ROHIRRIM GUARD. Oh! Elves! Wow, I didn't expect that.
> PEOPLE WHO READ THE BOOK. Neither did I . . .

Molly expects her readers to be fluent in the language of Jackson's imagery. As in *The Very Secret Diaries*, Molly's "The Condensed Parody Version of the FOTR Script" alludes to the Weathertop scene in order to offer a comical critique of Jackson's presentation of a helpless Frodo.

> SAM. Go away! Shoo!
> RINGWRAITH bats him aside.
> MERRY. We kindly request that you go away!
> PIPPIN. In the name of common decency!
> RINGWRAITHS bat them aside.
> FRODO. I haven't had time to practice using this sword yet, so I think it's safer if I just drop it and roll around on the ground.
> SAM. No, Mr. Frodo! That's if you're on fire!
> FRODO. Oh, damn it, I always mix those up.

This section of script is funny only if readers remember how Elijah Wood looked and behaved during the scene in *The Lord of the Rings: The Fellowship of the Ring* film. It is funnier still if they also recognize how this interpretation differs from Tolkien's original understanding of Frodo as an inexperienced and yet valiant Hobbit.

Molly J. Ringwraith and Cassandra Claire underscore the ways in which Jackson's narrative differs from Tolkien's, yet it is evident that both fan fiction writers have great knowledge of and affection for the two competing texts. By examining the rift between the bookverse and movieverse, they create a new opportunity for their own creativity and self-expression. Both authors choose to fill the divide between Tolkien's literature and Jackson's imagery with references to popular culture, diverting attention from the sore spots of narrative incompatibility and towards the funny bones of readers. For instance, Claire creates puns; her Arwen laments, "Went all the way to the Gap of Rohan only to find there is no Gap in Rohan. Not even a Banana Republic. False advertising!" ("The Very Secret Diary of Arwen Undómiel"). Molly J. Ringwraith includes similar references to contemporary life, out of place and anachronistic in Middle-earth:

> FRODO flings himself onto the ground and writhes in
> agony.
> FRODO. I can't bear it. Life is horrid. My heart is shriveled
> and my soul is dead. The blackness of despair shrouds
> my eyes. I choke on pain and anguish.
> SAM. That's it—no more listening to The Cure for you.
> SAM picks FRODO up, slings him over his shoulder, and
> carries him up the mountain.
> ("*The Return of the King*: Condensed")

Even as these fans poke gentle fun at Peter Jackson's film trilogy, they, like Baylor and Thevina, also give the movies their blessing. They do this in three ways: by investing time and creativity in engaging Jackson's work, by returning audience memory to key sequences and images in his films, and, most importantly, by reacting to Jackson's departures from Tolkien's texts with genuine laughter. Irreverent, even absurd comedy in the face of Jackson's successes and failures suggests that adapting *The Lord of the Rings* to film does no real harm to the bookverse, while it introduces the joy of the movieverse to many. Thus Jackson provides a common language of laughter, as well as terminology and imagery, to unite the online Tolkien fan fiction community.

BRIDGING THE GAP

Tolkien fan fiction writer Ana begins her poem "How Figwit Was Born" with the following lines: "There once was a casting director for *Lord of the Rings* / Who said 'Who needs guidelines? I'll take care of things!' / . . . Oh no here comes Jackson, I'd better look busy / Oh Sir, how bout this kid? He's not elvish, is he?" The reader discovers that Ana does not mind some of Jackson's directorial decisions, because her verse celebrates the character Figwit, one of most unexpected products of Jackson's film trilogy. Figwit fan fiction—or Figtion, as some practitioners call it— provides just one illustration of another impact Peter Jackson has made on the Tolkien fan fiction community (*Fans of Figwit*). The disjunction between aspects of his story and Tolkien's opens a new literary playing ground for some fan authors. These writers choose to adopt a visual cue from Jackson's films and explore its story in detail in order to bridge the divide between his cinematic narrative and Tolkien's written one.

Ana's "How Figwit Was Born" alludes to a character portrayed by actor Bret McKenzie. His original appearance as an unnamed Elf extra in *The Lord of the Rings: The Fellowship of the Rings* is limited to mere moments of silent screen time during the Council of Elrond sequence (*Fellowship*, scene 27). Immediate online reaction led fans to dub the mysterious figure Figwit, referring to the supposed gasps many uttered when they first saw him: "Frodo Is Grea . . . Who Is THAT?" Websites and mailing lists followed; the groundswell of appreciation led Peter Jackson to ask Bret McKenzie to revisit the part as a speaking role in *The Lord of the Rings: The Return of the King*. Jackson officially adopted the fan name for the character. The licensed trading card series for the third installment of the trilogy even includes a Figwit autograph card (*Figwit Lives!*).

Of course, Jackson's choice to allow Figwit's leap from informal fan icon to official film character makes Figwit "real" only in the movieverse. J.R.R. Tolkien never writes of an Elf named Figwit. This poses a challenge some fan fiction writers are glad to tackle. By providing Figwit a back-story grounded in the bookverse, these authors find imaginative ways to make Tolkien's and Jackson's visions speak to one another. For instance, writer Kid Frock suggests in the story "His Lordship" that Figwit is the son of Elrond by a forgotten first wife. Figwit only discovers this through a conversation with Erestor, Elrond's chief counselor, a figure from Tolkien's books only briefly glimpsed in Jackson's trilogy. In the story Erestor explains that Elrond's first wife perished after an attack by Orcs, and then Elrond married his second wife, Celebrían. The chronology Erestor relates about the second marriage fits Tolkien's storyline about Elrond as found in *The Silmarillion*, *The Lord of the Rings*, and *Unfinished Tales*. Kid Frock adds the character of the late first wife in order to forge a link between Tolkien's Elrond and Jackson's Figwit, displaying knowledge of both the books and films in the process.

Similarly, Neon Star revives Tolkien characters lost to the film trilogy—the powerful Elf Glorfindel, and Elrond's twin sons Elladan and Elrohir—in the story "Son of Silence." This piece suggests that Glorfindel found an orphaned young Figwit wandering in the woods and brought him to Elrond in Rivendell for care. The author theorizes that young Figwit went mute from the trauma of watching Orcs attack and kill his parents. This silence, Neon Star implies, explains his quiet nature as an adult, including his lack of comment during the formal discussion at the

Council of Elrond. Here the fan not only links the movieverse to the bookverse, but also covers the simple fact that Bret McKenzie was as a non-speaking extra in the first film with a credible literary reason for Figwit's quiet during a pivotal debate.

Tolkien fan fiction about Figwit is not the only example of how authors bridge the gap between Jackson's imagery and Tolkien's literature. Other writers choose different visual clues to help tie together the two narratives. For instance, most of the film trilogy shows Pippin wearing a particular scarf around his neck. This wardrobe piece has no recurring parallel in Tolkien's fiction; nonetheless, it is linked with Pippin in Jackson's movies. The scarf motif appears repeatedly in online Tolkien fan fiction, where is used for everything from a symbol of Pippin's childhood bond with his cousin Merry in Murron's tale "Little Bird" to a signal of Pippin's death in Hope's story "Bauble." Once again, authors provide a back-story to the image in order to reconcile the movieverse and bookverse.

Robin Girl's story "The Scarf" gives one possible origin for the piece and its meaning for Pippin: Merry makes it for his cousin when the younger Hobbit is only seven years old. Pippin wants to play outside in the cold with Merry, but the Took parents will give their permission only if Pippin wears a scarf. By providing one, Merry makes Pippin's play possible. In a tale that introduces other Tolkien book characters not seen in the films, such as Esmeralda Brandybuck and Eglantine Took, Robin Girl gives the scarf a poignant history inextricably linked to Tolkien's literature.

Red Autumn's "Untitled Drabble About Pippin's Scarf" also links the piece to Merry; in this case, the scarf belongs first to the older Hobbit, who hands it down despite the fact it is a favorite of his. The author takes the connection to Tolkien's bookverse a step further than Robin Girl, however. She suggests that it is Pippin's scarf, along with his foot, that catches Gimli's eye when searching for the Hobbit after the last battle of the War of the Ring. Peter Jackson's film does not depict Pippin fighting against the troll or crushed beneath its dead weight as Tolkien describes. In following this section of the storyline from the book *The Lord of the Rings*, Red Autumn puts a visual cue from Peter Jackson's costuming into the specific points of Tolkien's narrative. In the process, Red Autumn makes Merry's selfless gift the agent of Pippin's salvation when "the worn piece of green knit" brings Gimli to the rescue in time to save Pippin's life. In the end, Red Autumn achieves what many fans wish to accomplish by reconciling Jackson's and Tolkien's texts: in her story Tolkien's bookverse is satisfied, while an image from the movieverse becomes even more meaningful.

EXPLORING AN ALTERNATE UNIVERSE

In the prologue to the Tolkien fan fiction work "Trust to Hope," self-proclaimed "newbie author" Novedelion writes, "I tried to follow canon where possible but did take some artistic license. If PJ can put Elves at Helms Deep [sic] . . . " Fan writer houses makes a similar statement in the preface notes to "Courtly Behavior": "Hey, if Peter Jackson can have a troop of elves show up at Helm's Deep and Faramir try to take the Ring (grumble), I can mess with things too. If I change certain things, I know I'm doing it—this is fanfiction after all." Both Novedelion and houses reflect the most radical way in which Jackson has influenced the Tolkien fan fiction community. As these two reveal, some fan fiction writers take Jackson's artistic freedom with *The Lord of the Rings* as a challenge to produce their own "alternate universe" realities based on Tolkien's fiction but free to stray from its storyline in original directions. These stories view movieverse and bookverse Middle-earth as a springboard from which to launch into new and imaginative tales unencumbered by preexisting narrative boundaries.

For instance, much as Jackson discards the "Scouring of the Shire" book sequence in favor of what he considers a more climactic conclusion to *The Lord of the Rings* trilogy, some fan authors deny the bittersweet parting of Frodo at the Grey Havens in favor of an ending that allows Frodo to remain in the Shire with Sam, at least for a time. Perhaps the most interesting phenomenon in this kind of alternative universe fan fiction is the development of the "Pretty Good Year" series.

Begun by Mary Borsellino after the debut of Peter Jackson's *The Lord of the Rings: The Fellowship of the Ring* film in 2001, "Pretty Good Year" follows a polyamorous arrangement between Rosie Cotton, Sam, and Frodo over the year following the end of the War of the Ring. In this universe Rosie loves Sam and Frodo and takes both as de facto husbands. Children follow from this union, and friends and neighbors react differently to the alternative lifestyle Bag End represents. At the core of the series is not the sexual experimentation implicit in the three-way marriage, however, but rather the daily challenges the three face in raising the next generation, renewing the Shire, and restoring Frodo's health. The series dwells to a surprising degree on domestic concerns and emotional conflicts. In the sequel "West of the Moon," Frodo chooses to stay with his family and postpone departure for the Grey Havens, thus permitting the saga to continue.

Mary Borsellino's productivity with this series is impressive. To date she has penned in the "Pretty Good Year" canon alone one prologue, forty-three stories, and two sequels with their sixty related stories. What possibly is even more compelling, however, is the resonance that this hopeful and unusual series has found with other fan fiction authors. At the current time, "Pretty Good Year" has spawned sixteen sequel stories by a total of five guest authors, seven "canon" stories by a total of five authors, and nineteen contemporary stories, one in six parts, by a total of eight guest authors.

The sequel "West of the Moon" has inspired thirty-seven contemporary stories by a total of eight guest authors, ninety-four "next generation" stories by a total of thirteen guest authors, and eight related stories by a total of six guest authors. The sequel "East of the Sun" has led to five contemporary stories by a total of three guest authors. Additionally, the series as a whole also has prompted eighty other related fictional works such as fairytales, poems, and parodies written by a total of thirteen guest authors and set in the "Pretty Good Year" universe.

The series ends with Mary Borsellino's story "East of the Sun," which tells of Rosie's death. In the tale Rosie's daughters Elanor and Goldilocks, or "Elly" and "Goldy," consider the ending Tolkien leaves his readers in *The Lord of the Rings*: an aged Sam following Frodo across the sea, and a deceased Rosie buried in Hobbiton, forever estranged from the other two Hobbits of Bag End. Goldilocks despairs at this final exile for her mother, saying, "She's not with them, Elly, not now and never again."

"East of the Sun" rescues Rosie from this fate, however, and offers her a reunion with Sam and Frodo. As Elanor tells her sister, "I don't know how I know it, Goldy, but the story's all played out in my head. My heart knows it, and it's a happily ever after." At Goldy's insistence that "Nobody gets a happily ever after," Elly replies with the following: "Well, this is so close the difference can't be told, anyway. And that's enough." Elanor's pronouncement summarizes the series as a whole: though this alternative universe Middle-earth is not ideal, love and patience make it seem as close to perfect as possible, a fairytale ending to an epic legend.

The aforementioned works, along with a related visual art gallery and links to foreign language translations of "Pretty Good Year" material, all exist on the *Pretty Good Year* website. Yet other spin-off works by "Pretty Good Year" fans published online remain uncollected. Clearly many fans feel the desire to revise the ending of *The Lord of the Rings*; although the online archives for the "Pretty Good Year" series mixes many images, it is fitting that the signature title illustration is a screen capture depicting Frodo, Sam, and Rosie as shown in Peter Jackson's *The Lord of the Rings: The Fellowship of the Ring* film.

Like Mary Borsellino, fan writer Sally Gardens denies the Grey Havens ending to *The Lord of the Rings*. In a 2003 novella spanning twenty-eight chapters plus a prologue and epilogue, Gardens has Frodo visit the Undying Lands only to learn that the true cure for his hurts exists back in The Shire. "The Road Ahead" brings Frodo home in order to begin a new life for himself, restoring his relationship with family and friends, finding lasting healing, and even discovering true love and marriage.

Using Pippin's voice as narrator for the epilogue, Gardens reveals how her story breaks the rules of the original bookverse with regard to Frodo:

> It is a wonder that he is here at all. Never will I, can I allow myself to forget this. He left me, once, left us all with the anguish of parting and naught but the thin hope of his healing to console us. He left, forever, to seek healing in a place from which return is said to be neither permitted nor possible.
>
> And yet it was permitted and made possible for him to return.

Here the audience can read "he left me, once, left us all with the anguish of parting" as a personal statement by Sally Gardens, an acknowledgement of how the original ending to *The Lord of the Rings* left her emotionally wrenched. This passage reveals the motivation for her work, in which she gives both the characters and the reader new closure by seeing Frodo reunited, whole, and happy. The novella is a departure from the bookverse, yet it is Gardens's deep love for Tolkien's characters that compels her to rescue and restore them. To illustrate her site, she draws on movieverse imagery, choosing a photograph of the New Zealand set used to portray The Shire in Peter Jackson's films.

The desire for a happy—or perhaps happier—ending to *The Lord of the Rings* is not the only factor behind the "alternative universe" phenomenon. Other fan fiction writers are drawn to different thought experiments. For example, in 2002, "The One Ring Challenge," a fan fiction competition, began. The organizer called for writers to address "what if" scenarios based on the premise that different Tolkien characters had gained possession of the One Ring before it was destroyed. Authors responded with works starring a myriad of Middle-earth personalities from Shelob and Thorin Oakenshield to Tom Bombadil and Gríma Wormtongue, with pieces ranging from light comedy to dark horror.

Though the initial phase of the challenge ended on October 31, 2002, new submissions by latecomer writers currently are accepted in the online archive. The stories collected thus far reflect a wide mix of movieverse and bookverse inspiration. The banner for the contest and website recognizes Peter Jackson's influence in particular, though, employing the image of Elijah Wood as Frodo Baggins as seen in the promotional posters for *The Lord of the Rings: The Fellowship of the Ring* film. It seems that many of those participating in "The One Ring Challenge," much like Mary Borsellino and Sally Gardens, consider Jackson's movie trilogy as permission, even a challenge, to experiment artistically with Tolkien's premise.

CONCLUSION: GIVING JACKSON HIS DUE

In "The Making Of" essay regarding the story "Gift of Men," SoldierBlue articulates sentiments at the heart of much of online Tolkien fan fiction today:

> So, this is a sort of hybrid . . . a story which started in the pure spirit of Tolkien but lost itself somewhere along the way, in part willingly. I can say only this, I had lots of fun (cathartic, you know) while writing it, and I did it out of love for the inspiring work of Tolkien, for Peter Jackson's movies and for the characters that make both so unique; therefore I hope that a little of this love will shine through, and that you too will enjoy it.

As SoldierBlue suggests, the online Tolkien fan fiction community as a whole rests on the shoulders of two forefathers: the first, obviously, is J.R.R. Tolkien, but the second is Peter Jackson. The advent of the film trilogy has expanded the terminology writers and readers use about the fiction they write. Even those fans interested in mining the great depths of the bookverse find the images from Jackson's films useful to set the emotional stage for their stories. Some authors focus on the areas where Tolkien's writing and Jackson's visualizations intersect. Others emphasize the divides between the two, sometimes with laughter, in the desire to play in both traditions despite their differences, and sometimes in reconciliation, with the hopes of helping one text speak to the other. Still others consider Jackson's artistic license a model to emulate in their own alternate universe works. Each of these phenomena points to a single conclusion: Peter Jackson's films are responsible for a remarkable degree of fan creativity, production, and dialogue.

One particular anecdote underscores this. The Official *Lord of the Rings* Fan Club, the cinema-sanctioned vehicle for fans of Jackson's trilogy, hosts several online discussion boards as part of its service. Members began posting works of fan fiction—stories, poems, even songs—as soon as the first movie in Jackson's trilogy debuted. The fans quickly determined to produce more than an online archive for these pieces, and "The LOTRfanclub Scrapbook" was born. An editorial panel assembled to evaluate and choose among the posted works. Together a team of fan volunteers produced two identical 12"x12" scrapbooks of 101 pages each, handmade and embellished, fully illustrated and divided into sections for tales, top ten lists, poetry, songs, musings, and other interesting Tolkien-related fan creations. The completed volumes represented the work of 125 different contributors ("The Fan Club Scrapbook Project").

At The Gathering of the Fellowship event in Toronto, Fan Club members raffled off one of the two scrapbooks on December 17, 2003, the day the final installment of the film trilogy debuted in theaters. The raffle earned $1,889 for the charity ProLiteracy Worldwide ("The Fan Club Scrapbook Project"). The event seemed to herald an end not only for the scrapbook project, but also for the many months of fan fiction activity on the Club discussion boards. But it did not. If anything, it gave the community a second life. Fans immediately began submitting new works for the next scrapbook, which has been dubbed "A Second Edition of Offbeat and Profound Products From the Slightly Deranged Minds of the LOTR Fan Club" (*LOTRfanclub Scrapbook*).

As for the other copy of the original scrapbook of Tolkien fan fiction, the Fan Club members made that volume as a gift—for Peter Jackson.

WORKS CITED

Ana. "How Figwit Was Born." n.d. *Figwit Lives!* 16 March 2004 <http://www.figwitlives.net/hfwb.htm>.
Award Winners: Mithril Awards 2003. 2003. 16 March 2004 <http://www.viragene.com/tolkien/shortlist.html>.

Bacon-Smith, Camille. *Enterprising Women: Television Fandom and the Creation of Popular Myth*. Philadelphia: University if Pennsylvania, 1992.

Battlefields Press. n.d.16 March 2004 <http://www.thebattlefields.org/bfpress.htm>.

Baylor. *A Short Cut To Mushrooms: Lord of the Rings Fanfiction by Baylor*. 16 March 2004 <http://home.comcast.net/~baylorsr/>.

___. "Baylor's Notes" to "I Always Know You." [c. 2002]. *A Short Cut To Mushrooms: Lord of the Rings Fanfiction by Baylor*. 16 March 2004 <http://home.comcast.net/~baylorsr/>.

Blackfly Presses. n.d. 16 March 2004. <http://www.t1goold.net/Blackfly/>.

Borsellino, Mary. "East of the Sun." [c. 2002]. *Pretty Good* Year. 16 March 2004 <http://muse.inkstigmata.net/eastofthesun.html>.

Brobeck, Kristi Lee. "Does Gender Matter? Women, Tolkien and the Online Fanfiction Community." 19 March 2003. *Thrihyrne: Thevina's Mountainous Fanfiction Archive*. 16 March 2004 <http://www.thrihyrne.net /FanfictionPaper.html>.

Claire, Cassandra. "The Original Pervy Hobbit Fancier's Journal." 30 December 2001. 16 March 2004 <http://www.livejournal.com/users/cassieclaire/>.

___. "The Very Secret Diary of Aragorn, Son of Arathorn." [c.2002]. 16 March 2004 <http://www.ealasaid.com/misc/vsd/aragorn.html>.

___. "The Very Secret Diary of Arwen Undomiel." [c.2002]. 16 March 2004 <http://www.ealasaid.com/misc/vsd/arwen.html>.

___. "The Very Secret Diary of Théoden." [c.2002]. 16 March 2004 <http://www.ealasaid.com/misc/vsd/theoden.html>.

___. "The Very Secret Diary of Ringwraith No. 5." [c.2002]. 16 March 2004 <http://www.ealasaid.com/misc/vsd/wraith5.html>.

DomLijah dot Com RPS FanFiction Archive. n.d. 16 March 2004 <http://www.domlijah.com/>.

"DomLijah Lovers" LiveJournal Community. 5 January 2003. 16 March 2004 <http://www.livejournal.com/userinfo.bml?user=domlijah>.

Emyn Arnen. 12 December 2003. 16 March 2004 <http://www.emyn-arnen.net/>.

"The Fan Club Scrapbook Project." n.d. *LOTRfanclub Scrapbook*. 16 March 2004 <http://lotrscrapbook.bookloaf.net/other/project/project.html>.

"Fan Fiction Groups." n.d. *Yahoo!Groups*. 23 March 2004 <http://dir.groups. yahoo.com/dir/Entertainment___Arts/Humanities/Books_and_Writing/G enres/Science_Fiction_and_Fantasy/Authors/Tolkien,_J.R.R./Fan_Fiction>.

"Fanfic/dom Terms." August 2003. *The Fanfiction Glossary General Version 3.0*. 16 March 2004 http://www.subreality.com/glossary/terms.htm.

Fanfiction.net. 16 March 2004 <http://www.fanfiction.net/>.

Fans of Figwit. n.d. 16 March 2004 <http://www.geocities.com/figwit_x/>.

Figwit Lives! n.d. 16 March 2004 <http://www.figwitlives.net/>.

Foster, Robert. *The Complete Guide to Middle-Earth*. Reprint edition. New York: Ballantine Books, 2001.

Gardens, Sally. "Epilogue to *The Road Ahead*." 2003. *The Road Ahead*. 16 March 2004 <http://www.geocities.com/sallygardens63/TheRoadAhead Epilogue.html>.

___. *The Road Ahead*. 2003. 16 March 2004 <http://www.geocities.com/sally
    gardens63/>.

Harris, Cheryl, and Alison Alexander, eds. *Theorizing Fandom: Fans, Subcultures,
    and Identity*. Cresskill, N.J.: Hampton, 1998.

Henneth Annûn. n.d. 16 March 2004 <http://www.henneth-annun.net/>.

Hills, Matt. *Fan Cultures*. New York: Routledge, 2002.

Hope. "Bauble." [c.2002]. *The One Ring Challenge*. 16 March 2004. <http://www.
    oggham.com/ring/archives/000597.html>.

houses. "Courtly Behavior." n.d. *Twisting the Hellmouth*. 16 March 2004
    <http://www.tthfanfic.com/story.php?no=1350>.

Jenkins, Henry. *Textual Poachers: Television Fans and Participatory Culture*. New
    York: Routledge, 1992.

Keigh, Emma. "Saddle Sore: a Legolas/Éomer story." 12 December 2003. *Library of
    Moria*. 16 March 2004 <http://www.libraryofmoria.com/legolasaragorn
    /saddlesore.txt>.

Kid Frock. "His Lordship." 3 December 2003. *Fanfiction.net*, 16 March 2004
    <http://www.fanfiction.net/read.php?storyid=1626559>.

Legomance Rex. n.d. 16 March 2004 <http://www.helical-library.net/legomance/>.

LOTRfanclub Scrapbook. n.d. 16 March 2004 <http://lotrscrapbook.bookloaf.net/>.

Mithril Awards for Tolkien Fanfiction Home Page. [c. 2003]. 16 March 2004
    <http://www.viragene.com/tolkien/>.

Murron. "Little Bird." n.d. *West of the Moon: A Tolkien Fanfiction Archive*. 16 March
    2004 <http://www.west-of-the-moon.net/servlet/ReadGenStory?
    storyID=64>.

Neon Star. "Son of Silence." 5 May 2002. *Fanfiction.net*, 16 March 2004
    <http://www.fanfiction.net/read.php?storyid=761828>.

Novedelion. "Trust to Hope: Prologue." n.d. *Shieldmaiden's Library*. 16 March 2004
    <http://www.arandor.com/loss/walkstories/tthprologue.html>.

The One Ring Challenge. [c. 2002]. 7 July 2003 <http://www.oggham.com/ring/.>.

The Original DomLijah Archive. n.d. 16 March 2004 <http://eldo.unite-or-fall.org/>.

Penley, Constance. *NASA/Trek: Popular Science and Sex in America*. New York:
    Verson, 1997.

Parma Eruseen. 2 March 2003. 16 March 2004 <http://www.parma-eruseen.net>.

Pretty Good Year. [c. 2002]. 16 March 2004
    <http://muse.inkstigmata.net/prettygoodyear.html>.

The Protectors of the Plot Continuum Online Archives. n.d. 16 March 2004
    <http://www.misssandman.com/PPC/archives.html>.

Red Autumn. "Untitled Drabble About Pippin's Scarf." 15 November 2003. 16
    March 2004 <http://www.livejournal.com/users/redautumn/81432.html>.

Ringwraith, Molly J. "The Condensed Parody Version of the FOTR Script." n.d.
    Lemon, Lay of the Nitrice. 16 March 2004 <http://home.earthlink.net
    /~ladyirony/FOTRparody.html>.

___. *Lemon, Lay of the Nitrice*. n.d. 16 March 2004 <http://home.earthlink.net
    /~ladyirony/home.htm>.

___."Literature." *Lemon, Lay of the Nitrice*. n.d. 16 March 2004 <http://home. earthlink.net/~ladyirony/Literary.html>.

___. *"The Return of the King*, Condensed." n.d. *Lemon, Lay of the Nitrice*. 16 March 2004 <http://home.earthlink.net/~ladyirony/ROTKparody.html>.

___. "The Ten-Minute *Two Towers*." n.d. *Lemon, Lay of the Nitrice*. 16 March 2004 <http://home.earthlink.net/~ladyirony/FOTRparody.html>.

Robin Girl. "The Scarf." 6 November 2002. *Fanfiction.net*. 16 March 2004 <http://www.fanfiction.net/read.php?storyid=1051867>.

"Smith, Coltrane Confirmed for Potter." 15 August 2000. *jam!Showbiz*. 16 March 2004 <http://www.canoe.ca/JamMoviesArtistsC/coltrane_robbie.html>.

SkyFire Press. 15 December 2003. 16 March 2004 <http://www.melethryn.net/ SkyFirePress/>.

SoldierBlue. "The Making of *The Gift of Men*." February 2004. *The Osgiliath Library*. 16 March 2004 <http://www.darkover.it/00sb/toclibrary.html# makinggift>.

SpiderWeb Press. n.d. 16 March 2004 <http://www.skeeter63.org/~silvablu/ Spider_web/Index.htm>.

Thevina. "Author's Notes" to "A House Divided." 2003. *Thrihyrne: Thevina's Mountainous Fanfiction Archive*. 16 March 2004 <http://www. thrihyrne.net/AHDAuthor'sNotes.html>.

___. *Thrihyrne: Thevina's Mountainous Fanfiction Archive*. 2003. 16 March 2004 <http://www.thrihyrne.net/>.

Tolkien, J.R.R. *The Lord of the Rings*. 2nd ed. With Note on the Text by Douglas A. Anderson. Boston: Houghton Mifflin, 1994.

___. *Letters of J.R.R. Tolkien*. Ed. Humphrey Carpenter. Boston: Houghton Mifflin, 2000.

___. *The Silmarillion*. Ed. Christopher Tolkien. Second edition. Boston: Houghton Mifflin, 2001.

___. *Unfinished Tales of Númenor and Middle-Earth*. Reprint edition. New York: Ballantine Books, 1988.

Verba, Joan Marie. *Boldly Writing: A Trekker Fan and Zine History, 1967-1987*. Minnetonka: FTL Publications, 1996.

The Very Secret Diaries. December 2001-March 2003. 16 March 2004 <http://www.ealasaid.com/misc/vsd/>.

PART VI:

THE LUCKY NUMBER

THE LORD OF THE RINGS:
A SOURCE-CRITICAL ANALYSIS

MARK SHEA

Experts in source-criticism now know that *The Lord of the Rings* is a redaction of sources ranging from *The Red Book of Westmarch* (W) to Elvish Chronicles (E) to Gondorian records (G) to orally transmitted tales of the Rohirrim (R). The conflicting ethnic, social, and religious groups that preserved these stories all had their own agendas, as did the "Tolkien" (T) and "Peter Jackson" (PJ) redactors, who are often in conflict with each other as well but whose conflicting accounts of the same events reveal a great deal about the political and religious situations that helped to form our popular notions about Middle-earth and the so-called War of the Ring. Into this mix are also thrown a great deal of folk materials about a supposed magic "Ring" and some obscure figures named Frodo and Sam. In all likelihood, these latter figures are totems meant to personify the popularity of Aragorn with the rural classes.

Because *The Lord of the Rings* is a composite of sources, we may be quite certain that "Tolkien" (if he ever existed) did not "write" this work in the conventional sense, but that it was assembled over a long period of time by someone else of the same name. We know this because a work of the range, depth, and detail of *The Lord of the Rings* is far beyond the capacity of any modern expert in source-criticism to ever imagine creating themselves.

The tension between source materials and the various redactors is evident in several cases. T is heavily dependent on G records and clearly elevates the claims of the Aragorn monarchy over the House of Denethor. From this it is obvious that the real "War of the Ring" was a dynastic struggle between these two clans for supremacy in Gondor. The G source, which plays such a prominent role in the T-redacted account of Aragorn, is significantly downplayed by the PJ redactor in favor of E versions. In the T account, Aragorn is portrayed as a stainless saint, utterly sure of his claims to the throne and so self-possessed that he never doubts for a moment his right to seize power. Likewise, in the T account, the Rohirrim are conveniently portrayed as willing allies and vassals to the Aragorn monarchy, living in perfect harmony with the Master Race of Númenóreans that rules Gondor.

Yet even the T redactor cannot eliminate from the R source the towering Amazon figure of Éowyn, who is recorded as taking up arms the moment the previous king of Rohan, Théoden, is dead. Clearly we are looking at a heavily reworked coup d'état attempt by the princess of the Rohirrim against Aragorn's supremacy. Yet this hard kernel of historical fact is cleverly sublimated under folk materials (apparently legends of the obscure figure of "Meriadoc"). Instead of the historical account of her attempt on Aragorn's throne as it originally stood in R, she is instead depicted as engaging in battle with a mythical "Lord of the Nazgûl" (apparently a figure from W sources) and shown fighting on Aragorn's side. This attempt to sublimate Éowyn does not convince the trained eye of the source-criticism expert, who astutely notes that Éowyn is wounded in battle at the same moment Denethor dies. Obviously, Éowyn and Denethor were in league against Aragorn but were defeated by the latter's partisans simultaneously.

This tendency to distort the historical record recurs many times in T. Indeed, many scholars now believe that the so-called Madness of Denethor in T (which depicts Denethor as a suicide) is, in fact, a sanitized version of the murder of Denethor by Aragorn through the administration of poison (possibly distilled from a plant called *athelas*).

In contrast to T, the PJ redaction of Aragorn is filled with self-doubts and frequently rebuked by PJ-redacted Elrond. Probably this is due to PJ's own political and religious affiliations, which seek, in particular, to exalt the Elvish claims to supremacy against Númenórean claims.

T suggests some skill on Aragorn's part in the use of pharmaceutical (and hallucinogenic?) plants, which may account for some of the more "visionary" moments of mysterious beings like "Black Riders" who appear to have been tribal chieftains hostile to the Aragorn dynasty. PJ, however, exalts Elrond's healing powers over Aragorn's. This is probably rooted in some incident of psychosomatic healing repeatedly chronicled in different sources. Thus, the G source also has an account of Frodo's "healing by Aragorn" on the Field of Cormallen, but E places it at Rivendell and attributes the healing to Elrond. Since we know that "Frodo" is likely just a figure representing the rural population and not a historical personage, most scholars therefore conclude that "Frodo's" healing is T's symbolic representation of Aragorn's program of socioeconomic appeasement of the agrarian class, while his healing by Elrond is a nature myth representing the renewal of the annual crops.

Of course, the "Ring" motif appears in countless folk tales and is to be discounted altogether. Equally dubious are the "Gandalf" narratives, which appear to be legends of a shamanistic figure, introduced to the narrative by W out of deference to local Shire cultic practice.

Finally, we can only guess at what the Sauron sources might have revealed, since they must have been destroyed by victors who give a wholly negative view of this doubtlessly complex, warm, human, and many-sided figure. Reasonable scholars now know, of course, that the identification of Sauron with "pure evil" is simply absurd. Indeed, many scholars have undertaken a "Quest for the Historical Sauron" and are searching the records with growing passion and urgency for any lore connected with the making of the One Ring. "It's all legendary, of course," says Dr. S. Aruman, "especially the absurd tale of Frodo the Nine-Fingered. After all, the idea of anyone deliberately giving up Power is simply impossible and would call into question the most precious thesis of postmodern ideology: that everything is a power struggle on the basis of race, class, and gender. Still, I . . . should . . . very much like to have a look at it. Just for scholarly purposes, of course."

ABOUT THE CONTRIBUTORS

Cathy Akers-Jordan is a Lecturer of English at the University of Michigan-Flint where she teaches writing. Her Master's degree is in Liberal Studies/American Culture; her thesis was *Ellery Queen: Forgotten Master Detective*. As an undergraduate the focus of her Bachelor of English was Medieval, Renaissance, and Fantasy literature. She has presented and published a variety of papers on topics ranging from the role of women in modern mystery fiction to the RMS Titanic disaster.

Susan Booker was until recently the Fine and Applied Arts Librarian at the University of Oklahoma. Her research interests focus on the written word, its dissemination, and the impact of popular culture figures upon amateur authors, and in particular, how the Internet fosters the ancient story-telling tradition in the modern world. She continues to study and document with photographs historically important buildings and styles of architecture in Oklahoma.

David Bratman has written on Tolkien for *Mythlore, Mythprint, Mallorn,* the Greenwood Press essay collection *Tolkien's Legendarium,* and other publications. He has been occupied, more than he'd like, critiquing the Jackson films since the first trailers appeared, and his first article on the subject, "The Case Against Peter Jackson," appeared in *Beyond Bree,* October 2001.

Jane Chance, Professor of English, teaches medieval literature, Medieval Studies, and Women and the Study of Gender at Rice University. She has published nineteen books, editions, and translations; among them are *Tolkien's Art: A Mythology for England* (1979) and *The Lord of the Rings: The Mythology of Power* (1992), revised for new editions (2001) and translated into Japanese (2003, 2004). She has also edited two issues of *Studies in Medievalism,* on the Twentieth Century and on the Inklings, and two collections, *Tolkien the Medievalist* (2002) and *Tolkien and the Invention of Myth: A Reader* (2004).

Janet Brennan Croft is Head of Access Services at the University of Oklahoma libraries. She is the author of *War and the Works of J.R.R. Tolkien* (Greenwood Press, 2004), and has published articles on Tolkien in *Mythlore*, *Mallorn*, and *Seven*. She has also written on library issues for several professional journals, and is the author of *Legal Solutions in Electronic Reserves and the Electronic Delivery of Interlibrary Loan* (Haworth Press, 2004).

Victoria Gaydosik completed her Ph.D. at the University of Rochester, writing a dissertation on Ben Jonson's use of imitation and innovation. She teaches in the Language Arts Department at Southwestern Oklahoma State University.

Judith J. Kollmann is Professor of English at the University of Michigan-Flint, where she has taught English literature since 1968. Her field is medieval literature, which has given her a strong interest in medievalism and fantasy. As a consequence she has published a number of articles on the Inklings member, Charles Williams, as well as articles on Brother Cadfael, on Centaurs, on Sheridan Le Fanu, and other assorted interesting writers and themes.

Diana L. Paxson is the author of twenty-four published novels, including re-tellings of the stories of King Arthur, Siegfried, Tristan and Iseult and Fionn MacCumhail, and over seventy-five short stories in the fantasy genre, most of them with mythic themes, and thus understands the process of revision only too well. Her most recent novels are *Ancestors of Avalon* and the forthcoming, *Golden Hills of Westria*. She received her M.A. from the University of California in comparative literature with an emphasis on the Middle Ages, and has given many presentations at meetings of the Mythopoeic Society, of which she has been a member since 1972.

Mark P. Shea is a popular Catholic writer and speaker, and the author of *Making Senses Out of Scripture: Reading the Bible as the First Christians Did* (Basilica), *By What Authority?: An Evangelical Discovers Catholic Tradition* (Our Sunday Visitor) and *This is My Body: An Evangelical Discovers the Real Presence* (Christendom Press).

J.E. Smyth, an Andrew W. Mellon Fellow in the Humanities, is a Ph.D. candidate in the Departments of Films Studies and American Studies at Yale University. Smyth's work has appeared in *Rethinking History*, *Film and History*, and *Film Quarterly*. She has lectured on film historiography and British cinema.

Amy H. Sturgis teaches science fiction/fantasy studies, media studies, and Native American studies at Belmont University, including the courses "J.R.R.

Tolkien in History, Political Thought, and Literature" and "Fan Participation in Media and Culture." Her works have appeared in journals and magazines such as *Seventeenth Century*, *Reason*, *Winedark Sea*, *The LockeSmith Review*, *Mythlore*, *CSL*, and *Parma Nölé*, among others, and she has contributed multiple articles to the popular *Revolution Science Fiction*. In 2003 she was named a scholarly Guest of Honor for the international *Gathering of the Fellowship* Celebration of J.R.R. Tolkien.

Maureen Thum has published articles on the Grimm Brothers, Chaucer, Milton, and the German literary fairy-tale writer, Wilhelm Hauff, in *The Germanic Review*, *The Philological Quarterly*, *Milton Studies*, and the *MLA Children's Literature Annual Journal*. She has presented numerous papers on topics ranging from Shakespeare to children's literature and the Victorian novel. She is also the Director of the Honors Program at the University of Michigan-Flint.

Daniel Timmons received his Ph.D. from the University of Toronto and has published several articles and reviews on the work of J.R.R. Tolkien. With George Clark, he co-edited the essay collection *J.R.R. Tolkien and His Literary Resonances: Views of Middle-earth* (Greenwood, 2000). Timmons is also the writer, director, and producer for a literary documentary, *The Legacy of The Lord of the Rings*. The program has been broadcast on **Bravo!**, **SPACE: The Imagination Station**, **Canadian Learning Television** and **Book Television**. For a description and video clip, see: https://www.scriptsandscribes.com/TVproj.htm.

Kayla McKinney Wiggins is the chair of the English department at Martin Methodist College in Pulaski, Tennessee. In addition to numerous articles on film, drama, and folklore, she is the author of *Modern Verse Drama in English* (Greenwood Press, 1993).